FOR YOUR TOMORROW

Canadians and the Burma Campaign
1941 – 1945

D1535266

FOR YOUR TOMORROW

Canadians and the Burma Campaign
1941 – 1945

Robert H. Farquharson

Bob Farquharson

The author gratefully acknowledges a grant in aid of publication from the Senate Research Committee of Victoria University in the University of Toronto.

NOTE FOR LIBRARIANS: A cataloguing record for this book that includes the U.S. Library of Congress Classification number, the Library of Congress Call number and the Dewey Decimal cataloguing code is available from the Library and Archives of Canada. The complete cataloguing record can be obtained from the National Library's online database at:
www.collectionscanada.ca/amicus/index-e.html
ISBN 1-4120-1536-7

Printed in Victoria, BC, Canada.

FRONT COVER PHOTO: Photo depicts members of 436 Elephant Squadron resting on a pagoda near Mandalay, April 3, 1945. Bottom row (*l to r*) E. M.Waring, D. H. Millar; second row, D. L. McIntosh, W. F. Minnie, A. E. Nunns, R. H. Perry; top row, K. Bennett, all from British Columbia. (*RCAF photo by F/L Jim March courtesy A. Adams*)

BOOK AND COVER DESIGN: Maureen Morin, Digital Studio, University of Toronto.

TRAFFORD

This book was published on-demand in cooperation with Trafford Publishing. On-demand publishing is a unique process and service of making a book available for retail sale to the public taking advantage of on-demand manufacturing and Internet marketing. On-demand publishing includes promotions, retail sales, manufacturing, order fulfilment, accounting and collecting royalties on behalf of the author.

Suite 6E, 2333 Government St.,
Victoria, B.C. V8T 4P4, CANADA
Phone   250-383-6864
Toll-free 1-888-232-4444
Fax   250-383-6804
E-mail   sales@trafford.com
www.trafford.com/robots/03-1914.html

10   9   8   7   6   5   4

For all Canadians who served in Burma, and especially

For those who did not return,

But above all for Anne

Who doesn't believe in war

But still edited, proofread and encouraged throughout.

Contents

Maps

Photos

Following Page 90

The Burma Road • Fighter Wing • Canadians in the British or Indian Army

Kohima • Chindits • 413 Squadron

Following Page 220

Air Supply • Bath Night • Squadron Life

Operation Dracula • Burma Bombers • Rangoon Jail

Action at Shwebo and Toungoo • Building Roads

Acknowledgements

Awork such as this cannot be written without the cooperation and encouragement of other people. I have been heartened by the readiness with which Burma veterans dug into their attics and their memories to share stories, pictures, memoirs and memorabilia with me. And I have been humbled by the willingness with which families gave me open access to collections of personal letters. I thank everyone who helped.

I thank John Kowles, Stickney Harris and Dave Bockus for helping me tell the Chindit story, and Wally Frazer, George Hosegood, Stan Johns, John Dey and Roy Borthwick for information about the activities of Liberator squadrons. Art Coy let me read his diary and his logbook, and Harry V. Smith told me of his visit at the Royal Palace in Siam. Len Birchall added details to the oft-told tale of the Japanese fleet steaming toward Ceylon. Dunstan Pasterfield generously opened all his Burma letters to me. My thanks to Atholl Sutherland Brown, Stan Johns and Bert Madill for telling what Beaufighters, Mosquitoes and Thunderbolts did in Burma, to Harry Ho, Fred Kagawa, Herb Lim and Willie Chong for filling out the story of the irregular side of war, and to David Rodger for a doctor's story. Dave Small, Hal Snell and Bill Corcoran shared their experiences on radar and Cedric and Albert Mah enlivened the Hump narrative. Walter Anderson, despite being very sick, took time to tell me of his adventures on the River Kwae.

The story of air supply takes up a good part of this narrative and here I am indebted to a number of my old comrades — Lou Duffley, Bob O'Brien, Aubrey Dutch, Derek Salter, John Harvey, Ross Huston, Mel Little, Herb Coons, Frank Cooper, Moe Falloon and Al Rosati. Howie Cuming was very helpful in telling of the Rangoon paradrop. My navigator, Norman Collins, shared his diary and his logbook and my co-pilot Chas Swift jogged my memory with his story. Peter Brennan very generously gave me free use of all the material he had collected for a proposed 435-436 history. I am particularly indebted to Art Adams, Honorary Colonel of 436 Squadron, for pictures, stories, and enthusiastic encouragement.

It is surprising how much archival material about Canadians in the Burma campaign is still treasured by veterans and their families. Barbara Brouse gave me free access to the wealth of material she holds relevant to the life of her father, Andrew Taylor. Marion Goodchild helped with the story of her brother, Walter Anderson. Andrew Duncanson went to great lengths to provide copies of his father's material from the Canadian Officer Party as did Mary-Ann Kinloch, the daughter of William Bramley-Moore. And I am indebted to Major-General George Spencer for filling in details and for directing me to the official report in the National Archives. Donald MacPherson generously let me use his memorial to his brother Ian. And I am indebted to so many more — to Mrs. R. Bates, Bob Bates's widow; to Jo Taylor, Bob McLure's daughter; to Peter Bolsby for information about his brother James; to James Broughall, Mrs. S. Paterson and Mrs. B. Pearson for information about Seton Broughall; to Michelle Levesque, daughter of Roger Caza and to Anne Faulkner, daughter of George Faulkner; to Barry Corston for showing me his father's logbook and diary; to Isobel Cuddy for writing me about her husband Keith; to Bill Curtiss, brother of Joe; to Bert De Leeuw and Greg De Cruyenaere for the little book about "Bing" De Cruyenaere; to James Everard, Headly's son; to Muriel Kempling for her husband's logbook; to Thomas Markowitz for help with his father's story; to Isabel Mendizabel, sister to Rudy; to Dr. E. R. Simpson for giving me Keith Muir's memoirs; to Douglas MacGillivray for information about John Scott MacGillivray; to Jack Oulette for helping me with Roy MacKenzie's story; to Bea Corbett, Jack Pike and Jennifer McKendry for putting the Norman McLeod tale together; to Dorothy Walker for information about her husband, William Arthur "Bud" Walker; and to Elsa Dickson for the story of her father, Roland Bacon.

I am particularly grateful to Gerry Beauchamp and Karl Vincent for permission to quote from *Mohawks over Burma*, to The Honourable Roy Maclaren for permission to quote from *Canadians Behind Enemy Lines 1939 – 1945*, to Viscount John Slim for permission to quote from General Slim's *Defeat into Victory*, and to James Everard for permission to quote from Hedley Everard's *A Mouse in my Pocket*.

There were others too. Will Chabun of the Regina Leader-Post gave many leads and enthusiastic encouragement, as did Ernie Neufeld of the Weyburn Times. Owen Cooke, bibliographer in Ottawa, and Ian Lyall Grant, author in Britain, took the time to answer my inquiries. Others wrote from England to tell of their Canadian encounters in Burma, John Williams (whose brother wrote the history of 194 RAF Squadron), Ken Yabsley, George King, Denis Gudgeon, Clifford White, C. Fairweather and H. F. W. Pickett. T. W. Melnyk, author of *Canadian Flying Operations in South East Asia 1941-1945* generously agreed to read the manuscript. I thank Jane Davie of the Cartography Department for the maps and Maureen Morin of the Digital Studio at the University of Toronto for expertly and enthusiastically tackling the design problems. I was blessed with two able editors, Gordon Elliott of Vancouver and my wife Anne. I owe them both great thanks for improving my text. There are undoubtedly others whom I have neglected to mention; I apologize to them and thank them. Indeed, I have had so much help from so many people that it is only the mistakes that I can rightfully claim as altogether my own.

Although I have based part of my book on the first-hand information the people named above have given me, it will be obvious that much of what I have written has been gleaned from other books. Despite that, I thought it proper not to impede the reader with footnotes; instead I have tried to recognize my sources within the text and in the Bibliography. I envisioned this book, not as a scholarly undertaking, but as a popular record intended primarily for Burma veterans and their families and for others who are interested in the little known but significant role that Canada played in the Burma War. I hope it fulfils that purpose.

Toronto, March 2004

Glossary

OR A book such as this, set in a distant land, dealing with an esoteric existence, and telling of events that happened sixty years ago, a glossary is well nigh indispensable. There are many words that are so peculiar to service slang or to the Burma Campaign that not to use them would be unnatural, and not to explicate them would be inconsiderate. The phrase "pukkha sahib" could be rendered as "proper gentleman," but it would widely miss the mark. In service slang in Burma "tik" or "tik hai" (pronounced "teek hi") altogether replaced "okay" as a signal of approval or assent. These expressions appear in this text because the flavour of those days requires them. In addition, there are natural features of the landscape that only the native language can convey – if this were not so, the Inuit would not need one hundred words for snow. I use the word "chaung" because a chaung is a chaung and nothing else. Similarly, I use the older place names — Siam instead of Thailand, Rangoon instead of Yangon — because those were the names we used. And then there are abbreviations and acronyms; in the military these are unavoidable. Time has rendered many of these obsolete, e.g., the RCAF no longer exists, and all the Air Force rank designations have disappeared. I hope this glossary dispels some of the lexicographic darkness.

PLACE NAMES

After independence in 1948, the Burmese government renamed many places to obliterate the traces of colonial days when the British had corrupted the original name or highhandedly given the town an English name (eg, Maymyo, named after General May).

Old Name	New Name	Old Name	New Name
Akyab	Sittwe	Moulmein	Mawlamyine
Arakan	Rakhine	Pagan	Bagan
Burma	Myanmar	Pegu	Pyay
Irrawaddy	Ayeyarwaddy	Salween	Thanlwin
Karen	Kahin	Siam	Thailand
Maymyo	Pyin u Lwin		

ABBREVIATIONS

ABDA or **ABDAC** = American, British, Dutch and Australian Command

AMES = Air Ministry Experimental Station (a radar station)

AFC =Air Force Cross (AFM = Air Force Medal, for non-commissioned ranks)

AVG = American Volunteer Group (The Flying Tigers)

BCATP = British Commonwealth Air Training Plan

BOR = British Other Rank, IOR = Indian Other Rank (a private soldier)

CNAC = Chinese National Aviation Corporation (flying the Hump)

CO = Commanding Officer

DFC = Distinguished Flying Cross (DFM for non-commissioned ranks)

MiD or **MID** = Mentioned in Despatches

MO = Medical Officer

NAAFI = Navy, Army and Air Force Institute (brought tea and cakes to the troops)

NCO = Non-commissioned officer

POW = Prisoner of War

RAAF = Royal Australian Air Force; similarly, RAF, RCAF, RNZAF

SAAF = South African Air Force

USAAF = United States Army Air Force

VCO = Viceroy Commissioned Officer

2/i/c = second in command

AIR FORCE RANKS

LAC = Leading Aircraftsman

F/S = Flight Sergeant

P/O = Pilot Officer

F/O = Flying Officer

F/L = Flight Lieutenant

S/L = Squadron Leader

W/C = Wing Commander

SERVICE VERNACULAR

Ack-ack = anti-aircraft fire

Basha = hut of woven bamboo and thatch

Bithess = Hessian cloth (a strong, coarse cloth woven of hemp and jute) impregnated with bitumen and used to surface roads and airstrips. Pronounced "bit-hess".

Bowser = refueling truck

Burra = big

Charpoy = rope bed

Chaung = water course or stream bed

Chota = small

Dacoits = lawless gangs

Dah = large knife carried by Burmese hillmen

Dahl = lentils

Dak = Dakota aircraft

Dak Bungalow = a government rest house

Erk = an aircraftsman

Flak = anti-aircraft fire (from the German, *Fliegerabwehrkanone* = anti-aircraft gun)

Ghee = clarified butter (a favourite of the Indian troops)

Godown = warehouse

Khud = cliff or hillside

Kukri = large knife carried by all Gurkhas

Mayday = call for help (from the French, *m'aidez*)

Sepoy = a private soldier in the Indian Army

Sprog = a greenhorn, rank beginner

Strafe = to machine gun ground troops from the air (from the German *strafen* = to punish)

Zhu = native rice beer

3/2 Gurkhas = designation of the Third Battalion of the Second Gurkha Rifle Regiment (spoken Third Second Gurkhas or Ninth Fifteenth Punjabs)

Introduction

When Dorothy Walker of Lancaster, Ontario tells people her husband was killed in Burma they often look bemused and ask "What was he doing there? What war was that?" The questions sadden Dorothy. Don't they know there was a war in Burma? Don't they know that Canadians were fighting there? Did her husband die in a war and in a place that are completely unknown or forgotten? It seems he did; for many Canadians the Burma Campaign is but a vague awareness and the role of Canadians in that Campaign is almost completely unknown. It is the purpose of this book to shed some light onto that unknown.

Even while it was being fought, the Burma Campaign was known as the Forgotten War. The generals and air commodores named it so because when the tanks and planes and other armaments were being distributed, Burma was repeatedly set to the end of Santa's list. For the troops it was the forgotten war because they were far from home, mail was slow and undependable, entertainers rarely visited, and home leaves were impossible. It was very easy to feel forgotten. When Admiral Mountbatten, newly appointed Supreme Commander in South East Asia Command (SEAC), first addressed the troops he made the point emphatically: "I hear you call this the Forgotten Front. I hear you call yourselves the Forgotten Army. Well, let me tell you this is *not* the Forgotten Front, and you are *not* the Forgotten Army. In fact, nobody has even heard of you." He then vowed that this would change, that they would do deeds that would make the whole world notice. Although his charismatic and flamboyant personality did somewhat elevate awareness of the Burma fighting, the campaign remained, and still remains, relatively unknown, its distant light eclipsed by the brighter glow of the European theatre and the American campaign in the Pacific. If the Burma Campaign was unknown in Britain, it was even more unknown in Canada.

The British press occasionally carried stories from the Burma front, but only rarely did Canadian newspapers pick them up. Moreover, whereas in World War I young Canadians had flocked to the Front to defend the Empire, in World War II few Canadian hearts quickened at the thought of Britain's imperial might spread all across the map in red. Britons still sang "The Empire too, We can depend on you," but in Canada the notion of Empire had been almost completely replaced by the concept of Commonwealth. Indeed Prime Minister Mackenzie King did not want to hear of Canadian troops involved in imperial causes, well aware that every such involvement would cost him votes in Quebec. Not until late 1943 was there a functional RCAF administrative headquarters in the theatre and as late as mid-1944 a Canadian Air Liaison Mission to India had recommended that "the Royal Canadian Air Force not participate in the war in South East Asia."

In these circumstances it is perhaps understandable that the Canadian public should be ignorant of Canadian involvement in the Burma War, but it is hard to understand how little it is acknowledged by the British. Churchill became quite emotional when he told the story of the airman whose reporting of the Japanese fleet approaching Ceylon turned the course of the war, but he did not know that the "Saviour of Ceylon" was a Canadian. Dave Bockus and Eric Loken, two Canadian pilots who used a salvaged light plane to rescue abandoned Chindits, yearned for a Canadian flag so they could stop the troops from calling them Americans. Even historians after the war often overlooked Canadians when they told their story. In *The Forgotten Air Force* Air Commodore Henry Probert gives gracious recognition to the valuable contribution made by the fighter, bomber and transport crews of the RCAF, but S. Woodburn Kirby, in *The War against Japan*, the final volume of the official *History of the Second World War*, merely mentions the two Canadian transport squadrons, while Hilary St. G. Saunders in *The Fight is Won*, volume three of the *Official History of the Royal Air Force*, tells the Burma story without any mention of the RCAF at all. Most shocking is the reticence of Lord Louis Mountbatten. When he took over as Supreme Commander in South East Asia he boasted of the diversity of his command: there were Indians, British and Gurkhas, Americans and Chinese, East and West Africans, Burmese, Australians, French and Dutch. But apparently no Canadians. Given that Canadians in Burma outnumbered Australians six to one, one wonders if the omission is not more intentional than inadvertent. Mountbatten arrived in India still smarting from criticism about the Dieppe raid and therefore somewhat allergic to the word Canadian.

Since the ordinary Canadian knows little about the war in South East Asia, it seemed necessary to tell the story of the Burma Campaign. It is told here in a general way with only enough detail to make the geography and chronology of the various events and expeditions understandable. The serious scholar of military history will want to turn to a book like Louis Allen's *Burma, The Longest War* where the campaign is chronicled in detail. Similarly although a number of worthy leaders played prominent roles at various levels of command — General Sir George Giffard, General Sir Archibald Alexander, General Sir Claude Auchinleck, and others — I have tended to refer to General Slim in a "generic" sense as the leader on all occasions, in part because it was so much his campaign, and in part because he was the one commander the soldiers, and the airmen, knew by name and respected.

I have used the names of the countries and places that were current at the time — Burma rather than Myanmar, Rangoon instead of Yangon, Siam instead of Thailand. For the reader who is confused in this regard there is a glossary.

I have been careless, even cavalier, in indicating rank, in part because a man's rank changed, sometimes with startling speed, and in part because Canadians were not notably rank conscious. Moreover, while for professional military men rank is important, for the wartime soldier or airman it is a temporary distinction, laid aside with his uniform at the war's end.

Admittedly this book has its genesis in my experiences in Burma during the war, but it is not my story except in a few instances where my personal experiences seem particularly relevant. I was in South East Asia Command for a scant ten months, time enough to finish a tour of operations with 435 Squadron, a Canadian transport squadron. After the war I occupied myself with my career and almost forgot about the war. In 1995, fifty years after the war with Japan ended, I joined a number of my war-time comrades on a Pilgrimage to Burma sponsored by the Department of Veterans Affairs. Standing at attention among the neat rows of white markers in the Taukkyan Commonwealth War Cemetery at Rangoon while the bugler played the *Last Post* stirred personal memories and activated in me a latent interest in my war experiences. The next Remembrance Day I went to Ottawa and marched to the Cenotaph with the Burma Star vets. Spectators clapped and said "Thank you" as we passed, and that was the first time I realized that my war experiences represented, not merely youthful adventures that were mine alone, but a small part of our country's heritage and history. The thought kept turning in me: "Canada should know about the Canadians in Burma. Some one should write their story." But no one did, and I realized if I wanted that story to be heard, I would have to tell it myself. Thus this book, more than four years in the making. About 8000 Canadians served in the Burma Campaign, no one knows exactly how many, and about 500 are still there, lying in well-tended Commonwealth War Cemeteries or in unknown, unmarked graves in the hills and jungle. These men, those who returned and those who did not, deserve to be remembered.

PRELUDE TO WAR

LTHOUGH EACH of the campaigns of World War II was unique in one way or another, none was as unique in as many different ways as the campaign in Burma. First, it was longer than any other campaign. It began in December 1941 when Japanese troops crossed into Burma from Siam and it did not end till General Slim, Commander of the British Fourteenth Army, accepted General Kimura's sword at the signing of the "Local Agreement," the unofficial surrender of Burma, at Rangoon, August 28, 1945. For over three and a half years the two forces had been at each other's throat, sometimes with animal ferocity, sometimes with baleful watchfulness, but always with deadly malevolence. The campaign was unique too in that a good part of it was fought in wild terrain, unmapped and unknown, striated by mountain ridges deepfolded on each other, with swift coursing rivers in their valleys and tangles of forest and jungle growth on their slopes. Moreover, from the Allied railhead in north east India, no roads led inward to the front, no railways supplied the army's needs. Indeed, frequently there was no front, only pockets of protected strength facing fortified bunkers somewhere on the other side. The jungle where men fought was an unhealthy place. Malaria was almost unavoidable, dysentery, typhoid, cholera, beriberi struck down twice as many men as enemy fire. Small cuts and scratches became deep festering wounds that would not heal. Leeches crawled into the eyelets of the soldiers' boots and fastened themselves to legs and ankles so that when the men finally had a chance to take off their boots, they found them full of blood. And there was the weather. During the monsoon season from mid-May to mid-October the rain was incessant, as much as 400 inches in a year. Night and day men lived in clothes that never got dry and fought in slit trenches half filled with water. Towering thunderheads roiling with lethal air currents and dragging their rain-filled

Map 1 — Burma and Her Neighbours — 1941

skirts across the mountain tops made flying extremely hazardous. During the dry season, the heat and humidity of the central plain were unbearable and the dust was choking, while on the northern mountain tops the winter nights were frigid. Moreover the local population, apart from the Kachins of central Burma, the Karens of the southeast and the Naga hill men of the northwest, were at best unreliable and at worst treacherously hostile. In short, the greater part of the Burma Campaign was fought far removed from the amenities of normal life and under rigours of geography and climate that were unique to the Burma theatre.

But above all the Burma Campaign was unique because of the twisted and criss-crossed political purposes that launched it and guided its course. Of all the combatants on Burmese soil, only the Japanese were sure of their purpose. For them invasion of Burma was easily understood. First, it accorded with the aims of the Greater East Asian Co-Prosperity Sphere, their ambitious plan for uniting all Asia against the foreign devils. It also accorded with the tantalizing dream of "freeing" India of its colonial oppressors and then reaching into Persia to join hands with their Axis friends. But immediately, and more importantly, it promised a source of natural resources that Japan's fast growing population and expanding industry desperately needed. Burma in 1939 was the world's leading exporter of rice and the Yenangyaung oil fields stood ready to deliver 15,000 barrels of petroleum products each day. Burma offered in addition teak, tungsten, tin, rubber, and cobalt, as well as rubies, jade, and sapphires. The final and by far the most important reason for Japanese aggression in Burma however was the hope of permanently closing the Burma Road and shutting off that flood of American lend-lease supplies streaming into Kunming.

For the Allies — British, American and Chinese — it was a different story. The Chinese, for example, had little reason to fight in Burma, except that the Americans wanted them to. They did delight in receiving American aid, but foremost in Chiang Kai-shek's mind was the desire to save his troops and hoard supplies for the internal war that would follow this "incident" with the Japanese. For this reason the Generalissimo proved to be a thorny and erratic ally; neither the British nor the Americans could ever count on his doing what they wanted him to do, and certainly not when they wanted him to do it. Stilwell was never sure that he was actually the Officer Commanding. In the Chinese Order of Battle he was listed merely as Chief of Staff, and for more than a year Chiang Kai-shek refused to give him the *chop*, the official seal that signified imperial sanction.

Nor had the Americans reason to fight in Burma, except for their desire to secure a safe land route into China. Immediately after Pearl Harbour President Franklin D. Roosevelt had promised Chiang Kai-shek 1.5 billion dollars of Lend-Lease aid. With the loss of Rangoon, the thousands of tons of matériel that this money could buy had to be ferried to China over the Hump, that extremely expensive, dangerous and inadequate air supply route that led from Assam in north east India over the Himalayas to Kunming. From Ledo, their railhead in north east India, the Americans were feverishly building a road and pipeline to Myitkyina and on to Lashio so that they could be ready to pour supplies into China as soon as the Burma Road was re-opened.[1] Their attention therefore was centred in northern Burma. The rest of the Burma Campaign they saw only as a British effort to reclaim lost glory, a thought that was anathema to the anti-colonial soul of all Americans. Cynically the American soldiers construed SEAC, the acronym for South East Asia Command, as "Save England's Asian Colonies."

Ironically, the British were also not very enthusiastic about reconquering their lost colony. In Winston Churchill's estimation, fighting in the precipitous mountains, the tangled jungle, and the hideous monsoons of Burma was like "munching on a porcupine quill by quill." Both he and his machismo Supreme Commander, Lord Louis Mountbatten, would have preferred to bypass Burma altogether, launch an air-sea invasion on Sumatra, and then a direct attack on Singapore, which, after all, was the true symbol of past glory. Moreover, Sir Stafford Cripps in his 1942 trip to India had more or less promised independence to India once the war was won and the notion was abroad that Burmese independence would soon follow. One fights half-heartedly for a treasure that is already promised away.

India's position vis-à-vis the war in Burma was even more anomalous. On the one hand, there was the Indian Army with its strong and long tradition of service to its King-Emperor in London. Generations of Sikhs, Jats, Dogras, and Gurkhas had proudly served in regiments with a long history of devotion to the Raj and two thirds of all the troops who fought in Burma were Indians in the Indian Army. Despite a policy of "Indianization," begun in earnest when the Indian Military Academy was opened in 1932, almost all their officers were British; Indian soldiers who were promoted to officer rank were commissioned, not by the King as all other British and Commonwealth officers were, but by the King's second-in-command, the Viceroy. The Indian Army swallowed this discrimination and fought loyally and bravely throughout the Burma Campaign, often bearing the brunt of the battle and winning the bulk of the medals. Of the 60,000 Allied men killed, wounded and missing in Burma, 41,600 were Indians. Of the 174 Victoria Crosses awarded in all of World War II, 31 went to men of the Indian Army.

---

[1] The centrality of the Burma Road to American thinking is emphasized by the fact that just seven weeks after Pearl Harbour the film *A Yank on the Burma Road* appeared on American screens. In it a New York cabbie leads a convoy of trucks through landslides and over bombed bridges to China.

However, even this model of colonial loyalty was not without its contradictions, for there was another Indian Army in the field, the Indian National Army. Subhas Chandra Bose, Ghandi's lieutenant in the Congress Party, had become impatient with non-violence and turned to war. With the help of the Japanese he eventually recruited an army of 20,000, mainly from among the sepoys taken prisoner at Singapore, and about 10,000 of these were armed and sent into the 1944 attack against Imphal. It is indicative of the ambivalence of the Indian people at this time that the leaders of Bose's Indian National Army were charged with treason after the war, eloquently defended by Jawaharlal Nehru, and finally cleared and proclaimed national heroes.

So there it is. From the Allied side at least, none of the major combatants in the Burma Campaign were fighting *pro patria*, no objective was straight ahead, no motive unalloyed.

There was however one person on the Allied side who did have a clear vision of eventual victory in Burma and that was General William Slim. He had taken over the Fourteenth Army just after the fall of Rangoon and had had to command the ignominious withdrawal all the way from southern Burma to the very borders of India. A determined professional soldier with a growing reputation, Slim found it hard to swallow what the American China expert, General Joe Stilwell, colourfully but correctly stigmatized as "a helluva licking." His soldiers understood how the retreat rankled; as one of them remarked: "Wherever Uncle Bill took a licking on the way out, he's going to give them a licking on the way back." In the final days of the Burma Campaign, Slim drove with obsessive intensity toward Rangoon, determined to do everything he could to see that his 17th Indian Division, the last out of Rangoon in 1942, should be the first back in 1945. In the end it did not turn out that way, but Slim made it a very close race.

Even before the Burma War started, relationships between the various nations involved were curiously crossed and contorted. The differing attitudes of the British and the Americans toward China illustrate this well. Britain's East India Trading Company had naturally extended its activities from India into China, and opium, grown in India under government supervision, proved to be an alluring medium with which to procure Chinese tea, cottons and silks. Chinese attempts to outlaw this trade were met with righteous indignation: had not Warren Hastings in 1783 proclaimed opium to be "a pernicious article of luxury which ought not to be permitted but for the purpose of foreign commerce only?" Repeatedly between 1852 and 1860 the British fought to preserve their notion of free trade and eventually the Opium Wars resulted in the occupation of Canton and the legal importation of opium. The Americans reacted by sponsoring a mission to tour European capitals to argue for the reinstatement of full Chinese sovereignty. They promised not only to respect Chinese territorial integrity but also to allow free immigration of Chinese labourers. The British gave grudging and inconsequential concessions and then demanded extended "spheres of influence." It began to look as though China was going to be partitioned and fall under European colonial domination as British India, Portuguese Goa, French Indochina and the Dutch East Indies had done.

This state of affairs prompted the United States to articulate, in 1899, its first ever foreign policy declaration, the policy of the Open Door, basically a public assertion that all nations should have equal right to trade in China with no special concession and no discrimination. At the same time, the Chinese themselves began to take an interest in their own welfare. Revolutionary groups, shouting the slogan "Protect the country. Destroy the foreigner," began to kill foreign missionaries and Chinese Christians. This was the start of the Boxer Rebellion, so-called because the symbol of the revolutionaries was a raised, clenched fist. The rebellion however was short-lived. By August 1900 the French and English had suppressed the patriots, occupied and looted Canton, and forced China to sign a protocol that granted further trade concessions and allowed free missionary activity. She was also required to pay indemnities amounting to £67,500,000. Once again the United States broke with its European friends; the Americans returned a good part of their share of the indemnity and with the rest of it established scholarships in the United States for Chinese students.

While all this was going on in China, a quite different scenario was playing out with the Japanese. For decades Japan had pursued a policy of rigid isolationism, so rigid that the construction of ocean-going vessels was prohibited and foreign ships that approached Japanese shores were driven off. If foreigners landed, they were executed. Even Japanese fishermen who had been rescued from the sea by foreign vessels were not allowed to be landed on their native soil. When the Dutch authorities from nearby Java plaintively asked for "some openness," the response was prim and pert: "Henceforth pray cease corresponding."

All that changed in 1854 when the American, Admiral Mathew Perry, sailed into Tokyo Bay with his 10 "black ships" and 2000 troops. Five years later the United States pressed upon the reluctant Japanese a Treaty of Amity and Commerce. It turned out there was more commerce than amity in the treaty, but it did awaken in the Japanese the realization that isolationism was not an option in the modern world, and she began an intense program of modernization, especially in the area of military preparedness. Her generals turned to Germany for their model, her admirals to England.

From the beginning, all the western nations, including Canada, regarded the Japanese differently from the Chinese. Whereas the latter were seen as tractable and docile, the Japanese were regarded as curious, clever, ambitious, and aggressive. This view became manifest when Japan insinuated herself into the Boxer Rebellion on the side of the western powers and thereby earned recognition for her role in helping rescue western nationals in Canton. Still it seemed as if, though all were equal, some were more equal than others. Thus, for example, in the Sino-Japanese War of 1895 Japan won from China the Liaotung Peninsula with its important naval harbour at Port Arthur. Germany, France and Russia however refused to support Japan's claim to the ceded territory. Added insult came three years later when Russia pressured China into leasing the same territory to her.

Seen against this background the importance of the Anglo-Japanese Alliance, especially to the Japanese, can be more easily understood for it seemed to grant them the recognition and equality they had previously been denied. Signed in 1902, it provided that each signatory would help the other if it were attacked and remain neutral if either attacked a third party. Fear of Russian aggression lay behind the Alliance, Britain anxious about an attack on North West India and Japan about an attack on Korea. Three years later, in 1905, little Japan, up to this time a bit player on the world stage but now emboldened by the assurance of the Alliance, took on the giant Russian bear. To the surprise of the world, she destroyed the Russian fleet and again occupied the harbour of Port Arthur. In 1914, obedient to the terms of the Alliance, Japan declared war on Germany and then seized the German-held port of Tsingtao. When China protested, Japan presented her with Twenty-One Demands, a series of requirements so outrageous that they would have come close to depriving China of her independence. The U.S. forced Japan to modify her demands. At Versailles in 1919 Japan once again tasted the bitterness of discrimination when her friends and allies rejected her request for the recognition of "racial equality."

The audacity of Japan's Twenty-One Demands against China and the rapidity with which her navy grew convinced the Americans that Japan was an international force that had to be contained. They convened the Washington Naval Conference of 1922 and forced Britain and Japan to accept limits to naval growth. The three nations were to maintain major battleships in the ratio of 5:5:3, with Japan, of course, limited to 60% of the naval power of the other two. David Lu in his book *From the Marco Polo Bridge to Pearl Harbor* describes the events and consequences that ensued from this agreement. On a rainy afternoon in July 1924, Japanese spectators on shore watched with growing resentment as their own planes bombed their warship *Ishimi* and sent it to the bottom. On that same day, *Nagata* and *Mutsu*, two of the Japanese Navy's proudest ships, opened fire on their sister ships *Satsuma* and *Aki* and sank them. "From this day," muttered Commander Kanji Kato, "we are at war with the United States. We shall avenge."

Japan now began to pursue an open policy of expansion. In 1931 a Japanese express train in Manchuria was bombed — probably by the Japanese themselves — and Japan used this incident as an excuse to invade Manchuria. Condemned by the Western Powers for this act of aggression, she withdrew from the League of Nations. In 1934 she signed the Non-Comintern pact with Germany and Italy, and a year after that repudiated the Naval Limitation Treaties. In 1937, on the excuse that the Chinese had killed a Japanese soldier at the Marco Polo bridge (it turned out the missing soldier had simply gone for a pee), she began full-scale war with China. The western powers reacted with outrage. Japan argued she was simply follow-ing the colonial plan set by Britain, France and Germany, and even by the U.S. in its occupation of the Philippines, but once again she found that the rules for those who were in the club did not apply to those who were not

President Roosevelt's reaction was mild; he suggested a "quarantine" to contain the disease of war, but the American public was more than a little annoyed. Ogden Nash put their feelings into rhyme:

> *How courteous is the Japanese,*
> *He always says "Excuse it please."*
> *He walks into his neighbour's garden*
> *And humbly says "I beg your pardon."*
> *He bows and grins a humble grin*
> *And asks his wife and family in*
> *He grins and bows a humble bow*
> *And says "So sorry. This my garden now."*

The emotion in the public response derived from the home front as well as the international scene. Over the years, immigrants from the Orient had been flooding into the western states, particularly into California, to feed the appetite for cheap labour in the gold mines and on the railways. Now the fear was that all the jobs were going to the Chinese and Japanese. The Immigration Exclusion Act of 1924 strictly limited the number of Orientals allowed into the U.S. each year and those already in the country were refused citizenship. California denied Orientals the right to own property, even through the proxy of American-born children. This anti-Oriental sen-timent at home, coupled with anxiety about aggression in China, gave par-ticular point to America's anti-Japanese bias. In 1939 Cordell Hull refused to sanction Japan's "brazen expansion in the Orient" and banned the sale of aircraft and aircraft equipment to Japan. Japan reacted by signing a Tripartite Pact with Germany and Italy in 1940 and by occupying French Indochina the next year, thus depriving the U.S. of the Hanoi-to-Chunking Railway as a supply route to China.

Quite a different attitude developed in Britain. The immigration factor of course was simply not there. The British were pleased that their Navy had become the model for Japan and they were satisfied that the Anglo-Japanese Alliance was working in their favour. In March 1921 Crown Prince Hirohito set out on a state visit to England, stopping at Hong Kong to tour, among other things, the Victoria Reservoir (which in 1941 turned out to be the Achilles heel of Hong Kong's defences). In Singapore he borrowed a yacht and circumnavigated the fortress, taking particular note of the huge naval guns fixed to fire only out to the sea. In London he was the guest of honour at a march past and even had his picture taken in the uniform of a British general. Next summer the Prince of Wales, accompanied by his very good friend Louis Mountbatten, visited Tokyo to finish the golf game he and Hirohito had begun in Britain. Mountbatten took the opportunity to make a secret report to his naval bosses about the huge and impressively armed Japanese battleship, the *Mutsu*.

In 1922, under pressure from Canada and the United States, Britain did not renew the Anglo-Japanese Alliance. Japan was vexed, but in fact not much changed in relations between the two. The Tientsin Incident makes the point. In July 1939 a political murderer sought by the Japanese authorities in Tientsin took refuge in the British concession. The Japanese demanded, not merely the delivery of the murderer, but also control of the concession. Britain, cravenly buying in to the notion that Japan had territorial rights in China, agreed to both demands. When, in March 1941, Vichy France granted Japan military access to the northern part of French Indochina, the Chief of the Imperial General Staff in London sent a telegram to Sir Robert Brooke-Popham, Commander in Chief Far East, "Avoidance of war with Japan is the basis of Far East policy and provocation must be rigidly avoided." In September Japan occupied the whole of French Indochina and the telegram was repeated.

Where did Canada stand on the Japan question? British Columbia in particular was as sensitive as California to the "threat" of Japanese immigration. During the 1880's, in response to the needs of the railway, oriental labourers flooded into the coastal regions. Here again, the Chinese and the Japanese were regarded differently. The *Victoria Colonist* claimed in 1900 that "the virile, civilized, and intellectual Japanese is an even more dangerous rival [to the European population] than the Chinese." The fact that Japanese fishermen held 20% of the Fraser River fishing licences in 1893 and 85% of them 20 years later reinforced this fear. Vancouver newspapers carried scare headlines about "Little Brown Men Swarming into Province," and in 1907 the Asiatic Exclusion League organized a full-scale riot against Vancouver's Little Tokyo. "Picture brides" began to appear and when people realized that the Japanese birth rate was three times the European birthrate, the fear of Japanese domination continued to grow. Even after Japan and Canada had concluded a "Gentlemen's Agreement" strictly limiting the rate of migration, the outbreak of the Sino-Japanese war triggered rumours of Japanese naval officers lurking on the Fraser River docks as spies and recruiters of spies. The BC Government petitioned the federal government to stop all Japanese immigration.

In Ottawa, on the other hand, there was a sense of obligation toward Japan. After all, during World War I Canada had entrusted Japan with the defence of the entire west coast. A lead article in *Saturday Night* maintained that, but for the presence of the Japanese Navy, the German Navy would have "shelled Victoria and Vancouver to fragments." And then there was the mundane matter of trade. By 1929 Japan was Canada's fourth largest trading partner and the balance of this trade was strongly in Canada's favour. With ostentatious panoply Canada had just opened a Trade Legation in Tokyo. Finally, despite all the talk of dominion autonomy replacing colonial dependence, Canada still remained in the shadow of "the Old Country" and Britain's twisted friendship with Japan was part of that shadow. When Japan officially protested the 1907 march against Vancouver's Little Tokyo, Prime Minister Wilfrid Laurier wrote to the mayor of Vancouver: "His Excellency has learned with the deepest regret of the indignities and cruelties of which certain subjects of the Emperor of Japan, a friend and ally of his Majesty the King, have been the victims and he hopes that peace will be promptly restored and all the offenders punished." A commission sent out from Ottawa (headed by a youthful Mackenzie King) investigated the Japanese protest and awarded a compensation of $9999. British Columbia again urged a total ban on Japanese immigration, but the Gentlemen's Agreement was working well and in Ottawa the motion was easily defeated. Despite increasing agitation for trade restrictions, Canada's exports to Japan were as high in 1940 as they had been in 1938. Although Mackenzie King — now the Prime Minister — could see war with Japan on the horizon and knew that when it came, Canada would fight on the side of America and Britain, his government still continued to treat its Asian friends with circumspection.

Meanwhile back in Burma things were closing in for the British. With the northern half of Indochina now in Japanese hands, the only supply route to China was northward from the port of Rangoon, through Burma, and then across into China via the Burma Road. The Americans wanted this route held open at all costs; the Japanese were equally vehement that it should be closed. Britain, pressed to the last wall in Europe, desperately needed supplies from America and just as desperately needed the assurance that Japan would not force her into an Asiatic war. What should she do with the pesky Burma Road?

THE BURMA ROAD

ALONG THE northwestern border of China about two thousand years ago one small feudal kingdom, the kingdom of Ch'in, overran the neighbouring kingdoms so that, in 221 BC, all the eastern empire lay under one command. King Cheng, who held the reins of that command, was not a prepossessing fellow, if we accept the description given by a later Grand Historian of China: "high-pointed nose, slit eyes, pigeon breast, wolf voice, tiger heart, stingy, cringing, graceless." One could add ruthless, too. He executed the conquered kings, then collected all their weaponry and melted it down to make bells and immense statues. He abolished the entire feudal system and set up 36 prefectures each ruled by his own appointee. For himself he took the title Ch'in Shih Yuang Ti, that is, First August Sovereign, and to this great new country he gave the name China in honour of the dynasty from which he came. He introduced a uniform system of weights and measures throughout the land, coded and unified the laws, ordered a common currency and a universal writing system. He also burned all the books (except those on agriculture and medicine) and when the scholars who wrote them protested, he had 460 of them buried alive.

Then he began to build. For the next ten years he put the hundreds of thousands of peasants available to him as corvée labour to work on his most ambitious project, the Great Wall of China. Having decreed a standard axle length for all wheeled vehicles, the First Emperor set about building a network of "speedways" so that his armies could move quickly to all frontiers to protect his kingdom. As well, he built enormous elaborate palaces and, most extravagant of all, his own tomb, an elaborate mausoleum surrounded by a moat of mercury in a bronze channel and guarded by thousands of life-size terracotta soldiers. Of his many accomplishments and achievements,

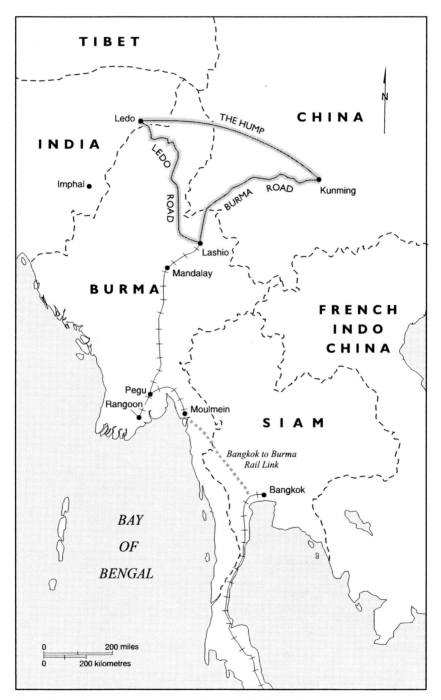

Map 2 — The Burma Road, the Ledo Road, the Hump, and
the Bangkok-to-Burma Rail Link.

however, it is the road that led southwest from Kunming that interests us, the Burma Road.

Like all the First Emperor's speedways, the Burma Road was built with huge granite slabs measuring seven to nine feet in length and as much as a foot in depth. It served to help subdue the restless tribesmen along the border, but it was also known as the Tribute Road, for spices, silk and cotton went down the road, along with salt from the Yunnan salt wells, and back up the road came rubies and jade, agates and amber, gold and silver, and even elephants, all contributed by the conquered tribes to acknowledge the Emperor's pre-eminence. (At one time, the British Consul in Kunming was housed in the pavilion that had originally been the elephant stables.)

Over the years the road was improved. The bridge over the Salween, originally slung from bamboo poles splinted together, was rebuilt with strong iron chains "five on each side and made to last forever," and they still swung across the wild current in 1930 when Dr. Bradley, a British medical missionary, set out to travel the Burma Road from Kunming to Bhamo. Little of the splendid granite-slab road that the First Emperor had laid down still remained. The first twenty-five miles westward from Kunming had been newly rebuilt with compacted earth, but since rain fell unremittingly on Bradley's departure day this was worse than no road at all. After that first day he travelled by mule, staying the night in primitive and unsavoury guest houses and at one point hiring a rag-tag platoon of mercenaries to protect his troop from local banditry. The track led up to heights of more than 8000 feet along narrow paths clinging to steep mountainsides; it took Bradley and his party thirty-one days to cover the 700 miles from Kunming to Bhamo. That was in 1930; by 1936 the Burma Road was once again an almost completely forgotten and abandoned mountain track.

Two years later it was a beehive, or, as one observer described it, an anthill of activity.

On October 21, 1938 when Japanese troops occupied Canton, China's foremost port for foreign entry, the last link between China and Hong Kong was severed. Now only one practicable supply route was available to Chiang Kai-shek's forces, the rail link from Hanoi in French Indochina to Kunming. There was also the uncertain trace of the Burma Road. When the Japanese pressured the French to forbid the transport of war materials on the Haiphon-to-Kunming railway, the Burma Road took on new significance and the Chinese secretly began to rebuild it.

The rebuilding of the road was no secret to the American Gordon Seagrave, who was later to become famous as the Burma Surgeon. His hospital at Namkhan on the border between China and Burma almost overlooked the road and the scurry of construction hugely piqued his curiosity. In 1937 he eagerly seized the excuse of a medical emergency in Lunglin to make a tentative excursion along it. The "road" was barely six inches wider than his second-hand Buick and in places he had to put down the top and lay the windshield flat to get under the overhanging rocks. The last twenty miles had to be accomplished on foot because there was no bridge. But the hill-sides were alive with thousands of coolies carrying baskets of clay on their heads, patting it down with their hands, cutting down sacred banyan trees, desecrating ancestral graveyards and jungle shrines that the road might be completed. On the Burma side, 17,000 conscript coolies were put to work in February 1938 with orders to hard surface the road from Lashio to the Chinese border by June. When he next travelled the Burma Road, Seagrave could easily drive the 700 miles from Bhamo to Kunming in three days .The new Burma Road was well on the way to being a reality.

But the real purpose of the road was as a military supply route from Rangoon to Kunming, and to date no one had shown that it was ready to serve that purpose. The first person to do so was Robert Baird McClure.

Robert McClure, the son of a Canadian medical missionary in China and eventually first lay Moderator of the United Church of Canada, followed in his father's footsteps. He was a man of unbounded courage and energy, of insatiable curiosity, indomitable spirit, and born with the absolute conviction that he could do pretty well anything he set his mind to. Once, in the middle of a serious operation he found that the husband, who was to give the blood vital to the success of the operation, had fled in terror. Without a moment's hesitation McClure climbed up on the stretcher, supplied the blood himself, then climbed down and finished the operation. On one of his rare home leaves he learned to fly, convinced that somewhere, some time, that would be a useful skill to have. In the same spirit he took para-training. Above all, he was a practical man, a trait that developed early and stood him in good stead throughout his life.

McLure spent most of his first fifteen years at his father's mission station in Yunnan province so that his command of the Chinese language was near native, especially in the rough, earthy vernacular of the working man. He came "home" to Toronto for his schooling in 1915, and seven years later graduated from the University of Toronto Medical School. His extracurricular activities were important too, for with them he developed his sense of practical engineering. In 1916 the sixteen-year old McClure took a summer job at the Russell Motor Car Company.[1] For twelve to fifteen hours a day he turned casings for artillery shells and thus learned at least the rudiments of machining and metal work. Later as a medical student

---

[1] The Russell Motor Car Company, formed by the merger in 1902 of Canadian Motors and the Canadian Cycle and Motor Company (CCM), produced one of the very few motor cars ever designed and built wholly in Canada. Its cars met with some international success, but design troubles led to its demise and the company went out of the auto business in 1913.

he acquired a strange conveyance consisting of four bicycle wheels with a fifth wheel behind driven by a small gasoline engine. The knowledge and experience required to keep this "pentacycle" on the road became the basis of the mechanical skills that served him well over and over again in the mission field and especially on the Burma Road. Some years later, in China, he even arranged to work for a fortnight in a Chevrolet engine factory so that he could recover and rehabilitate an ambulance that had sunk eight feet below the surface in quicksand. He also experimented with the production of methane gas from water steamed through a bed of hot coals which he then used to power all the equipment and lights of his mission hospital. All these unexpected and ancillary skills that McClure derived from these varied experiences he later put to good use on the Burma Road.

By 1937 the Japanese invasion of China had gained sufficient momentum that a group of missionaries and industrialists, foreseeing the need for some agency that could bring relief to civilian victims along the battle front, formed a branch of the International Red Cross and asked McClure to become Field Supervisor. He realized that his work as a medical missionary at Hwaiking would soon be in jeopardy, the United Church of Canada agreed to continue his salary, and Robert McClure took on the job. It was a job that kept him very busy tending victims of air raids and scrounging for supplies. W. H. Auden and Christopher Isherwood, travelling to report on the Sino-Japanese War, were worn out after spending ten days with him; he had, they declared "the energy of a whirlwind and the high spirits of a schoolboy."

On one trip to Hankow, now the "capital" of Free China, McClure got a mysterious message asking him to be at a certain street corner at a certain time. A green sedan drew up. He was swept into the rear seat and whisked down strange alleys and narrow streets, transferred to another car, to a small truck, and eventually conducted into a suburban residence and into the presence of a petite, charming Chinese lady who spoke excellent English, Madame Chiang Kai-shek. She arranged for McClure to tour Europe and America speaking about the valiant struggle of the Chinese people. She also suggested that on his way back he would do well to acquaint himself with the Burma Road.

A suggestion from the Number One Hankow Lady, as McClure took to naming her in his letters home, was pretty well a command, but for Bob the idea was irresistible in its own right. The Burma Road was still a military secret. Even a year later, the American journalist, Nicol Smith, trying to film the Burma Road, was warned: "You'll never go there. That's the secretest secret in all China." But with Mme. Chiang Kai-shek's backing there was no problem, and McClure set out to make the acquaintance of the new Burma Road. As far as McClure knew, only Gordon Seagrave had so far actually travelled it, and even Seagrave had not gone all the way to Rangoon.

On his way back from his European tour, McClure acquired in Rangoon two identical Dodge light trucks, one with a station wagon body, one with a small truck body. One was bought with Canadian funds, the other was provided by an American bishop, who was also to travel with them. In mid-January 1939 the small convoy set out for Kunming, a distance of about 1300 miles. Bob was driving the jitney bus and Bishop Ralph Ward of the American Methodist Mission the station wagon. Both vehicles were loaded to capacity and beyond, especially since the good Bishop had, at the last minute and without consulting McClure, added three extra passengers so that the bus was required to tow a trailer sway-backed under the weight of food, bedding, medical supplies and enough spare parts to build a third Dodge. The roof of each vehicle was piled high with the luggage and on top of the luggage the Bishop's car carried Bob's new bike, a Raleigh, "the best bike he had ever owned."

The first 600 miles, from Rangoon to Lashio, took just two days. The road surface was good, the road was level, and refuelling was no problem. One hundred and sixteen miles beyond Lashio the road surface changed from crushed gravel to round pebbles — they were in China. There were no formalities; the custom office had been moved back 65 miles into China because the original station had been burned by Kachin tribesmen and the attendants had been massacred. With this on the top of their minds, the mission convoy was not comforted to be told that the Shwaba, the local tribal ruler, expected them to pay a courtesy call on him as they passed through his territory. The entry to the Shwaba's village was through a gated portal. The station wagon went first, and McClure watched in anguish as the low roof of the portal swept the luggage and his new bike from the roof rack. Stoically he picked up the pieces.

The Shwaba fortunately was celebrating the funeral of his mother so that, instead of the hostility they feared, the convoy was hospitably received and it was four hours before they could get on their way. At Lunglin, the little village that was to be their stopping place for the night, McClure and his group waited and waited for the Bishop; after all, he had their bedding and their money. Finally they rented a few thread-bare, flea-infested blankets and bedded down for the night in the local school. Late the next morning the Bishop appeared. The Shwaba had invited them to spend the night and it seemed like too good an invitation to refuse. McClure summed up his reaction in a letter to his wife: "With the worry over them, the lack of our bedding, the lack of funds and the wreck of my bike, I was definitely not feeling fraternal toward the Bishop." His mood was not improved when, entering the low portal of the bridge over the mighty Salween the next day, the Bishop completed the destruction of Bob's wonderful new bike.

At the Salween their way was barred by a ragged troop of soldiers. McClure recognized that the illiterate officer in charge was an opium addict and that the soldiers were in fact brigands. He turned on them all the rough eloquence of his Yunnan upbringing and they backed down at once.

The terrain was now decidedly less tractable. In Rangoon they had been told that driving the Burma Road was akin to an ant crawling over corrugated iron and they soon came to appreciate the aptness of that simile. Again and again they climbed to seven and even eight thousand feet only to drop down again to three thousand feet within a few miles and then immediately begin to climb again. The road reached its summit at 9500 feet — at 10,000 feet aircrew are required to use oxygen. Gradients of 15% were common and more than once the jitney was stalled until all its passengers got out and pushed. At times the road clung by its toenails to precipitous mountainsides or snaked along the steep sides of valleys. To get down to the bridges over the Salween and the Mekong required an unbelievably torturous series of switchbacks. McClure noted with satisfaction that the bridges, suspended from long lengths of steel chain, were stressed for seven tons, sufficient for a fully-loaded lorry. In Burma they had counted seven steamrollers at work: in China there were coolies, male and female, large and small, toiling like ants. It is claimed that from 130,000 to 300,000 peasants were recruited for the road, and paid, for the most part, with opium. They worked with their hands and with baskets. Even shovels and wheelbarrows were rare and at one point McClure deciphered a perversely proud sign roughly painted on the cliff: "This road was built by the natives of this district without the aid of foreign implements."

On the sixth day the convoy came through the last pass and broke out above a beautiful plain. In the middle of an emerald green valley lay a blue lake and, at its eastern end, Kunming, their destination. They had travelled 1300 miles without a breakdown, without even a flat tire. McClure could now report to the Number One Hankow Lady that the Burma Road as supply route for the Chinese forces was a reality. He had shown that the thousands of dollars and the thousands of lives — it has been estimated that two coolies died for every six feet of road in the 700 mile stretch from Lashio to Kunming — expended on the road had not been wasted. The back door to China, by now the only door, was open for business.

That journey on the Burma Road was only the first of many for Robert McClure. In June of 1941 he was asked to take command of a Friends Ambulance Unit on the Road. He was delighted with the opportunity and was soon in Rangoon again, this time to receive twelve shiny new ambulances, two of them even outfitted as operating theatres. Everyone was elated — except Robert McClure. He alone realized that the vehicles were exactly six inches too wide for the bridges of the Burma Road. But he also knew the remedy. He persuaded the British Army that they needed his ambulances and that they should give him twenty-four new ambulances with bare chassis in return. He and his drivers then worked furiously to transfer the equipment to the new frames. But while waiting for the ambulances to be fitted, McClure completed twelve trips on the Road with other trucks modified according to his specifications and under his direction to burn charcoal rather than gasoline. Gasoline was expensive, hard to get and hard to handle; charcoal was inexpensive and available everywhere.

These trips were not uneventful. On one trip they came upon a coolie who had been hit by a truck. There was a hospital in the next town, but it was a "show place only" and its doors were locked. McClure broke in through the back door and while the so-called nurses and doctors looked on he clipped the hair with hair clippers and trimmed the wound with his razor. When the resident staff refused to provide a bandage McClure's companion grabbed a sheet and threatened to tear it. The bandage was found. On another occasion he was stopped by a ragtag band of soldiers demanding papers or money. As McClure tells the story: "the soldier was nasty and loaded his rifle in front of us and then pointed it at my head. I jumped out and we had a little disarmament conference. I took the bayonet off before it went into me and threw it over the precipice. Then I got the bolt out of the breech and the five rounds out, and finally by making a rather forceful argument under his chin, I took the entire rifle away in a very un-Quakerly style and put it in the cab of the truck."

Thanks to McClure's pioneering venture, the back door to China was opened and the American supplies that could no longer be delivered via Hong Kong or Hanoi began to pile up on the docks of Rangoon. By the end of 1939, 21,965 metric tons of American Lend-Lease war matériel had wiggled along the Burma Road to Kunming and in December of that year a thousand more three-ton Chrysler and General Motors trucks were on the way, paid for with $25,000,000 from the American Import-Export Bank.

This was a circumstance the Japanese could not tolerate and strong pressure was put on Britain to close the road. In March 1940 Sir Robert Brooke-Popham, the Commander-in-Chief for the Far East, again got the word: "Avoidance of war with Japan is the basis of Far East policy and provocation must be rigidly avoided." The same stricture bound the Chiefs of Staff in London as they weighed their options: their European allies were gone, the Army had not recovered from Dunkirk, Germany was flexing her muscles just across the Channel, no one knew where the Americans stood. There really were no options to weigh. They recommended that the road be closed and on September 18, 1940 the Government concurred. The understanding was that the closure should last for three months, time to either find a way of living with Japan or to find a firm ally in America.

The Japanese were not particularly appreciative. On September 23, 1940 they finished their occupation of French Indochina and three days after that, having seen the way the war winds blew in Europe, they signed the Tripartite Pact with Germany and Italy. Now Britain's course was clear and it took very little urging from the Americans to cause her to re-open the Road. There would be no more vacillation or appeasement, no more attempts to placate Japan.

For the next year the port of Rangoon was busier than it had ever been and the Burma Road was used to capacity. Sylvia Molloy, wife of an area administrator, witnessed the scene when she accompanied her husband across the Road in 1941: "We travelled in our 12 year-old Essex tourer via Lashio, which is where the Burma Road to China began. All along the road we met lorries either going to or coming from China. At Lashio we had seen thousands of them, many of them American and of the latest design." It was still not an easy passage. In many places the road was so narrow that trucks could scarcely pass and Mrs. Molloy describes how they came upon two trucks jammed together on one of the steepest parts and on a corner overlooking a precipice. Still, the Burma Road was there and, as Robert McClure had shown, it was ready to serve its purpose — at least for a time.

III

DAY OF INFAMY

IN THE 1940-41 period, Japanese foreign policy, particularly as interpreted by the Army faction in the government, focused increasingly on the aggressive implications of the dream of a Greater East Asia Co-Prosperity Sphere. To smooth the way toward this dream Japan signed a Tripartite Pact of neutrality with Germany and Italy on September 27, 1940, completed the occupation of French Indochina and signed a five-year Neutrality Pact with Russia. This overt sabre rattling could not be overlooked; the United States reacted by forbidding the sale of iron and steel to Japan and, later, of aviation fuel. On July 26, 1941 both the United States and Britain froze all the Japanese assets they held.

The oil and gas embargo particularly pinched. Japan had stockpiled sufficient fuel for two years, but that was far from enough for even a contained war. Negotiations with the Netherlands government-in-exile in London had been unsatisfactory; if the Dutch East India fields were to be seized, then they had to be seized swiftly before they could be demolished. And then there was that other irksome development, the flood of war matériel making its way along the Burma Road from Rangoon to Kunming, 15,000 tons of it every month, all in direct defiance of the Amau Doctrine of 1934 wherein Japan had declared herself to be the "guardian of peace and order in East Asia" and had forbidden any nation to assist China in its resistance to Japan.

For Japan the time for decisive action was coming closer. Any aggressive move now had in it the risk of war with both Britain and the United States, but that was a risk she had to take. Britain at least was impotent in the East, being fully occupied in Europe. For some time the Japanese Army had had its "Go South" plan ready, a plan for an assault against European colonial holdings in East Asia — the Philippines, the Netherlands East Indies,

Map 3 — Japanese Landings, December 7-8, 1941

Malaya, Burma and Guam plus the independent kingdom of Siam. A necessary adjunct to this plan was a synchronized attack on Pearl Harbour, with the object of neutralizing the American Pacific Fleet, accompanied by a broad sweep away out to the middle of the Pacific. This eastern thrust, reaching out to Midway and Guam, the Philippines and Papua New Guinea, was strategically important in establishing a wide defensive ring wherein the Japanese Navy could play freely. But the western thrust, encompassing Malaya, Sumatra, Java and lower Burma, was more important, for it would deliver to Japan not only tea, rice and sugar, but ninety per cent of the world's rubber, sixty per cent of the world's tin and an almost unlimited supply of oil and petroleum products. And it would close the Burma Road.

This plan was put into action on December 8, 1941 Japanese time, December 7 Washington time. Early in November all forces were warned to prepare for action and on December 1 they were told of the assault day. On December 4, eighteen Japanese troopships bearing 26,000 soldiers especially trained for beach assaults left Hainan harbour. At 2:15 am on December 8 Japanese time, they landed on the eastern shore of the Kra Isthmus. Seventy minutes later Japanese aircraft attacked Pearl Harbour.

Because American officials were still desperately negotiating in good faith with Japanese emissaries in Washington, trying to find an accommodation to the impasse even as the attack was being launched, Roosevelt called December 7 "the day that will live in infamy" and ever since history has equated this day with Pearl Harbour alone. And with good reason. On that day four American battleships were sunk, 188 planes were destroyed, 2334 American lives were lost, and on that day the United States finally declared itself a combatant in World War II, changing completely the course of the war. But it was the other attacks of that infamous day that spread like a cancer across the East Asian landscape. Seven strategically important landings were made along the eastern shore of the Kra Isthmus. The southernmost, at Kota Bharu in Malaya, struck at the head of the railway that led through the world's richest rubber producing area and straight to the island fortress of Singapore while the northernmost, in Siam, was just 25 miles from the Burmese border and Burma offered oil and control of the Burma Road. Over 26,000 troops were landed — a month later this number had risen to 110,000. This is the thrust that developed into full-scale invasion and eventually into the Burma War.

In a long history of military unpreparedness, Britain was probably never so unprepared as she was for the Japanese attacks in the Far East. Since 1923 her plans for the defence of her eastern empire centred altogether on the notion of a strong naval force based at the "impregnable fortress" of Singapore. From its conception the plan was suspect. When the then Prime Minister of Australia, S.M. Bruce, heard of it he remarked with touching faith and loyalty that, while he was "not quite as clear as I should like to be as to how the protection of Singapore is to be assured, I am clear on this point, that apparently it can be done." In 1938 the assurance was that nine capital ships, three carriers, and 19 cruisers would be available within 70 days. By June 1939 this assurance had dwindled to a carrier and a battlecruiser based in Ceylon plus an unidentified additional force available within 180 days. When the attack began on December 7, 1941, the actual strength of the British Navy at Singapore was 1 battleship, 1 battlecruiser and 7 destroyers. The Japanese Navy counted 10 battleships, 34 cruisers, 9 aircraft carriers, 110 destroyers and 64 submarines. As Raymond Callahan trenchantly remarks in *Burma: 1942-1945*, "from 1922 Britain's Far Eastern empire was in fact defenceless, unless the Japanese obligingly attacked at a moment of profound European tranquility."

As for Burma, Brooke-Popham declared in his Order of the Day for December 8, 1941: "We are ready.... Our defences are strong and our weapons efficient." This did not quite accord with reality. There were two British regiments of garrison troops, one in Rangoon, one in Maymyo, both under strength. They had Bren gun carrier platoons, but no Bren gun carriers, Thompson machine guns with 90 rounds of ammunition for each, 3-inch mortars and almost no ammunition. Two brigades of Indian Infantry were also available, but they were almost untrained and altogether untested. In addition there were four battalions of Burma Rifles and four Burma Frontier Force units, but these latter were basically police under civil control. Lacking radios, they communicated with semaphore flags and heliographs or through the public telephone and telegraph services. The anti-aircraft battery trained assiduously, but ineffectually, for they had no guns. There were four 18-pounder field guns left over from World War I but there were no shells for them. Air defence was entrusted to a motley collection of 140 antiquated aircraft. The Brewster Buffalo, the star of the show, was a tubby little low-wing monoplane that had been declared obsolete by the Royal Air Force in Britain in August 1940.

But — not to worry. There really was no problem. The High Command in Britain was convinced that Japan was concentrating for action against Russia (even though she had just signed the Russo-Japanese Neutrality Pact) and that she would not consider any aggression in the Far East that could bring down upon her the combined wrath of Britain, the United States, and the Netherlands. Duff-Cooper, Minister of Information, on an inspection tour of Singapore and Burma in mid-1941, unable to imagine a war in the Far East, commiserated with the Rangoon garrison: "I'm sorry for you chaps out here. You'll never have a shot at the Jerries or the Italians." And even if the Japanese Army did come, the British could handle them easily. After all, the Japanese soldiers were bow-legged little fellows who travelled by bicycle and were afraid of the dark. As for the Japanese Air Force, it was well known that their pilots were handicapped by poor eyesight, the consequence of a diet of seaweed.

The Japanese did come, of course, and the Royal Navy's *Repulse* and *Prince of Wales* — just arrived to defend Singapore — were sunk two days after Pearl Harbour. When Hong Kong capitulated on Christmas Day 1941, three hundred Canadians were killed, 500 wounded, and 1200 went into four years of brutal captivity. The Japanese forces that had landed at Singora and Kota Bharu spread down the Malaya peninsula and occupied Singapore. Troops from Indochina and southern China occupied Siam. On December 14, 1941, Japanese troops crossed the border from Siam into Burma.

At the forefront of the thrust into Burma there was a small element of the Burmese Independence Army. The "Quit India" movement that was gathering strength in India was echoed in Burma by underground freedom groups protesting the British occupation. In particular they resented the Indians who had immigrated as menials and then stayed to completely take over certain segments of Burmese society. There had been strikes — a students' strike in 1920, a peasants' strike in 1930, a strike among the oil field workers of Yenangyaung in 1938 — but the British had ruthlessly suppressed them. Then, in May 1940, Minami Masuyo, the affable correspondent for a Japanese newspaper, came to Rangoon. In reality he was Colonel Suzuki Keiji, posted to Burma by the Imperial Army HQ to organize a fifth column among the patriots and the disaffected. In February 1941 he formed the Minami Organ, an underground group whose express purpose was "to aid Burmese independence and to close the Burma Road."

As the threat of war came closer, Minami moved his organization to Bangkok and arranged for the leaders, the Thirty Thakin (masters), to go to Hainan, a small island off the southern coast China, for training. Among them was a young student named Aung San, an energetic advocate of Burmese independence and editor of the student newspaper in Rangoon. When war broke out 200 Burmese patriots and 74 sympathetic Japanese joined together to form the Burmese Independence Army (BIA), marking the occasion with a parade through the streets of Bangkok, with ceremonial oath-taking, and with the ancient ritual of "drinking the blood of the arm." Colonel Suzuki was the Commander in Chief, and Aung San was his Chief of Staff. The BIA became part of the Japanese Fifteenth Army with the understanding that it should be in the vanguard of the thrust into Burma.[1]

---

[1] While in the end the promise of freedom that came with the Japanese troops was chimerical and Aung San eventually switched to the British side, it is only fair to make the point that Colonel Suzuki himself was impressed by the patriotic fervour of the Burmese and came to believe in their cause to the point that he found himself strongly at odds with

Colonel Suzuki, now General Bo Mgyo, gave the battle cry: "The favourable opportunity for Burmese independence has now arrived. Rise up! The enemy is weak."

A small group of BIA soldiers crossed from Siam into Burma even before the Japanese invaded. Knowing the language and the people they could move ahead of the main force, gathering information, marking paths and jungle tracks, soliciting rice and bullock carts, and persuading the village youths to volunteer as porters and the local population to welcome the invaders as friends and liberators. A Japanese war correspondent described the arrival of the invading troops: "When we entered the village, the villagers greeted us with joy, brought us coconuts, presented us with brown sugar blocks and entertained us with plain tea.... When we announced 'We are Japanese troops and are now going to beat the English troops,' they literally danced for joy and many offered themselves as guides." Even among the Burma Rifles, ostensibly a mainstay of the British defence forces, soldiers now deserted to the BIA ranks.

The bulk of Burma forms an elongated wedge with India on the western edge and China and Siam on the east, but the tail of Burma stretches thinly southward along the western shore of the Kra Isthmus to end at Victoria Point. Along the 500 miles of coastline leading northward to Rangoon there were four important airfields, one at Victoria Point itself, others at Mergui, Tavoy and Moulmein. These were the objectives the Japanese forces that landed on the eastern shore of the Kra Isthmus headed for. The distance they had to cover was not great — the Isthmus is barely 50 miles wide — but so mountainous and so jungled was the terrain that they averaged only four or five miles a day. On December 14, one week after the Day of Infamy, they crossed the Burmese border, boarded trucks supplied by the BIA, and rode in triumph into Victoria Point. The defenders had withdrawn the day before. Mergui and Tavoy fell on January 19 and Moulmein, the city that looks westward to the sea, on January 30. The next major objective was obvious, Rangoon. But between the invader and Rangoon lay one more obstacle — the Sittang River.

---

his superiors and spoke out against the behaviour of his fellow countrymen. Remembering Colonel Suzuki's true sympathy for Burma and the BIA, Aung San never turned altogether against the Japanese. Still today a statue in Rangoon depicts him in the uniform of a British officer while in Prome he is depicted wearing a Japanese uniform.

DEBACLE AT SITTANG BRIDGE

W HEN THE Japanese invaded Burma, they had not planned on
conquering the whole of it but merely on controlling the oil
wells at Yenangyaung, the refineries near Rangoon, and, most
importantly, the Burma Road. They estimated that 15,000 tons of matériel
were reaching Kunming monthly, most of it American lend-lease and all of
it through the port of Rangoon. Without Rangoon, the Japanese could not
cut off these supplies nor hope to control the Burma Road. Between them
and their goal however lay one last barrier, the 600 yard wide Sittang River.
Inexorably the Japanese invaders fought their way northward, reinforced
now by troops who had struggled across a difficult mountain path from
northern Siam.

It was not a lack of fighting spirit in the defenders that enabled the invaders' inexorable advance. The 17th Indian Division fought with tenacity, but
the cards were stacked against them. Many of the troops were untrained
and newly recruited from their remote villages, while the rest were trained
for fighting in the north African desert, not in the jungle and hills of lower
Burma. They had little artillery and no armour (though that was coming)
and virtually no air support. Moreover they were mechanized and therefore
bound to the roads, and for the last twenty miles to the Sittang Bridge there
was no road, just country track.

But the main reason for the 17th Division's lack of success was command
confusion. Immediately after Pearl Harbour, Roosevelt and Churchill had
met and agreed upon a unified command for South East Asia. It was to be
called ABDA (for American, British, Dutch and Australian) and General
Archibald Wavell was to be the Supreme Commander. To satisfy all the
stakeholders, his mandate was to hold the line Sumatra — Java — Australia,
a mandate that left Burma out in the cold, and his headquarters were

to be in Java, 2000 miles from Rangoon. Wavell operated from the firm conviction that the Japanese were inferior soldiers and that they were outnumbered. Accordingly his insistent order was "Attack! Fight forward! Hold Victoria Point at all costs!" Or Mergui or Tavoy or Moulmein. And when each of these successively fell, he whined "The troops are not fighting with relish," an assessment picked up and echoed all the way to the Prime Minister's office in London.[1]

Wavell's "Fight forward" adjurations were passed to Lt. General "Jackie" Smyth, now in charge of the 17th Division. As a 23 year old subaltern Smyth had won a VC in France in 1915 and later an MC in the Afghan War in 1919. He was a soldier's soldier of the stiff-upper-lip variety. Perhaps a bit too stiff, for in his eagerness to remain in active command he persuaded a medical board to pass him fit despite an extremely painful and debilitating medical condition. But physical discomfort was not his only problem; he was also at odds with the battle strategy of his immediate superiors. In the first three weeks of February 1942 his troops fought, then disengaged, fell back, and fought again. Gurkhas, Sikhs, Pathans and Yorkshiremen, they battled with absurd bravery, resorting to bayonet and kukri (the knife used by the Gurkhas) when rifle and machine gun would no longer do. At the Bilin, a small river just north of Moulmein, they held up the invaders for four days, giving time for an armoured unit to disembark at Rangoon.

More reinforcements were desperately needed and Churchill, assuming colonial compliance, ordered that an Australian division heading home from the Middle East be diverted to Rangoon. John Curtin, the Australian Prime Minister, made it very clear that those troops were needed at home — Darwin had just been bombed by 100 Japanese planes — and Churchill rescinded his order. Smyth now knew there was only one way to save Rangoon; he had to consolidate and reorganize his scattered forces along the western bank of the Sittang with the river in front of them as a natural defence. Repeatedly he asked for permission to withdraw across the bridge and repeatedly Wavell refused it. In the end Smyth ignored Wavell and began to fall back on the Sittang bridgehead.

Through a series of forced marches, in searing heat, with no water, the troops slogged along the dusty track toward the Sittang in a race for the bridge. Unfortunately the long delaying action at the Bilin, rather than buying time for the British, bought advantage for the Japanese, giving them an opportunity to send an outflanking party wide around the track

[1] The Viceroy, Lord Linlithgow, cabled Churchill: "Our troops in Burma are not fighting with the proper spirit. I have not the least doubt that this is in great part due to lack of drive and inspiration from the top." General Alan Brooke, Chief of the Imperial General Staff, echoed this sentiment in his diary: "Burma bad news. If the Army cannot fight better than it is doing at present we deserve to lose our Empire."

and head through the jungle to the bridgehead. This tactic of holding the enemy's feet to the fire at the front while sweeping wide around his flank to establish a road block in his rear was one the Japanese used repeatedly in their march up Burma. Unencumbered by motor vehicles and guided by the Burmese Independence Army, it was a natural for them. At the Sittang they did it again arriving at the bridge almost as soon as the British.

The fleeing troops concentrated in a small level area in front of the bridge as they waited to cross. The bridge was meant only for trains and the British engineers were covering the eleven spans, each 50 yards long, with planking for road traffic even as the soldiers approached. The planking was scarcely wide enough for the vehicles and in places it bounced loudly and loosely. Passage was slow and tension was high, even higher when a three-ton lorry went out of control and two precious hours were wasted trying to free its nose from the girders. All the while, the engineers were preparing and placing their demolition charges and now, even as they clambered down to the piers and along the girders, the Japanese began to snipe at them from the hills that overlooked the bridgehead. The rearguard fought to keep the enemy off this ridge, but inevitably the moment would come when the plunger would have to be pushed and the bridge blown.

At 6:30 in the evening of February 22, the sappers of the Malerkotla Field Engineering Company reported that the demolition charges were in place. The rearguard was still holding off the Japanese and stragglers were still coming across. Smyth, called to a conference near Rangoon, gave his Brigadier full authority to blow the bridge when he saw fit. The brigadier fretted through the hours of the night. If he held out till dawn, could more men be saved? But if he held out till dawn, could the bridge be blown before the enemy attacked? If the enemy attacked, could the rearguard hold them off? The bridge had to be blown or the road to Rangoon would be an open highway for the enemy. But when? Where was that fine balance point that allowed the greatest number to escape while yet ensuring the successful demolition of the bridge? Smyth had decided that the bridge should be blown: Brigadier Hugh-Jones alone had to decide when. At 5:30 am on February 23, Hugh-Jones withdrew the covering troops and gave the order to push the plunger. There was a tremendous roar and then, for a brief moment, unreal silence as both sides took in the finality of the event. For the British it was near disaster. Headquarters and one brigade were safely across, but more than half of 17 Division was stranded on the other side. Of 8000 men, only 3300 had reached the western shore. Fortunately the enemy did not push its advantage and in the next week a further 1400 crossed by swimming, on makeshift bamboo rafts, or clutching empty petrol tins. Three hundred non-swimmers pulled themselves across on a lifeline an enterprising officer had strung across from the end of the bridge wreckage to the western shore.[2]

Controversy about the rightness or wrongness of the decision to blow the bridge raged bitterly in the weeks that followed, and rages still among military historians and Burma vets. We give the last word to a man who was there, John Hedley: "I'd like to meet the man who blew the bridge. He had a ghastly decision to make and I'd like to tell him that I think he was right. … I was almost the last man across, and so can't be accused of being an armchair critic, but I salute the man who made that courageous and ghastly decision." That man was of course Jackie Smyth, the Divisional Commander, and to the end of his days he bitterly fought the condemnation that other armchair critics, in particular Wavell, brought against him.

Until the end of February 1942 the ragged remnants of the 17th Division, lacking guns and even personal arms, many still lacking the uniforms and shoes they had abandoned to cross the Sittang, struggled toward Pegu. For the Japanese their first objective in Burma was straight ahead, the port of Rangoon.

---

[2] These figures are all rough estimates, the best the turmoil of the moment would allow. There is a further, ironic footnote to all this: the Japanese had no plans to attack the bridgehead on the morning of the 23rd. In fact, they were unable to regroup and cross the river until March 3rd.

V

THE FALL OF RANGOON

A PART FROM the heat and humidity of the monsoon season, Rangoon
was a rather pleasant place to be in 1938, especially if, like Keith
Muir, one were an officer of the Indian Army. Muir, born in Eureka,
Nova Scotia, had graduated from Dalhousie in medicine in 1931 and
interned for a year in Ottawa. Then, like many young Canadian doctors
launched into a Depression-ridden world in Canada, he succumbed to the
allure of employment and adventure with the British forces and accepted
a three year short-service commission with the RAF. At the end of his stint,
finding he liked the Services but also finding that the RAF would not
guarantee him a pension, he transferred to the Indian Medical Service and
was soon on his way to India. There were other young Canadian doctors
travelling with him, Lt. D. R. "Red" Nichol (Toronto '35), Lt. Ross McCul-
loch (Toronto '34) and Lt. Clifford Ash (Toronto '34), all bound for Urdu
language training at Rawalpindi.

Perhaps because everything was strange and exotic, Muir found that
Canada was strongly in his thoughts. Walking to the hospital each morning,
he mused about the green grass and yellow dandelions growing by the side
of the road. "Surely I liked Rawalpindi," he remarked, "because there were
simple things like these to remind me of Canada." And there were other
Canadians there; Lt. Ralph Crowe of the Royal Canadian Regiment was in
India on exchange and his Royal Military College classmate, Lt. Thomas
Gemmel, now with the Royal Artillery in India, came to visit him. Dr. Hilda
McNamara of Walkerton, Ontario was employed in the Holy Family Hospital in Rawalpindi. Yvonne Carter from Shelburne, Ontario, a vivacious
young Canadian nurse, became a close friend of Muir's wife Margaret. Capt.
Charles S. Gamble, a McGill graduate and now with the Royal Army Medi-
cal Corps, and his wife swelled the Canadian contingent.

In June 1938 Captain Muir was transferred to Rangoon. He and his wife sailed from Calcutta, down the Hooghly River and across the Bay of Bengal to Mingaladon, the cantonment city on the northern edge of Rangoon. Margaret had come to India from Ottawa and they had married in Bombay the previous October so this was their first real home, "a two story solid brick house with french windows, a covered front porch and morning glories covering its walls." White gardenias and red hibiscus nestled under the neatly trimmed bamboo hedge that surrounded the vivid green lawn. There was a gardener to mow the lawn with his "dah" (a machete-like Burmese knife), a cook and a dishwasher to tend the kitchen, a sweeper to clean the cool tile floors, the flush toilets and the "long" bathtub (as compared to the "knees under the chin" tubs usually found in India) of the western-style bathroom, and a butler to look after the whole household. The sweeper also tended the "dry room," a thoroughly sealed room where a charcoal fire burned constantly throughout the monsoon season to protect leather goods, paper and clothing from the ubiquitous mold and silver fish.

Captain Muir's duties were not onerous. His bearer wakened him early with a cup of tea and then, since he was the regimental medical officer for the First Burma Rifles, he cycled to their lines to hold sick parade. After that, it was back home for breakfast then a leisurely bike ride to the Military Hospital where he was in charge of the Brigade Laboratory. It was also his responsibility to climb the water tower once a week and check the water supply. One morning the red Waterman's fountain pen his mother had given him slipped from his pocket. He watched in despair as it twirled and twinkled to the bottom of the tank. That evening, the Hindu works superintendent handed him the pen. Moved and delighted, Keith exclaimed "You drained the tank just to get my pen?" "It had to be done anyway, Sahib," the superintendent lied.

The workday ended early and Margaret and he could then go shopping or to the cinema. Rangoon, just a few minutes away, offered shops where the Muirs could buy most things – a new frigidaire, an automobile, a choice of "Johnny Walker" or "Haig and Haig" whisky, and even fresh frozen BC salmon to celebrate their first wedding anniversary. Occasionally they went to the weekly dances at the officers mess or visited the night clubs of Rangoon, but often they preferred evenings of mah jong or bridge, or perhaps just a quiet time with the *Ottawa Citizen,* to which Margaret subscribed. Thanks to the "All Up, First Class" mail policy, letters from Canada now came in two weeks. "Here," sighed Muir contentedly, "we enjoyed such comfort as I never expected in the East."

Dropping calling cards at the homes of the other officers and at Government House, the residence of the Governor, was a social obligation which resulted in Margaret and Keith being entertained in the elegantly furnished home of Lt. Col. Roy C. Phelps, the medical superintendent. He was another Canadian, a University of Toronto graduate from Dunnville, Ontario who had joined the Indian Medical Service after service in the First World War. For the great social occasion of the year, the Governor's Ball, the ladies schemed for weeks about their long dresses, but the officers were the real peacocks in their white tropical mess kit with its short jacket, close-fitting trousers, scarlet cummerbund and black velvet cape with embroidered gold lion and crown.

In March 1939, the Muirs went to Canada on home leave. In June Keith returned to Burma alone, leaving Margaret in Canada. Then war broke out in Europe and threats and rumours of war filtering down from Japan made Rangoon an uncertain and uneasy place. In November 1941, Keith was transferred to Maymyo, a hill station in central Burma. A month later war had come to Burma, the atmosphere in Rangoon had changed and the pleasant, almost idyllic life the Muirs had known was gone forever.

What changed Rangoon most markedly and most abruptly was the Japanese air raid of December 23, 1941. On that day, 70 to 80 Japanese bombers with fighter escort attacked, not the docks and oil refineries, which the Japanese wanted to take intact, but the central part of the city and the airfield at Mingaladon. The one radar station in all Burma alerted the one RAF fighter squadron in all Burma and the squadron's total complement of serviceable aircraft, all 18 Brewster Buffaloes, took to the air. So did the 21 Tomahawks of the American Volunteer Group (AVG).

The AVG, popularly known as the Flying Tigers, was the brainchild of Colonel Claire Lee Chennault, an old China hand invalided out of the USAAF because of deafness. He was barnstorming through the mid-western states with a small group of stunt fliers when he began to ponder the perilous fragility of China now that her only lifeline was the Burma Road. Much abetted by the silken tongue and chic charms of Madame Chiang Kai-shek, he persuaded Roosevelt to turn a blind eye to neutrality and other diplomatic niceties and to finance the formation of an independent mercenary air force. Thus three squadrons of American fighter pilots, all seasoned veterans of air warfare, were training in Toungoo in central Burma when the Japanese invaded. Two of these withdrew to Lashio on the Chinese border but the third, in recognition of the importance of Rangoon to the American concern for China, was allocated to Mingaladon. There the flamboyant Americans acquitted themselves well. Their aircraft, made more intimidating by the fierce shark's teeth painted on their noses, were the equal of the Japanese planes and the Chinese government paid them $500 for each enemy plane destroyed. The raid of December 23 was repeated on Christmas Day and again the AVG proved particularly effective. In the two raids the Japanese lost at least 15 aircraft as against 10 for the defenders.[1]

Such strong resistance surprised the Japanese air force and it was a month before they returned to Rangoon. During that month, the meagre air defences of the city grew as aircrew who had been stationed at Singapore evacuated, first to Sumatra and Java and then to Rangoon or Ceylon, a number of Canadians among them. How these Canadians got to the Far East in the first place is a curious and complicated story.

Basically Canadian aircrew arrived in the Far East in one of two ways: either they had joined the RAF pre-war or they were in the RCAF but caught up in the RAF training flow and then posted to wherever the RAF felt they were needed. A surprising number of Canadians joined the RAF or other branches of the British services in the early 1930's. The reasons are not hard to find. During the 1920's and early 1930's the anti-war sentiment engendered by the First World War coupled with a laggard economy meant that England's armed forces had been massively underfunded, to the extent that even the Staff College, the source for all future senior officers, had been closed for two years. That changed in the last half of the 1930's when the clouds of war gathered over Europe and China, and Britain looked about in panic for a way to repair the damage of its neglect. Canada was still deep in the Depression. Well-educated young men were putting in time in relief camps or "riding the rods" in a vain attempt to find work. The regular army was not recruiting but many men joined the Non Permanent Active Militia just to earn a few dollars as Saturday night soldiers. Posted up in the Armouries, along with the Daily Routine Orders, was a notice of short-service commission opportunities in Britain. Unemployed young Canadians read the notice and found a new career.

In Victoria it was whispered that a certain Captain Henry Seymour-Biggs, late of the Royal Navy, could offer opportunity and adventure. Those who followed these mysterious rumours found that Captain Biggs had connections with the RAF. Whether he was a remunerated recruiter or a patriotic volunteer is not clear, but so many young Canadians volunteered under his patronage that the "Biggs' Boys" became an open secret among the youth of Victoria and eventually of all Canada.[2] Recruits had to find their own way to England — the cost from Victoria to Liverpool was $181.20 — where they were given mysterious instructions (on the order of "Go to the back door, knock three times and say 'Joe sent me'") that led eventually to attestation in the RAF. From that point on they became regular members of the British forces and only occasionally and inadvertently were they identified as Canadians.

---

[1] These figures are probably understated. The AVG alone claimed 35 enemy aircraft destroyed.

[2] Ken Stofer of Victoria in his privately circulated book *The Biggs' Boys* estimates that at least 250 young Canadians, and perhaps as many as 750, enlisted under Captain Biggs' auspices.

As for members of the RCAF who were swallowed into the RAF, theirs was from the beginning an ambiguous fate. Throughout the war, and despite repeated efforts at various command levels to untangle the administrative web, there was confusion as to whose pay, promotion, posting and repatriation policies would determine the fate of these orphaned airmen. Under Article 15 of the British Commonwealth Air Training Plan, signed December 17, 1939, the British government undertook to "identify" Canadian, Australian and New Zealand graduates with their respective homelands, but what this meant and how it was to be accomplished was left unsaid. Later the RCAF developed a Canadianization policy which envisioned Canadian aircrew being withdrawn from RAF squadrons to form Canadian squadrons. Considering that in the end almost one third of RAF aircrew were Canadians, the British became justifiably alarmed at the implications this policy had for the integrity of their squadrons. Unexpectedly, when "descrambling" began, and Canadian crews were withdrawn from RAF squadrons for posting to "nominated" squadrons, that is, those nominated to become Canadian squadrons, there was often unhappiness on all sides for the crews had become accustomed to the cosmopolitan camaraderie of a mixed unit.

Whether as Canadians in the RAF or as members of the RCAF swallowed up by the RAF, Canadian airmen had been involved in the war against Japan right from the first day. Alex Jardine of Victoria managed to join the Royal Air Force for pilot training in 1935. In 1937 he was posted to Singapore as second in command of the local Catalina flying boat squadron. His squadron was of course involved in trying to fight off the Japanese landings on the Kra Isthmus.

Another Canadian on the Squadron, P/O David Babineau from Saskatoon, was shot down when the Japanese attacked on Christmas Day. He spent seven hours in the water, the crew holding hands in a circle to support each other till another flying boat found them. Unable to land in the rough seas, the rescue plane dropped them medical supplies and a dinghy and promised to send help. Babineau had been severely burned when his aircraft was shot down and now the sun and the salt water added to their torment. Eleven more hours they waited and then, reports Babineau, "we got the surprise of our lives. A submarine surfaced nearby and took us aboard. They were Dutchmen and about the most pleasant sight I have ever witnessed." He returned to his squadron just in time to be evacuated to Java and then to Ceylon.

Sgt. J. D. Bonnar, an RCAF navigator, joined Jardine's squadron in Singapore on the last day of 1941. Twelve days later he became one of the first Canadians to fight against the Japanese when his crew took off in a Catalina to bomb the Japanese beachhead at Singora. While the skipper steered the big flying boat across the railyards to drop his bombs, Bonnar leaned out the waist blister and threw down incendiaries by hand. Not only was he one of the first Canadians to see action in the East, he was also one of the longest-serving. He had arrived at Singapore at the end of December, 1941. After evacuation from Java and then Sumatra, he rejoined his squadron, No. 205, in Ceylon and fought in the Burma Campaign until he was finally repatriated in July 1944 after two and a half years of fighting the Japanese.

Alex Jardine never did make it into the Burma Campaign. When Singapore fell, he flew for a time from Java. As the Japanese closed in and the Dutch commander threatened to blow up the base, Jardine tried to fly to Sumatra or Ceylon but the only two aircraft left were unserviceable and he was taken prisoner. The Japanese had no plans and no facilities for handling prisoners of war — a category unknown in their *Samurai* tradition of fighting to the death — and he easily led a small group away to attempt an escape. They were frantically trying to build a raft when the Japanese recaptured them and Jardine spent the next two and a half years in a POW camp.

Jardine, Babineau, Bonnar and a few other Canadians were thus in the Far East before Pearl Harbour. In the first months of 1942 more arrived, most of them members of the RCAF. With the belated realization that there actually was a war with Japan, High Command in Britain began a panic scurry to deliver troops to the area. A troopship intended for the Middle East was diverted to Singapore with its cargo of 51 crated Hurricanes, two army battalions and twenty-four aircrew. Among the latter were a few Canadians including Rudy Mendizabal, J. P. Fleming, and Joe Leetham. They were only in action for eleven days before being withdrawn to Java and Sumatra, but in that time they accounted for three enemy aircraft shot down and four probables.

The next wave of reinforcements arrived aboard an unusual troopship, *HMS Indomitable*, the Royal Navy's newest and biggest aircraft carrier. *Indomitable* ought to have been part of Z Force, the naval contingent sent out to save Singapore, but an accident in the West Indies delayed her coming and so saved her from the ignominious fate of the *Prince of Wales* and the *Repulse*. Thus it was that she was available to ferry aircraft and aircrew to the Far East. The 48 Hurricanes she carried were uncrated and assembled during the voyage and on January 27 they were flown off to Batavia in Java. Again there were Canadian pilots in the contingent, Gordon Dunn, Bill Lockwood, Tom Watson, Neil Scott and Art Brown among them. They did not know that another Canadian, Alex Jardine, was circling above them in his Catalina to guard them as they docked. Jardine, for his part, did not know that the nervous, inexperienced and trigger-happy pilots of *Indomitable's* Seahawks took him to be hostile and almost shot him down. *Indomitable* returned a month later with another load of Hurricanes and another contingent of Canadians. These, too late for Singapore, were diverted to Ceylon.

The fall of Sumatra on February 16 and Java on March 8 was marked by chaos and confusion and by valiant attempts at defence, all the more valiant for being almost futile. In the fog of war that now fell over the fighting, Canadian airmen, less bound by military tradition than their European comrades, easily adapted to the circumstance and became foot soldiers if the air was denied them. There are good stories of the daring and determination of individual Canadians and, though they are not directly concerned with the Burma campaign, some deserve a brief retelling.

Gordon Dunn began his Far East flying by taking off from the *Indomitable's* flight deck and groundlooping into a pile of stone when he landed at Batavia because his air speed indicator did not work. In the last days of Java he volunteered to drive a large petrol bowser (gas truck) loaded with the personal effects of the squadron's pilots across the island. He was captured and spent the rest of the war in a POW camp. Two Canadian sergeant pilots, Howard Low from Vancouver and Russell Smith from Kamsack, Saskatchewan found themselves leading a band of RAF ground crew in vicious hand-to-hand fighting against the Japanese attackers. Even after they were taken prisoner, Low and Smith continued to resist. With two others they tried to escape by stealing a Japanese aircraft from the field next to the POW camp. One engine refused to start; they were recaptured and executed.

John Tayler, a Canadian Squadron Leader in the RAF, must have thought that he had been transferred to the Army. Three days after he arrived on Sumatra from Egypt, the Japanese launched a paratroop attack, followed by a vicious air raid and then a full-scale assault on the beaches. The Dutch defences were inadequate and airmen suddenly found themselves forced to fill in as infantry. Tayler tried to lead a small group to rescue an airman trapped under an overturned petrol bowser that blocked the main escape route but he was turned back. He was then asked to take six officers and 80 men and establish a protected bridgehead at the ferry dock in Palembang. He had barely got into position when word came that the Japanese were about to enter the town. Commandeering a three-ton lorry, he drove to the docks at Oosthaven where most of his squadron were being evacuated, but rather than being embarked for Java, he was put in charge of 200 men and told to hold the road till the evacuation was completed. Next day, February 15, his roadblock was withdrawn and he climbed aboard a small ammunition ship for evacuation to Java.

But he did not find safe haven there. At midnight on March 1, the Japanese landed on the shores of western Java. Without warning, their troops and tanks burst onto the airfield where Tayler's Hudsons stood. In his scramble to take off Tayler bogged down in a bomb crater. He abandoned his aircraft and jumped into a truck with some of the ground crew and they fled across the drome. Two enemy tanks fired on them as they bumped across the field at top speed and they returned the fire, one of the airmen with a Bren gun and Tayler with his Tommy gun. Their truck took a direct hit and they fled into the bush. All that night they haunted the perimeter of the airdrome, hoping for the Allied counterattack that never came. Then they began to beat their way through the jungle, not knowing in which direction safety lay. On a narrow inlet they found a small boat and set out for the harbour. A Japanese plane strafed them, setting fire to the oil on the water. With all the speed their little launch power could muster they ran through the fire and into the harbour. There they stocked up from an abandoned ship — water, canned milk, bully beef, dried apples, and a bottle of whisky just in case — and set out for the open sea. Their harbour launch was not crafted for the long steep swells of the ocean and, reports one of the company, "Except for the Canadian, John Tayler, who hails from the prairies and has scarcely ever seen the sea before, we are all sick as dogs." In the end, all their travail was for naught. Their vessel foundered in a violent storm, they made their way to shore, and were then handed over to the Japanese. Thus ended John Tayler's valiant and dogged effort to escape.

Thus ended too the attempt to hold Singapore, Sumatra and Java. There were bright flashes of individual bravery and courage, but on the whole it had been a discouraging interlude of unpreparedness. Of the 54 RCAF men who ended up in Japanese POW camps, 26 were taken in this short campaign.

The order for the evacuation of Java was given on March 6 and all aircrew were instructed to fly off to Ceylon or Mingaladon, the air base at Rangoon. For two of the Canadian pilots, however, getting into the Burma fray was not that straightforward. Rudy Mendizabel, from Sarnia, Ontario and a geology student at the University of Toronto when the war broke out, was stranded on Java when the evacuation began. There were four other pilots in the same plight, a Dutchman, a New Zealander, and two Australians. Around them was a squadron of Lockheed light transport planes, all sitting squat on the tarmac, their undercarriage having been retracted to render them useless to the enemy. One plane still stood, saved by a flat battery from the ignominy of a crushed fuselage: instead its tail section had been stove in by a towing tractor. The five pilots got to work They replaced the smashed tail section of their plane with the intact tail of another using such makeshift devices as a coin for a screwdriver and bits of rope and bamboo to make sure it was secure. They installed the fuel tanks of an abandoned fighter in the fuselage of their plane and pushed a rubber hose through a hole punched in the wall to connect them into their wing tanks. Then they loaded extra cans of fuel and took off.

None of the five pilots had flown a Lockheed before and it took them ten minutes to raise the undercarriage. After that all went well, although topping up the wing tanks from their reserve was tricky. Lacking a fuel pump, they had to fly with one wing low and let gravity make the transfer. After two stops to refuel and one close encounter with Japanese fighters, they landed in Ceylon, having flown a total of 1400 miles and 15 hours in a plane of their own making.

Even more curious was the escape route fate forced on Tom Watson. He flew off the *Indomitable* on January 27, landed at Java, and was immediately sent on to Singapore. From that point on, every second day brought adventure and excitement. On February 5 he rescued a pilot from a burning Buffalo and drove him to the hospital; on February 7 his aircraft was damaged by enemy fire and he had to make a deadstick landing; on February 9 he got his own back by damaging two enemy aircraft; and on February 11 orders came to evacuate Singapore. Someone else had taken his Hurricane so Watson scouted out a battered Buffalo, persuaded the engineering officer to help him get it started, and took off for Sumatra. His was the last plane to leave Singapore. He had never flown a Buffalo before and, like Mendizabel, it took him ten minutes to raise the undercarriage and even longer to discover that the pitch control was on the dash. He had no maps so he followed the three Hurricanes ahead, one of them flown by his good friend Art Brown from St. John's. The Hurricanes were too fast and he lost them. He couldn't bail out since he had no parachute so he simply kept flying in what he hoped was the right direction. Coming finally to Palembang, he landed and rather proudly presented himself to the Commanding Officer, only to be reprimanded for flying an aircraft on which he was not checked out.

That was not the end of Watson's adventures. On Friday, February 13, the Japanese bombers attacked. A Hurricane stood by the readiness hut; technically it was unserviceable and unflyable for it had neither brakes nor guns. To save it from destruction on the ground, Watson flew it anyway. Six or seven enemy aircraft attacked him. He had the uncomfortable feeling that their bullets were smashing against the armour plate behind his back, but all he could do was run for it. Then the engine quit. He made a forced landing at the satellite drome but having no brakes he overshot, crashed into the jungle, and wrote off the aircraft that he tried so hard to save.

Then came another evacuation, this time to Java, and operational sorties that resulted in his claiming two enemy aircraft shot down. On March 2 he was shot down for the third time. Realizing he was behind the Japanese line, he threw away his flying helmet, smeared his face with dirt, found a native straw hat to protect his bald pate from the sun and hoped that he might be mistaken for a native. A young native boy with some English led him to the river, an old man helped him build a bamboo raft to cross it, and a Dutch cavalry officer gave him a horse to save his blistered feet. When the horse gave out, an Australian army officer drove him to a Dutch army camp and there a Dutch officer gave him a "letter of introduction" to his wife in the next town. Even though Watson came to her door at midnight she took him in, bathed his feet, and gave him a bed to sleep in. Next morning, in fresh socks and a pair of ill-fitting shoes, he set off to find his squadron. The car that picked him up was hit by a truck and Watson was thrown through the windshield. He awoke to find three beautiful young Dutch girls hovering tenderly over him.

He was taken to the military hospital where a skillful Australian surgeon saved his eye. Because the wounds were serious he was given priority passage on a hospital plane to Australia. When he recovered he joined an Australian squadron and did a tour of operations with them, then a stint of instruction at an Operational Training Unit before eventually managing a posting back to India to join a Liberator squadron. And that is how Tom Watson got into the Burma war.

As for Rudy Mendizabel, after safely landing at Ceylon in his makeshift plane, he was posted to 5 RAF Squadron at Dum Dum airport on the northern edge of Calcutta. He was pleased to discover that the Squadron emblem was the maple leaf, a remnant of World War I days when most of the squadron's pilots were Canadians. He was also pleased to discover three other Canadian pilots on the squadron, Tom Trimble, Rod Lawrence and Harold Seifert. Trimble was from Kenora while Lawrence and Seifert were both from Winnipeg, and indeed both lived on Lipton Street. Their common heritage drew them together and, moved either by an abhorrence of bully beef or nostalgia for their Canadian youth, Lawrence and Trimble borrowed shotguns from the Squadron armourer and went hunting. They came back with an armload of pigeons and the cook made them pigeon pie, with a bit of bully beef added for flavour. Thanks to a letter he had received from his mother in February 1943, Harold Seifert could give his chums the words to "White Christmas," though as yet they had not heard the tune.

The Squadron immediately went onto operations, flying their bulky little Curtiss Mohawks on strafing missions against locomotives, river traffic and troop encampments. Although enemy aircraft did not often come at them, Mendizabel was credited with two probables when six Mohawks tackled eight Oscars over Akyab in mid-January, 1942. On his next sortie he got another chance at one, but whether it went down or not, he could not say for his windscreen was covered with oil from his own engine. Tom Trimble collided in mid-air with another 5 Squadron aircraft and gained some fame as being one of only two pilots in Burma to bail out of a Mohawk. He was fortunate in that he landed on a small sand bar in the middle of the river and was rescued by an Englishman who had seen the accident. Three days later, when he walked into the Mess with his parachute slung over his shoulder, he was somewhat taken aback to find that his mates had held a wake to mourn his passing and then auctioned off all his kit. Rod Lawrence was elated when he got his first "kill," but subdued when the CO's congratulations were footnoted with a reprimand for breaking formation to do it. He was further subdued when the armourer sergeant scolded him for burning out all six guns by firing continuously rather than in short bursts.

The Squadron was then withdrawn from operational activity to convert from Mohawks to Hurricanes and to familiarize themselves with the habits and capabilities of their new machines. On August 10, 1943, as Rudy Mendizabel was making a mock attack on another aircraft, his Hurricane went into a high speed stall and he crashed into the Bay of Bengal. A month later Harold Seifert, on a familiarization flight, reported difficulty controlling his aircraft, then plunged down in a steep dive into the paddy field below. In a letter home Rod Lawrence mused on the deaths of his two friends: "last spring when the Canadian Public Relations fellow visited the squadron, he wanted a picture of the Canadians by a Mohawk… only Harold and Mendizabel were there. They had their picture taken and now they are both gone. Maybe there is something to that old superstition of the Royal Flying Corps that it is unlucky to have one's picture taken just before flying."

Seifert's death, caused when an access panel broke off and upset the aircraft's trim, "was a shock to all of us," wrote one of his mates. "Seifert was a consistent pilot. … I pressured the CO to get permission to fill the 12 foot hole and erect a stone cairn with a cross. Harold was a 'Mr. Nice Guy' who stayed with his plane just too long." From the condolence letter Harold's roommate and fellow Canadian, Lloyd Thomas, wrote to Harold's parents one can sense the close camaraderie the Canadian pilots felt for one another; it is not likely that many bereaved parents received as comforting a letter:

> *Harold and I visited Kashmir together and enjoyed long chats on every subject. He spoke of his homelife a good deal and mentioned the church and its ministers. They seem to have taught him well because Harold was a fine clean-living chap. It is impossible for me to write how much I will miss our long walks, cribbage games, dominoes and talks.*
>
> *On a bright sunny afternoon of 9th November, we held the burial ceremony at the scene of the crash. We drove for several miles through the bright green trees of a nursery. At the end of the road we had a walk of a half a mile. The path wound between paddy fields. In some fields the harvesters worked slowly at their tasks, cows grazed behind them.*

*Other fields bore a rich golden crop of rice and the wind stirred not a
blade. All was extremely quiet and restful. Coming to a small knoll we
found Harold's last resting place. There are lovely trees to the north and
east. To the south and west a long view of sloping paddy fields stretches
into the distance.*

*The officers lined up on one side of the grave, a twelve gun firing
party on the southern side and myself and an airman on the eastern
side. The Reverend Edwin Brush of the American Baptist Church
read the sermon. ... The firing party fired a three volley salute and the
earth closed in upon Harold. He is resting a few miles out of Khargpur,
where his aircraft plunged to earth.*

Of the other Canadian pilots who landed up in Ceylon, Tom Trimble
went on to command a flight in 9 Squadron of the Royal Indian Air Force,
while Rod Lawrence stayed with 5 Squadron till he was repatriated to
Canada in June 1944.

The Canadians who fled from Java and Sumatra to Mingaladon, the
airport at Rangoon, had a different experience, above all because they
were closer to the front, there was little organization, and there were no
amenities such as Ceylon and nearby Calcutta afforded. The airport buildings were burned out, the runway was bombed out, and the few remaining
aircraft, Brewster Buffaloes and AVG Tomahawks — were worn out. The
Australian, Bush Cotton, one of the first of the replacement pilots to arrive,
tells of finding a roughly printed sign "Fighter HQ," and behind it a shell-
torn building wherein the Commanding Officer, "a short stocky man in a
sweaty shirt and shorts with greying and diminishing hair, and bearing a
remarkable resemblance to W. C. Fields" greeted them in an unmistakably
Canadian accent.

This was Group Captain Herbert Seton Broughall, born at Toronto in
1898 of a long and proud military line and a strong Canadian heritage. His
great-grandfather, Samuel Proudfoot Hurd, had fought with Wellington
at the Battle of Waterloo, and later became surveyor-general for Upper
Canada just as his father, Seton's great-great-grandfather, had been surveyor-general for Cape Breton.

Seven of Samuel Proudfoot Hurd's grandsons served with the Canadian
Army in World War I, Seton among them. Like many young Canadians, he
transferred to the Royal Flying Corps. Five confirmed air victories earned
him an MC before he was shot down and taken prisoner. After the war he
remained in the Royal Air Force, as the Royal Flying Corps then became,
serving in Russia under the great Canadian air ace, Ray Collishaw, and later
in Kurdistan, where, in 1923, he was awarded the DFC. In 1941 he was
Collishaw's senior staff officer in the Western Desert Campaign when he
got the call to Burma.

Now in Mingaladon, it was not only the accent that set him apart but the sincerely casual friendliness, the total lack of swank or side, unexpected of a relatively senior RAF officer. His pilots all called him Seton, in the mess he was "one of the boys," holding with them pint for pint, joining in their games and singsongs, always ready with a wisecrack to ease the tension of the day. Above all, he was revered by the pilots who served with him because he was not afraid to stand between them and what they saw as the intractable stupidity of the upper echelons. One example will suffice. Even in these very early days, Hurricane pilots realized that, although they could not outmanoeuvre an Oscar, they could outclimb and outdive one. Their tactic therefore was to get above the enemy, make one swift diving pass and then zoom up for a second try. Unfortunately the Hurricane's range and endurance was only half that of the Japanese fighters and the Air Officer Commanding ordered that the Hurricanes carry wing tanks to compensate. Since the wing tanks could not be jettisoned, they remained not only as a further impediment to manoeuvrability but also to the rate of climb, thus depriving the Hurricanes of their only advantage. Not until some of the pilots were put in mortal danger and Seton had made himself an obnoxious nuisance at Headquarters was the order rescinded. It was because of Seton's sincere sense of identity with the junior ranks and his concern for their welfare that Ken Hemingway, one of his Mingaladon pilots, dedicated his book *Wings Over Burma* to "Group Captain Seton Broughall, MC, DFC."

Gradually Seton organized his battered and tattered station. The Brewster Buffaloes were gone, replaced by much more lethal Hurricanes. The sergeants had established their mess in a nearby mansion while the officers located themselves in a Catholic convent when the nuns withdrew. Over January 1942 the aircrew complement grew as pilots from Britain, Australia, New Zealand, South Africa and Canada arrived. As well as those who had fled from Singapore and Sumatra, Seton now had pilots who had hopscotched their Hurricanes across continents via Cairo, Habbaniyah and way stations. Bob Payn, Biff Viens, Maurice Cuthbert and Art Brown, all Canadians, were sent from England to Cairo on their way to an unknown Far East destination. Here they waited in the Hotel Riche, a filthy second-rate hostelry in the native quarter, while their officer tried to persuade the local commander to give them the Hurricanes they were to ferry out. Eventually he did so and they set off, a flight of 6 led by a navigator in an accompanying Blenheim, and early in January they arrived at Seton Broughall's Mingaladon station. They were disappointed when they had to give their brand new Hurricanes over to another group of Canadians who had arrived earlier *sans* aircraft, Ken Wheatley, Jack Gibson, Ricky Chadwick, John Barrick, Al MacDonald, Hedley Everard, H. S. "Happy" Armstrong, Clarence

Wisrodt, T.L. Lewis, C. S. Miller and Hank Forde. Actually, Gibson, Wisrodt and Barrick were Americans who had crossed the border to join the RCAF before Pearl Harbour.

Seton now had a decent number of pilots for the defence of Rangoon and he put them all to work as soon as aircraft were available so that, coincident with the Sittang Bridge affair, a sortie went out from Mingaladon to support the ground forces still fleeing across the river. Hedley Everard, an idealistic youth from the hardrock mining town of Timmins, Ontario, was on that first sortie. He had just arrived that day at Mingaladon, a "sprog," an absolute neophyte who had never been on operations before, but there was no time for a familiarization flight. Along with fellow Canadian Ricky Chadwick he was sent out to stooge up and down the Sittang and silence the enemy machine gunners who were shooting at the soldiers still trying to flee across the river. And of course the machine gunners shot at him as well. They had the advantage since they were hidden in the dense jungle that fringed the river while he was silhouetted against the sky. But his presence gave some comfort to the soldiers frantically crossing on makeshift rafts or clinging to empty petrol tins. When his ammunition was gone and his fuel was low Everard returned to base. The ground crew refueled him and pasted patches on the seven bullet holes in his weary Hurricane with bright red glue. "I'm glad it's not my blood," thought Everard, and returned to the patrol.

This time he and Chadwick were to patrol at about 12000 feet to keep enemy aircraft from annoying the troops below. They really should have been higher, but there was insufficient oxygen for that. Below him the British soldiers looked like "a lazy line of ants crawling uncertainly across a muddy ribbon of water." Now and then an inert speck left the line and floated lifelessly down the river. On the east bank of the river the guns and lorries destroyed by the retreating army still smouldered. Everard's blood boiled in futile frustration. That night, sitting on the ground around the campfire that served as the kitchen for the officers' mess — and the sergeants' mess and the airmen's mess, for Mingaladon was being bombed and strafed daily and there was as yet no semblance of an organized and comfortable station life — Bunny Stone, the lanky British squadron commander and Battle of Britain veteran, casually remarked to Everard that he had "behaved quite coolly on the day's operations," a comforting comment for the young Canadian on his first day of battle.[3]

While Everard and Chadwick were patrolling the Sittang, Bunny Stone was leading an offensive sweep in the Moulmein area. Despite the differ-

---

[3] Hedley Everard became one of Canada's air aces, credited with 5 enemy aircraft destroyed, 3 probables and 3 damaged. He was one of the very few airmen to have fought in three theatres, Burma, Italy, and Germany. After the war he continued his association with the RCAF and rose to the rank of Group Captain. He died in 1999.

ence in their ranks, Squadron Leader Stone always chose Sgt. Ken Wheatley, a young Canadian, as his number two, because "whatever situation one found oneself in, he was always there." On this day, February 25, 1942, Ken followed Stone across the Gulf of Martaban and up the Salween estuary. There, about to disembark, 200 Japanese reinforcement troops in full battle regalia crowded the deck of a small coaster. Stone went in first, strafing the deck from bow to stern. Wheatley followed and, looking back over his shoulder he saw that the boat "appeared to burst into a white sheet of flame from its funnel to its stern."

Tex Barrick began his career by shooting down two enemy aircraft shortly after he arrived at Mingaladon. When the Japanese attacked again a fortnight later, his was one of the six Mingaladon Hurricanes who went up to meet them. Tex was the first to spy the enemy and excitedly he shouted the alarm "Snapper! Snapper!" forgetting that it was not a code word known in Burma. The rest flew on so Tex turned alone to charge into 15 enemy aircraft. One fell immediately to his guns and he turned tightly to try again, so tightly that one of his gun panels flew open and caused him to flick over. The accident probably saved his life for it swiftly removed him from the sights of the enemy on his tail. When the squadron was forced to evacuate Mingaladon a week later, Tex undertook to fly out one of the war-battered Hurricanes so that it could be salvaged for another day. The aircraft had no airspeed indicator, in fact, no working instruments at all. Oil leaks in the engine block were stopped with wooden plugs. He sighed with relief as he settled onto the runway at Magwe. That was when a truck drove into the side of the aircraft he was trying to save and completely demolished it. Later Tex Barrick was awarded the DFM and was commissioned and in short order he was given a double promotion to Flight Lieutenant and appointed flight commander. In the end he was recognized as one of the air aces of Burma with a total of seven and a half enemy aircraft to his credit.

Thanks to the defensive action of the RAF and AVG, the disembarkation of the last reinforcements for the ground forces and the demolition of the Rangoon dock facilities could take place free from air harassment. Thanks to Allied air cover, not one ship was lost during the seaborne evacuation of Rangoon. General Slim, assessing the situation when he arrived in Burma, summed it up nicely: "Rarely can so small an air force have battled so gallantly and so effectively against the odds."

The Canadians, the largest ethnic component of this polyglot squadron, played a large part in this success, not only with their contribution to air fighting, but also because they, and especially the three "American Canadians," Barrick, Wisrodt, and Gibson, had been able to break down the standoffishness that had at first marred relations between the RAF and the AVG. As Hedley Everard remarked, "My RAF squadron mates gave me traitorous glances whenever I sauntered over to the AVG Operations Tent or their makeshift Club in the evenings, but they were like my true Detroit cousins to me." A truly symbiotic relationship developed between the two groups; the inexperienced RAF pilots learned a great deal about fighter tactics from the battle-wise Yanks and the Flying Tigers accepted ground crew help from the RAF. The AVG were entitled to collect bounty from the Chinese government for each plane they shot down. Sometimes they collected for an enemy aircraft shot down by the RAF, an arrangement apparently accepted if not condoned by the Chinese. In such cases, the free-and-easy Americans always split their bonus with the Canadian or RAF pilot who had given them a "present."

It was now the end of February. Japanese air raids were frequent and government offices began to evacuate Rangoon. Clearly the Air Force at Mingaladon would be well advised to move as well. Seton ordered a withdrawal to the dusty, second-rate drome at Magwe. Because Ricky Chadwick had a particular affinity for automobiles, the CO appointed him as Transport Officer and sent him off scouting for vehicles that could move them to Magwe. Ricky and the NCO in charge of maintenance concealed a dozen drivers in the back of a three ton lorry and went down to the Rangoon docks to find the transport they needed. Long rows of new American vehicles lined the area. When asked what he was going to do with them now that the enemy was at the door, the American sergeant in charge guessed that he would have to burn them. "Can we have some?" "Take what you want." The concealed drivers jumped out, appropriated the vehicles they needed, including a staff car for their Squadron Leader, and drove back to Mingaladon. On March 2, 1942 the fighter squadron at Mingaladon loaded into its newly acquired American vehicles and, together with the AVG unit, withdrew to Magwe.

As for the army, General Wavell was still blustering: "You must stop all further withdrawal and counterattack whenever possible!" Viceroy Linlithgow and the High Command in Delhi were so shaken by the news from Sittang that they ordered that ABDA be disbanded and Wavell's headquarters be moved from Java to Delhi. They went beyond that and ordered a shake-up of top level command. General Alexander, the commander who had successfully fought the last ditch action at Tobruk, was spirited in to take over as Army Commander. Major General Smyth, VC, MC was made the scapegoat of the Sittang affair. Wavell, implicitly putting the full blame for the Sittang Bridge debacle on his shoulders, removed him from his command, demoted him to Colonel, sent him back to Britain, and asked that he be discharged from the Army.

Immediately upon assuming command, Alexander went to Rangoon to assess the situation. He realized at once that this was not to be another

Tobruk. The air attacks on December 23 and 25 had resulted in "a general dispersal of the population." The Indian dock workers had fled up the Prome Road heading for home and leaving mountains of matériel on the docks. Many Burmese workers had fled to the jungle. The prison doors had been thrown open and the inmates of the mental home had been released for there was no one to care for them. Looters and arsonists and mad dogs roamed the streets until the Army took on a police role and restored a vestige of order. The Governor and the civil administration had fled to Maymyo. To top it all off, there were reports of Japanese patrols in Pegu, 35 miles northeast of Rangoon. They were obviously headed for Prome to cut off the escape route to the north. Alexander had no option but to withdraw from the city. He had entered Rangoon on March 5; at midnight, March 6, he gave orders for the city to be evacuated.

When General Alexander and the Rangoon garrison began their exit up the Rangoon-Prome road on the morning of the 7th they ran into a strong Japanese road block at Taukkyan, just 15 miles north of the city. Their first assault was thrown back as was their second, even though it was backed by tanks. The day was almost over and the Rangoon garrison dug in for the night. It began to look as if Alexander's command in Burma would be short and in no way sweet. Over night elaborate plans were made for a final desperate attack to be launched first thing next morning but even before the attack could begin the news came that the road block was abandoned, the road was clear, and Alexander's entourage could flee freely northward away from Rangoon.

Captain Arthur James Bolsby, a Toronto native in the British Army, was directing traffic at the Taukkyan intersection that day. He stood to attention in the rain and saluted smartly as General Alexander passed by. His grandfather had fought in the Boer War, his father had been a Colonel in World War I; Bolsby knew he wanted a soldier's life. But when he graduated from Royal Military College, Kingston, his only choice was to transfer to the Supplementary Reserve of the Canadian Army or accept a commission in any Imperial force. Jim chose the Indian Army. With his regiment, the 1/11th Sikhs, he had taken part in the chaotic retreat from Moulmein, so chaotic that he had had to pour gas on the first Canadian mail he had received in months and burn it unread on that ill-fated march to the Sittang Bridge. Now he was still retreating.

At the time the evaporation of the Japanese road block was not understood and there was jubilation at the narrow escape of the Commander and his headquarters as well as celebration of the stupidity of the Japanese at letting such a prize evade them. Information that came to light after the war revealed that the installation and removal of the roadblock were an intentional part of the Japanese plan. They had imagined that because of the importance of Rangoon and its docks the British would fight for the city street by street and they therefore planned for a strong column to sweep widely across the top of Rangoon and attack from the west, that is, behind the line of defence. The roadblock was put in place to allow the pincer column to cross the highway and it was removed when it had served that purpose. It was only after the Japanese forces had occupied the city that they discovered that the troops attacking their road block were not merely the perimeter guard but the whole of the Rangoon garrison, including the Commander in Chief of the British Army in Burma, trying to get out. Belatedly they gave chase, but with their energy, their supplies, and their ammunition exhausted, they had to abandon the pursuit. Still, they had what they wanted, the port of Rangoon.

VI

THE LONG RETREAT

W HEN THE Japanese flag went up on the Governor's Residence in Rangoon at 10 am on March 8, 1942 it signalled a fateful turning point in the Burma war. One hundred thousand tons of vital war matériel were lost on the Rangoon docks and the port as a major point of re-supply was gone. Worse still, it was now available to the enemy, allowing them to bring in formidable reinforcements — two infantry divisions, two tank regiments, plus boatloads of supplies. Moreover, the aura of invincible splendour that had emanated for decades from the British raj was gone forever, a realization that greatly heartened the freedom fighters of Burma and the Quit India leaders in India. The fall of Rangoon betokened too the eventual loss of all Burma; from this moment on the Allied forces were never able to take the initiative and mount a meaningful offensive until the tide of battle turned in 1944. Most damaging to the morale of the troops was the developing myth that the Japanese were wily little warriors who could live on next to nothing, slip through the jungle unseen, march for days without rest, kill even after they had been killed, and who regularly tortured and executed their prisoners.

That is the negative side. The positive side, though not yet fully appreciated by either the troops or their commanders, was the arrival in Burma of General William Slim. Unlike many senior officers of the British and Indian Army, Slim was of solidly middle class stock. Unable to attend university because of faltering family fortunes, he had through some slight subterfuge associated himself with the Birmingham University Officer Training Corps and been commissioned on the outbreak of World War I, later transferring to the India Army. A blunt, determined man of intense common sense and resolute nerve, he had steadily advanced till, though not well known in army circles, he had nevertheless caught the eye of General Alexander and

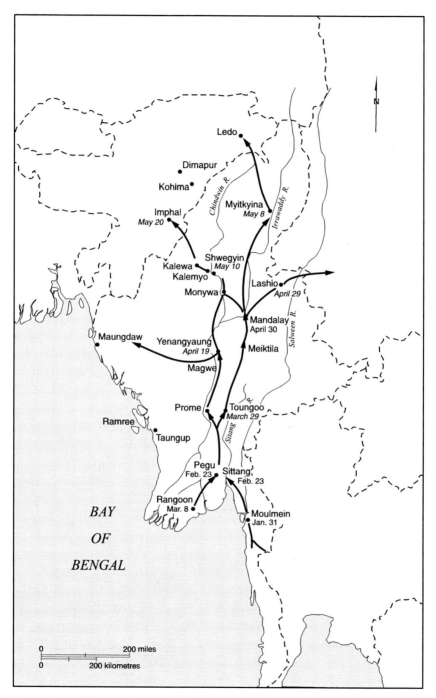

Map 4 — Chronology of the Retreat, 1942

won the nod to command the newly organized Burma Corps (Burcorps) with that most unenviable of all martial mandates, overseeing the fighting withdrawal from Burma to India.

When General Slim took command of Burcorps on March 19, 1942, his troops held a line from Prome to Toungoo. Alternately fighting and fleeing they withdrew up the Irrawaddy and up the Sittang to Mandalay and then westward to Imphal. Their withdrawal was hampered by the thousands of Indian refugees trying to reach Akyab and sea passage to Bengal or streaming north to Myitkyina in the wan hope of getting out by air. The Chinese troops fled in undisciplined and disorganized bands northeastward through Lashio and back to China. All who were fleeing, British and Indian Army, Chinese Army, civilian refugees, were subjected to unopposed air attack every day, for the RAF had withdrawn from Burma a week after Slim took command.

On March 20 Wing Commander Seton Broughall, having resettled the tattered remnants of his wing at Magwe, discovered that the Japanese Air Force had usurped the airport he had just abandoned and he launched a full-strength attack against the Mingaladon strip. "Full strength" must be understood with some qualification — the RAF at Magwe could muster only 9 Blenheim bombers and 16 Hurricane fighters. Early on the morning of March 21, all 9 Blenheims and 10 of the 16 Hurricanes took off from a dirt runway lined by a few kerosene lanterns and set course for Mingaladon. Hedley Everard, the idealistic young man from Timmins, Ontario, and Shorty Miller from Cape Breton Island were given the job of taking out the anti-aircraft defences around the drome. The Japanese defenders, sitting in the sun on the sandbags that protected their gun emplacement and sipping their morning tea, were taken completely by surprise. Everard could see the astonishment on their faces as he came down on them and opened up with his eight machine guns. That gun crew was now out of action.

Shorty Miller too had done his assigned job and now both were free to attack other targets. Everard lined up on a Japanese fighter just beginning to move down the runway. One vicious burst from his guns and the enemy aircraft tipped up on its nose as he passed over a few feet above it. He turned toward the railway where Japanese soldiers were scrambling to get their rifles into action and strafed along their ranks. With his fuel low, he joined another Canadian, Al MacDonald, and headed back to Magwe.

The Mingaladon raid was a great success — four and a half tons of bombs dropped on the runways and a total of 27 enemy aircraft destroyed. Two Hurricanes were shot down, but in both cases the pilots got back to base. Seton was elated and immediately began to plan a second raid. But the hornets had been disturbed and even as all aircraft, including five new Blenheims just arrived from India, were being readied to renew the attack on Mingaladon, a strong enemy force of about 60 bombers and 25 fighters appeared over Magwe. In an unrelenting hour-long attack, three waves of Japanese aircraft bombed and strafed the airdrome. Of Magwe's meagre air strength, 7 were destroyed on the ground as well as a 1000 gallon oil depot. In addition two Hurricanes were shot down, one of them piloted by Ricky Chadwick, the Canadian who had commandeered transport for the squadron from the Rangoon docks. Both pilots landed on sandbars in the river and later returned to the squadron. Of the losses suffered by the Japanese that day, two fell to Canadians, one to Al MacDonald and another to Hedley Everard. Everard chanced upon an enemy plane separated from its fellows and held his eager trigger finger till the rising sun rondel almost filled his gunsight, then watched it spiral to the ground.

The ground crews worked throughout the night to repair the few aircraft that could be made flyable, to restore trunk-line communication, and to fill the badly bombed runway, but early the next morning the enemy came again, and again after that. In three waves 113 bombers dropped 167 tons of explosive on Magwe's humble runways and its fragile wooden sheds. The AVG had already pulled back to their main base at Lashio on Burma's northeast border and now Seton got permission to follow them. Six Blenheims and eight Hurricanes, all that remained of the Royal Air Force in Burma, flew off to Akyab, an island just off the Burmese coast, while the rest of the squadron personnel toiled up the length of Burma by lorry. Five days later they wearily straggled into Lashio.

A short *excursus* on the withdrawal from Magwe is in order at this point. The Army, not appreciating the utter toothlessness of the Air Force, complained bitterly that the RAF had let them down. Stung by this accusation, the Air Force upper echelons tried to turn the blame back on Seton Broughall, claiming that the Magwe evacuation had been carried out in panic and disorganization. The official account of the withdrawal, however, completely exonerates Broughall: "The movement was carried out under complete control, the movement order was in writing and completely understood by all concerned, and the general behaviour of the RAF and the convoy discipline were excellent. ... There can be little doubt that Burwing Commander's decision to move his flyable aircraft from Magwe to Akyab was correct."

For the personnel who fled to Akyab life was difficult. Their fighter aircraft were obsolescent Hurricanes marked "For Training Only" and most of the refuelling was done by pouring petrol from four-gallon cans through a chamois-lined funnel. Nevertheless, when the Japanese attacked again over the next three days, four Canadian pilots rose against them. After an eleven day flight from Cairo, Edward "Biff" Viens of Brittania Heights, Ontario had arrived in Mingaladon in the middle of an air raid, had followed the retreat to Magwe and then to Akyab. Now he found himself in the middle of another air raid. This time he was able to claim one enemy aircraft probably destroyed. Verne Butler too claimed one probable before he was shot down. Slightly wounded, he was still able to walk home next day. Lorne LeCraw from Norland, Ontario was shot down over the sea and found he could not inflate his Mae West because a gun shot wound had perforated both cheeks and deprived him of his puff.

Bob Payne was the fourth Canadian to scramble that day. He got onto the tail of a Japanese fighter, a Japanese got onto his tail, one of his mates got on that fighter's tail, and another enemy on his tail. Round the airstrip they went, foe-Payne-foe-friend-foe in a deadly game of follow-the-leader, till Bob Payne was shot down and crashed into the sea. That night one of his mates remembered him: "The biggest blow to all was losing Bob. He was a grand pilot — the best we had — and the keenest man I knew. He was mad-headed and it cost him his life."

Those intense raids on Akyab on March 23, 24 and 27 marked the end of Allied air support for the next year. The few planes that remained at Akyab were flown off to Calcutta leaving Slim's Burcorps with no tactical air support and no photo reconnaissance. Army personnel muttered bitterly that the Air Force had pulled out prematurely and let them down, but these complaints ignored the facts: Japan could now put upwards of 250 aircraft into the skies; the RAF fewer than 50, none of them operationally airworthy. The Air Force, like the Army, had been ill-equipped and ill-prepared from the beginning, but had nevertheless outfought the enemy five to one, having shot down 233 enemy aircraft for a loss of 46. And let it be said that the Flying Tigers, the American Volunteer Group, accounted for more than the tiger's share of the enemy's losses.

The first week of April 1942 was probably the bleakest moment of the war in the Far East. The RAF had been forced out of Burma, allowing the Japanese Air Force to attack Mandalay unopposed and kill 2000 people. The British army was retreating up the Irrawaddy with no prospect of being able to regroup and make a stand. Elsewhere in the theatre, the Japanese land forces, having already secured their hold on the Dutch and British East Indies, Malaya, Sumatra, Hong Kong and Singapore, were wiping up the last resistance on the Bataan Peninsula. The Japanese Navy had landed on the Andaman Islands, only six hundred miles from the Indian coast, and was hunting almost at will in the Bay of Bengal. On April 5 at 1:40 pm a huge flight from her aircraft carriers attacked the cruisers *Dorsetshire* and *Cornwall*. Within a half hour, both were sunk. Next day carrier-based planes attacked the south-east coast of India, the first time the Indian main-land had been bombed. Over the next five days, the Japanese sank 28 ships, a total of 144,000 tons. Alarm spread throughout Ceylon and Madras and panic followed as civil administrators and non-essential military personnel fled inland.

Back in London Churchill realized that the loss of Ceylon could "close the ring," giving Japan control of the Bay of Bengal, the port of Calcutta, the Java Sea, the Indian Ocean and the sea route to Australia. Fearing that Japan could possibly link hands with her European allies in the Middle East and cut off oil supplies from the Persian Gulf, he named this moment "the most dangerous moment of the war." In his diary for April 7, Alan Brooke, later Lord Alanbrooke, Chief of the Imperial General Staff, echoed those forebodings: "I suppose this Empire has never been in such a precarious position throughout history. I do not like the look of things. And yet a miracle saved us at Dunkirk and we may pull through this time."

The miracle was worked by a Canadian pilot of 413 RCAF Squadron flying his first mission in South East Asia a scant 48 hours after arriving in the theatre. 413 Squadron had been formed in Scotland in June 1941 and operated for a few months in the Shetland Isles where it rained for 260 days of the year, the average temperature was 40 degrees Fahrenheit and fierce winds were incessant. Squadron personnel were delighted when the word came through of a move to sunny Ceylon.

When 413 established itself at Kogalla in Ceylon in May, 1942 it became the first Canadian squadron to be stationed overseas beyond the British Isles. Although it was designated "Canadian" within the definition of Article 15 of the Empire Air Training Plan[1], the RCAF lacked personnel with flying boat experience and many RAF men were included. One Canadian pilot, however, Squadron Leader Len Birchall, had had considerable flying boat experience and, in the early days of the war, had been involved in the capture of an Italian freighter. In April 1942 he piloted his ponderous Catalina flying boat eastward via Gibraltar, Cairo and Karachi and eased it down onto the tricky landing path at Koggala Lake in Ceylon. Two days later, with barely time for a night's rest, he undertook an urgent patrol to look for a Japanese flotilla that British intelligence suspected was steaming toward Ceylon.

With fuel for 32 hours, Birchall and his crew took off early on the morning of April 4 to cover a designated area south east of Ceylon by flying 150 mile east-west search lines 50 miles apart and at a height of 2000 feet. Even a periscope could be detected at that height. All day long they thumped back and forth and saw nothing. The day ended and dusk came, but since Birchall had never tried the tricky approach at Koggala by night, they would have to "stooge" all night to make a daylight landing. Still, they

[1] It is significant that the scheme known in Britain and Australia as the Empire Air Training Plan was stubbornly referred to in Canada as the Commonwealth Air Training Plan.

could at least head for home. Warrant Officer G. C. "Bart" Onyette, the Canadian navigator, had a request: "Skipper, if we fly one more line, the moon will come up and I can take a moon shot to cross with my sun shot for a fix." Birchall agreed and they turned for one last sweep. Then the waist gunner, Sergeant L. A. Colarossi, saw it — the Japanese fleet! Birchall steered in close to identify and count the ships. Phillips, the wireless operator, hurriedly coded his message and sent it off, and sent it off again. Three transmissions were required for verification; halfway through the third sending the aircraft carriers below loosed their terriers. With ships firing up at them, Navy Zeros diving down on them, and no place to hide in the cloudless sky, the Catalina was an easy prey. The radio operator and the two air gunners were seriously wounded, the radio set was destroyed, Birchall was hit, his controls damaged and the internal tanks were set afire. It is a credit to Birchall's skill that he was able to bring the badly damaged craft to a controlled landing amid the chaos of that melee.

As the crew swam from the burning petrol, the Zeros continued their attack. The two wounded gunners, buoyed up by their Mae Wests were unable to duck and were killed in the water. The rest of the crew were taken aboard one of the Japanese vessels and thrown into a scarcely ventilated paint locker where three could lie down, two could sit, and one had to stand. In the brutal interrogation that followed, Birchall almost had the Japanese convinced that they had not had time to send a message when the ship's radio picked up a request from Ceylon for confirmation of the last, garbled transmission. The interrogation became even more brutal; then they were thrown back into the paint locker without food or medical attention.

At eight in the morning of April 5, Easter Sunday, the attack on Ceylon began. Before 9 o'clock it was over. Although Birchall's message had given the island's defences a general warning, there was no immediate alert for the radar installation was still unfinished. The attackers, a mixed force of 127 fighters and bombers, concentrated on the docks, the railyards and the airport. Thirty-six Hurricanes, at least eight of them manned by Canadians, rose belatedly to meet them. Dodging in and out of the rain and cloud, Jimmy Whalen managed to shoot down three dive bombers to add to the three victories he had chalked up in earlier action in Northern Europe. F/L R. T. P. Davidson had already shot down three enemy aircraft in the Middle East before he came to Ceylon. On this day he claimed two more. P/O D. A. MacDonald shot down one attacker just before the enemy aircraft next in line shot him. Forced to land on a grassy spot in front of the elegant Galle Face Hotel, MacDonald strolled in and ordered a drink, only to be told that the waiters had all fled, and besides "the bar wasn't open yet." Bob Davidson and Jimmy Whalen each got the DFC for their action over Ceylon, as of course did Birchall.

After flying Spitfires in England, Ken Moorhouse went by troopship to Lagos, then by Pan Am Airways to Cairo. Here he was given a Hurricane and instructed to fly to Port Sudan. In due course, which in the Forces meant after some weeks of waiting, Ken and his Hurricane, along with 50 other Hurricanes and pilots, were loaded onto *Indomitable,* and told they were going to Singapore. Midway through the voyage they were told that Singapore had surrendered and that they were to go to "another island." On March 6 Ken's aircraft was lifted from the hangar deck and he made his first and last carrier takeoff and set course for the distant smudge on the horizon, Ceylon. Now at dawn on Easter Sunday, April 5, 1942 he sat in readiness in his aircraft. At 8:40 enemy aircraft were overhead and Ken scrambled to meet them. At 3000 feet a nimble little Japanese fighter came straight at him, firing as he came. Glycol from the cooling system streamed across Ken's windscreen. He landed wheels up on the grass of the race-course which was their drome and fled unhurt from the wrecked aircraft. Next day he came to view the wreckage and counted 74 bullet holes in the fuselage, but the glycol leak was caused, not by a Japanese bullet, but by a blown gasket.

At the end of the day, the defenders claimed 27 enemy aircraft destroyed for a loss of 19. The attackers admitted to a loss of only 7 aircraft and insisted they had destroyed 41 RAF planes. That leaves a largish range wherein the truth can dwell. What we do know is that the Japanese made only one more assault on Ceylon.

On April 9 the Canadian F/L Rae Thomas, one of 413's most experienced pilots, began an early morning patrol just as Len Birchall had done a few days earlier. At 7 am, five hours into his patrol, he spotted a large Japanese naval force and began to transmit the news to his base. The message broke off before he finished and Thomas and his crew were never heard of again, but the warning had been received. When aircraft from the Japanese carriers attacked the naval base at Trincomallee the RAF was ready. Again Canadians were strongly represented in the Hurricanes that climbed up above the invaders and then dove down on them like banshees. The enemy losses were considerable but so too were the British, the two cruisers *Dorsetshire* and *Cornwall* and the carrier *Hermes.* After this attack, the Japanese fleet withdrew and did not molest Ceylon again. The alarm that Birchall had sounded and the subsequent air battles not only saved Ceylon, it also frustrated the Japanese dream of controlling the Indian Ocean, immobilizing the Eastern Fleet and severing the delivery line for oil from the Persian Gulf.

Len Birchall and the two unwounded members of his crew eventually ended up in a prison camp near Yokohama. As the senior officer among the prisoners, Birchall became camp leader, responsible, to the extent a prisoner could be responsible, for the welfare of the others. Conditions were execrable but morale, he sensed, was even worse than conditions warranted, in part because of the "rank has its privileges" attitude among the other officers. He tackled this problem head on, insisting that "We are all in this together," that the small quantities of vegetables and rice they were given be shared equally by weight, even to the point that a soldier, if he felt that an officer had got a bigger portion of the watery soup or boiled rice that was their only fare, could insist upon an exchange. Birchall also interposed himself between the prisoners and the brutal guards and often took the beatings himself, once even physically attacking the guard and breaking his jaw. The other guards stood by, mouths agape, in a momentary paralysis of unbelieving consternation. He badgered the prison officials ceaselessly for better food and for medical attention. On one occasion he absolutely refused to allow the sick and undernourished to go on a work party and his obstinacy won the day. It also won for him days of solitary confinement, merciless, sadistic beatings, a reputation as a trouble-maker, and in the end the grudging admiration of his captors.

In addition to the DFC he had already won for his courage and skill in landing his badly damaged aircraft, Len Birchall was awarded the Order of the British Empire (OBE) for his selfless and courageous leadership in the prison camp. The citation for this latter award is longer and more detailed than is usual and generous in its praise, but no more generous than his actions deserve. He retired from the RCAF with the rank of Air Commodore.

There is a coda to this tale. Shortly after the war, Churchill was a dinner guest at the British Embassy in Washington. Lester Pearson was also present. Someone asked Churchill what he considered was the most fateful and dangerous moment in the course of the war. His answer was surprising: the moment when he felt most alarmed was when he was told that the Japanese fleet was heading for Ceylon. He explained that the capture of Ceylon and with it the control of the Indian Ocean, coupled with the German occupation of Egypt, would have "closed the ring" and put everything in jeopardy. He then went on to give thanks for that unknown airman whose courage and determination had so changed the course of the war and who lay now in the depths of the Indian Ocean. He was delighted when Pearson told him that the airman in question was still alive and indeed was with the Canadian Military Mission just down the street. Len Birchall still treasures the letter from Pearson that tells this tale.

The defeat it had suffered at Ceylon persuaded the Japanese Navy to withdraw from the Bay of Bengal area. 413 Squadron then turned its attention to less sensational, though no less important matters, such as lengthy anti-submarine patrols. In a sense these were tedious flights tinged with a sense of futility; the chance of spying a periscope or even a surfaced submarine in the wideness of the Indian Ocean seemed remote. Sometimes however, the unexpected happened. On December 27, 1943 F/L S. J. Grandin and his crew spied the distant wake of a submarine. Speeding to the spot — a Catalina's top speed, full out down hill, was about 200 miles per hour — they found only the swirl left by the submerging vessel. Still, they dropped their depth charges and turned to observe the results. Something like the end of a submarine rose out of the water then sank again below the surface. Grandin and his crew were credited with a "probable" kill.

Even if the excitement of an encounter came but rarely, these long patrols, often as long as 20 hours, paid off in other ways — the mere presence of patrol aircraft constrained the wide-open hunting habits of the German and Japanese submariners and comforted Allied sailors, no small consideration in an ocean where the shipping did not travel in convoy. Moreover, since the flying boats sought their quarry wherever a ship had been sunk, they were often on hand to help survivors. In April 1944 when faint flashlight signals were reported on the open sea, F/L Gelmon and his crew set off to investigate and found two rafts each bearing survivors. They dropped food, water, cigarettes and books and then circled till their fuel ran low. Three days later, having spent fifty days on life rafts, the sailors were taken aboard a rescue boat. They were gaunt and stiff but alive and in good spirits, thanks to a flying boat that did not give up the search. The Air Officer Commanding sent a commendation to the Squadron with special mention of F/L Gelmon and his navigator, F/O Rankin.

In December 1942 the Squadron was asked to bomb an airfield and two harbours on the tip of Sumatra and gather information about the Japanese activities there. Sending a Catalina 1500 miles to bomb an airfield made little sense; obviously the information gathering was the important part of the mission. After eight and a half hours flying, W/C J. C. Scott found the airfield, then the first harbour, then the second. Only the first harbour presented any worthwhile targets. Scott dropped six bombs and a few incendiaries and began the long flight home. The damage the bombs had done was minimal, but the information must have been valuable. The crew were praised for their "superb" navigation and Wing Commander Scott received the DSO and was cited as "a brilliant captain whose determination to complete his allotted task, whatever the circumstances, has been outstanding."

At first the men of 413 Squadron revelled in the bright sun of Ceylon after the dreary chill of the Shetlands, although they were taken aback to discover that they were to be housed in a dirty camp recently vacated by a group of Italian prisoners and that they had to catch a train at 5:30 in the morning to go to work. Gradually living conditions improved, but for the

Canadians the feeling of being isolated and forgotten was strongly with
them. They had not even the consolation of an administrative structure
dedicated to their care and feeding. There was no one to whom they
could turn with questions about pay, promotion, repatriation or, most
importantly, mail. With typical Canadian energy and ingenuity, they took it
upon themselves to improve their own lot. The Canadian Overseas Radio
Network, call letters CORN, had gone on the air first in the Shetlands
when radio techs Jumping Joe Soper from Edmonton and Glen Farrell
from Woodstock, Ontario got hold of an old phonograph pick-up. They
brought the system to Kogalla and with wires strung from palm to palm
their "radio" delivered sprightly news and jivey tunes to the Squadron three
times a day. Other airmen put out a camp newspaper, Tropic Topics. One
issue carried a nostalgic item: "A visit to the local NAAFI reminds one of a
Montreal grocery store. Sitting on the shelves you can find peaches from
Hamilton, canned cherries and pears from Niagara, biscuits from London,
Ont., pickles, relishes and gum from Toronto, and best of all, beer from
Montreal."[2] To celebrate their first anniversary at Kogalla the Squadron
contracted for two coaches on the local train to take all personnel and
their friends for a day-long outing in the hills above Colombo. Kogalla, the
Squadron historian remarked, was "a beautiful place to spend a week, but,
for a permanent stay, the perfection of each day became tedious." Be that
as it may, it seems unarguable that squadron morale was high and that the
men had done their best to conquer the tedium of perfection.

In late 1944 the Canadian Government asked that 413 Squadron
be released from South East Asia Command. Aircrew were becoming
tour-expired, ground crew were becoming eligible for repatriation and
the strategic need for flying boats was dwindling. Honours had come to
them. They had been visited by the Commander in Chief, Lord Louis
Mountbatten, and by the Duke of Gloucester. They had received a Group
commendation for outstanding service from the Air Officer Commanding
and a second commendation for their excellent record of aircraft serviceability. The RAF agreed that the Squadron had served well and now they
could go home. In January 1945, after two and a half years on Ceylon,
squadron personnel climbed the gangplank of the Durban Castle to begin
their journey back to Canada.

Although Birchall's determined sortie into the midst of the Japanese
flotilla changed the larger course of the war, it did nothing to ease the
plight of the soldiers on the ground. The loss of air support, and par-

---

[2] NAAFI is the Navy, Army and Air Force Institute, a British organization that brought tea,
cakes, chocolate and such amenities to the troops. The passage is quoted from the RCAF
newspaper Wings Abroad.

ticularly of the intelligence that air reconnaissance could have supplied, was a problem that plagued General Slim throughout the retreat. For the moment however greater problems were on his mind. The Japanese, having consolidated their hold on Hong Kong, Singapore, Sumatra, Java, Siam, French Indochina and the Philippines, now had resources to divert to Rangoon and with them they were pressing hard toward the oilfields at Yenangyaung. Although Slim had received some reinforcements just before Rangoon fell, in particular an armoured regiment and an infantry battalion, he had not yet been able to replace all that was lost at the Sittang Bridge nor reorganize what remained. He would have liked to consolidate around Prome to defend Yenangyaung, but the Chinese had now joined the fray and were holding the Sittang valley sector around Toungoo so that Slim had to stretch his line thinly eastward to protect their right flank.

The Chinese troops were in fact a mixed blessing. Part of the problem was their commander, the American general Joe Stilwell. Slim got on well with him, but Vinegar Joe had few kind words for the other commanders, be they Chinese, whom he considered "pusillanimous bastards," or even fellow Americans. His special scorn and most acidic vitriol however he directed at the "Limey stuffed shirts and pompous monkeys." He was further irritated because Chiang Kai-shek had never fully accredited him so that the Chinese generals felt no obligation to obey his orders unless they were confirmed by one of their own leaders. When the Japanese attacked Toungoo, a major communication and supply depot, the Chinese 200th Division, though they defended with outstanding skill and bravery, found themselves surrounded and cut off. Stilwell called for the reserves. No one moved, and Toungoo was lost. On other occasions however, when they had resolute leadership, the Chinese forces showed their potential. A British unit, cut off and surrounded at the oil fields of Yenangyaung, was saved when a Chinese group wheeled up in enormous lend-lease Studebaker trucks, deployed with textbook crispness, and swept the Japanese from the perimeter.

Despite the small comfort the Chinese intervention had brought, the British had to give up Toungoo and shortly after that Yenangyaung, leaving its derricks as twisted wreckage and its oil wells so thoroughly plugged that they delivered no more oil till long after the war was over. Toungoo was a main supply depot, and its loss was for Slim a disaster almost equal to the debacle at Sittang Bridge. He yearned for the opportunity to meet his foe face-to-face, to hold the line Prome-Toungoo or, failing that, the line Yenangyaung-Meiktila-Taungyi, but each in turn had become impossible. Now there was almost no hope of reorganizing and consolidating and none at all for a counteroffensive. Burcorps was forced into one of the most difficult and dangerous manoeuvres that can be asked of an army, a fighting withdrawal. The front-line troops had to hold off the attackers, then break off the action and withdraw while a small rearguard protected their backside. Then the rearguard leapfrogged through while the front line protected them. Each disengagement was a moment of particular and peculiar danger.

For the troops, a fighting withdrawal meant unending tension and uncertainty. Japanese aircraft harassed them by day and mortar fire and artillery searched for them at night. They had to stand-to each evening, eat their scant meal of tea, hard tack and soya sausage, then curl up on the ground under the insufficient warmth of the half blanket they carried and hope there would be no night attack or jitter raid.[3] Before dawn there would be another stand-to before the column could eat, pack up, and move off. Even if they felt their rear securely covered by the rearguard, stragglers were always vulnerable to heartless attacks by roving bands of Burmese. They were perpetually hungry, perpetually tired, plagued, not only by the enemy, but by every disease and pestilence the jungle could throw at them. All units were below half strength. Enemy action accounted for many casualties, and ill health for many more. The usual ten-minute-per-hour break was abolished because, once the men got down, the officers often had to be brutal to get them up again.

All the time the Japanese advance continued. It developed into a twofold thrust with the eastern attack directed northward toward Lashio to push the Chinese back into Yunnan province. When Lashio fell on April 29, the Japanese finally had complete control of the Burma Road from Rangoon to Wanting on the Burma-China border. The second attack went straight up central Burma to overrun the enormous supply depot at Meiktila and head for Mandalay. Just six miles below Mandalay was the Ava Bridge, the only bridge in all Burma that spanned the broad expanse of the Irrawaddy. Remembering the Sittang, Slim took care to see that the Chinese, his tanks, and most of his infantry were over the river before he ordered its demolition. It was not rebuilt for thirteen years.

With the Irrawaddy behind them and the enemy not pushing as hotly, obviously the best course for Burcorps was to head northwest and get back to Assam with as much of its manpower and equipment as possible. The enemy divined this strategy and jumped ahead of the British to occupy Monywa, a small town on the Chindwin. Now the situation for the British was perilous; their first choice for an escape route lay through Monywa and then by boat up the Chindwin to Kalewa and thence, via Tiddim, to Imphal. With Monywa gone, the retreating troops would have to beat their way

---

[3] In all sectors of the Burma Campaign the Japanese made good use of jitter raids, small attempts at infiltration, sometimes made in eerie stealth, sometimes with unearthly howls, always in the depths of darkness. These raids were meant to unnerve men rather than to win ground.

northward along the river where no track existed and then take the ferry across the Chindwin at Shwegyin.

The object of all Slim's endeavours now must be to rescue as many men and salvage as much matériel as possible. It was not an easy job. The army was no longer falling back on its supply depots but was retreating away from them. The troops went on half rations. It was May 2, the monsoon could be expected within a fortnight, and the *chota* (small) monsoon was already starting to fall on their heads. Because the enemy controlled the skies, and made very good use of that control, the British had to march off the road or move at night. The tanks ran a shuttle service, taking a platoon forward a few miles then coming back for another load, and there were a few bullock carts to carry the sick and wounded, but basically it was a matter of slogging out on foot along the Chindwin, the last river between them and Assam.

Crossing the Chindwin was not a straightforward tactical exercise. On both shores the banks were steep and high; on the east the only flat land that could accommodate a ferry dock was at the small town of Shwegyin. Here, in this tight basin around the jetty, crowded all the remnants of the British forces in Burma as well as thousands of civilian refugees, mostly Indians fleeing desperately back to India. Five or six ferries, each capable of carrying about 1200 men, chuffed sluggishly six miles upstream to disgorge their load and six miles downstream for another portion of the frantic mob. The Japanese Air Force bombed and strafed the masses in the basin and the ferries on the river. The Japanese Army barged silently upstream and attacked from the south. The ferry crews fled and refused to return. The commanders gathered their scattered troops and the frightened refugees and began another cross-country march. Now everything that could not be carried in the hand had to be abandoned. The armoured regiments used their tanks to crush the trucks and then sorrowfully drained the oil from their vehicles and let them run till the engines seized. (One tank however survived the long retreat. Stripped of its turret and bearing the proudly perverse name *The Curse of Scotland*, it butted its way out to Imphal and butted its way back into Burma two years later.) The artillery turned their few remaining guns toward the enemy and, in one loud twenty minute barrage, fired off their scant supply of ammunition. Then the sad remnants of the 1ˢᵗ Burma Corps packed up their mules and took to the Getaway Path, a narrow trail along the Chindwin, more suitable for mountain goats than mules, for the 12 hour trek to Kalewa. Fortunately the Japanese were too interested in the booty in the basin to follow up.

After the ferries at Kalewa had set the column across the Chindwin, the end of the 900 mile retreat was tantalizingly close, just an 80 mile stroll up the Kabaw Valley, reputedly the most deadly malarial valley in the world, to Tamu and the beginning of the newly built road. There transport was surely waiting to take them on to Imphal. On May 12, when the last troops left Kalewa, the monsoons broke in fury. Within minutes the path was a slime of mud. Every slope meant fighting forward for one step and sliding back for two. Even the mules, surefooted through miles of dry mountain paths, fell from these slippery trails. From the teak trees high overhead the rain continued to fall long after the furious pelting of the monsoon had stopped. Whenever the soldiers brushed against bushes and foliage, leeches fastened on them and sucked their fill, unnoticed till the soldiers removed shoes and clothing at night and found these tenacious creatures swollen to three times their normal size. Where the leeches had fed, deep jungle sores that would not heal developed. There was virtually no food left. Belts were cinched beyond the last notch and the rags that insufficiently covered them drooped loosely on their wasted frames. All the diseases that had been barely held in check — dysentery, dengue fever, malaria, and among the refugees, even smallpox and cholera — began to rage. Hour after hour the troops plodded on, foregoing all rest stops in the certain fear that many would not rise again. At night a few hours fitful sleep on the wet earth under a wet half blanket did little to restore energy or revive spirits. Somehow, with heads down and feet plodding forward, they kept going, brute testimony to what the human spirit can do.

It was a ragtag, bare-bones army that had crossed the Chindwin and started that hell-march up the Kabaw Valley toward Tamu and Imphal, but when the moment came to show themselves in public their pride shone forth again. When the British officer, Captain Gerald Fitzpatrick, led his mud-spattered, exhausted, emaciated men into India and saw General Alexander standing on a small mound by the track, he became a soldier again: "I gave the order 'Kings Own Yorkshire Light Infantry, Mortar Platoon! March to attention! Eyes right!' I whipped up my first salute in weeks, and nine wonderful men did Alexander proud, turning eyes in unison." Fitzpatrick did not recognize the man standing beside General Alexander. It was William Slim and he too felt the pride that comes from recognizing men who were doing more than men can do: "All of them, British, Indian, and Gurkha, were gaunt and ragged as scarecrows. Yet they still trudged behind their surviving officer. They still carried their arms. They might look like scarecrows, but they looked like soldiers too."

VII

FLEEING FROM THE ENEMY

Aᴛʜᴏᴜɢʜ Bᴜʀᴄᴏʀᴘꜱ was plagued by disease and hunger throughout the long retreat, it was never altogether abandoned. Even in its most ragged moments, some semblance of Army administrative structure remained. Rearguard units controlled and directed traffic, and the RAF flew air supply missions as often as it could. But thousands fled from the enemy without even that attenuated support, without food or protection, without knowing where they were going or how they were going to get there. This chapter tells the story of these thousands, most of them Indian civilians fleeing in terror from Rangoon. It also tells of General Stilwell leading his party of American and Chinese troops from Indaw, and of two Canadian doctors who walked out from Maymyo. First is an account of the civilian exodus.

Throughout the years of their colonial management of Burma, the British had encouraged the influx of Indian labourers to do the day-to-day chores that a modern city requires. The Burmese were charming people, carefree and easy-going, but the British felt that they could not be counted on to load and unload shipping at the docks, to sweep the streets, to drive the trolleys, to serve in the clubs and hotels, or to take up police duties of directing traffic and patrolling the streets. For these tasks, Indians by the thousands came to Burma hoping to find their fortune. And this they did, moving upward from street sweeper to shop owner, from shop owner to land owner, and from land owner to money lender, the most lucrative trade of all. Of Rangoon's pre-war population of 500,000, 200,000 were Indians. Their industry and entrepreneurial skills made them indispensable and influential in the economy of lower Burma, but it did not endear them to their Burmese hosts.

When the first air raid came on December 23, the populace flocked onto the streets to watch and 2000 were killed. Only 60 were killed when the sec-

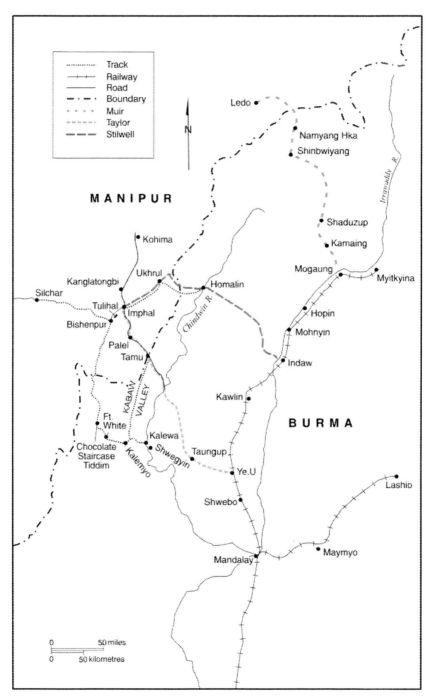

Map 5 — Walk-Out, Muir, Taylor, Stilwell. Imphal and Environs

ond air raid came on Christmas Day but thousands fled from the city. As the Japanese advanced, the tempo of flight increased until the road to Prome and northward was thronging with Indians frantic to get back to India.

The estimate of the numbers involved in this flight range from 250,000 to one million, and, as one writer has said, either figure could be correct. Not only Indians from Rangoon were involved, but Indians from all parts of Burma as well as the families of civil and military personnel. The British refugees had at least the assurance that whatever remnant of officialdom remained would be doing what it could to expedite their escape. The Indians had only the assurance that they would have to take second place behind the British, that they would undoubtedly be robbed, and that, if they were ever to find themselves at the mercy of a band of Burmese dacoits, they would probably be killed.

The most immediate and obvious escape route from Rangoon was by sea and 25,000, mostly Europeans, fled in this manner before the docks were closed to them. As long as Rangoon held, a daily train ran to Mandalay and many refugees, here again mostly Europeans, were on it. Many of them eventually flew out from Myitkyina. The Indians fled on foot, flocking on the road north to Prome then turning west to cross the Taungup Pass and reach Akyab where ships could take them, for a price, to safety in Calcutta. For a time the Government, in a cynical and futile attempt to hold them to their Rangoon duties, closed the pass, but eventually at least 100,000 reached India via this route, despite a threat of cholera at Akyab and a breakdown in civil administration that caused thousands to starve to death.

Those who were turned back from the Taungup Pass were herded on to Mandalay where a refugee camp sheltered 100,000 souls with more accumulating daily. From Mandalay the second preferred route of exit was the Kalewa-Tamu-Palel path. Thousands, British and Indians, fled along it. The suitcases of the British women, one suitcase for a woman alone and two for a woman with children, were carried by elephants of the Bombay Burma Trading Corporation[1]; the Indian women carried all they now possessed in this world on their heads. For three days the road was closed altogether to allow the feces on the roadside to dry up and thus abate the threat of a cholera epidemic. One day when it was found that there were 2400 Indian women at Tamu and only 8 sacks of rice to feed them, a temporary quota

[1] As early as January 1942 the Bombay Burma Trading Corporation, a teak extraction firm, ignored jibes about "The Corporation first in Burma and first out" and secretly began to survey escape routes to Assam. Along the route, the Corporation built and stocked rest stations and deployed a skeleton staff to aid the evacuation. At the same time, workers from the Assam Tea Estates and the Indian Tea Association were improving the various escape routes from the other end. These were people knowledgeable about jungle paths and jungle travelling in a way that the Army was not and it is no exaggeration to say that whatever success attended the flight from Burma, especially for civilians, was due to the help of these volunteers.

of 750 persons per day was imposed. Despite the hardships and difficulties, the official estimate for refugees fleeing through Tamu was 191,000. A further 25,000 to 30,000 refugees escaped through Myitkyina, either by air or along the track that would later become the Ledo Road.

For civil refugees the Ledo Road was the most fearful path to freedom. In *Through the Jungle of Death: A Boy's Escape from Wartime Burma* Stephen Brookes tells the story of his Anglo-Burmese family struggling through the Kumon Range, across the monsoon-deluged Hukaung Valley and then up and down the steep ridges of the Patkai Range. Twice they are brutally robbed by a band of Chinese soldiers and for weeks they are detained by the authorities at a dirty primitive camp in the middle of the jungle. Here Stephen learns to scour the forest for roots and "green things" to supplement their meagre diet of rice and his father dies of blackwater fever. In the hut with them are other refugees, driven mad by hunger and disease. They cannot escape the peculiar stink of corpses that no one has the strength to bury. It is five months before the Brookes family reaches the relative safety of India.

Stephen Brookes tells us that the Indian Government estimated that between 500,000 and 600,000 "British Asiatics" reached India from Burma and that approximately 100,000 died. However one estimates and adds up the numbers, the conclusion is inescapable that the flight from Burma was one of the most massive displacements of humanity that World War II engendered. But no statistics can measure the heartache and human suffering that plodded along with the despairing marchers.

The story of General Stilwell's doughty march from Burma began with the disintegration of his Chinese army. Throughout the campaign the Chinese forces that Stilwell nominally commanded had been an uncertain strength on the Allied side. General Slim generously acknowledges that when the Chinese soldiers were well equipped and well led, they were brave, obedient, and determined, "cheerful rascals" with whom he would happily go into battle. But their usual state was to be without any of the second echelon support a modern army required, no administrative support, technical services, communications, medical services, transportation, or ordnance supply. They had not even a pay corps to ensure that their wages came to them with even a shadow of dependability. Their greatest handicap however, was the lack of leadership and an assured chain of command. In such circumstances Stilwell did his best to hold the eastern end of the British line but found he was forced to fall back through Mandalay and Shwebo. More and more his control over his forces was evaporating, more and more the three Chinese armies in Burma were disintegrating, one of them to the extent that it never again appeared on the Chinese order of battle. In the end, scattered remnants of the Chinese force made their own

way back to China independently and as best they could, brutally commandeering trains, scavenging, foraging, robbing and pillaging whenever
the opportunity presented. There was one exception to this sorry story. The
38ᵗʰ Division, the one that under the excellent leadership of General Sun Li
Jen had rescued the British troops at Yenangyaung, withdrew in relatively
good order through the Kabaw Valley to Tamu and Imphal.

As for Stilwell, in early May he was at Shwebo with a miscellaneous band
of about one hundred followers — American soldiers and civilians, Chinese
soldiers, a war correspondent, a seven-man Quaker ambulance team, and
Colonel Seagrave, the Burma surgeon, with 19 Burmese nurses. Stilwell's
plan to take the train to Myitkyina and hope to fly out from there had to be
abandoned after a Chinese general commandeered the train at gunpoint
and then wrecked it 25 miles up the line. The American Air Force sent in
one last plane to spirit Stilwell back to India. Thirty-seven officers of his
headquarters contingent climbed aboard, but Stilwell scorned the rescue
attempt, assembled a convoy of jeeps and trucks and set off by road. As
vehicle after vehicle gave up the ghost, he simply ordered "Burn the damn
thing" and carried on. At Indaw he learned that pressing on was no longer
possible. The track ahead was impassable and the Japanese were threatening Myitkyina. Now the only option was to take to the jungle and beat across
the two hundred miles of steep mountains and wild rivers that lay between
them and India.

On the morning of May 7, Stilwell sent his last message, destroyed his
radio, and set out at the head of his strange troupe. At the tail of it came
Dr. Seagrave and his nurses, petite young ladies in dainty native dress. The
soldiers feared these girls would be an impossible burden on the march,
but surprisingly the girls were better than the men at tolerating the fast
pace, the scarcity of food and the rigours of the trail. More than that, their
light-hearted rendition of "Onward Christian Soldiers," their playful spirits
and their solicitous care for the sick and lame did more for morale than
an extra ration of rice. Stilwell himself, on the point of turning sixty, led
the band, calling the cadence and setting the tempo, 105 paces per minute.
Civilian groups walking out on the Ledo Road were lucky to make ten miles
in a day; Stilwell insisted that his column do at least 18 or 20. When one
of his officers felt he could not keep up, Stilwell was heartless: "Dammit,
I'm telling you to keep up with this column and that's what I mean!" The
officer kept up. Always Stilwell led the column and set the example that
he expected the others to follow. "He's made of steel, wire, rubber and
concrete," his public relations officer admiringly declared.

When they reached the Uyu River they hoped that two days on a raft
would give them a rest but the rafts kept getting caught and breaking apart.
Finally, with almost no supplies in their larder, they reached Homalin on

the banks of the Chindwin, but there was still a two day march before a relief party found them, gave them food and put them on the track to Manipur. On May 22, fifteen days after they set out, Stilwell and his followers marched into Imphal. Someone asked him how many he had lost on the march out. "Not a one," replied Stilwell gruffly, "Not a single one."

A few days later he was interviewed by the American press in Delhi. In a war where good news was in short supply, here was the hero the American press and the American public yearned for. Through his determination and persistence, through his physical stamina and by mere strength of character he had led his band of Americans, Chinese, British soldiers and his colourful bevy of Burmese nurses out of the jungle and into safety. Characteristically, Vinegar Joe was not about to seek the limelight or glorify his exploits: "I claim we got a hell of a beating. We got run out of Burma, and it's humiliating as hell. I think we ought to find out what caused it, go back, and retake Burma." General Slim was thinking along the same lines, but it was going to take a while to get started.

Still to be told are the stories of the two Canadian doctors who were forced to flee from the central Burma town of Maymyo as the Japanese advanced. Through accidents of fate, they fled on different paths and had different experiences. Each of them wrote a diary of his flight and the somewhat detailed accounts that follow are based on those unpublished diaries. One of the men we have met already — Major Keith Muir, the doctor from Eureka, Nova Scotia who had established himself so happily in Rangoon. The second is Major Andrew Copeland Taylor. His story comes first.

Andrew Taylor was the son of Canadian missionaries active in rural India. At the age of 14 he, like Robert McClure, was sent back to Canada for his education. After completing his medical degree at the University of Toronto, finishing an internship at Detroit and marrying Miss Marion Gauld of Mimico, he returned to India to begin his work as a medical missionary. His skill and dedication earned him the respect of the populace. "The whole of Malwa," so one tribute runs, "knows your reputation as an expert surgeon and a skillful physician who works with unfailing assiduity for hours at a stretch in the day and gets up at any hour of the night to relieve the suffering of the sick, be they rich or poor, prince or peasant, high caste or untouchable." "All baloney," said Andy Taylor with self-effacing modesty.

In 1935 the Taylor family went back to Canada for a well-earned furlough. Then the blow fell — the United Church could no longer support him. In default of other employment, Dr. Taylor accepted a commission in the Indian Medical Service and returned to India. When war came, he sent his family back to Canada and joined 41st Indian General Hospital as Chief of Surgery. In mid-December the newly-formed unit was ordered to prepare in all haste for embarkation for North Africa. Leaving Taylor in charge, the Commanding Officer took four days leave to say good bye to his family. The day after he left, secret orders came for immediate departure, not for the West, but for the East, for Burma, and Taylor had only three days to collect equipment for a 1000 bed hospital from all over India. The hospital was far from fully equipped when, on December 23, 1942 he and a pipe band led his men to the station. Medical officers are not often called upon to lead parades and Dr. Taylor was a bit diffident: "It's the first time I've done that," he wrote to his wife, "and I did feel a bit of a fool trying to play the soldier."

The 41st Indian General Hospital arrived in Rangoon just one week after the air raids of December 23 and 25. The cranes in the harbour were still working, but the sheds were burned out and all the dock hands had fled. Throughout the night and on into the next morning Taylor and his troops slaved at the unloading, slipping and sliding on docks that were slimy with maggots that had crawled out of the burning warehouses, holding their noses against the stench of decaying corpses buried in the wreckage. That was their New Year's Day, 1942. The next day they entrained for Maymyo.

Pre-war visitors to Maymyo were always struck by how greatly the air of the place evoked the feeling of a provincial English town — quiet tree-lined streets, lawns protected by hedges and filled with the roses and lilacs of an English garden. The houses in the cantonment area were of frame and stucco construction with a gabled dormer projecting from the dark brown roof tiles. If the civil administrators and army families felt at home here that was because General May, who founded the town in the 1880's, planned it so. And at an elevation of 5000 feet, it was an ideal hill station where one could escape the heat and humidity of Rangoon. It is no wonder, especially after the grisly experiences of the Rangoon docks, that Major Taylor wrote to his wife: "I never expected to be dropped into a place like Maymyo for active service."

There were difficulties getting the operating room set up and the nights were "cold as blazes," but apart from that life was genial. He and an English doctor shared a bungalow where each had his own room and bath and, once Taylor got his fireplace going and the blackouts up, it was quite cosy. They had found a tea room that served the fresh strawberries for which Maymyo was famous with thick cream from the government dairy, and there would be fresh pineapples when the strawberries were over. Major Taylor learned that Bob McClure had passed through just the week before he arrived and he met the "other Canadians," Major Muir and Colonel Phelps, both recently arrived from Rangoon. Colonel Phelps, though he had been out of Canada since World War I, still took on the role of mentor to newly arrived compatriots. Just as he had entertained the Muirs when they first arrived in Rangoon, he now invited Taylor in Maymyo. "We had a nice dinner with very good strawberry shortcake for dessert," Taylor wrote to his wife. "It was refreshing to talk 'Canada' with someone."

In the bazaar down the road there were a few European shops, branches of the stores in Rangoon. The path around the lake was lined with cherry trees just coming into bloom and at the end of the trail there was a quiet Botanical Garden. Taylor's only complaint was that mail from Canada was not getting through. Apart from that "It is all so peaceful and quiet," wrote Taylor, "that it seems hard to believe this is a 'Field Service Area' with the Japs and ourselves fighting it out somewhere over the horizon."

Gradually that horizon closed in on Maymyo. On February 2 Taylor notes that he removed his first Jap bullet. A fortnight later he is so busy with the first big batch of casualties from the Sittang battle that he misses lunch with Colonel Phelps. Over his battery-operated radio he is depressed to hear of the fall of Singapore and of the Japanese being uncomfortably close to Pegu and Rangoon. On February 22, a Sunday, he is cycling past Burma General Hospital and sees planes high over head in perfect formation, then a series of loud bangs and clouds of dust and smoke rising from the other end of town. Maymyo has had its first air raid and Taylor immediately cycles to his hospital to tend the casualties. The worst case is a man with a smashed leg and abdominal wounds. "We could have saved him," wrote Taylor wistfully, "if we had had plasma or blood."

In the weeks that follow, the order and neatness of life in Maymyo begins to break down. The officers' wives and families are sent off to Shwebo to be airlifted to India. Three days later they are back in Maymyo. The airstrip in Shwebo has not even been constructed; they have had to sleep in the bug-infested beds of a police barracks crowded with squalling children. The Colonel's wife is furious. In the mess the diet is becoming less varied, rice and curried bully beef each day, and no eggs. At least there are still strawberries. The casualties from the Sittang Bridge debacle are flooding in and Major Taylor schemes to get down to Mandalay to collect medical supplies "before some one gets the bright idea of blowing them up."

On April 8 Maymyo has its second air raid. Twenty-seven Japanese bombers come over in perfect formation and drop 90 bombs on the town. The hospital staff has time to get into their slit trenches and from there Major Taylor notes that the whiz of the falling bombs is worse than the actual bangs, but even worse is the total lack of any air defence. "What is exasperating," he complains, "is that the blighters can sail over and do pattern bombing onto us without any interference." The raid is over in a minute, but for the next twelve hours Taylor is operating nonstop on its victims. He is particularly pleased that the casualty whose spleen he had removed is recovering nicely.

Despite the air raids, the evacuation of dependants, and the news of the relentless advance of the Japanese Army, a torpor and inertia persists in Maymyo, a reluctance to surrender the idyllic dream. Then reality hits quickly. On April 24 all patients, nurses and volunteer aides are ordered to leave. Taylor and his fellow officers work throughout the day and late into the evening loading, indeed, overloading the train. He counts 13 nurses in one second-class compartment and notes with disapproval that the Matron insists that her large camphor wood chest be loaded in with her and is then annoyed that she has to share her compartment with 3 other nurses. The officers return to a subdued supper and in the night they hear shots and explosions in the distance. The entry in the 41st Indian General Hospital War Diary, hurriedly handwritten, catches the mounting tension of the next day:

26-4-42   *8 am Maymyo. Orders from DDMS (Deputy Director of Medical Services) — Hospital to be ready to move with 10 % of equipment leaving rear party to load balance if train transport can be arranged.*
11:17 am Orders from DDMS — only essential equipment to be taken.
1 pm Orders from DDMS — be ready to move at once.
3 pm Personnel to march to station for entraining, leaving party of 45 men and one officer under Major Taylor, IMS, as rear party to come out by road with vehicles.
8 pm — entrained all personnel except rear party in the last train to leave Maymyo.

That last train to leave Maymyo was packed with over 900 men, most of them jammed side by side into goods wagons. The officers, after going through the train throwing out kit to make room for one or two more, crowded into one third-class compartment. Taylor watched the train pull laboriously out of the station and then went back to the hospital to sleep. Early next morning his rear-party convoy of eight ambulances, two trucks and three cars drove through the deserted streets of the town and down the road to Mandalay. He brought up the rear of the little cavalcade in the Ford staff car, the last doctor to leave Maymyo.

It was a shock to see Mandalay. For a half mile on either side of the main street there was nothing but rubble, twisted wires and the charred remains of buildings. The whole place was deserted and quiet as death. They passed over the Ava Bridge, well aware that there were charges on the structure below ready to blow at a moment's notice. Driving toward Shwebo they encountered a casualty clearing station and Andy Taylor spent half a day operating and plastering "under most appalling and uncomfortable conditions." Shwebo itself was still burning as they slowly manoeuvred through its rubble-strewn streets to get their ambulance patients onto an evacuation plane. Others of his troop are taken to the station to catch the last train from Shwebo.

From this point on Major Taylor's path through the fog and chaos of war is difficult to trace. He has been charged to lead the rear party out — that surely is his first duty — but on the way he repeatedly encounters suffering that cries out for his attention. The tension that arises from the pull between the duty that has been laid upon him by his commanding officer and the professional duty that is imposed upon him by the circumstances of war underlies all the rest of his account. He is ordered to report to a casualty clearing station, but first he must ferry half his men along to a rendezvous and arrange for the rest to march to it. Then even before he can find the casualty clearing station he is stopped by another medical officer who asks him to take some patients to a hospital up the road. With two ambulances filled with wounded he sets out. The night is pitch black and it is raining. One ambulance goes off the road but they manage to set it right again. At the Ye-u River they become embroiled in a huge tangle of trucks, cars, ambulances, artillery tractors and tanks all milling about to get over the river and all, apart from the tanks, getting deeper and deeper mired in the sand. Dawn is breaking — "a most unpleasant feeling," says Major Taylor, "to be sitting helpless in the open bed of a wide river, knowing that the daylight would bring the Jap bombers." Finally, at 6:30 they are able to cross the river and streak for cover. When they find where the hospital had been, it is gone, leaving six wounded lying on the verandah without food or water. Taylor then seeks out Burma Corps HQ, hoping to find what is required of him, but he is told by the Assistant Director of Medical Services that he and his men are on their own. He tries to get another ambulance filled with wounded to the airstrip at Shwebo. The last plane has left so he takes the patients on to Ye-u and then has to take his companion back to the casualty clearing station at Shwebo. Driving back again toward Ye-u to join his own men, he spies a British officer crawling out of the canal that parallels the road. The man had fallen asleep while speeding to the Camp Commandant at Shwebo with urgent orders for its immediate evacuation. Taylor turns again to drive the officer to Shwebo, his third trip down this road today. On the way back to Ye-u he stops long enough to wade into the canal and salvage a wheel from the drowned vehicle as a spare for his own.

When he finally gets together again with the men of the rear party he finds that they have chosen to bivouac with the 37 Field Ambulance. That is a mistake, for casualties from the battle at Monywa are streaming in and Taylor feels obliged to help out throughout the night. Still his professional pride shines through: "Worst case Captain Innes, gun shot wounds to face, fracturing jaw, plus wound left shoulder joint and had a job fixing him up."

He goes on, "This was my second night without sleep and toward morning I was dead tired." Just before breakfast he got a chance to curl up for an hour in a corner and go to sleep.

It is now the first week of May. Major Taylor's convoy is reduced to one 15 cwt (hundredweight) truck and the staff car. Five men ride with him in the car, a few more are in the truck, and the rest are somewhere on the trail marching toward India. Their rations are in the truck and they eat if they and the truck come together at the end of the day. Otherwise they go hungry or depend upon others to share their scant supplies. They sleep without blankets on the ground, or often under the car to escape the rain of the *chota* monsoon. Once they are dive-bombed by the Japanese Air Force, once Taylor sees British troops take three Burmese collaborators off to the side of the road and then he hears three shots. On May 4 he finds himself held up by about 200 vehicles, all waiting to make their way down a particularly steep hill. Taylor's turn comes and he sees before him a series of sharp switchbacks leading down at a 45 degree angle. There is no room to make a turn at the bottom of the switchbacks so he goes alternately forward down one stretch, then backward down the next.

The road surface is bone-rattling rough and cut every mile or so by steep-sided sandy *chaungs* littered with abandoned, burnt out vehicles. The radiator of their car is steaming and has to be refilled at every puddle. Among the marching troops there are civilian refugees, hundreds of them, pitifully ragged and dirty and hungry. Taylor will never forget two little girls, about five and three, standing by the body of their dead mother, their father having died the day before. A truckload of British Tommies picks them up.

All this rag-tag throng of fleeing troops with trucks and tanks, sullen marchers, civilians on foot, wounded on bullock carts or carried by their mates, all are headed for Shwegyin, a small port on the Chindwin. Just short of their destination, Taylor and his crew are stopped by the Military Police and ordered from their vehicle. Their car is unceremoniously pushed over a hill to join hundreds of others in a mass of wreckage at the foot of the cliff. "It was sad," Taylor records, "to see the old Ford that had puffed and steamed its way so far, over such foul roads, end up in this way." What little kit he still has he must now abandon, including his fine green battle dress. Taking nothing but what he can carry in his small haversack, he hitches a ride in a small four-wheel drive truck that can manage the sand of the dry *chaungs*. In the dark of the night they abandon the truck when the road takes an unexpected turn and leaves them half hanging over a steep declivity. They walk the last mile to Shwegyin, find a spot on the steep hillside among all the other troops and refugees, wrap themselves in their groundsheets and hope for a bit of sleep tonight and a place on the river steamer next morning.

The steamer did take them across the Chindwin next morning, and then six miles up the river to Kalewa. Here Major Taylor found a Field Ambulance overwhelmed with wounded and felt conscience-bound to stay and give them a hand. For three days he stood under a tree, stripped to the waist, dressing and plastering the wounded who lay all about on the hillside. Most had gun shot wounds with compound fractures, but worst of all were three burn cases who cried out all night in a delirium of pain. There were literally hundreds of wounded lying on the ground around them and all the doctors could do was to keep working on the most severe cases and let the rest lie.

By May 9 the Field Ambulance had done all it could do and it was ordered to evacuate. Late in the afternoon they set out on foot with Taylor leading the column toward Kalemyo. They were relieved when they turned north up the Kabaw valley toward Tamu before they reached the town, for rumour had it that Kalemyo was already in Japanese hands. At two o'clock in the morning they stopped for tea and a short rest then marched on till noon the next day. Taylor and the other officers bedded down in a small native hut. It was filthy and stinky, but they were too tired to care. For the next two days they walked and stopped to eat bully beef and drink tea and then walked again. It was raining every day now; they were at an altitude of 3000 feet and were unendingly miserable and cold. Japanese planes came over but spared the fleeing troops in favour of a battery of artillery in a nearby wood. Despite his own misery, Taylor checked to see that the victims of the bombing had been evacuated before toiling on to Tamu.

Along the north-west border of Burma lies the Kabaw Valley, reputedly the most malaria-ridden area in the world, and on its edge, directly on the Burma-India border, is the village of Tamu. Thirty-four miles to the north-west of Tamu and well within the Indian province of Manipur lies the even smaller village of Palel, gateway to the Imphal plain. Before the war no road had connected Tamu and Palel, partly because such a road would serve no commercial purpose commensurate with its cost, but more importantly because the Burmese did not want one. It would only serve to bring in more Indian workers and there were far too many of them in Burma already. Now of course, it was a far different situation. A road connecting Tamu and Palel could mean the salvation of an army as well as a quarter of a million civilian refugees.

With trucks, bulldozers and elephants, the Royal Engineers set about building a road through the pinched valleys and up and down the steep slopes of the Chin Hills to join the two villages. Under the double threat of the Japanese advance and the monsoon rains, they worked wonders, but they would have worked miracles if their Canadian-made Fords had not had so much petrol pump failure. When an urgent request to have 400 cork gaskets air- lifted from Canada went unanswered, the mechanics plastered the pumps with soap and improvised with washers cut from cigarette packages or from the soft leather of the drivers' jerkins.[2] The Canadian trucks were a worry to the road builders, but the elephants were a godsend. As a Forest Manager with the Bombay Burma Trading Corporation, "Bill" Williams had made himself an expert in the extraction of teak and a wizard with elephants. He now contributed his wizardry, his elephants and his "oozies," Burmese elephant drivers, to the building of the Palel road. With a dexterity no machine could match, the elephants went into the jungle, brought out teak logs each weighing a quarter of a ton, and deftly placed them just where they were required for the building of a bridge. Thanks to them, trucks stuck axle-deep in mud came out like corks from a bottle. Even bulldozers teetering on the edge of a sheer cliff were rescued by these intelligent beasts. The only thing that interfered with their work was the number of HQ visitors who came up to the construction site to marvel at the wonders the elephants were performing.

With such dedication and ingenuity, the engineers managed to build a passable road and to keep the trucks moving. Providing drivers was more difficult. The major in charge of transport had been given 400 new drivers. They had come straight from small rural villages in southern India and of course had never driven any vehicle before. The major's officers spoke English and Urdu; the sepoys spoke six different languages, none of which was English or Urdu, and the major had only three months to make soldiers and drivers of them. At the best of times the road, an unending series of sharp curves and steep slopes, was a challenge even for experienced drivers; now the rains turned it to deep and slippery mud. The Royal Engineers calculated that every time they sent a convoy up the Palel road they lost 20% of their vehicles.

Taylor's diary for May 13, 1942 takes up the story: "Left Tamu in a 10-wheeler truck driven by a terrified and inexperienced Madrasi. Road hilly and steep — a hair-raising experience, with many trucks over the edge. We had to pick up the injured from one of these which crashed just before us. Finally a BOR took over the wheel."[3] They reached Palel at one o'clock the next morning, having completed their terrifying journey in pitch darkness. It is now May 14, seventeen days since Major Taylor had left Maymyo.

Next morning Taylor allowed himself the luxury of a haircut, then searched through the scattered tents and camp areas of Palel to find his

---

[2] Despite these difficulties, the Canadian-built trucks lingered on. A 1993 visitor to Burma saw a Canadian Chevrolet, vintage 1944, hauling teak in the Burmese forest. (*Dekho,* Summer 1993, p.15)

[3] BOR, British Other Rank, that is, a private soldier. IOR is Indian Other Rank.

party and bring them together in a "Rest Camp" where they were fed, given an opportunity to bathe in the river and settled down under tarpaulins for the night. Two hours later they were roused, marched five miles and loaded into trucks for an all-night journey to a jungle camp near Imphal, the end of their retreat. It was not, however, the end of their travail. In his diary Taylor records what happened next: "We all had visions of nice comfortable beds and good food ... but the first thing we found was that there were no medical arrangements. We had to open up and work like stink because practically everybody who came into the camp — and they came in thousands — had sore feet, big sores on their legs, or malaria or dysentery. We had to go on short rations. Our supper the first night was gluey boiled rice with a spoonful of jam. Breakfast next morning the same with a tinned sausage." Now the monsoon proper had set in and it once rained without stopping for three days. The camp became a quagmire and, while Taylor and his medical party had acquired a small tent, hundreds of wounded were lying unprotected in the ceaseless rain. With all the strength he could muster he threw himself into his work.

Of the thousands of soldiers who struggled back across the Chin Hills almost none reached the Imphal valley in good health. The scant and incomplete diet meant not only extreme weight loss but also beriberi with its concomitant of swollen limbs. Leeches and broken skin meant deep-festering jungle sores. The Kabaw Valley march almost guaranteed a siege of malaria with its alternation of debilitating high fever and shivering chills that no blankets, had they been available, could warm. Given the scarcity of uncontaminated water it is no wonder that many of the men were suffering the severe cramps and bloody stools of dysentery. Some had cut the seat out of their trousers to accommodate the constant diarrhea that came with that disease, others simply dispensed with trousers altogether. Major Taylor had been no more able to avoid malaria and dysentery than the rest of the men. One night when he went out to answer a call of nature, he passed out. The rain revived him and he crawled back to his tent. Delirious with fever, shaking with chills, plagued by constant bloody diarrhea, he was eventually evacuated to where medication and proper treatment were possible and then sent on five months sick leave. Thus did his walk out from Maymyo conclude.

In November 1941 Keith Muir, the doctor from Eureka, Nova Scotia, arrived in Maymyo on his posting from Rangoon. He was delighted with the brilliant bloom of the tall poinsettia trees along the roadways and the towering oak with its mistletoe in the front lawn, but even more by the nasturtiums and sweet peas, "just like those we had in Nova Scotia." The hospital and the laboratory, which was his particular charge, were just up the road. A rambunctious white ram was kept in a pen beside the lab to supply white blood cells for his Wasserman tests. The cold bothered him a bit, but he lived in the Mess, there was usually a fire in the grate, and he was among friends from previous postings. Roy Phelps, the hospitable Canadian colonel, had also been transferred from Rangoon to Maymyo, and there was a new Canadian doctor, Major Taylor.

Another Canadian Muir met in Maymyo, Lieutenant Gordon Bruce, was a bit of an enigma. According to the story he told Major Muir, he had at one time been in the Canadian Army, then had joined the American Army and been sent to China. There he had married a Chinese girl and taken his discharge from the Army to start a radio sales and service business in Tientsin. Having experienced the Japanese occupation of Tientsin, he felt strongly moved to get into the war. He left his wife and child with her family, found his way across into Burma and persuaded the British to commission him as a radio officer. He was a free spirit and liked to strap to his belt a hunting knife he had made for himself and hike off through the surrounding hills, "just like the boys in Nova Scotia," remarked Muir. With an unconscious premonition of trouble ahead, Muir joined Bruce on these walks, to toughen himself up, he told himself, in case a much longer walk was in his future. Then Gordon Bruce disappeared from Maymyo as mysteriously as he had come

Just as Major Taylor had noticed the persistence of a peacetime calm in wartime Maymyo, so Major Muir wrote of a "pretended carefree attitude." One could fill the long evenings with golf and tennis. Strawberries were still in season, large red luscious fruit served with thick cream just as good as he had at home. Every evening front line troops with a few days leave and wanting to forget the unpleasantness and stress of battle initiated parties at the Maymyo Club that lasted until the night's allotment of liquor had been consumed. Major Muir preferred a quiet evening of conversation in the mess.

Then in February of 1942 the enemy air raids began. In a park near the hospital there were two circles of sandbags with large green bamboo logs angled up out of them to resemble gun emplacements. They did not fool the Japanese. In the evening calm a biplane would float impudently over the town taking photos and next day there would be an air attack. After all, the enemy had complete control of the skies now.

Throughout March awareness of the fighting grew in Maymyo. Muir sold his car to the Army and took some of his kit to the nuns in the near-by convent for safekeeping. His reasoning was that the nuns were Austrian, Austria was now part of Germany, Germany was an ally of Japan, *ergo* his kit would be safe. Following the same logic, he entrusted the laboratory's rambunctious white ram to them. Lt. Colonel Malone, the McGill graduate who had been principal of the Medical College at Rangoon, visited briefly

on his way to set up an evacuation centre near Lashio. Muir warned him of
the rumours of Japanese advances in that area but the Colonel carried on.
Toward the end of April the situation deteriorated and on Sunday, May 26,
the evacuation order came. Muir and his staff killed the guinea pigs and
rats from their laboratory, packed their equipment in a truck, and set off
to drive to Shwebo, where they hoped to catch a train to Myitkyina. As they
drove out of Maymyo, the air raid warning siren announced another visit
from the Japanese air force and it began to rain.

The truck they had scrounged barely made it to Shwebo. They had to
abandon it and an Army mechanic ferried Muir to the station in a beaten
and battered auto which Muir recognized as his own, the one he had sold
to the army a few weeks before. The station had just received a direct hit
and the platform was lined with corpses in rough uncovered coffins, a grisly
reminder of the dangers that lay ahead. Muir and his men loaded their
equipment into a goods wagon . He was uneasy that it was not hooked onto
their train but the Rail Transport Officer assured him it would follow the
next day. They were crammed into an already overfilled coach connected
to a train that was already too long for one engine. All night and into the
next day it toiled northward toward Myitkyina.[4] On April 30, three days
after leaving Maymyo, the train pulled onto a siding at Mohnyein, ninety
miles short of their destination, and they were told they were to establish
a medical centre here, "a good mission hospital where patients could, if
necessary, be left." Unspoken was the suggestion that, if the retreat got too
hot, the wounded were to be left here at the mercy of the Japanese.

If there was to be a medical centre, Muir would need his lab equipment.
For two days he trudged the length of each incoming train but never did his
goods wagon arrive. On the second day he was taken to visit the site of this
putative medical centre and found there only a few half-finished buildings
in a small jungle clearing. Discouraged and downcast, he returned to the
station. Some one handed him a note scribbled on the back of an envelope.
It was an order from his brigadier to proceed to Mogaung, fifty miles up
the line, and to march from there through the Hukaung valley to Ledo
in Assam. The message concluded with the encouraging words: "If you
organize your party well, most of you should get through alive." Muir was
disconcerted to note that the message had been written two days earlier.

When Major Muir and his party landed in Mogaung, they were met by an
executive of a rice and teak exporting firm. The executive was astonished
when he heard their plan. It would be folly, he declared, for a party of
this size to try to march out through the Hukaung Valley starting from

---

[4] Pronounced "Mitcheenah," with the accent on the middle syllable. In English orthography
"ky" renders the Burmese "ch" sound and "gy" renders the Burmese "j". Thus the Yenangyaung
oil fields are at "Yenanjong," and the Taukkyan Military Cemetery is at "Tokchahn."

Mogaung. He strongly urged, indeed, as much as ordered them to go back to Hopin and start their march from there. On that route they would at least find some civilian support. And he further urged haste, for if they did not reach the Chindwin in eight days, there was a good chance they would be overrun by the advancing enemy. Alarmed and angry, Muir and his party got back on the train and started back through the dark night the way they had just come. It was only a twenty-five mile journey, but the train stopped for fuel and water, and all able-bodied men were required to take a shift feeding wood into the hungry maw of the locomotive. It was midnight when they reached Hopin. Muir spread his ground sheet and blanket on the ground and went to sleep.

Next morning he prepared for the walk out. He put on his best cotton underwear and his best khaki shorts and shirt and set about lightening his load. His Dalhousie and Mount Allison diplomas, his London Medical College certificate, his insurance policies, the loose leaf diary he had been keeping — all had to be discarded. The only possession beyond the necessities that he allowed himself was a small leatherette notebook wherein he would write a few words each day as a record of the march. The "necessities" included two blankets, a rubber ground sheet, a mosquito net and a full water bottle. The column was given a few sacks of rice and a bullock cart to carry them for the first few miles of their journey. Under a bright sun in a clear sky they began their march. The Colonel who had assumed command of the column divided it into four or five companies and asked Muir to lead off with the first group. "You will be the first to get to Imphal," he joked. The path led uphill but Muir was keen to get on with it and he set a decent pace. He was grateful now for the toughening up walks he had taken with young Gordon Bruce in Maymyo.

A halt was called at about four o'clock. The bullock carts were to leave them now and the rice would have to be divided out so that each carried a share. Muir, wet with perspiration, flung himself down in the shade to rest. The Colonel in charge regarded him for a moment, then called another doctor over. There and then, without any preliminaries or explanation, the Colonel gave him an impromptu medical board, declared he was unfit to proceed and that he must return with the bullock carts. Muir protested that the "medical board" was wrong, that it was comprised only of surgeons, not physicians, that he was quite fit to go on, that there was nothing wrong with him that a good night's rest would not cure, but the decision stood. He was to return to Hopin with the bullock carts. Aware that if he, a senior officer, continued to defy the Colonel it could have an effect on discipline and jeopardize the safety of all, he finally accepted the order in seeming good grace. But the decision rankled and to the day he died he kept the scrap of paper on which the pseudo-Medical Board had inscribed its verdict.

The road back was all down hill, the bullocks moved at a good trot, and he was back at the railway station just before dark. The streets of Hopin were absolutely deserted but a Chinese tea shop next to the station was still open. Muir ate a clear noodle soup served in a flowered porcelain bowl with a matching ladle then settled in to wait for a train, any train.

A train arrived a few hours later. Muir found a spot on the floor and slept. When he awoke early next morning, he was told they were at Mogaung. Now the word was that Myitkyina was in Japanese hands and the train was going no further, they would have to walk out from here.[5] Here, of course, was Mogaung, the head of the trail that, four days earlier, he had been advised not to take because it was too difficult. But there was at least some semblance of organization for the trek. A Burmese civil servant opened a large canvas bag filled with silver rupees and invited them to help themselves. Another passed out notes outlining the trail and the amenities it provided. Muir kept his copy:

Mogaung	Mile 0. Shelter for 1000 coolies etc. at 1st mile up Kamaing road. Along Kamaing Road are villages at frequent intervals – Shan, Burman, Kachin and Gurkha.
Kamaing	Mile 25. HQ of Asst. Supt. Kachin Hills – Dak bungalow. Rice is stored here. Available on application to Asst. Supt. Road beyond for next 9 miles is good fair weather Public Works Dept. road.
Pakhrenbum	Mile 34. Road to jade mines branches to left. Route to Manipur down Uyu River. 18 days march. Rice in godown. Shelter for small parties.
Tin Kawk	Mile 80. At about 75 miles the divide is crossed and one enters the Hukawng Valley. Rice godown.[6]
N'Kyaw	Mile 129. The Tarung Hka crossing to Yurang on the opposite bank. Rice in godown both. Ferry easy in low water, very difficult in floods. Very swift stream. Halfway to Ledo. No rice beyond this point.
Shingbwiyang	Mile 152. Officer on duty. Rations dropped by air here. Road now enters hilly country. From S'Yang to Namyang Hka is 40 miles climbing and descending. No villages on route.

[5] Myitkyina fell May 8, 1942. From Muir's diary I calculate he left Maymyo April 26, arrived Mohnyin April 30, arrived Mogaung May 3, started the aborted march out from Hopin May 4, was back in Mogaung on May 7 and began the march out that same day.

[6] A "godown" is a warehouse or storage area. The etymology is uncertain but it is speculated it derives from trading company employees being told to "go down" to the warehouse to fetch something.

Namyang Hka   Mile 192. Main road to Pangsau Pass goes due north from here. 10 days hard marching to Ledo. Road rises to 5000 feet. Cold and wet. Rains daily.

It was a daunting itinerary, particularly for Muir who was alone and without supplies. He was relieved to meet an old army friend. "Join us," said Colonel Hey, "We've got rations enough and you can ride our ration truck for the first twenty miles." The truck took him to Kamaing and there he settled down on the verandah of a makeshift jungle hospital to await the column. He waited through the evening and through the night. By noon the next day there was no sign of Colonel Hey. "There was nothing I could do," says Major Muir's diary. "I took up my pack and started off alone."

A few miles down the track he became aware of a tall man overtaking him with long purposeful strides. It was a missionary whom he had met on the train from Hopin. "What are you doing here?" cried the missionary. "I thought you would be in India by now." Muir explained and declared his intention to persevere on foot. "But you have no food. Go back. Go back. Surrender to the Japanese. You'll die on the road." "No," replied Muir. "I have a family at home." "Then God help you," exclaimed the missionary as he splashed boldly through a small stream and disappeared into the tall teak forest. Somewhat disheartened by this unexpected encounter, but spurred by the fear of a Japanese prison camp on the one hand and the memory of home and family on the other, he plodded on.

With the help of another lift in a rice truck Muir came to the village of Shaduzup, mile 64 of the track to Ledo. About 1000 refugees were gathered here and there were rations. He collected boiled rice and dahl in his mess tin and ate the first food he had had since the noodle soup in Hopin the night before.

A strange torpor briefly overtook Muir in Shaduzup. A benevolent government provided food; the wildlife — fireflies and butterflies, birds and flowers — was intriguing. He might have dallied if an army column had not asked him to accompany them as their medical officer. For a time they proceeded by truck but within a day both the truck and the road gave out and they were back to marching. By this time the low shoes which Muir had been wearing were cutting his ankles and cramping his toes quite seriously. A coolie, who preferred at any rate to go barefoot, sold him his boots. They were almost worn out and did little to relieve his viciously painful toes, but they were better than the shoes. Hampered by his painful feet, Muir could not keep up with his comrades and again he found himself marching on alone, counting "one-two-three-four" over and over again in time to his slow laboured steps. Almost in a dream he noticed things as he passed— a horse, a mere gaunt skeleton abandoned by its rider and lacking even the energy to shake off the huge flies that buzzed all over it; a pink silk night gown draped over the bushes; two freshly made graves marked by sticks roughly tied together to form a cross; a barefoot girl of eight or nine leading a blind man by a string tied round his neck.

He was now in the Hukawng Valley. The chota monsoons had begun and the clay path was wet and slippery. Whenever he fell going down an incline the incessant caw of the brain-fever bird seemed to mock his weary efforts to rise again. Climbing hills meant seizing twigs and grass or scrambling on all fours. Yet when he reached the top, Muir still had the strength to notice the view and match it to the memory of his Nova Scotia home. Down in the valley he met villagers selling tins of sardines, coffee and milk, all salvaged from a recent airdrop. Fair enough, thought Muir, they gleaned it, why shouldn't they sell it.

Unable to keep up with the soldiers, Muir dropped back to join a motley crew, partly civilian, partly army. The leader was Mr. Macdonald, a teak company officer with his bearer, an Indian known simply as "Coolie." The army component included two privates known as Snub and Ginger. They offered no other name. They can add sugar and tinned ham to the group's rations, but when asked how they had acquired these luxuries, they simply say "Don't ask." Later on, Muir encountered Colonel Hey again. The Colonel was angry because some of his troops had absconded with his rations and Muir conjectured that he now knew where Ginger and Snub had got the ham and sugar.

When the group reached Shingbwiyang Mr. Macdonald estimated they were now half way to Ledo. From this point on the path went up and down over a series of sawtoothed ridges for this was Naga country and Nagas are hill people who know nothing of switchbacks or gradual slopes. Their notion of surveying is to stand on a mountain ridge, fix on their destination on the next ridge and head straight for it. The rains have brought out an additional plague, leeches. Ubiquitous and insidious, these loathsome creatures drop down from branches, slip off leaves, or emerge from the grass and insinuate themselves into the least opening or orifice, undetected till the victim disrobes at the end of the day.

On May 15 the group is at Namyang Hka, 192 miles from their starting point according to the notes they were given in Mogaung. If Muir's record keeping is accurate, they have been on the trail for eight days. Even given that a truck carried them for parts of the trek, it is amazing that they covered that distance in that time. They camp that night on the banks of the river and set out to ford it at daybreak next morning. For a change the sky is clear and the sun is bright and because it did not rain during the night, the river has not risen. Still, Muir finds it is up to his armpits. Ginger is only five foot three and it is up to his chin. Unfortunately he had been entrusted with the salt and the sugar and both dissolved in the water. A hard blow. But it could have been worse; they learn later that just after they crossed, the rains resumed, the river rose, and it was not fordable for a week.

With their salt and sugar gone and their rice supply dwindling fast, the future looks bleak. Muir thinks back to the Hukwang Valley route notes they had been given at Mogaung: "Mile 192. Main road via Pangsau Pass goes due north from here. 10 days hard marching to Ledo. Road rises to 5000 feet. Cold and wet. Rains daily." There was scant comfort in the thought. They are not alone of course. Daily they encounter other refugees and evacuees. In fact Muir once meets a British soldier wearing an Indian Medical Service officer's mess-dress hat, dark blue and adorned with a lion and crown badge embroidered with gold thread on a black velvet backing. He easily identifies it as his, but he does not reclaim it. Still, the encounter makes him wonder — the hat had been in the suitcase that he put in the goods wagon with their lab equipment in Maymyo. Where was his suitcase now? Where was the lab equipment? What did it matter? They walked fifteen miles that day and when they sat down for their evening meal, each took a spoonful of boiled rice from the cup as it was passed around.

The next day Muir reached the Pangsau Pass on the border between Burma and India. From the summit he stopped briefly to admire the bright sun shining on the glistening tree tops of the Assam rain forest that stretched as far as he could see. There were a few wild raspberries growing there and they tasted just like the ones at home. Then he hurried down the slope into Assam, one stage closer to the end of the flight. The descent was very steep, every handhold and foothold was needed to keep upright, and when he reached level ground it was a matter of wading through the puddles of a swampy marsh, crossing two rivers and then — wonder of wonders — coming to a relief camp set up by the Indian Tea Association. It was a scene from another world. Men were walking about in freshly laundered, stiffly starched khaki shorts, there was a substantial administrative building with radio connections to the outside world, and there was food. It was only bully beef stew with hard tack biscuits and tea with sugar and condensed milk, but it was hot and it was served to you and there was as much as one liked. Ironically, Muir found he had no appetite. But he was overjoyed to find some one who could treat his poor tortured toes and he bedded down that night in a sturdy, well-built basha. The groundsheet laid on the dry, bare floor with a flannelette blanket on top looked as inviting as a feather bed and Muir would have slept like a baby if the enteritis had not interfered. When, he wondered, would the diarrhea stop?

Even though they are now in India and there is a camp at each stop, the going is not much easier. It is still raining frequently and, if anything, the hills are steeper and longer. Particularly trying were the Golden Stairs, a series of steps formed by bamboo logs set into the hillside. Each step was two feet high and there were reputed to be a thousand of them going up one side and a thousand coming down the other. Muir came into camp that night panting and perspiring and was immediately conducted to a bed in a tent. He heard one of the soldiers outside the tent say "Poor Doc is done for." "Far from it," he thought to himself, and after a day's rest he was on the trail again.

There were more camps — Warner's, Buffalo, Wilkie's, Kumalo, Tirap. At this last camp Muir said goodbye to Mr. Macdonald and his coolie and to Ginger and Snub, and set off on the last sector of the trail. The road was fairly level but the mud was above his ankles and indescribably sticky. Every step required a prolonged tugging to free his foot for the next plunge into the morass. Suddenly he emerged from a forest of great trees and there, two miles ahead, he glimpsed a group of white and red buildings and the tall chimney of a powerhouse. It was Tipong, a coal mining centre, the terminus of a small gauge railway and the end of Major Muir's long walk from Maymyo. That afternoon, May 25, 1942, he was issued a new khaki shirt and shorts, enabled to send a telegram to his wife in Nova Scotia and transferred to a military hospital nearby. The bed was an Indian charpoy, rope stretched on a wooden frame, but there were clean sheets and he had the room to himself. For the present, that was enough.

They were two Canadian officers of the 41st Indian General Hospital. Major Muir left Maymyo with the main party on April 26 and reached Ledo 29 days later having covered over 700 miles, at least 400 of that on foot. Major Taylor's trek was 300 miles long, only 100 miles of that on foot, and it took only 21 days. There is no question but that Muir's escape was more punishing in all ways than Taylor's, and certainly the chance decision that assigned him to the Ledo route rather than the shorter Tamu route is in part the reason for that. But there are other reasons as well. Taylor is moving out to India with the Army, with people he knows. He falls in with a casualty clearing station, a field ambulance, a field hospital. Each time there are wounded who need him so that his life has purpose and finds support, even in the chaos of the trek. For Muir it is the opposite. At that moment when the impromptu Medical Board in the middle of the jungle finds his heart inadequate, he is cut off from the Army, the environment he knows, and he is on his own. He is diffident about thrusting himself on other groups because he has no food, nothing to offer. Surgeons could be useful, but who needs a pathologist in the middle of the jungle? And when-ever he does find a group willing to take him on, his crippled feet prevent him from keeping up. Time and again he has to pick up his pack and walk on alone. In such circumstances the wonder is not that he felt despondent, but that at the end he finished in style: "Breaking out into a quick march and swinging my arms in parade ground style, I did the last hundred yards as smartly as I could although each step was sheer agony."

VIII

AN UNQUIET INTERLUDE

IRTY AND ill clad, but still carrying their personal arms, the ragged remnants of the King's Own Yorkshire Light Infantry, the Gurkha Rifles, the Baluch Regiment, the Rajputs, the Cameronians, and all the other regiments marched into Imphal in the third week of May, 1942. General Slim was proud of them just as, exactly two years earlier, all Britain had been proud of the survivors of Dunkirk. But in the week previous to their coming other groups of soldiers had straggled into Imphal, undisciplined, leaderless, dispirited bands, some simply lost from their formations and instinctively trying to survive, others deserters wanting only to save their own skins. Lt. General Nöel Irwin, Area Commander, watched them come and formed his opinion: these were not heroes, they were cowardly creatures who had turned their backs to the enemy and fled. Contemptuously he consigned them to open fields with no tents or blankets, no cooking facilities or sanitary arrangements. When Slim and the remnants of his battered force arrived, they received the same treatment, and when Slim protested Irwin's rudeness, Irwin haughtily replied, "I can't be rude to you. I'm your superior."

Slim's motto had always been "The Lord helps those who help themselves." Accordingly his troops immediately dug in, either using truck tarpaulins to make their own rude protection from the incessant monsoon rain or moving into houses vacated by local inhabitants fleeing the Japanese air raids. Hospital facilities and medical services were desperately needed, for all the diseases barely held in check on the march now bloomed among the enfeebled, exhausted troops. Eighty per cent of the refugees were felled by one or another of the many diseases that thrived in the dank and fetid jungle. Because replacements were arriving slowly those few men of the 17th Division who were still on their feet were required as the major line of defence should the enemy continue their offensive. Soon, however, it became obvious that the Japanese were so exhausted and disorganized by their long advance, so uncertain of their attenuated supply line, and so apprehensive about the coming monsoon that they were not going to launch a further attack. Only then could the soldiers who had struggled out of Burma be sent back to India to find the rest and the medical attention they needed and deserved.

No sooner was Slim fairly secure about his Burma front than he discovered insecurity on his India front. Quite apart from the open warfare that Gandhi's erstwhile lieutenant Subhas Chandra Bose was stirring up with the Indian National Army in Burma, Gandhi and the Congress Party were now taking advantage of Britain's precarious position in Europe to push the "Quit India" movement in Bengal. Thus when the British government sent Sir Stafford Cripps from London to negotiate domestic peace and cooperation now in return for the promise of possible independence when the war was over, Gandhi called the idea "a post-dated cheque on an overdrawn account" and summarily dismissed it.

What followed was impassioned resistance to the British raj, particularly in Bombay and Calcutta. Mobs took to the streets, barricading thoroughfares, tearing up streetcar tracks, burning trams, and looting stores. Railway staff and isolated English servicemen were showered with gasoline and set afire. Activists exhorted factory workers to strike in the name of national pride and the cause of independence. In rural areas, telegraph lines were torn down, railway trains blocked by mobs, passengers hauled from the carriages and mauled or even murdered. For ten weeks Harry Wilkinson, now a Vancouver resident but then an officer with the 9/15 Punjab Regiment, was in charge of an armoured train patrolling the Indian rail lines. In a letter to the author he gave a vivid picture of the tension of those days:

> I was with a group of officers travelling to Saugor, central India and we were told 6 air force pilots were massacred after being dragged from the train they were on and their remains thrown in the river. Strangely enough our train stopped at a small station and the platform was crowded with an unruly mob shouting and yelling. It was a scary moment I can assure you. Windows and doors of our compartment were closed but the mob could easily have broken the windows and dragged us out as we could see the leaders in the crowd urging the mob on and yelling insults. I reckon we were very lucky and it was an incident all of us will always remember. I know I have.

At Patna Station two Royal Canadian Air Force officers were taken from a train by a hostile mob, torn apart and thrown in the river. The whole of India was teetering on the edge of insurrection and for the British the fear that the Japanese were purposefully enflaming it was always lurking within the fury.

Slim stepped into this seemingly hopeless situation charged with the task of reestablishing law and order. He did it in his thorough, no nonsense way. Soldiers rode on all the trains and armed guards patrolled the rail lines. In Calcutta and other cities the Army marched through the streets and made it clear that mob action and defiance of the law would not be tolerated. Gandhi and other Congress leaders were imprisoned as were the anti-British malcontents who tried to interfere with recruitment or suborn the sepoys already serving. The Hurricanes of 607 Squadron, nine of whose 24 pilots were Canadian, regularly patrolled the rail lines to persuade the saboteurs that tearing up the tracks was not a healthy exercise. Blenheims flew "Internal Security Reconnaissance Flights" to spot blocked lines and disperse unruly crowds. Little by little, calm was restored as rabble-rousers realized that any show of civil disobedience would be met with resolute force.

Slim then took up his next task, the reorganizing and retraining of his troops. He began with the basics — physical hardening and the discipline of the drill square. The experience of the past five months had shown him that *all* soldiers had to be fit, for in jungle warfare, medical orderlies, clerks, storemen, and cooks could quickly be required as front line troops. With dry humour he recorded the protests of the support staff who had previously been spared parades: "The drill instructors are harsh men who use rude words;" or "Our boots will wear out." But nevertheless they went on parade and in time everyone began to feel some pride in being tough and soldierly. As replacements and reinforcements arrived they had to be integrated into the ranks of the old Burma vets and the whole corps trained to regard itself as an elite fighting unit.

The emphasis was on fieldcraft, night patrols, on being at home in the jungle, and above all on mobility. To that end, Slim devised the Indian light division. It had jeeps and light trucks, but animal transport took the place of heavy vehicles. There were machine guns and mountain artillery, but no heavy artillery. Behind all the training and reorganization was the intent to restore the morale and *esprit de corps* that was shaken and destroyed by the experience of retreat and defeat, and to install in the troops the conviction that they were going to go back into Burma and seek revenge. Slim had made a careful note of all that he had lost in the retreat. As he regarded the final tally, he remarked, "Some day I hoped to balance the account with perhaps a little interest added."

In the meantime, Stilwell was similarly involved in the training of his Chinese troops. Despite continual trouble with Chiang Kai-shek, trouble usually revolving around the Chinese leader's efforts to extort more aid from the Unites States, Stilwell managed to bring troops from China to India. Here, in bases set up especially for them, Chinese soldiers were issued new uniforms, given sufficient food, paid regularly, and transformed into smart and alert infantrymen. Their American instructors were surprised at how quickly the Chinese, once they were given the appurtenances of modern war — tanks, trucks, radios and signal equipment — mastered their mysteries and understood their uses. Eventually 66,000 Chinese soldiers were trained in India, and China had an army far more efficient and effective than it had ever had before. Stilwell had less success with Yoke Force, the thirty divisions Chiang Kai-shek kept promising to make available for training at Kunming. Promise after promise was made but month after month went by with none of them fulfilled. In frustration Stilwell wrote to his wife: "If I last through this job and get back to Carmel, it will be as an old man of eighty and you'll have to push me around in a wheelbarrow."

The Army and the Air Force both knew that the lack of air support had been a large factor in the unhappy outcome in Burma and both recognized that whatever the next move was to be, a huge build up in air power had to be a necessary part of it. But the infrastructure needed to support an air force was sadly lacking. When the war began there were only four decent airports in all of India and none possessed a runway longer than 1,100 yards. More were being built, but breaking stone by hand and delivering it in baskets meant airstrips were slow to appear. There was only one repair and maintenance unit in the whole area, scarcely the skeleton of an observer corps, and one early warning radar station. As for aircraft, when the retreat ended the RAF had two front line squadrons, one just converted to Hurricanes and the other flying Blenheims and using them as bombers or transports as the day required. London promised 25 squadrons by August 1942 and indeed by December, 12 squadrons of Hurricanes were on hand and more or less combat ready. They were not new aircraft, but thanks to ground crew who worked from dawn to dusk cannibalizing wrecked aircraft for spares, they were kept serviceable. It would have been much better if the fighters had been Spitfires that could outrun the enemy's Oscars, but the RAF would have to wait a few more months for them. They did get a new fighter however. In the first few months of 1942 the Mohawk, a 1934 Curtis-made fighter with a radial engine, began to appear in the Indian skies. Only in India-Burma did the Mohawk fly operationally so that all Mohawks were consigned to that theatre. Thus when ten new ones intended for the Iranian Air Force were captured, they turned up in India. "The petrol gauges were in Arabic" one pilot noted in his log book, "with the petrol consumption rated at something like a couple of beetles and an inverted half moon per hour." Still, the pilots were delighted that they finally had a plane that could turn inside a Japanese fighter.

Bomber planes came as well. There were now seven or eight medium bomber squadrons flying Blenheims and even one squadron flying Liberators. Because the next campaign in Burma would have to be supplied by air, transport planes were high on General Slim's wish list. They were also hard to come by. All through 1942 and most of 1943 there was only one Dakota squadron in Burma; not until July 1944 did that number increase to four. RAF personnel strength was growing too, from 11,600 in September 1941 to 50,000 a year later.

At this time, the number of Canadians in the area increased substantially. Much to the chagrin of RCAF HQ in London, who tried to keep tabs on the whereabouts of Canadian airmen, the RAF HQ insisted upon treating Canadians as regular members of the RAF. This insistence created administrative problems for regional HQs who were trying to sort out mail deliveries, repatriation rosters, and promotions, and at times it also caused problems for individual members who felt the RAF was reluctant to recognize that Canadians were somehow different. The problem was particularly acute on training stations where Canadians were liable to resent the *hauteur* of the superior officers, a resentment that was exacerbated when they lost their national identity and were addressed simply as "colonials." On the whole however Canadian aircrew in RAF squadrons fitted in well and even enjoyed the diversity of various nationalities flying together. On an operational station there was no parade-square swank to offend the democratic sensibilities of the New World psyche and only infrequently did Canadian aircrew feel that their Limey bosses were slow to recommend an award to a colonial hero.

One result of the RAF's policy was that Canadians continued to come to Burma, not only in the 1942-43 period but throughout the War, despite the fact that the thought of Canadian service men fighting for the imperial cause was anathema to Prime Minister Mackenzie King. In the first six months of 1942 the venerable 136 Squadron, one of the Mingaladon originals, received 6 Canadian pilots and in the month of June 1942, 9 Canadians came to 607 Squadron: on these two squadrons nearly half the pilots were Canadians. Number 31 Squadron, the first transport squadron in Burma, boasted 7 Canadian aircrew in August 1942, 15 in August 1943, and over 50 in February 1945. Roy Borthwick of West Vancouver estimates that when he was on 159 Liberator Squadron in 1945 half the aircrew were Canadians. In fact, over the entire war a total of 237 Canadians served with that squadron. Had they all been there at the same time, they would have comprised the aircrew of the entire squadron.

While the Air Force build-up during 1942-43 continued with vigour, the prospect for the ground forces looked dismal, especially in the area of command administration. The overblown stodginess of Army Headquarters in Delhi was legendary. Stilwell commented on it when he first came to India: "This GHQ is an enormous affair, big enough to run our War Department."

Then, with his characteristic blunt and biting acumen he added, "And only three brigades at the front." Coming again to Delhi in June, 1942, immediately after his walk out, he was still impressed, in the Stilwell way: "The Limey layout is simply stupendous, you trip over lieutenant generals on every floor, most of them doing captain's work, or none at all." The judgment is harsh, but not unwarranted; even Slim and his commanders spoke scathingly of Delhi as a storehouse for old brigadiers and "curry colonels," while Churchill characterized India Command as "a welter of inefficiency and lassitude."

Slim could not reform Delhi, but he could transform his own Headquarters and he did. Motor transport was strictly limited, and all messing and office impedimenta were packaged for immediate transfer by boat, plane or mule. The staff was accommodated in tents and practised striking and setting up till they could leave one bivouac and set up at the next within twenty-four hours. The new Air Officer Commanding, Air Chief Marshal Sir Robert Peirse, recognizing that jungle warfare required close cooperation between air and ground forces, set up his HQ next door to General Slim's.

All that remained now was to develop a plan for the reconquest of Burma. Such a plan would not have been so problematic if the High Command in London and Washington could only agree on a goal. Churchill was all for bypassing Burma altogether and going straight to Sumatra and Java and thence to Singapore. But that required that landing craft and crews be taken from the European Theatre and the European Theatre could not spare them. The Americans were insistent that the next action should be in northern Burma with a view to reopening the Burma Road and getting supplies to China. Finally, Wavell and Stilwell agreed on a compromise plan.

Code-named *Anakim*, it envisioned X Force, the Chinese Stilwell had trained in India, sweeping southeast from northern Assam while Y (Yoke) Force, the original Chinese army, was to thrust southwestward from Yunnan province. Their pincer was to close below Myitkyina and then sweep southward through Central Burma to join with the British forces that, operating from the Calcutta — Chittagong area, were to take Rangoon and then turn northward. Thus was the Burma Road to be reopened and eventually all Burma reconquered. At the Casablanca Conference of January 1943 the President, the Prime Minister and all the Chief of Staff ratified *Anakim* and accepted November 15, 1943 as the provisional launch date.

The Americans added a supplementary to this plan. They would build a road from Ledo to Myitkyina and thence onward to link up with the Burma Road at Lashio and thus ensure a land route to deliver to China the millions of dollars of Lend-Lease matériel that had been promised.

There was much to-ing and fro-ing connected with *Anakim* and while that was going on, the powerful China Lobby in Washington was shrill in

The Burma Road

Top: In 1930 the bridge over the Mekong was stripped for repair. Bottom left: In 1940 a series of twenty-one switchbacks led down to the Salween River. Bottom right: The bridge over the Mekong 12 years later.

Seton Broughall as a young Flight Lieutenant, ca 1932.

Hal Seifert and Rudy Mendizabel pose before a Mohawk. *Courtesy DND, Canada.*

"Bing" De Cruyenaere with his Spitfire, named for King Leopold of Belgium. *Courtesy DND, Canada.*

Jimmy Whalen with his Hurricane.

Canadians in the British or Indian Army

Roland Bacon (extreme right) with the six Korean officers he led to the front line.

As Training Officer, Dunstan Pasterfield sits in the middle of young recruits — Sikhs (with a sharp Vee in their turbans), Muslims (with a flash sticking up) and Hindus (with flat-topped turbans).

Andy Taylor accompanies Lady Mountbatten on a tour of an Indian Military Hospital.

Kohima

All that is left of the Commissioner's bungalow and the tennis court when the siege is lifted. *Courtesy Imperial War Museum, London.*

The memorial erected at Kohima by the 2nd Division. The epitaph can be deciphered on the stone.

Chindits

Dave Bockus and Eric Loken with the light plane they salvaged and flew throughout the Chindit campaign.

A Japanese newspaper featured Bill Kempling with the flag he returned to the dead man's family.

A reluctant mule goes to battle in a Dakota. *Courtesy Imperial War Museum, London.*

A 413 Squadron Catalina moored in the tropical paradise of Ceylon. *Courtesy DND, Canada.*

Len Birchall in the office of his Catalina. *Courtesy DND, Canada.*

its demands that supplies to China must go through. The Ledo Road was a great idea, but it was obvious it was not going to be built for some time. After all, seventy per cent of the right-of-way was still in enemy hands *(see map p. 12)*. Some better interim answer to the China Lobby shrillness had to be found, and that answer was the innovative and daring air transport project which history now recognizes as the Hump.

The massive force of the American industrial machine was producing prodigious amounts of war equipment and, even though the Anglo-American command had agreed upon a Germany-first policy, Madame Chiang was determined to get her share. The China Lobby asked for an airlift guaranteeing 7600 tons per month and settled for 5000. To get to its destination these supplies followed the most attenuated and taxing supply route of the war.

From factories everywhere in the United States, trucks, tanks, artillery, munitions and all war supplies for the Pacific and the China-Burma-India theatres were collected at the great Utah General Depot at Ogden. The Overseas Supply Division, one major, three captains and 7 lieutenants, all harried and overworked, forwarded each shipment to the port of San Francisco or one of the subports, Los Angeles, Portland, Seattle or Prince Rupert, BC[1] for transshipment to Karachi or Bombay. In India the cargo was loaded onto rail cars that rattled along single line trackage to the point where it had to be laboriously unloaded and transferred to the narrow gauge tracks of the Bengal-Assam Railway. To cross the Brahmaputra, the train was uncoupled car by car and coach by coach, pushed onto a ferry, and shipped to the other bank, there to be reassembled and sent on its rambling, shambling way. Twelve thousand miles and many months after having left North America the supplies arrived at Ledo, the western terminus of the Hump route to China.

The Hump derives its name from the terrain it passes over. Immediately upon leaving Ledo, the pilot is faced with the Naga Hills, a misnomer for they reach 10,000 feet. The real challenge, however, the real Hump, comes after that when the Santsung range, a south-reaching arm of the Himalayas, pushes across his flight path at a height of 15,000 feet or more. From Ledo to Kunming was only 500 miles, but every mile was spiced with danger. Although enemy fighters were a worry for the unarmed transports, the weather posed a greater and more constant threat. Freak winds of over 250 miles per hour and turbulence that could hurl a plane up or throw it down at 3000 feet per minute were fairly common and often the peaks were shrouded in cloud. Down below there were no emergency landing

---

[1] The official history of the US Army in World War II calls it Port Rupert. See Stauffer, II: 140.

strips, just jungle-covered cliffs and the deep, steep gorges of the Irrawaddy, Salween and Mekong rivers.

Stilwell imagined the route would be serviced by the venerable Douglas C47, known to the US Air Force as the DC3 and to the RAF as the Dakota (derived from the manufacturer's name, *D*ouglas *A*ircraft *Co*rporation *Tr*ansport). While the Dakota was a tried and trusted aircraft already established as the workhorse of the air, it was slow, had a limited ceiling and a load capacity of only two and a half to three tons. Scarcely had the Assam-Burma-China Ferry Command, to give it its official name, begun operations than a newer and larger transport appeared, the Curtis Commando or C46. It was faster than a Dakota, carried just over four tons, and best of all had a service ceiling of 24,000 feet. This was important, for the aircraft flew at 15,000 feet in clear weather and at 18,000 to 20,000 feet at night or in cloud. But the Hump operations began in April 1942 and the US Air Force did not take delivery of its first 25 Commandos until July. Thus the aircraft was very new and it had its bugs. It was susceptible to carburetor icing, it often suffered broken fuel lines, and it leaked like a sieve in rainy weather. Soon so many Commandos were splattered across the mountains of the Hump route that the pilots began to call it the Aluminum Trail. Although the bugs were eventually worked out and pilots affectionately nicknamed it Dumbo (because of its awkward, elephantine shape), to the end their faith in the Commando remained uncertain.

In other ways too the Hump operation got off to a slow start. No sooner had flights begun than planes and crews were diverted to aid in the retreat from Burma, flying supplies and evacuating refugees. Then came the monsoons, the most treacherous enemy on the India-to-China route. At first the group scarcely averaged 60 flights per month, but a year later, in September 1943, 228 aircraft delivered 5390 tons of much needed war supplies from Ledo to Kunming. In the month of December 1943, 13,000 tons were delivered, and in December 1944 an almost incredible 35,000 tons. Over the three years that the Hump flights operated, a total of 600,000 tons were landed in Kunming. It was however an expensive business. In all 600 aircraft were lost and more than 1000 fliers lost their lives.

Who were these fliers? In the beginning the Assam-Burma-China Ferry Command was a quasi-military organization. Many of the pilots were members of the US Air Force Air Transport Command, others were from the Chinese National Aviation Corporation (CNAC), a subsidiary of Pan American Airways. The CNAC pilots came from the United Sates, from Australia, China, Great Britain, Denmark, and from Canada. They were mercenaries in a sense, civil aviators working on a military contract. They were paid $800 per month — if they were Caucasian. Those of Chinese origin, regardless of their citizenship, were paid $325 per month.

A good few Chinese Canadians were among the latter. The Canadian Army and the RCAF had a sorry and spotty history in the recruitment of Canadians of Oriental ancestry. Most Chinese lived in British Columbia and the word among RCAF recruiters there seemed to be that Chinese Canadians were not to be signed up or they were to be taken on only as ground crew. Persistent young Chinese who made their way to Alberta or more easterly recruiting centres stood a better chance, but here too there was no clear policy. One young Chinese Canadian who volunteered at the Toronto recruiting centre was instead threatened with internment as an "enemy alien." Even licensed pilots, and there were a surprising number of these among young Chinese Canadians, were turned away. Some of these were eagerly taken on as instructors in the British Commonwealth Air Training Plan (BCATP). Others joined the Chinese National Aviation Corporation and flew the Hump.

Harold Chinn was one of these. He was born in Vancouver in 1912. When he completed his pilot training in 1933 few firms in Canada were hiring pilots, and none were hiring Chinese Canadian pilots. Chinn paid his own way to China and joined the Chinese Air Force, later transferring to the CNAC. He flew between Chunking and Hong Kong until Hong Kong fell in December 1941 when he began to fly the Hump route. When the Hump route ended in 1945 he had flown it over 600 times, more than any other pilot. After the war Chinn continued to fly commercially in China until the Communists took over. He then returned to Canada but once again was unable to find employment in the land of his birth. He emigrated with his family to the United States and stayed there for the rest of his life, though retaining his Canadian citizenship.

In her book, *The Dragon and the Maple Leaf: Chinese Canadians in World War II*, Marjorie Wong tells the story of more Chinese Canadians who flew the Hump, men like Enoch and Luke Bunn, Jack Dong, Stanley Fong and C. T. Fung, all wireless operators with the CNAC, and pilots Kuo Lim Mah and Tommy Wong. Two other Mahs, the brothers Albert and Cedric, came a bit later to the CNAC. Born in Prince Rupert, they both took pilot training in California at their own expense and for a short time flew commercially in Canada. When the war came, they were rejected by the RCAF and so settled for instructorships with the BCATP. In 1943, as the Air Training Plan was winding down, they found their way to China and joined the CNAC. In all, Albert made 420 flights over the Hump and Cedric 400. They carried ammunition, explosives, aviation fuel and money into China and on the return trip brought back tin, tungsten, tea, mercury, silk, and hog bristles, as well as Chinese troops who were to be trained in India. At one point two hundred million dollars in gold bullion was to be transported from Calcutta to Kunming. Cedric made three Hump crossings with a cargo of gold. On another occasion the fierce weather of the Himalayas caught up with him. Carburetor icing and wing icing attacked him together. One engine quit and to maintain height Cedric jettisoned his cargo, $800 million dollars in Chinese paper money.[2]

In general the Chinese Canadian Hump pilots felt underappreciated on their return to Canada, but Cedric Mah's experience was different. As a reward for his post-war flying in Western Canada a peak in the coastal range was named after him "for outstanding service transporting and supplying a government survey party under difficult flying conditions."

Apart from the Chinese Canadians with the CNAC, few Canadians flew the Hump except as unofficial hitchhikers. Peter Boldt of Victoria tells how he did it:

> It was quite easy to get a lift over the Hump. On August 4, 1945 I flew to Myitkyina with Art Jeal and climbed up to the control tower to ask about a flight. The controller was somewhat surprised but directed me to a plane about to take off. I rushed over and explained my intent. "It don't make sense to me, but come along." So I boarded the Curtis Commando which at that time was the world's largest two engine air-craft. I noticed that it displayed a few dozen camel stencils [one for each Hump flight completed] plus the name "Curtis Abortion," which did little for my well being. The flight took us to Liping and was unevent-ful. We were carrying some ammo. I recall that the Chinese were very handsome, especially the lasses. There were thousands of them carrying flat baskets of crushed rock for a runway extension.
>
> I spent that night in a tent that housed four. One chap was in sick bay allowing room for me. The food was considerably better than what we were used to and there were Life and Look magazines only a week old. Quite a treat. … I took a flight back to Tulihal the next day and can honestly say that I have flown the Hump.

As a supply line into China, the Hump was quite clearly an inadequate stopgap measure. It was expensive in terms of aircraft and crews lost and of aviation fuel consumed; in terms of matériel delivered, the most one can say is that it was the only choice available.

The Americans and the Chinese remained fixed on the notion that the Ledo Road had to be built as a supplement to the Hump. The British were extremely doubtful. Their prognostications of woe were legion: the entire work force would succumb to malaria; nothing could be accomplished before the monsoons broke; the monsoons would wipe away every vestige of

---

[2] A curious cargo, but in actuality 9% of all tonnage carried over the Hump in the eight-month period, July to February 1943, was Chinese paper money engraved in the US under Lend-Lease arrangements.

the road; the project would gobble up all the engineering resources available in the whole of India. Churchill summed up all the negatives: "An immense, laborious task, unlikely to be finished until the need for it has passed." This negativism simply challenged Yankee determination and on December 7, 1942, one year to the day after Pearl Harbour, President Roosevelt gave his blessing and elevated the Ledo Road to the highest priority.

With their customary zeal the Americans threw themselves into "the greatest military road job in history," disdainful of the fact that most of the route was, in theory at least, still held by the enemy. Crews worked night and day. Gravel pits were established and gravel crushers set up. Landing strips were built alongside for light planes, and bulldozers appeared in quantity, not the big ones the engineers yearned for, but big enough to impress Lt. General Sir Henry Pownall. "I have just returned from a good round trip – Ledo – Imphal – Arakan – Comilla," he wrote in his diary in April 1944. "The Americans have made fine progress with their Ledo road thanks largely to their wealth of mechanical equipment. It is pathetic to watch our humble efforts at road making, coolies, picks and shovels, even small children with little buckets of water; the Americans with dozens of bulldozers, angle dozers, graders, scrapers and heaven knows what all."

It was a big job. In the end a total of 105 miles of culvert had been laid and enough earth had been moved to build a wall a yard wide and ten feet tall from New York to San Francisco. It was a difficult job too. As one of the engineers saw it, the Panama Canal was child's play compared to building the Ledo Road. From an altitude of 200 feet at Ledo the road began at once to climb steeply up the Patkai Range. Then came three rivers, one immediately after the other and each down in a gorge with difficult access. Steadily and steeply the road continued its climb up to the Pangsau Pass, the pass on the India-Burma border that Major Muir stumbled over in 1942. The average gradient to this point was 5000 feet in 10 miles, better than 1 in 12. From the height of land the road wound down into the Hukawng Valley, that waterlogged, malaria-ridden swamp that had almost been Major Muir's undoing. Here the monsoon rains flooded miles of the survey trace so that bridges had to be a hundred yards long just to span what was in the dry season a gentle stream. A bulldozer that slid off the trail could quickly disappear altogether in the bottomless ooze.

There were other challenges. Labour was one of them. The British undertook to supply the many porters and coolies that were needed. The trouble was, they were recruited from various parts of India and they all insisted on a short term contract so that they could get home with their newly acquired wealth. Not that they were that well paid. Coolies got only 16 cents a day plus 8 cents for subsistence. At first the Americans paid for the full term of the contract, but when they discovered that many coolies were "riding the sick book," they began to pay only for days worked. Nature too was a challenge. Leeches were everywhere and there were 300 varieties of snakes, though only 40 of these were poisonous. Mosquitoes of course abounded. The Americans took all precautions and were relatively free of malaria, but the indigenous workers were often infected. As the work progressed the danger of enemy action increased and an estimated 100 or more Americans were killed by Japanese snipers. In all at least 1100 Americans lost their lives in the building of the Road.

Was it worth it? On January 12, 1945 General Lewis Pick, the engineer in charge, lined up a caravan of 113 vehicles at Ledo and ceremoniously sent them off to Kunming, 1100 miles eastward. There was a pause at Myitkyina while the convoy waited for a week for the road to be cleared of Japanese, and there was some consternation when a much smaller convoy found a jeepable short cut and got ahead of them, but theoretically the Ledo Road could be declared a reality. A crude, hand-written sign proudly declared: "With the opening of this road America is implimenting [sic] her promise made to China in the dark days of retreat to give our allies the means to Victory." As a symbol of America's ability to "get things done," the Ledo Road was a unique success. As a strategic factor in the Burma Campaign it was less so. The first convoy had arrived in Kunming January 28, 1945. The last convoy reached Kunming on October 8, 1945, and the last fuel delivery through the pipelines that had been built along the right-of-way was on October 25. The construction costs were estimated at $137 million. In the nine months it was in operation, the Road delivered 137,000 tons of war matériel. The comparable figure for Hump deliveries was 500,000 tons. Hilary Saunders, writing in the official history of the RAF, was brutally frank in his assessment: "Looking back it is now possible to say that the Ledo Road, on which so much material, so many men and such great resources of skill were lavished, was, for the purpose of supplying the armies in Burma and China, almost entirely useless." Today the Ledo Road has so much grown back into the jungle that it is no longer marked on current maps. American and Chinese officialdom decreed that the Ledo Road and Burma Road together should be known as the Stilwell Road. It would be altogether forgotten today if the Chinese had not built at Kunming a memorial museum in honour of both General Stilwell and his Road.

In telling the story of the Hump operation and the building of the Ledo Road, we have been concentrating on the action in Assam and northern Burma, the American and Chinese sector of the Burma theatre. The British sector, centred on Imphal, was quiescent as the Indian and British armies continued to train for the forthcoming return to Burma and the Japanese continued to hold and consolidate behind the Chindwin. The British command was however apprehensive about air attacks on Calcutta and to counter the threat, fighter squadrons were stationed in the area, at Alipore and Dum Dum. More to reassure the citizens than for tactical efficiency, the RAF made one of the most unusual assignments of the war — a detachment of fighter planes, Spitfires and Mohawks, was stationed in the very heart of the city. Like many Far East cities, Calcutta had in its centre a large park or parade ground area designated by the Urdu name *maidan*. The maidan in Calcutta was bisected by an elegant promenade called, because of the colour of its surfacing, Red Road. Leading from the immodest monumentality of the Victoria Memorial at its southern end to Government House in the north, it was intended as a *grande allée* for imperial parades. Now, throughout November and December, 1942, it became the landing strip for the Spitfires and Mohawks of 17 and 155 Squadrons, with the aircraft dispersed along Ochterlony Road, a small street connecting Red Road to Chowringhee, Calcutta's main thoroughfare.

The Canadian pilots we previously met in Mingaladon were there, Harold Nicholson, J. F. "Tex" Barrick, Jack Gibson, Hank Forde, T. L." Slim" Lewis, Ken Wheatley and Hedley Everard. They were housed in the Grand Hotel, the poshest accommodation in the whole city. The posting definitely had its perks. Pilots on readiness could stay in the hotel lobby, while the CO had it worked out that he could be in Firpo's, the four star restaurant on Chowringhee, get notice of a "scramble," and get to the strip in time to join the rest of the squadron on take off. Years later Harold Nicholson, originally from Regina, remembered another perk those days afforded: "It was great girl bait to trudge through the lobby of the Grand Hotel with a parachute over one's shoulder and one's face smeared with cordite from two synchronized machine guns."

As an airfield, Red Road had its drawbacks. For one thing, the smoke and haze that habitually hung over the city often made it hard to locate. Not only was it narrower than a regular runway, it was lined on both sides with marble balustrades and, like any well-engineered road, it crowned in the middle. The resultant camber required that the pilots land square on the centre line and hold to it or ground loop into the marble. There was a high building at the north end of the strip and pilots taking off toward it could wave to the office girls as they flew past. Landing from the north however meant they had to come in high, then cut the throttle and land as short as possible. Under normal circumstances Red Road was just long enough, but circumstances were not always normal. Ken Wheatley, a young pilot from Banff, Alberta, had barely touched down when he realized his brakes had failed. He shouted and waved at the airmen lounging by the strip and then recognized that, even if they saw the trouble, there was nothing they could do to help him. A flimsy bamboo barrier marked the end of the strip and beyond that there was a busy cross-street. Ken's aircraft was rapidly approaching it. He crowded to the side, turned off the switches, and rolled toward the barrier with his wheel rubbing hard along the curb. The aircraft came to a stop just six feet short of the bamboo.

The anticipated bombing attacks on Calcutta came on December 21 and 23, 1942. These were small raids, nine bombers each time, and though they concentrated on the docks, they did little damage beyond frightening the coolie labour out of the city. The fighters had patrol lines up in readiness but the intruders came at night and neither Spitfires nor Mohawks were night fighters. Still, Jack Gibson, one of the Americans in the RCAF, did shoot down one Japanese fighter.

Wavell recognized that the Hurricanes were not the right tool for the job and he asked for night fighter aircraft. A squadron of Beaufighters arrived from the Middle East on January 14, 1943; the very next night they shot down three enemy aircraft. A few nights later the Japanese came again and this time they lost two of the four aircraft they sent over. That ended the enemy's interest in Calcutta for some time.

In theory at least, *Anakim*, the plan for a coordinated British-American-Chinese attack converging on Myitkyina, was still on, but more and more it became obvious that it could not be launched during the 1942-43 dry season as had been planned. In April 1942 Wavell was called to London to discuss what was to be done. The facts that came to light in that discussion were not encouraging. The worsening situation in North Africa had required that a good portion of the trained troops in India be sent to the Middle East. Wavell estimated he would need 477 landing craft for the assault on Rangoon and the European Theatre could spare him none. Air supremacy over Burma was a *sine qua non* for success on the ground and air supremacy was far from established. The decision was to defer the operation. In January 1943 Chiang Kai-shek declared that he would not be part of *Anakim* unless the British could guarantee naval dominance in the Bay of Bengal. When that guarantee was not forthcoming he withdrew from the operation.

A further complication in the planning for operations in Burma arose from the growing dissension and disagreement between Stilwell and Chennault. As an old infantry man, Stilwell was certain that he could win the war against Japan by fighting on the ground, first in Burma and then in China itself. He had trained the Chinese soldiers and he knew what they could do, though he had as yet little evidence to offer. Chennault was equally certain that air attack offered the swiftest and surest means of defeating the enemy. Stilwell had under his command the Tenth Air Force, a well trained and experienced group that he was using to defend the transports on the Hump and intended to use in the future to back up his land forces in Burma. One sector of the Tenth Air Force, however, the China Air Task Force, was under

Chennault's command and Chennault intended to use that to bring Japan to her knees through air attack alone. As proof of the effectiveness of his plan he claimed that in 1942 his Air Task Force had sunk 49,600 tons of enemy shipping.[3] He stoutly asserted that, given 105 fighters, 30 medium bombers, and 12 heavy bombers, he would win the war against Japan. At the same time he complained to Chiang Kai-shek and to the President that Stilwell was taking all the Hump deliveries to build up his army and thus robbing the Air Force of what it needed for ultimate victory.

The usual practice of underlings reporting to the Generalissimo was to tell him only what he wanted to hear. Stilwell never followed this practice and in consequence he lost favour in the Chinese court even as Chennault gained it. In Washington as well, the President preferred the reports he got from Chennault to the ones he got from Stilwell and he ordered that the first 4700 tons of Hump delivery each month were to go to Chennault's air force rather than Stilwell's Y Force. Stilwell's position was awkward and ambiguous in all respects. He wore three command hats: as Chiang Kai-shek's Chief of Staff in Burma he was equal to Mountbatten; as Mountbatten's second-in-command he was subordinate to Mountbatten; as the President's representative and officer in charge of Lend-Lease he was at least equal to Chiang Kai-shek. Somehow he suffered through these complications, but eventually the dispute with Chennault would come to the point that the President had to make a choice. Before that point came however, Stilwell was given the opportunity to do what he most wanted to do — return to Burma with Wingate's Chindits and seek revenge for the "helluva licking" he took in 1942.

Anakim was never formally rejected. In the way of military decision making, it was simply postponed and deferred and allowed to wither unattended. In consequence there was no accepted plan for the furtherance of the Burma war; instead there were individual actions of a limited scope such as Arakan I, the 1942-43 expedition into the Arakan to retake Akyab.

---

[3] A check made after the war could only discover 7000 tons sunk by Chennault's Air Task Force in 1942. (Romanus and Sutherland, I:313n)

RENEWING THE BATTLE

WHILE THE Americans worried their road eastward from Ledo, Wavell, determined not to waste the 1942-43 campaigning season, planned for an assault in the Arakan. His purpose was twofold, first to occupy Akyab and thus secure a forward base for air action against central and southern Burma and second, to achieve a victory that would raise morale, take away the bitter taste of defeat, and dispel once and for all the myth of Japanese invincibility. He gave his orders to Lt. General Nöel Irwin, the General Officer Commanding the Eastern Army, and Irwin passed them on to Major General Lloyd, his divisional commander. The circumstances looked favourable: the British were numerically superior to the Japanese, they were closer to their source of supply, and their air power was at least equal to that of the enemy. There were however two unfavourable factors: first, Wavell was still underestimating the Japanese, and second, Irwin, the inhospitable host of Imphal, was constitutionally unable to delegate. Despite the fact that his circle of concern stretched all the way from Fort Hertz to Rangoon, he could not resist interfering with each detail of the attack he had ostensibly assigned to Lloyd.

The Arakan is the large coastal province on the northwest edge of Burma. It is separated from the Central Plain by the Chin Hills and the Arakan Yomas, a series of knife-edge ridges that rise to six and eight thousand feet. Lloyd's expedition, now known as Arakan I, was concerned only with the Mayu Peninsula, a narrow finger of land that pointed straight down to the port and airfield at Akyab. The peninsula was basically a mountainous spine, two thousand feet high and heavily covered with jungle vines, thorns and trees. On the west side of the spine was a littoral shelf of varying width and on the east a broader alluvial plain that merged uncertainly into the Mayu River. Both shores of the peninsula were swampy and frequently cut

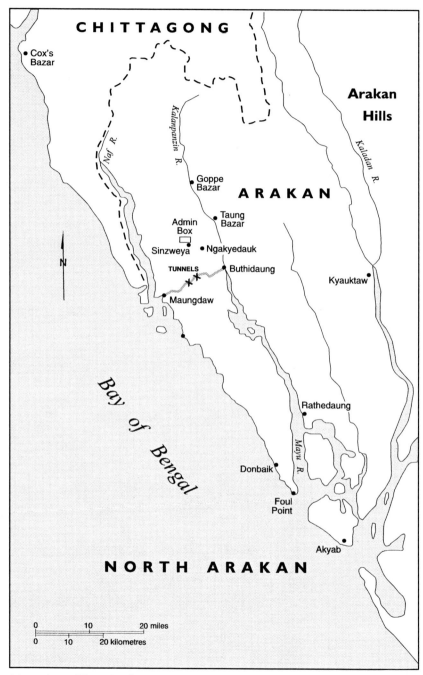

Map 6 — The Arakan

by *chaungs*, the creeks or water courses that represented a significant barrier to tanks and even to marching soldiers. There were tracks down both sides of the peninsula, but only one road cut across the spine from east to west, an all weather road that, with the aid of two small tunnels at the summit, joined Maungdaw on the west with Buthidaung on the east. One more fact must be mentioned: the Arakan is one of the most rained-upon regions in the world. Even in the dry season it is not dry and in the monsoon months of July and August it averages more than 50 inches of rainfall per month. On November 5, 1942 thirteen inches of rain fell. A few weeks later, Lloyd began his 90 mile thrust to Akyab.

The Japanese forces occupying the Maungdaw-Buthidaung Road and the tunnels drew back when they realized an attack was coming and by early January Lloyd's western push was at Donbaik and his eastern assault at Rathedaung, both within a few miles of Foul Point, the tip of the peninsula and the jumping off point for Akyab Island. There the advance stalled, for the British had met something new — bunkers. To this point in the Burma campaign the Japanese had been on the offensive, pushing forward as fast as they could. Now they were in a defensive position and they had had ample time to prepare their defences. Dug six feet into the ground where possible, built above ground where the water table was high, then covered with logs and with four to five feet of earth, the bunkers were sited to give each other covering fire and built into the jungle so that they were almost invisible. Nor were they vulnerable to mortar fire or air attack. In the cease-less rain the logs had become soft and punky and readily absorbed bullets and explosives, even a direct bombing from above. Secure within, a platoon firing from small apertures could easily hold off any attack. Crawl trenches connected the bunkers to each other and to the command post behind the bunker line. The command post could be as much as thirty feet below the surface and made comfortable with electric light and forced air.

Constrained by water on one side and mountains on the other, Lloyd decided he could do nothing but attack straight ahead toward this carefully constructed and artfully concealed line of defence. Attempts to sneak up in the blind area to either side of the firing slots were defeated by the mur-derous crossfire from the neighbouring bunker. Even when one loyal and fearless Gurkha by luck or divine protection worked his way to the very lip of the bunker and threw in a grenade as his bullet-riddled body slumped, there was no one behind him to follow up. The corpses on the slope piled up and the shaken troops withdrew. A small troop of tanks arrived, but in the darkness they found themselves entrapped in the deep and steep-sided *chaungs* and then an easy prey to Japanese gunners. Reinforcements arrived from India but that only meant that more men were lost in a series of stub-born head-butting attacks against formidable defences.

Wavell insisted that Donbaik and Rathedaung be taken: "A strong blow on the Mayu Peninsula and a real success here will do more than anything to help the situation. I should like to finish up this campaigning season with a real success which will show our own troops and the Jap that we can and mean to be top dog." Irwin sent more men and ordered Lloyd to attack again. Again the attack was repulsed. This stalemate continued into March when Irwin sent Slim down "just to have a look around." Slim was to take no action, only to observe, but he could not help observing to Lloyd that perhaps he should try to infiltrate troops over the spine and come back down behind the bunkers. Lloyd was absolutely convinced that the spine was impenetrable. At the urging of Wavell and Irwin he made another frontal attack. When that failed Irwin sacked Lloyd and took over the campaign himself

At this point Japanese troops from central Burma entered the fray. Unaware that the Arakan Yomas and the Mayu Range were impenetrable, they scrambled over the mountains and moved in behind the British troops, threatening to cut them off. Even in these perilous circumstances Irwin would have stubbornly persisted in trying to butt forward if Slim had not insisted that withdrawal was a much wiser course. Fighting, withdrawing, trying to fend off the attackers on his left flank and wearily reminded of the 1942 retreat, Slim asked Major General C. E.N. Lomax, who had replaced Lloyd as divisional commander, to launch a harassing and intelligence gathering raid into the village of Maungdaw. "B" Company of the First Battalion of the Lincolnshire Regiment was chosen to carry out the raid. The company commander was Major Charles Ferguson Hoey of Duncan, British Columbia.

To the principal of Duncan Grammar School, Charlie was "an all-round good lad," full of intense interest and enthusiasm. He was on the first cricket XI and the rugby XV, played in tennis tournaments and was a keen member of the Quamichan Scout troop. Above all he liked hiking and fishing and gathering souvenirs of his natural surroundings – butterflies, birds' nests, the skeletons of the forest animals, an interest that stayed with him into his adult life. When he died his fine collection of Indian butterflies was presented to the Bombay Museum of Natural History.

In 1934 at the age of 20, Charlie went to England and joined the British Army. After graduation from the Royal Military College at Sandhurst he chose to join the Lincolnshire Regiment, a choice undoubtedly influenced by the fact that his maternal grandfather had been the Colonel of that regiment for 25 years. The Regiment was sent to India in September 1937. Harry Wilkinson, a former member of the Lincolnshires now living in Vancouver, remembers Major Hoey: "As Brigade Orderly Officer of the 71st Brigade, I had the privilege and honour of knowing Major Hoey and considered him a friend. He was a quiet, retiring man and very pleasant to talk to compared to most of the other officers I met." The First Lincolns were posted to Burma just in time to become involved in the Arakan expedition.

The raid assigned to "B" Company was a rather complicated one involving sampans floated into position by upriver tides and cooperation with a local guerrilla force.[1] Their objective was to enter Maungdaw village, destroy supplies, gather information, and bring back a prisoner. On July 5 the column moved out for what was to be a week-long operation. From the beginning things went wrong; it was raining and very dark, a sampan capsized, a reconnaissance patrol got lost, a sentry fired a shot in error. It seemed likely the surprise element had been lost, but Major Hoey decided to carry on. At 5:30 on the morning of July 13 they attacked the enemy camp. The Japanese sentry was taken completely by surprise and belatedly opened fire. The Japanese guard platoon, nine men and an officer, dashed out to investigate and all were killed. The alarm had now been raised and machine guns fired fiercely at them while mortar bombs rained down. One man was wounded and the crown (designating his rank) was knocked off Major Hoey's shoulder. A Japanese attack on their position was easily repulsed, but when the enemy artillery joined in, backed up by a threat of a much larger infantry attack, Major Hoey decided it was time for a strategic withdrawal. Hoey Force returned to the Battalion with no prisoners but they had identifications and a Japanese post bag full of mail, rich grist for the intelligence officer's mill. They had wounded approximately 28 Japanese soldiers and killed 22. Their own casualties amounted to one killed, two wounded, and the crown lost from Major Hoey's shoulder. For this action Major Hoey was awarded the Military Cross. The citation accompanying the award concludes with the sentence: "Major Hoey's determination, courage and skill during the whole operation were beyond praise."

Major Hoey's operation was one of the few bright spots for the ground forces in the First Arakan offensive, but the RAF put on a more creditable show. It will be remembered that Seton Broughall's rag-tag force had disappeared from Burma in March 1942, had reappeared to defend Ceylon in April and then Calcutta in May. Now, in March 1943, the Air Force was able to offer 8 fighter squadrons and two bomber squadrons in support of the faltering troops on the ground. It was an opportunity for the 48 Canadian fighter pilots involved to come into their own. Tex Barrick had left Mingaladon as a flight sergeant with three and a half enemy aircraft to his credit. He was now a flight lieutenant and flight commander wearing the ribbon of the DFM and leading his flight of six Hurricanes in a strafing

---

[1] This was actually V Force; we shall learn more of them later.

mission in support of the beleaguered soldiers at the Ngakyedauk pass. He lined up on the enemy trenches and pushed the button — and the 50 mm cannon exploded, tearing away a good portion of the upper covering of the wing. Only by flying at full throttle could he keep the aircraft from stalling, and only by using all his strength to hold the stick full right could he keep it flying straight and level. Straining till his muscles ached he held this contorted position for half an hour until he reached a forward strip and landed safely.

The early days of March were glory days for Homer "Hap" Armstrong, in civilian life a salesman from Toronto. At nine o'clock in the morning of March 5 the radar discovered enemy bombers over Akyab. Armstrong scrambled to 20,000 feet and screamed down upon them. Closing to 350 yards he opened fire and nine seconds later, a scant 50 feet from his target, he broke off. He was aware that the bomber had gone down, but he had no time to watch it. Teaming up with one of his mates, he aimed a four-second burst at a second Japanese plane and saw it hit the ground in flames, then with two others from his squadron he turned on the rest of the bombers and together they got two more. Hap Armstrong's tally for the day was two and a half enemy aircraft destroyed. Four days later he scrambled to tackle a flight of enemy fighters. Closing from the starboard quarter he pushed the button and saw white smoke streaming from the Japanese fighter. Quickly Armstrong pulled sharply up and stall-turned back onto his target. A short burst from dead astern and the enemy plane spiralled to the ground. That brought Hap Armstrong's total to three and a half victories in five days.

In 1940 Albert Joseph De Cruyenaere of St. Boniface, Manitoba was 18, a tall and lanky prairie boy when he volunteered for the RCAF. When he joined 136 RAF Squadron at Akyab in the Arakan in February 1942, his fellow pilots had trouble with De Cruyenaere. It came out something like "de crooner" so they called him Bing and the name stuck. In his diary, Guy Marsland, a Flight Commander with the Squadron, remembers Bing as six feet three of bones and skin: "He was a good pilot but always into mischief.... [H]e had a generous nature; he was younger even than his years and he did not understand when he was doing wrong. I am quite sure that out of any worry he may have caused his seniors, he never once knowingly did a mean thing to any other man."

Bing's first adventure took place on February 28, 1943 when he was shot down over the Bay of Bengal. He managed a wheels-up landing on a small island near the Arakan coast and was greeted by a band of natives who had never before seen an aircraft, or at least, not one on the ground. Having assured himself that the natives were friendly, Bing got the headman to put a guard on his "bird" and then went to their village for food and drink. They gave him a bath and a bed "with silk pillows and cotton sheets". When

he awoke he was taken to a boat and rowed back to Akyab, surely one of the
pleasantest forced landings one could imagine. On March 15 Bing, with
three of his mates, was escorting Blenheim bombers on an attack on Donbaik at the extreme south end of the Mayu peninsula, unaware that a strong
flight of Japanese fighters was protecting the area. On the ground Guy
Marsland watched as a massive dogfight developed and four Hurricanes
tore into ten Oscars. His diary tells how the first two RAF planes each got
their man and of how the battle ended: "Freddie Pickard and Bing De Cruyenaere did their job very well indeed. A number of Jap aircraft were found;
Bing and Freddie obviously shot them down, but neither returned to fill in
combat reports. Poor Bing died as he had lived, not giving a damn for any
man and certainly not afraid of the whole Jap air force. I am convinced that
if there had been a hundred Japs, Bing would have remained until either all
of them had been shot down, or he himself had been destroyed." Thus 136
Squadron lost the man they thought of as "our French Canadian," although
he was actually of Flemish descent. In the no man's land between the lines
the wreckage of nine Japanese planes was found along with the wreckage
of Bing's Hurricane. His body had plummeted deep into the ground and
was identifiable only by the serial number of the engine. A RAF padre went
forward to conduct a small graveside ceremony in the Arakan jungle.

There is a bit more to tell of the Bing De Cruyenaere story. One very hot
afternoon in June 1942 Owen Hearn, manager for the Calcutta provision-
ing firm of Jardine Matheson, had a visitor, a very tall, very thin airman
who announced himself as Flight Sergeant De Cruyenaere and inquired
about getting beer for his mess. Beer was scarce, but Owen, an old sweat
himself, always tried to find some for men in the service. Besides, he was
taken from the first by his visitor's appearance: "Tall, thin, a small head of
beautiful shape carried erect over a long thin neck, dark brown hair well
brushed, and a pair of grey eyes flashing eagerness and friendliness." They
settled on one case of beer, then, as Bing counted out the bills and coins
that cluttered his pocket book, he looked up with an eager smile, "I guess I
could manage two cases if you would take some stamps?" With a grin and a
chuckle, Owen Hearn agreed and thus began a close friendship that lasted
for Bing's life and beyond.

The next time he came, Bing brought his friend, Verne Butler, a
Canadian from Calgary and the "quiet, appraising half of an unbreakable
partnership." They were an interesting pair, Bing eager, quick, impulsive,
Verne thoughtful, earnest and sincere. Soon they were weekly visitors at the
Hearn apartment on Chowringhee. The Hearns exploited Bing's height
to decorate the Christmas tree; he in turn invited them to the airfield and
introduced Owen to "Leopold," his Hurricane, named for the King of
Belgium. The two young Canadians became great favourites of the Hearn's

nine year old daughter Lesley and of all the girls at her school. Lesley liked
Verne because he talked to her about horses, but the other girls preferred
Bing because he was "naughtier."

By this time Verne and Bing were heavily involved in the Arakan action.
At 10 in the morning of the last day of 1942, twelve Hurricanes scrambled
to seek out a Japanese force attacking four Royal Navy minelayers along the
Arakan coast, Verne Butler and another Canadian, Lorne LeCraw among
them. Both had been shot down and forced to bail out earlier in the year
and now they were out to get even, or even get ahead. From a height of
30,000 feet, Verne saw them first. "Bandits 8 o'clock below," he called. "I'm
going in. Follow me!" So furious was his dive that he screamed past the
first bomber without seeing where his fire was going. No matter. Another
bomber filled his sights; he fired again and a second enemy plane went
down in flames. There were enemy fighters above him but they did not
seem to see him so he had a go at a third bomber. Before he could mark its
fate, he saw a fourth 1000 feet below and he fell down upon it. This time
his attack was more controlled and he saw it make a forced landing on the
beach. Verne's blood was up and, remembering how the Japanese pilot had
strafed him when he had crashed, he turned on the downed aircraft and
scattered it with lead.

Lorne LeCraw also shot down an enemy bomber that day, a total of four
for the two Canadians. For LeCraw the revenge was particularly sweet for
he was the pilot who had been shot down at sea and could not inflate his
Mae West because he had been shot through the cheek.

Shortly after this adventure, Verne Butler had a bad accident and went
on convalescent leave. He was visiting in the Hearn household when the
Calcutta papers told of a warrant officer pilot killed in combat. For two days
Verne and Owen Hearn hovered in uncertainty, hoping that it was not Bing
and yet almost knowing that it was.   .

All this is told in *Bing*, a small book Owen Hearn wrote and had privately
printed. It ends with an eloquent elegy: "I confess there have been bitter
and rebellious moments when I have said — Why? Why? Why? But stronger
than that, there wells up from the very centre of one's heart, pride and
gratitude that such young men should be. At the going down of the sun
and in the morning, we will remember them." Almost exactly one year later
Verne Butler was killed in action near Imphal. Owen Hearn wrote another
little book; this one entitled *Verne*.

Overall, the RAF had shown that it could hold its own against the Japanese Imperial Air Force. That, along with Major Hoey's gallantry, was one
of the few bright spots in the Arakan I operation. By May 1943 the British
force had to withdraw to Cox's Bazaar, leaving Maungdaw, Buthidaung
and the Tunnels once again in enemy hands. The expedition had gained

nothing, it had lost 5000 men, killed, wounded and missing, and far from raising morale, it had completely shattered the confidence and pride that Slim had worked so hard to restore. Now the need for some show of success was greater than ever. At this juncture Orde Wingate came to Burma.

Before we take up the tale of Wingate and his Chindits, we must mark time for a moment to tell the story of how air supremacy passed from the Japanese to the Allied side, for until air supremacy was assured the Chindit expedition was impossible.

Since the withdrawal of Seton Broughall's Burwing from Magwe in March the RAF had been busy reinforcing and reorganizing. There had been the successful repulse of the attack on Ceylon in April 1942 and the happy victory of the Beaufighters over Calcutta in January 1943 but apart from that the Air Force was able to do little but attempt to fight off the Japanese attacks. The Japanese had no more than 200 planes in Burma now, but as soon as the 1942 monsoon ended in October they turned their attention to the American Hump bases in the Ledo area and to the RAF forward bases at Feni and Chittagong. On one such raid against Feni, Flight Sergeant Harry Gill from South Devon, New Brunswick got off tardily and found himself alone in front of 15 enemy bombers and their fighter escort. He set upon the fighters first and saw one of them explode before him. Then he turned on the bombers and, though he saw clear strikes, he was chased off before he could do further damage. Early on the morning of January 11, the Japanese came to Feni again, and again Gill scrambled to meet them. At 10,000 feet he attacked but this time his luck ran out. Harry Gill was only 20 and already the holder of the Distinguished Flying Medal when he was killed.

Throughout the spring months of 1943 the Japanese air campaign grew increasingly aggressive but so also did the ability and confidence of the RAF defenders, much abetted by the growing efficiency of the early warning stations, many of them manned by Canadian radar technicians. Soon it became apparent that the losses were more than the Japanese could bear and even before the new monsoon began in May the frequency of their attacks decreased. Air dominance seemed to be passing to the Allied side. Blenheim bombers with Hurricane and Mohawk fighter escort poked and pecked at Akyab, Magwe and Mingaladon so that the enemy sought to avoid the annoyance by withdrawing his air forces to Siam and Malaya, using the Burma strips as staging posts only.

As early as December 7, the first anniversary of Pearl Harbour, the RAF had sufficient faith in its re-organized air power to lay on what passed in the Far East for a large air raid, 12 Blenheim bombers with 24 Hurricanes as fighter escort. The target was to be Mandalay. Unfortunately, the weather was not favourable and the mission had to be recalled, but in the dense cloud that covered the route, two Hurricanes did not return. One pilot was never heard of again. The second, the Canadian Bobby Bates, eventually found his way home the hard way. Preoccupied with a balky motor Bob blundered into the clouds and lost the formation. Occasional glimpses of the ground told him that he was east of the Irrawaddy. That probably meant that he had insufficient fuel to return to base so he set course for Paoshan in the northern, the Chinese, sector of the front. Flying low to escape the cloud he calculated that he was now close to the Salween River and about to enter the Chinese zone. With his fuel almost gone, he made a dead stick landing on the river bank and found he had landed about 75 yards from a Japanese gunpost. He fled at once from his damaged machine. "They fired a couple shots at me," Bates recalls, "so I bunked off to a nearby creek."

Lying low in the jungle Bobby Bates watched the Japanese searching for him. After nightfall he crept out and stumbled north along the river till he came to a few huts. The natives — he took them to be Chinese — gave him rice and a small meat cake. Further along the river he met a patrol of Chinese soldiers who took him to their farmhouse outpost. "No one understood Canadian," says Bates, " but they gave me a little rice and vegetable and led me on." After two days they came to a larger troop concentration and a Chinese officer who spoke a little English. They led him to the Paoshan hospital and to Robert McLure.

The flying boots that Bates had worn throughout his march were not ideal for jungle hiking and his feet were much abused. McClure treated them for a few days and even took his patient to a banquet where the Chinese generals received him as an honoured guest. Bates enjoyed the food but he was taken aback to watch these exalted persons spit the chicken bones onto the floor. McClure arranged for the pilots of Chennault's AVG to fly him home and Bob Bates had quite a tale to tell when he walked into the Squadron mess.

Bob McLure had a tale to tell as well. In a letter from the 71st Field Hospital in Paoshan, dated December 17, 1942, he wrote to his family back in Toronto:

> *The surprise here was to meet a chap from Hamilton, Robt. W. Bates of 290 Cannon Street East, Hamilton. He is a Ft. Sgt. of the RCAF. His Hurricane ran out of gas some 3 days walk from here in the Upper Salween.*
>
> *I wired to his folks this morning. I went over to the airfield here and got it fixed up with them to send a plane down here for him. He is to take this letter up to Kunming for me. He is reported missing, but it is rather nice to be able to be of some help to these chaps. We loaned him clothes. He must be a good flyer for he landed in hill country and only broke his prop. He did not hurt himself one bit.*

In March 1943 three Spitfires landed at Dum Dum airport in Calcutta. They had long pointed wings, huge fuselage fuel tanks, no guns, and they were painted blue all over. They were intended only for photo reconnaissance but they were Spitfires and now for the first time, the RAF in India had an aircraft that could match the Zeke, the Oscar and the Dinah. By June the Spitfires had been augmented by two squadrons of Beaufighters and four of Vultee Vengeance divebombers. All this strength was a sure sign that the balance of power in the air was changing. If by the onset of the 1943 monsoon the Allied air forces could not claim absolute supremacy, they could at least hold their own and hope with justification to do better than that. Now, with the balance of air power teetering in the right direction, with the land powers stabilized on either side of the Chindwin, with the nationalist urges of the Indian patriots controlled, but with a huge deficit in morale gloomily hanging over the whole British front, now the time was right for Orde Wingate to appear.

Wingate was born in India. His father, a remote and austere man, was a colonel in the Indian Army and a devout member of the Plymouth Brethren Church, an intense, earnest sect, darkly loaded with the thought of judgment and damnation. Eventually Orde broke from the family religion, but an earnest religiosity remained with him. Throughout his life a messianic mysticism infected his demeanour and Old Testament language coloured his utterances. Even as a youth he had a sense of apartness, a sense of destiny and purpose. One anecdote makes the point. At the Royal Military Academy at Woolwich the cadets were entrusted with their own discipline. Wingate had somehow offended and the consensus was that he was to be "run," that is required to run between two rows of senior cadets while they struck at him with swagger sticks. At the appointed hour the cadets lined up and Wingate appeared. But he disdained to run. Instead he marched staunchly down the length of the line and scarcely a cadet swung his swagger stick.

Posted to Palestine as staff intelligence officer in 1936, Wingate developed an affinity for the Zionist cause that made his Army masters uneasy. He also developed a system of night patrols that effectively curtailed the activities of rebel Arab bands. Posted next to Ethiopia, he led a combined force of British troops and native "Patriots" against a much stronger Italian army and restored Haile Selassie to his imperial throne.

Wingate had been awarded the DSO for his role in the Palestinian campaign, and then he had been prohibited from returning to Palestine. In Ethiopia he was given a Bar to his DSO and then he was not allowed to attend Haile Selassie's victory banquet. He had been granted the acting rank of Colonel when he began in Ethiopia, but when he finished, having won a stunning victory against a vastly superior force, he was reduced to the rank of major. The military establishment was developing a pattern of eagerly accepting any victory this scruffy and irreverent eccentric delivered them, but refusing him a seat at the table.

Wingate did not help his cause when, in his report of the Ethiopian campaign, he referred to his superiors as "military apes" and his British NCO's as "the scum of the army." Shunted off to Cairo on leave, he brooded in his hotel room, not only about the injustice done to him, but also about his suspicion that the English were going to betray Haile Selassie and annex his nation into their empire. At the same time, his malaria had developed into a cerebral form wherein the malarial parasites attack the brain. Rather than go to a military doctor and risk being put on the sick list, he doctored himself hugely with Atabrine, a medication that controls malarial fever but, in large doses, is a severe depressant. With a temperature of 104 degrees, he stumbled out into the beating heat of the Cairo streets looking for more Atabrine, lost his way, somehow returned to his hotel and to his room. Fever-crazed, heat-stricken, depressed, befuddled, and certain that God had forsaken him, he tried to commit suicide by cutting his throat. In the hospital his cerebral malaria was diagnosed and treated. Soon he was ready for a new crusade.

Wingate was a complex person. Many words have been assigned to him — strange, excitable, moody, impossible, brilliant, anti-authority, mad, unorthodox, charismatic, intense, eloquent, articulate, bloody-minded, ruthless, uncompromising, brutal, scruffy, unsoldierly, uncouth, arrogant, assertive — none has captured him wholly. Because he was such a prickly personality, he had many enemies and few friends but somehow his friends and advocates always turned out to be persons in high places. His report of the Ethiopian campaign, rewritten and much toned down, came into the hands of Sir Alan Brooke, Chief of the Imperial General Staff and of Lord Ismay, Churchill's military advisor. Very soon an urgent message came from Wavell, Commander-in-Chief in India, that Wingate should come to him "by the fastest route at the first opportunity." He met with Wavell in New Delhi March 1942 and was told his new job was to take charge of all guerrilla operations in Burma, just the sort of assignment Wingate thrived on.

After a few months of reconnoitering and thinking, Wingate devised a plan. The enemy's front line, if such it could be called, was scattered and porous, and his line of communication wavering and insecure. Behind the line there were vast areas of mountain and jungle that the enemy could not patrol. A mobile force could penetrate far into that area and there do damage out of all proportion to its size. It could blow bridges, rails and trains, ambush troops and convoys, destroy ammunition dumps and so much plague the enemy that a whole battalion or even a brigade might be employed in hunting it down. Only three things were needed, a force trained to strike quickly and then melt back into the jungle, a wireless that could order supplies as they were needed, and an air force that could deliver the supplies as they were ordered. Wingate got a promise of these things from Wavell and began to train his force.

He was not given elite commando-type troops, just ordinary soldiers, but he trained them hard and he trained them well. Life at base camp meant tents, mud, hard rations, and everything done on the double. Exercises that began with twenty-mile jungle marches in the rain for three nights running and ended with a river crossing and the mock assault of an "enemy" stronghold were standard training drill. He instilled in his men the notion that they were going to do something very extraordinary, something that would change their lives, that is, if they lived. From the first they understood that a sick or wounded man would have to struggle out on his own or be left to his fate. He also instilled in them the notion that they were going to prove that an ordinary Englishman could live and fight in the jungle as effectively and as bravely as a Japanese. Such was Wingate's charisma that most soldiers believed and followed him willingly; those that did not were dropped from the force. By mid-February 1943 Wingate's 77th Indian Brigade[2] was ready to move across the Chindwin into enemy territory.

For a moment though the whole venture seemed in danger of being cancelled. The original plan envisioned a three-pronged offensive with one British force driving down the Arakan on the west, a second fighting toward Mandalay in the centre, and a third, the Chinese, pushing down from the north. The Wingate expedition would then be the gadfly, flitting here and there behind the enemy lines to throw him off balance and prevent him giving his whole attention to the front line action. When the Chinese offensive was cancelled, Wingate's expedition would have been cancelled as well had he not argued that his men, trained to razor sharpness, could never be used at all if they were not used now when they were so ready for action. Because Wavell too was keen to test the theory of long range penetration he reinstated the Wingate plan.

Wingate's calculation of a Chindit's[3] daily nutritional needs could best be described as frugal: twelve Shakapura biscuits (hard tack), two ounces of cheese, one ounce of milk powder, nine ounces of raisins, three quarters of an ounce of tea, a packet of salt, four ounces of sugar, one ounce of

---

[2] There were no Indian troops in the 77th Indian Brigade. The name was intended to confuse or deceive the Japanese. The brigade consisted of one British and one Gurkha infantry battalion with a battalion of Burma Rifles who, in native garb, could infiltrate a village and bring back intelligence.

[3] Chindit is a corruption of *Chinthe,* the Burmese name for the mythical beast, half lion, half dragon, that guards a Burmese temple. Wingate himself chose this appellation for his expedition.

chocolate, 20 cigarettes, and a box of matches. That was reckoned to supply 3000 of the 4000 calories a man would need. Officers were issued a shot gun with the expectation that they should make up the deficiency by hunting, an altogether vain expectation, for the Burmese jungle is almost devoid of edible game. Each man carried on his back rations for seven days, one change of clothing, rubber-soled shoes, mess tins, and water sterilizing tablets. In addition he carried in his hands or about his person his rifle and bayonet, ammunition, hand grenades, water bottle, a dah or kukri (Burmese or Gurkha machete), water wings, toggle rope and jack knife. All this weighed just over 70 pounds. Officers were further burdened with revolvers, binoculars, maps, Verey pistols, compasses, and flashlights, but they were each allowed a horse so that they could patrol the column as it marched. Mules carried blankets, and other camp impedimenta, including the bulky, heavy wireless and its equally heavy batteries and charging engine. Carrying all this, three thousand men and a thousand animals slithered and slipped along the muddy track that led to the banks of the Chindwin.

The plan was that one column was to cross with great noise and clamour to deceive the Japanese into thinking it was the main thrust, while the other seven columns were to cross in great secrecy at various points thirty–five miles further north. From the Chindwin the columns would make their separate ways eastward to begin their tasks of harassment and demolition. We can get some idea of what those tasks were and how they were to be carried out if we follow the fortunes of Captain Roy McKenzie.

It has not been possible to discover how or why Roy McKenzie left Sarnia, Ontario and ended up in Burma. The only information the family can offer about his military career is that he made his own way to England and joined the British Army about the time the war started and that he came back from India some time before the end of the war with vivid tales of jungle warfare and a pair of Gurkha kukris as souvenirs. From the *History of the Second King Edward VII's Own Goorkha (sic) Rifles* we learn that in January 1941 a fresh influx of officers seconded to the Third battalion of the regiment from the British army "included Lieutenants McKenzie and Gudgeon." Dennis Gudgeon still remembers Roy McKenzie for, as he wrote to the author in October 2000, " I had a special affinity with Mac as I worked in the London buying office of the T. Eaton Co. from September 1935 to 1957."

The 3/2 Gurkha Rifles was newly formed and untried. Apart from a scattering of older men "milked" from other battalions to provide a cadre of experienced soldiers, the other ranks were very young Gurkhas recently recruited from their remote Nepalese villages and scarcely trained. In June 1942 they began the arduous toughening and training scheme Wingate had devised. The training was made even more arduous when rain flooded their bivouac and forced officers and men to perch in the trees for three days. After that experience the battalion was happy to move by rail, steamer and on foot to Imphal from whence they were to launch their foray into Burma. On February 13 the launch began. Their task was to cut the rail line between Myitkyina and Mandalay and to cause confusion and havoc in the enemy's rear in any way they could. If things looked favourable, they would then cross the Irrawaddy and try to cut the Mandalay-to-Bhamo line of supply.

Roy McKenzie, known always as "Mac" to his fellow officers, had by this time become a captain. He was assigned to 3 Column under the command of Major "Mad Mike" Calvert and, perhaps because it was assumed that all Canadians are cowboys, he was named Animal Transport Officer for the Column. His first task in that capacity was to get the mules over the Chindwin. Mules are good swimmers once they are persuaded to enter the water, but they need coaxing and cajoling. Mac got his mules into the river, but when they were turned loose in midstream, they headed back to the shore they knew. Eventually, with patience, persistence and profanity, he got the mules across.[4] The horses were easier to handle. Mac tied two of them to the sampan so that they had to swim. When the other horses saw their mates on the far side, they jumped in and crossed on their own. The bullocks too, intended both as pack animals and as "rations on the hoof," made a relatively easy crossing. The elephants however reneged and were sent back to base. Once all his charges, eighty mules and twenty horses, were over, Mac himself crossed elegantly astride his charger. The men of the column swam across if they were able or were ferried in native boats.

It was an audacious move, to camp for two days on the banks of a river in enemy territory amid all the noise and turmoil of a river crossing, but the Japanese seemed to have no notion of what was happening beneath their noses. The column took its first supply drop a few days after crossing the Chindwin, but one of the aircraft, caught in a storm, dropped a bag of mail into the enemy's hands, so that the Japanese soon knew a good deal about the size of the expedition and its purpose. Fortunately the intelligence so alarmed the local commander that he withdrew his defence post, allowing the column to advance unopposed to the foot of the Zibyu Taungdan escarpment, a geological formation characterized by a long hard climb up the western slope and a steeply precipitous plunge for 1200 feet down its almost perpendicular eastern face.

By this time the Chindits had been two weeks underway. The route had been difficult and the one air drop had barely been sufficient. The animals, the horses in particular, were suffering and the day came when

---

[4] One of Mac's fellow Animal Transport Officers did it differently. He asked the regimental bugler to call "Feed" from the far bank. The hungriest mules swam across and the others followed.

Mac acknowledged that the big black assigned to the doctor would have to be shot. He turned to a junior officer: "Would you do it? Just shoot him here." Then he walked quickly down the track so that he did not have to hear the shot.

After another river crossing, this one smaller and easier than the Chindwin, the column was drawing near its first objective, the railway between Mandalay and Myitkyina. They had still not encountered the enemy, but patrols and friendly natives warned of their presence and the column moved forward with great caution, detouring widely to avoid enemy garrisons at Wuntho and Indaw. The objective Wingate had assigned Calvert was to destroy a series of railway bridges near Nankan, a small station halfway between these two larger towns. On March 5, eighteen days after crossing the Chindwin, the column prepared to carry out its task. The Commando platoon was ordered to destroy a small, three-span bridge just east of the station, while a second platoon was to blow up the tracks in a number of places with one pound slabs of gun cotton. Calvert, the eager engineer, took on the main bridge. To protect the area of operations, an ambush was set to the east and to the west. Mac was in charge of the westerly ambush.

In the noonday sun Calvert scrambled gleefully among the girders and beams of the three-hundred-foot long structure, expertly placing his charges. Mac waited tensely on the rail line, watching and listening for any sign of the enemy. The gunfire, when it came, came from the eastern road block. Even as Calvert was setting his last charge shots rang out and the road block, forty strong, found it was fighting a force of about 100 Japanese. Fortunately the Japanese had blundered into the ambuscade so that many of the attackers were killed before they got out of their lorries. They brought up an armoured car with heavy machine guns, but the Gurkha mortar section hit it squarely before it got into action. For some time the rattle of machine guns, the whump of mortars and the crack of rifles continued, till the heavy boom of two separate explosions told the Chindits that their main task was done. As darkness fell, they faded back and escaped to the agreed-upon rendezvous six miles into the jungle. Mac's men however stuck to their post throughout the night and did not get to the rendezvous till next morning. When the roll was called, not a man was missing. A cautious return to the scene of the action revealed two bridges were down, the rail line had been cut in seventy places, three enemy trucks were destroyed and fourteen Japanese soldiers were dead. It had happened on Calvert's thirtieth birthday and no present could have delighted him more.

Even as Calvert's Three Column was destroying the line at Nankan, Five Column was dynamiting the gorge and blowing the bridge at Bonchaung. All in all, a good day for Wingate's Chindits. On the enemy's main supply line, three bridges were destroyed, miles of rail line blown up, tons of debris dumped into the gorge that carried the rail line, and a good few Japanese soldiers killed or wounded. But more importantly, Wingate's theory of long range penetration had been tested and proved. A light mobile force could disrupt the enemy's line of communication and hold off an enemy attack, then disengage and fade into the jungle to fight again.

There were however briers in Wingate's rose garden. Two and Four Columns had lost men and lost their radios in encounters with the enemy and thus deemed it expedient to turn back. The columns that persevered found it hard to keep their morale high when they had to shake hands with wounded comrades and leave them to the enemy or, in extreme cases, deliver a fatal shot of morphine. They had all heard of wounded who had fallen into Japanese hands and been used for bayonet practice. In all the regiments the tradition was strong that the wounded would be cared for and brought to medical attention as soon as possible. With the Chindits that was never possible. On the plus side, air supply was working very well. It was reassuring to know that, if the weather held, ammunition, rations and mail, even false teeth or eye-glasses, could be delivered on demand.

Once the Mandalay-to-Myitkyina railway was blown the column continued eastward across the Irrawaddy and entered a treeless, arid area. Until they reached the river, thirst became a torture. And once they were over the river, they were confined by its enormous breadth on the west, the Shweli River on the north and east and the road from Mongmit to the Irrawaddy on the south. The Japanese now knew exactly where they were and could easily hunt them down.

Within this arid area there was one assignment that tempted Calvert mightily, the blowing of the Gokteik viaduct, a spindly structure strung dramatically across a 1200 foot deep gorge about thirty miles east of Maymyo. Its destruction would mean a major disruption of the Japanese supply line from Lashio to Mandalay, but even before they reached it, word came from Delhi that the Chindits must return.

The return would not be easy. All the native boats on the Irrawaddy had been confiscated by the Japanese and the river was closely watched. The question now was, should the column stick together or should it disperse and evacuate in small groups. Calvert himself favoured staying together, but he did the democratic thing and put the question to his officers. The consensus was that small groups could more easily slip through the jungle and feed off the land. Accordingly Calvert broke the column down into nine groups of about forty men each and suggested each group choose its own path out. Mac McKenzie, given charge of one group, elected to exit on the path by which he had entered. The column received a final supply drop — maps, compasses, tommy guns, pistols, ammunition and rations for ten days. It would take at least a month to walk out; obviously there would be lean days ahead. They would have to buy food from the villagers and each leader was given 400 silver rupees for that purpose. On March 29, 42 days after the columns had crossed the Chindwin and entered enemy territory, Calvert gathered the officers into a circle, thanked them for their loyal service and wished them God speed. With the last ration of rum they toasted the King, then they shook hands and went their separate ways.

There are virtually no documents or official records of the exodus and though there are personal accounts written by those involved, none of these tells of the fortunes of Captain Roy McKenzie's troop. It is not hard to imagine their adventures however. There were long hours of struggling through thickets of elephant grass or tight groves of bamboo, of toiling up steep mountain paths and of slipping and sliding down the other side, all the while shaking with exhaustion and parched with thirst. Every turning in the path held the threat of a Japanese patrol ready to fall upon them with bayonets and exultant yells. The villagers they encountered were often sympathetic or at least as sympathetic as their fear of their conquerors allowed. In some villages a feast was served up for them, on one occasion a feast that was intended for the enemy, but in other villages they were betrayed to the Japanese and had to fight their way out of an ambush. It was hard on Mac to have to turn the mules loose and chase them away when they followed the group. It was a good deal harder to simply walk on and leave the sick and wounded behind. Whenever possible they were entrusted to the care of friendly natives, but even then their fate was doubtful. When the troop had to abandon a comrade in the jungle they prayed that he would die rather than fall into the merciless hands of the enemy. In the story of the withdrawal there were a hundred tales of compassion, suffering and courage that went well beyond the ordinary, but what was needed above all was leadership that kept its head whatever happened.

When he finally got back at the Regimental Depot in India, Mac felt he had earned some rest and relaxation. With another Chindit officer from the Regiment he set off for a houseboat holiday at Srinagar in Kashmir. Throughout the withdrawal, the 400 silver rupees they had been given had ground and bounced in the ammunition pouches at their belt. Now they took the remaining silver on their holiday and, as Mac's companion reports, "I didn't think the King would mind and on the assumption that I had his blessing, Mac and I drank his health every day and night in Kashmir until the very last silver coin had been spent."

When Wingate planned his columns, he provided that each should have an aircrew officer who could select dropping zones and talk knowledgeably to the crew of the supply planes. The word went out to the squadrons asking for volunteers for a secret and dangerous mission. Ken Wheatley was the only Canadian volunteer chosen for the expedition and he was assigned to

8 Column. We have met Wheatley earlier as the young Canadian pilot who always flew as Number Two to the leader of 17 Squadron at Mingaladon because "whatever the situation one found oneself in, he was always there." Wheatley survived the six weeks of the Chindit expedition and, when the recall order came, he began the walk out with his group. At one bivouac he went off with a party of four men to cut firewood and was taken prisoner. It was April Fool's Day, 1942. He escaped briefly, but was recaptured and taken by train to Rangoon jail. In the jail the Japanese segregated air crew from Army prisoners and treated them with particular brutality, maintaining that the air force men were devils who bombed innocent women and children and therefore deserved a vicious punishment. Wheatley spent five months in a cell about four feet by nine feet with one small window high on the wall, a stone floor, a leaky old ammunition box as a latrine and a single blanket as the only other furnishing. He was not allowed to talk nor was he taken out except for interrogation, and interrogation always meant being slapped and beaten with a club. Despite the "persuasion" to tell all, Wheatley stuck to his story that he was a sprog, a newcomer, and had nothing to tell. Eventually he was released to the general barrack cell.

The end of the first Chindit expedition was torture for those who walked out, but it was hell for those who were so depleted by sickness, disease, wounds, exhaustion, starvation and malnutrition that they fell by the way. Only one group was able to air lift its casualties. That column was without rations, the mule that carried their radio had died, and seventeen of their number were so seized with fever or immobilized by wounds that they could not continue. The column was 170 miles into enemy territory and within 20 miles of a Japanese fighter base. The radio operator drained his batteries to send a last appeal for food and for a rescue plane, then destroyed his set. Hoping against hope, they set out markers for the drop and added a message: PLANE LAND HERE. The Dakota pilot who made the drop next day surveyed the small clearing, shook his head, and dropped a note: "Mark out 1200 yard landing ground to hold 12-ton transport."

Two days later Mike Vlasto, an RAF pilot, and Jack Reeves, his Canadian wireless operator, loaded their plane and took off for the little jungle clearing. Before they left, the supply officer gave them each a new pair of boots, cheerily suggesting, "You may need these to walk home if you don't make it." They found the clearing and saw the sign: LAND ON WHITE LINE. GROUND V G." Reeves, known on the squadron as a sound and sober man, and also known as "Happy" because no one had ever seen him smile, was not a pilot, but he could easily see that the strip was at least 400 yards too short. There were tall trees just 200 yards beyond the end of the white line. They might get in; they might not get out again. "Here goes nothing," said Vlasto as he lined up on the clearing. Touching down as short as he could and using the brakes hard, Vlasto made his landing. Eighteen casualties were loaded and the door was closed. Then one corporal protested that he did not want to be evacuated: "I came in on my feet and I want to go out the same way," he said. The door was opened again and he jumped out. Vlasto went back as far as he could, put all his weight on the brake pedals and ran up his engines until the old Dakota trembled and the debris of the jungle flew out behind. He released the brakes, the Dakota jumped forward and sped toward the towering line of trees. At the last moment Vlasto pulled the aircraft off the ground and the trees just scraped their undercarriage. "Thank God for number eighteen," murmured Jack Reeves. For Mike Vlasto, for Jack Reeves, and for the seventeen Chindits April 13 was a very lucky day.

There was another Canadian on the first Chindit expedition, Major George Faulkner of the Indian Medical Service. George Faulkner had trained at McGill and, after interning at London, Ontario, had become interested in researching the silicosis problem among miners in northern Ontario. He was in Britain when the war broke out and immediately joined the British Army. Fearful of being stuck in a base hospital in Britain, he said nothing about his medical qualifications, joined the Argyle and Sutherland Highlanders as a private, and was sent to the Continent, escaping back to Britain after France fell. When the war with Japan broke out, he saw another opportunity to get on to active service, confessed his medical degree, and transferred to the Indian Medical Service with the rank of Captain. In January 1943 he volunteered for Wingate's expedition and a month later was on his way into Burma, taking with him 300 pounds of medical supplies and six hand grenades, explaining they were "for the Japs and as sure-catch fishing tackle, as occasion presents."

On the expedition his concern of course was for the physical well being of the soldiers. Wingate, with his typical heartlessness, insisted that sick parade be held at six in the morning and that platoon officers be held responsible if there was even a suspicion of malingering among their troops. Faulkner eased that restriction and received the sick for treatment whenever they appeared. He recognized there were malingerers, but in his experience, "laggards disappear on getting into enemy country." Not that he mollycoddled the troops. When, on the never-ending march out, a starving, emaciated and bone-weary soldier felt he could not rise to take another step, Faulkner did not hesitate to use a strong arm and a short stick to get the man up again and on his way. They thanked him for that after it was all over.

Faulkner's final report on the medical aspects of Chindit I is a down-to-earth, straightforward document that deals in everyday, common-sense language with the problems he encountered and gives suggestions for solving them. He scolded Wingate that, in his desire to reduce baggage, he had scanted the scale for medical supplies. At the very least, he insisted, snake serum and anti-anthrax vaccine should be added to the medical kit. He noted that castor oil is an excellent substitute for dubbin for waterproofing your boots and in a pinch it would keep the rust off your revolver. He recommended going without socks. He was concerned about the nutritional deficiency of the rations but acknowledged that under the circumstances a more liberal food allowance was difficult. On one point he was emphatic: tea, tinned milk and sugar must be a part of every meal, not merely for medical reasons but for morale as well. "Hot sweet tea," he declared, "is only laughed at by those who have never been without or felt the need."

This claim is sufficiently important to warrant a short digression. No one can read far in the literature of the Burma Campaign without hitting upon a paean to the restorative power of tea. Chindits prevented from lighting a fire by the closeness of the enemy would boil their tea water on the muffler of the generator that charged their batteries. One troop, finding themselves cut off without food or ammunition and closely surrounded by the enemy, asked "What shall we do now?" "Brew up," was the reply, and they did. Even Americans fighting with a British guerrilla force behind the lines reluctantly confessed that, though they yearned for the smell of coffee, there was more survival and revival value in a mug of hot sweet tea. And that is why Major Faulkner insisted that there be tea in the ration box.

By May of 1943 the skin and bones remnant of the First Chindit Expedition was back out and Faulkner, on convalescent leave in Calcutta, gave his understanding of what it takes to be a Chindit: "One must be physically fit, enjoy roughing it, and be a wee bit daft."

Twenty-five years later, Mike Calvert, addressing the medical staff of St. Mary's Hospital in London, summed up George Faulkner's contribution to the First Chindit expedition: "Captain G. V. Faulkner, IMS, a Canadian, and Senior Medical Officer on Wingate's staff, a man of magnificent physique and realistic brilliance, went in on the operation marching 1500 miles or so behind the Jap lines in the jungle, and wrote a report on the expedition which helped revolutionize the attitude throughout the Burma Army to disease and casualty treatment and the problems of evacuation."

But what had the expedition accomplished? It had blown a few miles of rail line and destroyed a few bridges and all the damage was put right again within a few weeks. It had taken three thousand men brazenly two hundred miles behind the enemy lines and kept them there for three months, but it had lost one third of them, and of the two thousand who returned, fully half were unfit for further active service. It had shown that air supply could keep a column going when it was cut off, if the radios could be kept working and if the weather were co-operative. Perhaps General Slim was justified in his wry appraisal: "If anything was learned of air supply or jungle fighting, it was a costly schooling."

But it had had other results — and for these there is no negative qualifier. It had shown that ordinary British and Gurkha troops, properly trained and led, could move and fight in the jungle as effectively as the best of the enemy forces. In its audacity it had ended forever the myth of the invincible Japanese. It had lifted morale, not only of the troops in Imphal and Calcutta but of the civilian populace in Britain as well. It also prodded the Japanese leaders to initiate a counter-move that eventually led to their complete defeat. And, most importantly for the immediate course of the Burma War, it gave Churchill a rousing tale of British triumph to take to Roosevelt in Quebec in August 1943.

X

BATTLE OF THE ADMIN BOX

L ACKING THE equipment that was needed for any combined operations
in Burma, Mountbatten and Slim settled for a modified version of
Anakim. There was to be a second go at the Arakan, a general advance
from Assam at least to the Chindwin, and a drive by Stilwell's Chinese forces
toward Myitkyina. Wingate, bucked up by the all the encouragement he
had received at Quebec, was ready to provide the fourth prong of the
attack, a second Chindit expedition penetrating into north Burma to harry
and harass in support of Stilwell. Although these four sectors of operation
were geographically distinct, they were of course strategically connected
since whatever happened in one area could not help but affect what happened in the others. Moreover because they were all planned for the 1944
"hunting season," the pre-monsoon months, they were to take place almost
simultaneously. By a scant month the Arakan attack preceded the others
and therefore we treat it first. Before we do that, however, we have to look
at what was happening in the enemy camp.

Slim was aware that the Japanese were bringing reinforcements to the
Chindwin front and were perhaps planning an assault too. The develop-
ment that accelerated the Japanese build-up was the completion of the
Bangkok-to-Burma railway, the railway best known for its bridge over the
River Kwae. In March 1942 the Japanese completely routed the Allied naval
forces in the Battle of the Java Sea and occupied the Andaman Islands.
That meant she controlled the southwest Pacific area and could bring in
supplies to her Burma army and take back the oil and rubber of Malaya,
Java and Sumatra. But sea supply was slow and vulnerable to Allied naval
action. A supply line from Bangkok to Burma would be much shorter, and
all that was needed was 250 miles of railway to join the Burmese railhead
at Thanbyuzayat on the Burma-Siam border with the stub of track that

ended forty miles north of Bangkok *(see map p. 12)*. In September 1942 Tojo ordered that the missing 250 miles of railway be built. The prisoners taken at Singapore were to be used as slave labour to build the railway. Dr. Walter Anderson was one of the prisoners.

Walter Anderson's parents had been missionaries to India from College Street Presbyterian Church in Toronto since 1901. Walter was born in China and lived there until he was old enough to be sent back to Toronto to go to university. He knew he wanted to be a missionary like his parents, but because he didn't like writing sermons, he enrolled in Medicine and in time became Dr. Walter Anderson. In September 1937 College Street United Church dedicated him as their medical missionary to India; to the end of his life he wore the engraved watch given to him by the Church on that occasion. For the next four years he worked as a medical missionary. When the Japanese invaded Burma in 1941 he was called into the Indian Medical Service and sent to Singapore. Anderson's initiation to war was immediate; as his troopship steamed into the harbour it passed the Canadian Pacific's *Empress of Asia* with black smoke billowing up between her funnels as she sank. Nine days later, the impregnable fortress of the East capitulated and 64,000 British, Australian and Indian troops went into captivity, Walter Anderson among them.

As Anderson remembers it, his group was concentrated into Raffles Square in central Singapore. Through February 14 and 15 they heard the incessant sounds of battle; when they awoke on the 16th there was only a frightening silence. Soon the Japanese troops entered the square and ordered the British to pile arms and stand back. Dr. Anderson managed to snatch a towel from the ruins of Raffles Department Store to add to the meagre store of medical supplies in his zealously guarded Red Cross pannier. Then they were marched away to Changi prison camp. Over the gate of the camp there was a defiant sign in Latin: QUI ULTIMA RIDET OPTIMA RIDET (He who laughs last, laughs best). Anderson treasured the memory of that sign in the years that followed.

Five soldiers escaped and were recaptured. The Japanese executed them on the spot and then required that all prisoners sign an undertaking not to escape. Their own officers warned that to sign was treason. The Japanese responded by making all the prisoners sit packed together under the hot sun on one third rations until they did. For three days this stand-off con-tinued until at last the senior British officer declared that they could sign, since any promise given under such duress need not be honoured.

After a short stay at Changi the prisoners were taken away to work on the railway. Anderson still recalls the horror of that trip. "We were crowded into metal box cars and with the sun beating down, it was like being in an oven. There was scarcely room to stand and absolutely no thought of lying

down or even squatting. We were given a handful of boiled rice once a day
and there were no sanitary facilities. By the end of the second day urine
and feces were floating around our feet. You can imagine the stench." After
three days on the train they were transferred to a launch and taken up the
river to a camp housing Dutch prisoners. He was the only medical man in
the camp.

The route of the Bangkok-to-Burma railway had been surveyed years
earlier by the British but had been rejected because of the high hills, deep
gorges and pestilent swamps. The Japanese looked again and decided that
with prisoner– and slave–labour it could be done. Work began in October
1942 with a projected finish date of December 1943. Midway through a
"speedo" order came from Tokyo and the line was actually completed three
months ahead of schedule, a phenomenal record for rail laying, even in
ideal conditions. In the end 60,000 prisoners and 270,000 slaves from
Malaya, Burma and Siam toiled around the clock in 12 and 14 hour shifts
under the sharp eye of Korean guards who were even more brutal than their
Japanese masters. For the prisoners conditions were unbelievably primitive
and punishing. They lived in hastily built jungle lean-to's and ate the same
meal every day, boiled rice with weevils and maggots as protein enrichment
and sometimes a wee bit of salt fish or spinach or a token taste of stewed
pumpkin. For the indentured workers from Malaya and Burma conditions
were more deplorable. They were fed even less than the prisoners and
sickness was everywhere. The usual jungle maladies of malaria, dysentery,
and beriberi, intensified by malnutrition and exhaustion, were rampant
but never an excuse for missing a shift at work. Even shivering, sweating,
feverish malaria victims who could not get up off the sleeping shelf were
beaten to their feet and sent out to break rock. Those who could not stand
were required to sit in a row and pull rails into position.

Dr. Anderson protested that the "hospital" patients at least should be
excused from work but the only response was to be beaten on the side of
the head with a scabbarded sword. His pleas for medicines and medical
supplies were scorned, though vaccine was forthcoming when cholera
appeared, for the threat of cholera sent shivers of terror through the Japanese tent. His one medical success was in the treatment of the suppurating
jungle sores that plagued most of the prisoners. A Dutch prisoner had
presented with an ugly open carbuncle on the back of his neck. Anderson
stole some kitchen scraps, rotted them in a length of bamboo and grew
his own private colony of maggots. Discarding the hairy black maggots, he
tweezered out the white ones, since they ate only morbid flesh, and planted
them in the enflamed opening. Next day, the wound was a healthy pink.

Once the railway was finished the POW's were withdrawn, but the
Malayans, Burmese and Siamese were kept on to maintain it. Anderson

was kept on as well, but now he was allowed to sleep in the tent with the Japanese officers. "We can't speak," his diary records, "but I am treated respectfully and there is no interference with my work." Also he now ate Nip food, "rather tasteless, but much better than coolie food, *white* rice, miso soup. Miso fried with onions was very good and most tasty of all (one spoonful enough for a bowl of rice)". Somehow he got hold of a copy of Shakespeare plays. He read it through twice, memorized long passages, and commented in his diary: "What a boon in this Burma jungle in the monsoon rain." The Japanese soldier in charge of the cookhouse had a Roman Catholic wife back in Japan and he surreptitiously gave Dr Anderson a bit of khaki cloth to patch his shirt and a pair of wooden clogs to replace his worn out Malayan running shoes. The clogs didn't last long, for the white ants ate them at night. As his captivity stretched on, Dr. Anderson saw in the repeated bombing of the railway bridges signs that the sway of war was turning against his captors. On one occasion they suffered a raid by nine Liberator bombers and he cursed and blessed the RAF as he ran around a tree trying to escape the strafing.

His afternoons were fairly free and he once wandered off, following the overgrown remnants of a fence. It led him to a row of small crosses bearing English names, the last and lost resting place for a few of the railway's many victims. He tried to clear it, but he didn't dare let the Japanese know what he was doing.

When the war ended, Anderson was called to Rangoon to testify about "good and bad Japs." His one happy memory of that time is of being able to testify positively about a Japanese sergeant interpreter who had treated them well. The man had once hummed a Negro spiritual, "Lord, I want to be a Christian," when he noticed Dr. Anderson alone with him in the area.

Walter Anderson is a gentle man and one who tries to live his Christian faith. Pressed about the brutality and torture he experienced, he diffidently tells of being forced to go down into a six foot deep grease pit near the kitchen and scoop out the filth with his bare hands while the Japanese stood round the rim and laughed at him. Bitterness is not in him, but it is easy to see that the memories are strong. With a two inch stub of a pencil he made a calendar and kept a "diary," a few scrappy notes hidden in a length of bamboo. Today he still treasures an aluminum mess tin that a British sergeant had etched for him. On it is the crest of the Indian Medical Corps and a few significant dates, "Singapore 5.2.1942; Prisoner of War 15.2.1942; Changi 17.2.1942; Selarang Incident 2/5.9.1942."[1]

Prisoners who were so sick or incapacitated that they were absolutely unable to work and yet refused to die, were sent back to a "base hospital" at

---

[1] Dr. Anderson died shortly after this account was written. He was 96.

Chungkai, 100 kilometres north west of Bangkok. Eventually the camp held 7000 patients, a good many of whom owed their lives to the ministrations of Major Jacob Markowitz. Marko, as he was called by everyone in the camp, was born in Toronto in 1901 and graduated from Jarvis Collegiate Institute in 1918. After obtaining a medical degree and a PhD in physiology from the University of Toronto, he worked for a few years in the United States then came back to Canada to become Dr. Best's surgeon on the insulin project. As a result of his work with Dr. Best's dogs he wrote *A Textbook of Experimental Surgery*, a publication that quickly went through six reprints and became a standby for veterinary surgeons. He was well recognized and had a thriving practice in Toronto but when war broke out he felt compelled to join up. Because the Canadian forces did not welcome him — he suspected there was anti-Semitism involved — he went to Britain, joined the Royal Army Medical Corps and was sent to Singapore. Two months later he was a prisoner of the Japanese.

Every patient in the Chungkai camp ought to have been considered a medical emergency but there were almost no facilities and no supplies. Because of malaria, pellagra, tropical ulcer, dysentery, debility and malnutrition, the prisoners were dying at the rate of ten a day. Although Marko and his colleagues worked 18 to 20 hours a day, their effectiveness depended greatly upon their ability to experiment and improvise. The ulcer ward was Marko's prime concern. The undernourished state of the patients and the filthy conditions under which they lived meant that every little skin break developed into an uncontrollable ulcer that ate its way to the bone and soon became a stinking pulp of necrotic flesh. Marko attempted to scrape the wound with a sharpened spoon, but frequently the gangrene won out and there was no cure but amputation. When they ran out of chloroform, Marko found dental novocain was an adequate spinal anaesthetic.

When he was ready to amputate, the cook loaned him the kitchen saw, with the injunction: "Sterilize it before you return it." Sterilization was of course a problem, but he improvised again, brewing alcohol from spittle, rice and a rotten banana. In nine months Marko did 120 amputations and despite the primitive conditions in his surgery, he did not lose a patient. Sometimes it was touch and go. An Australian soldier about to have an amputation at the thigh stopped breathing. Harking back to his Old Testament studies, Marko remembered "the method used by Elijah the Tishbite when he resuscitated the widow's child." He seized a length of tubing and breathed directly into the patient's lungs. When the patient began to breathe again, his first remark was "I'm glad you guys don't eat onions." Marko's most daring medical exploit was the improvisation of blood transfusions using a wooden spoon to stir the bucket of blood to prevent coagulation, multi layers of gauze to strain it into a funnel made from a bottle with the end broken off, and a length of stethoscope tubing to introduce it into the patient.

Jacob Markowitz suffered just as all the prisoners did from inadequate nutrition and sadistic bullying, but he kept his spirits high and dedicated himself always to helping others. The citation which accompanied the MBE he was awarded in 1946 mentions all his brilliant medical improvisations and achievements, but it ends with recognition of his humanity: "He has shown great disregard for personal danger and the risk of brutality in order to serve his patients." That is the dry language of the *London Gazette*. The *Canadian Forum*, to which he had contributed brilliant articles in the Thirties, better captures the spirit of the man: "In whatever circumstances those quick eyes and deft fingers and that understanding and infectious laugh might have been placed, they would be found to the last in the serene and tireless ministration to the suffering of others."

After the war, Marko returned to Toronto to share his knowledge, his experience and his enthusiasm for the healing art with generations of future doctors at the University of Toronto medical school.

Dr. Anderson is reticent to tell of the horrors of the railway camps, and Dr. Markowitz does not dwell on them. Less charitable accounts of life on the Bangkok–to–Burma railway tell sickening tales of camps flooded with rain and latrine filth, of Japanese and Korean guards who are inhumanly brutal, of starving men shaking with malaria and weak with dysentery whipped out to build a railway. For the least infraction of discipline, even for not bowing promptly or to a properly respectful angle when a Japanese soldier passed, prisoners were forced to stand all day under the searing sun holding a heavy rock above their heads, or were beaten senseless with a club. For good reason the project is called the Death Railway. Of the 330,000 men working on the railway about 100,000 died, one corpse for every twelve feet of track. Eleven thousand of the dead were Allied prisoners of war. From those in charge of the camps all the way up to the Emperor, the culpability of the Japanese commanders for this useless waste of human life cannot be avoided. When the British medical officer at one camp pointed out that the dysentery epidemic could be stopped if only the fly-blown latrine were replaced by a bench suspended out over the ocean, the camp commandant brusquely rejected the suggestion. The ocean belonged to His Imperial Highness and must not be defiled by the bodily wastes of slaves and prisoners.

At this cost the Emperor had his railway. As soon as it was finished, in October 1943, it began to deliver troops and supplies to Burma. Throughout the 1943 monsoon period there had been four Japanese divisions in Burma. By the end of November there were seven and indications that more were coming. Warned of this build-up, the Allied planners accelerated the 1943-44 campaigning, and immediately upon his return to India from Quebec Wingate began to assemble and train the columns for his second expedition. Even while he was doing that, Mountbatten and Slim launched another initiative, a second attack on the Arakan.

The first Arakan thrust had been a dismal failure, mainly because the attackers had butted straight down the narrow isthmus against the unassailable bunkers of the Japanese defence. In some respects the situation had not changed. The constraining geography had not changed, the bunkers were still there, and Akyab, the port at the end of the Arakan peninsula, was still a supply port and airstrip worth striving for. But three things had changed: the ridge down the centre of the peninsula was now recognized as penetrable, the morale of the attackers, thanks to Wingate, was now high, and most important of all, the British had a secret weapon — air supply.

Where the notion of air supply first came from is a disputed question. In his early days with the Indian Army Slim had mooted it for the North West Frontier, the troops and refugee columns retreating toward Imphal in 1942 had seen it briefly, and Wingate had promised his first Chindits that they would be sustained from the sky "like Father Christmas." Whatever its beginnings, its fulfilment was certainly in the First Chindit expedition, for at the end Wingate could claim that as long as the wireless and the weather did their part, the Air Force never let them down. Now air supply was to be tested again. In the Second Arakan campaign Mountbatten issued a dictum: "If the enemy try their old trick of hooking in behind, stand firm. Never let go. We will supply you from the air." He added a second dictum: the campaigning would continue right through the monsoon season, a heretical thought to all old India hands.

The immediate object of the Second Arakan thrust was to occupy Maungdaw on the west and Buthidaung on the east and the Tunnels that lay between, an action that would also bleed off some of the enemy forces on the Central Front facing Assam (*see map p. 101*). As in First Arakan, one thrust was down the west shore and the other down the east, but this time a third thrust would go down the spine as well. In addition, to ward off the threat of interference from the Mandalay area, the 81st West African division was to advance down the Kaladan River on the extreme east flank.

The attack began in mid-November of 1943. As it progressed, history seemed about to repeat itself. Resistance was minimal and by Christmas the thrust down the spine had reached the main line of the Japanese defence, the Maungdaw-Tunnels-Buthidaung road. There the attack faltered in the face of obstinate resistance and those impassable bunkers covered with a roof of logs and mounds of earth and now backed up by supply and ammunition dumps as much as 35 feet underground. Mitchell and Liberator bombers, newly arrived in the theatre, dropped tons of bombs on the fortifications. Vultee Vengeance dive bombers strafed and pounded them.

The tanks of the 25th Dragoons blasted the emplacements point blank. Convinced that the Japanese backbone must be completely broken, the British troops moved in to finish the job. To their surprise the defence was as determined as ever. The Japanese called the area the "Golden Fortress" and it was obvious they meant to stay in their Golden Fortress for a long time. There were also signs that they were about to use it as a launching pad for a not insignificant counter attack employing the reinforcements that had been flooding in.

At the beginning of February 1944 the counter offensive (code-named *Ha Go*) began, a wide sweep that would encircle the attackers from behind, the same tactic that had served so well in the 1942 campaign. This time, however, the British were prepared. Mountbatten had said "No withdrawal. Stand firm and we will supply you by air." Ten miles north of the tunnels road, a rough track utilized the Ngakyedauk Pass[2] to traverse the spine of the Mayu Range. In a mile square clearing midway along it, a supply and administrative area complete with ordnance and medical services had been established. Here the encircled British forces consolidated to receive the support that Mountbatten had promised and to fight back with a stubborn bravery that has made the Battle of the Admin Box forever a byword for valour and courage in British military history.

Because the Box was surrounded by hills and the jungle pressed in on every side, it was not an ideal defensive position. Naturally the Japanese assessed its inadequacies and exploited them fully. Almost constantly their mortars and artillery installed on the surrounding hills directed a deadly hailstorm of shot and shrapnel onto the motor transport, the mules and the ancillary troops concentrated in the centre of the Box. By day and by night the Japanese infantry ran screaming from the jungle to launch fierce attacks on the perimeter.[3] One such night-time attack captured a field hospital where the doctors were still operating. When the area was retaken next morning the Allied troops found that the wounded had been slaughtered on their stretchers and the doctors had been lined up and shot. The Indian orderlies were forced to carry the wounded Japanese back to the Japanese lines and then they too were shot. Such bestiality backfired; the British and Indian soldiers were enflamed with anger and fought back with raging determination. Patrick Turnbull in *Battle of the Box* tells a small anecdote that illustrates the spirit of the Indian troops. When the commander of a Sikh regiment was asked how long he could hold his outlying

---

[2] The British troops soon christened it the Okeydoke Pass.

[3] Elements of Subhas Chandr Bose's Indian National Army were also in the perimeter attacks but for the most part they contented themselves with shouted attempts to suborn their Indian Army compatriots. They were answered with laughter and jeers.

position he replied; "Without food, six days. Without ammunition, as long
as you like. We have our bayonets."

Nor did the defenders limit themselves to defence only. Nightly they sent
out their own patrols to harass the enemy and to interrupt his supply lines.
One patrol encountered a large enemy supply column, killed the escort,
and marched the local porters back into the Box with a goodly supply of
ammunition, a large quantity of rice and a complete field ambulance. Not
only did the British benefit from the supplies, but thanks to the labour of
the captured coolies they got a light plane strip from which American L5's
then evacuated 200 wounded.

One of the biggest and most important of these offensive sorties involved
Major Hoey, the Canadian officer from Duncan who had won the Military
Cross at Maungdaw the previous year. Overlooking the northern edge of the
Box was a particularly troublesome promontory known as Point 315. The
strength of the Japanese force holding it was not known, but the damage
they were doing to the troops below was considerable. When word went out
that the point must be neutralized, Charles Hoey and B Company of the
First Lincolnshires were nominated to do the job. With each man carrying
a small haversack and a day's rations, and with ten mules to carry mortars
and the wireless, they set out at moonrise down the centre of the valley,
hidden by a thick ground haze. They tried to move in absolute silence but
cutting through the jungle and then clambering down and up the steep
banks of Laung Chaung made that difficult. Nevertheless the Japanese
were completely surprised; some were still wrapped in their blankets when
B Company fell upon them. Soon however the Japanese machine gunners
at the summit found their range and directed a deadly fire down on the
attackers. Without hesitation Major Hoey seized a Bren gun and charged
straight up the hill, all the while exhorting his men to follow him. His mad
charge carried him right into the middle of the enemy gunners. Even
though he was twice wounded, he struck out right and left, killed all the
enemy and took the post, but at the cost of his own life.

Major Hoey's valour was recognized with the award of the Victoria Cross;
his memory was honoured in other ways. In a Special Order of the Day
issued March 18, 1944 the Commanding Officer of the Lincolnshires wrote:
"Let us go into our future battles with confidence and courage and with the
knowledge that we are better than our enemies. We have recently been set a
very perfect example by Major Hoey. His grim determination, his supreme
courage, and his willing self-sacrifice for his cause and his Regiment should
be an inspiration to all of us." Back in England the altar rail of Lincoln
Cathedral was dedicated to his memory. In Duncan a school was named
after him and nearby a wilderness area was designated as Arakan Park. In it
is a replica of the monument at Kohima in Burma and on it the names of

Charles Hoey and his brother Trevor who was killed at Caen. On occasion the British Columbia branch of the Burma Star Association gathers there to honour him.

The siege of the Admin Box was lifted when, on February 23, a Lee tank clattered over the Ngakyedauk Pass and halted under the tree that sheltered the area Headquarters. Still fired with the arrogance of their 1942 advance, the Japanese had started Operation *Ha Go* with only ten days rations per man. At the end they had not captured a single supply depot, nor had they won a significant encounter. The British and Indian troops, staring in astonishment as Japanese soldiers broke and ran from their formidable bayonet assaults, continued to push southward. On January 3 they took Akyab unopposed and on the 21st they attacked Ramree Island. The Japanese defenders, realizing that further resistance was futile, fled through the mangrove to reach the mainland. Naval patrols and air attacks hampered their escape, but not as much as the voracious Estuarian crocodiles that infested the swampy water. Almost 1000 Japanese entered the swamp in an attempt to gain the mainland. All night long the British troops heard the frenzied roaring and thrashing of crocodiles and the anguished screams of the victims. By morning scarcely twenty were still alive.

On May 10, after three years of bloody combat, the Arakan was finally free of Japanese occupation. In a very real sense the Battle of the Admin Box can be named as the turning point of the Burma war. Patrick Turnbull puts it succinctly in his book *Battle of the Admin Box:* "For the first time in history a Japanese army had been defeated on level terms in the jungle that it had made its own. And from that moment till the final triumph of VJ Day, the Japanese were never to win another major victory." It is not unreasonable to make the more precise claim that the unexpected attack on Point 315 and Major Hoey's single handed charge to the summit can be named as the point where the turn began.

But all the determination of the infantry, all the valour of heroes like Charles Hoey could not have won the Arakan if the allied forces had not had superiority in the air, and that superiority was very shaky as long as the Hurricane remained the dominant fighter plane in Burma. Canadian pilot Al Corston knew first hand the frustration of trying to outfight a Japanese Oscar with a Hurricane.

Al was from Chapleau in Northern Ontario. His logbook, still treasured today by his son, has a tooled leather cover with an ornamental RCAF crest on the front and a sleek Spitfire in flight on the back. The pages are adorned with delicate and detailed drawings of Spitfires in formation or executing operational manoeuvres. The logbook reveals its owner, an imaginative, artistic and thoroughly committed fighter pilot. In his diary Al explains his ancestry: "My grandfathers came from the wild islands of the north of Scotland. They were voyageurs and worked for the Hudson's Bay Company and they took Indian women of that barren country for their wives and to this day up in our far north there are many Cree Indian families with names such as McCauley, Fraser, Linklater, Turner, Fletcher and Corston." When he arrived on the squadron in late August 1943 the RAF ground crew thought he looked Japanese and nicknamed him "Tojo." His aircrew chums called him Chief, and affectionately continued to call him that years after the war was over. Al took no offence at either name; rather he delighted in the good humoured camaraderie that engendered them.

He was a newcomer to 67 Squadron in September 1943 and the flight commander eased him into air warfare. His first operation out of Chittagong was to fly the "Upper Air Observation" plane, climbing on track out over the enemy lines to 25,000 feet, noting the outside temperature at various altitudes as recorded by an oversized thermometer attached to the wing and then repeating the process on the return descent. After that he graduated to a seemingly endless series of convoy patrols, escorting supply ships into Chittagong harbour. Next he flew escort to Dakotas dropping supplies to the Army: "We had to circle round and round above the Daks till the last bale was kicked out and then escort them back to friendly territory. Hundreds of cans of bully beef. Thanked by Army, poor devils. Three hours! My ass was numb!" His next sortie was a bit more exciting. Six Hurricanes set out to strafe Akyab. The purpose of the sortie was to drop their long range fuel-tanks on the enemy and then to set them afire with incendiaries. As far as Al could see the experiment did not work.

Repeatedly in his Arakan experience Al felt unhappy about the performance of the Hurricane. It was rugged and dependable, but, as he wrote in his diary, "it can't do the job." The extreme frustration was to scramble when the Japanese reconnaissance plane came over and then feel totally inadequate as it flew tauntingly away. The recce plane, code named Dinah, was a sleek twin-engined aircraft with a top speed of 365 mph and a range of 1400 miles (against 325 mph and 460 miles for the Hurricane). To illustrate the problem, Al reproduced in his diary the flight leader's exchange with the Controller. The Controller first directs them to enemy fighters just ten miles away, then twenty, then "Thirty miles. Return to base." Sadly Al comments "Our poor Hurricanes just couldn't cope. It was irritating and sure frustrating."

At the end of November 1943 the squadron was pulled back to Alipore near Calcutta to receive its Mark VIII Spitfires, but Al was to know one more humiliation before the Hurricanes were taken from them. On December 5 the Japanese attacked Calcutta in strength. Along with his squadron, Al scrambled to meet them. As they climbed he realized he was not hearing anything in his headset and he got his head down in the cockpit to check the various connections. When he looked up, his mates had all disappeared and a few hundred yards behind him two unfriendly radial-engined fighters were aiming straight at him. At once he recognized — these were naval Zeroes, a more deadly foe than the Army's Oscar. Get out of here! Stick forward, hit the deck! He did escape his pursuers, but the aircraft was spewing glycol and overheating, so he sought a field for a forced landing. An Indian officer and a few soldiers approached but, as soon as they saw him climb out of the aircraft, they encircled him with menacing pistols and rifles. Al knew what was happening; they had taken him for a Japanese. Waving his dog tags, the only identification he had with him, and shouting "Canadian, British," he finally persuaded them to lower their rifles and help him back to the squadron.

Hurricanes did not disappear from Burmese skies in the first months of 1944 but from now on they were relegated to ground support, strafing and bombing. The new star of the show was the Spitfire; with a top speed of over 400 mph it could easily overtake the Japanese fighters. For Al and for all his mates it was a happy moment when, at the end of June 1944, they headed back to the Arakan with their trim new Spitfire VIII's. His log book for the last half of the year tells what air supremacy means, unopposed strafing sorties against the Japanese lines:

August 8 – strafed Japanese troop and supply positions, Donbaik. Hit in left aileron by Jap light machine gun fire. OK

August 15 – strafed Jap machine gun positions. Not much seen. Sure are masters of camouflage.

August 18 – strafed Jap troop positions at Mowdock. Going in too low. They damaged my radiator. Good thing they never hit coolant pipes.

September 6 – Gave Alechaung a going over for three days. Lots of Jap activity here.

September 7 – Support for West Africans. Strafed positions south of Chaung believed to be 300 soldiers of the Indian Nationalist Army (traitors).

That is the tempo of fighter operation the RAF squadrons were able to maintain, and Al Corston thrived on it. At the same time, because all action was tightly concentrated, the troops on the ground were well aware of what their comrades in the air were doing and were heartened by it. It truly was air support.

When 136 Squadron got its long-awaited, desperately-yearned for Spitfires in October 1943, F/L R B "Joe" Edwards itched to be the first to try one, but his squadron commander exercised his *droit de seigneur*. Joe was satisfied to be second. Joe was from Glace Bay, Nova Scotia. His regimental number, C1605, indicated a long association with the RCAF, an association intensified by the fact that his uncle was Air Marshal Harold Edwards, Air Officer Commanding in Chief, RCAF Overseas. Joe had come to the

Far East by way of Cairo, having flown his own Hurricane out to join 136 Squadron at Ceylon. That was in February 1942 so that he was there when Dizzy Mendizabel arrived from Java in his home-made Hudson. He was also there to take part in the defence of the island and claim a "probable" when the fateful Easter Sunday attack that Len Birchall warned of came.

In the months that followed, Joe was involved in air support for the First Arakan campaign, mostly bomber escort work to Akyab, Magwe, Pakokku (a village on the Irrawaddy) and the marshalling yards at Mandalay. On December 29, 1942 the squadron had its first offensive mission, an attack on the airfields of Akyab. To ensure surprise they flew in as low as possible. The sea was mirror-smooth and somehow the squadron commander flew right into the water and disappeared without a ripple. Sadly the squadron made its attack and flew home. Next day the CO's possessions were shared out among the pilots; because Joe Edwards took over as squadron commander, he got the staff car, an immaculately polished Chevrolet. Four days later, as the officers sat in the Mess, some one looked to the door of the basha and exclaimed "Look! The CO!" And indeed there he was. His Mae West had inflated as he popped up out of the water and he had been rescued. All his possessions were returned to him, Joe Edwards a bit shamefaced that he had to return the staff car spattered with mud and limping with a broken spring.

In October the Squadron was posted to the Calcutta area to receive their new Spitfires. The CO did a few circuits and bumps and then gave Joe a turn. He was a bit apprehensive about the narrow undercarriage. It didn't feel as stable as the old Hurricane, but after a week or so of ciné-film attacks and 400 mph chases, the squadron felt operational with them and they were ready to return to the Arakan. But not Joe. At the end of November he had finished his tour and was posted back to Canada without having had a chance to match his new Spitfire against a Japanese Oskar.

Robert William Rouviere Day arrived in Burma just as Edwards was leaving. He was from Victoria and had been working in insurance when the war broke out. After instructing for two years in Canada he did a short tour on Spitfires over Europe before coming to India. Bob Day had begun his operational flying in Burma as a flight commander with 81 Squadron before coming to 67 Squadron. On his first sortie he was scrambled to intercept a wave of Japanese fighters over Buthidaung, by now one of their rare appearances in the Arakan. From 20,000 feet, Bob Day picked his target, came down on it out of the sun, gave it one short burst, and saw it catch fire and spin down into the jungle below. That was his first victory. He was promoted to take command of 67 Squadron, Al Corston's squadron, just when the battle of the Admin Box was at its height. The two Canadians often flew together. Al's log tells of one such sortie when Bob chose him as his Number Two (wing man) for a reconnaissance over the Kaladan River sector. Al's aircraft was hit in the wing root by Japanese anti-aircraft fire. Day called for assistance, but the rest of the squadron had already returned to base and Al and Day had to escape from the hostile fire alone.

The coming of the Spitfires greatly changed the tempo of the battle in the Arakan skies for here was an aircraft that, though it could not outmanoeuvre the nimble little Oskar, could outfly it in every other respect. When Noel Constantine, the Australian commanding officer of 136 Squadron, tested a Mark VIII Spitfire his logbook entry glowed with enthusiasm: "Jan. 1. Spitfire VIIIB. HM-A. Test battle climb (40,000 ft) 12½ minutes !!!!!!!!" An encounter over Buthidaung in mid-January 1944 gave the Spitfire a chance to show its stuff. On that day the RAF shot down 16 enemy aircraft and damaged a further 18 for a loss of two Spitfires. A month later British airmen, and that includes a good many Canadians, shot down 10 enemy planes. In the 14 days of the Battle of the Admin Box the Japanese suffered 65 aircraft destroyed or damaged while the British lost only four Spitfires. By the time the siege was lifted on February 24 the Japanese probably had fewer than 180 aircraft left for the Burma fighting.

With air superiority fairly well established, Mountbatten's promise of air supply could now be fulfilled, provided the planes and crews were at hand to do the job. But air supply was a new concept, and while the RAF had been clamouring for Spitfire fighters and Liberator bombers, no one had considered that transport planes could become an operational priority. During the 1942 retreat 31 Squadron, the only operational transport squadron then available, had worked overtime to drop food and medicine to the refugees and to the retreating troops. With only six Dakotas on their roster, each crew had flown as many as five sorties a day to air lift 4000 weary refugees and wounded soldiers from Myitkyina. In the spring of 1943, flying its two Hudsons and three Dakotas, all that could be spared at that time, the Squadron had done a magnificent job of supporting the first Chindit expedition. Each of these actions had demonstrated the inestimable value of air supply and Mountbatten made it a priority to see that transport planes and trained crews were brought into the area. Before the Battle of the Admin Box was over there were four transport squadrons flying over the Arakan. About 550 aircrew were involved and 20 per cent of them were Canadians.

Among the misconceptions that surrounded the idea of air supply was the notion that flying a slow, awkward, overloaded and unarmed Dakota into enemy territory over the most inhospitable geography in the world and through the most treacherous weather in the world was a "cushy" job. When 194 Squadron, "The Friendly Firm," came forward into operations, Joe Curtiss was the first to learn how misconceived that notion was. Joe had been finishing high school in Delia, Alberta, a hamlet of 270 people, when the war began. He joined the RCAF, graduated as a pilot and was crewed up in England with a Canadian navigator and two wireless operator/airgunners, a Welshman and a Scot. They were flying Hudsons on internal communications in India when the CO of the newly-formed 194 Squadron picked them to join his "firm." Happy now to be flying Daks, Joe and his crew came forward just in time to do a few sorties in support of the first Chindit expedition and then to be on hand for the Admin Box. They arrived at their operational station at 10 o'clock in the morning of February 2, 1944 and at midnight that same day they loaded three tons of supplies and set out on their first sortie in support of the troops caught in the Admin Box.

That sortie went well. The crew got home at 3:30 in the morning, had breakfast and went to bed. At nine o'clock that night they were off again. This time they received no recognition signal from the ground and there-fore brought their load home, aware that the dropping zone (DZ) had probably fallen into enemy hands. On their third sortie a brief encounter with light anti-aircraft fire (ack ack) did not greatly perturb them, but when Doug Williams, the wireless operator, spotted a single engine plane darkly silhouetted against the night sky he dashed up to warn the pilot. Joe corkscrewed as violently as a Dakota allowed, lost the attackers and scurried for home taking their load with them.

Because night-time sorties were chancy, their take-off time next day was at 2:30 in the afternoon. An hour and a half later they were over the DZ. Huge puffs of smoke billowed out of the jungle, signs of a hot battle on the ground below. Joe steered into the midst of it, got down low, below 500 feet, and when the DZ came up ahead, he turned on the green light, the sign for the drop to begin. Everything they had been able to pile at the door flew out and floated down beneath the white parachutes. Then Joe pulled up and came round again while the kickers in the back piled the next bundle of supplies at the open doorway. On the third circuit the crew standing by to shove out the load could hear the crack of rifle fire above the roar of their engines. A heavy plume of black smoke flew past the open door and the wireless operator ran up to the cockpit to see what had happened. "The port motor has been hit," Joe announced almost matter-of-factly. "I've feathered the prop. Get the load out anywhere and ask the navigator for a course for home." They were low now, so low that trees were flashing past. With frantic haste the crew pushed everything out, hoping that it was falling into the right hands. Doug got a message off asking that a fire truck and ambulance stand by just in case. Once the load was gone, Joe could slowly gain height. A strong and capable pilot, for two hours he coaxed the Dakota onward on one engine while the crew stood on tip toe and yearned heavenward to lighten the load. Finally the base was before them. Joe set the aircraft down smoothly and Doug Williams in his book *194 Squadron, The Friendly Firm*, recorded the reception they got: "Our two fitters gave us a rousing cheer as we arrived at dispersal and the wide grins on their faces was a joy to behold. Counting our blessings later in the Mess over several bottles of Scotch, we were greatly saddened by the news that Joe had been reprimanded for not landing the crippled aircraft at the nearest satellite strip on the way home. We thought he deserved the DFC."

In their first ten days of operations over the Arakan, the Curtiss crew had flown six complete sorties and aborted two because of enemy action. More importantly, they had delivered a total of 14 tons of vital supplies to the besieged troops in the Box. In the month of March 1944 the four transport squadrons delivered 87,595 tons of supplies to the Arakan front. Supplies included everything — mail, cigarettes, uniforms, boots, ammunition, food, petrol, barbed wire, vehicle and ordnance spares, hay for the mules. On occasion even mules were dropped, but it was found they had to be tranquillized first, for they tended to land stifflegged and suffer broken limbs.

It does not require much imagination to realize what it meant to the troops on the ground to receive all these supplies from the air. It was like Christmas every day. Repeatedly the memoirs of 14th Army soldiers tell of the reverent awe with which the troops watched the necessities of war and life wafting down through the clouds. Dennis Sheil-Small's description of a drop is typical: "Without the air drop, all our efforts would have been futile. Those Dakotas, winging their way each day from the supply bases in India to nameless clearings in the Burmese jungle and paddy fields, were a delight to behold and one which never failed to thrill us. As they canted over on one wing to view our smoke signals, we could clearly see the figures, braced in the open hatchways, ready to bundle out their precious cargoes which would blossom behind them and float to earth, swinging gently under their silken canopies." But it was not just the supplies. Equally important was the troops' awareness that though they were besieged, they were not forgotten. Mountbatten was keeping his promise.

If air supply was a blessing for the British and Indian troops, imagine what effect it had on the enemy. This is the order that the Japanese infantry received as they entered the Admin Box Battle: "Advance straight into the enemy key area. Keep going ahead and do not take care of the fallen comrades. Carry seven hand grenades and as much as possible of other ammunition, but only three days rations. If the food is not enough, get it from the enemy." Before his time at the front was up, the man who received that order had been under mortar fire for two days with nothing to eat. When his troop was finally ordered to withdraw, morale was extremely low: "It was very difficult to go down the mountain carrying stretchers when we were so exhausted and hungry. The line of stretchers was a miserable sight of defeated men." Normally the Japanese soldier fought ferociously through all adversity; the despair that shows in these comments was undoubtedly engendered in good part by seeing the enemy so handsomely supplied while he had nothing. This contrast between the elation of the British and the despair of the Japanese lays open the whole dynamic that led to Allied victory, not just in the Arakan but eventually in the whole Burma campaign, and air supply was the key to it.

XI

THE SECOND CHINDIT EXPEDITION

IN HIS report of the first Chindit expedition Wingate acknowledged there had been difficulties, but his emphasis was on its successes and on the undeniable need for a repeat performance. "When long-range penetration is used again," he wrote, "it must be on the greatest possible scale and must play an essential role in the re-conquest of Burma." The report was finished in mid-July 1943 and Churchill read it shortly thereafter with ever-growing interest. Here was a man after his own heart, a man who devised wildly unorthodox plans and carried them out with courage and flair. In addition, he offered a plan for action against the Japanese, just what Churchill needed to take to the Americans when he met them at Quebec in August. They were always pressing him to "do something in Burma." He ordered that Brigadier Wingate be brought to London to tell his own story as soon as possible.

On the evening of August 4, 1943 Churchill was just about to dine when Wingate was announced. Still wearing the jungle khaki of the campaign, Wingate sat down at Churchill's table and began to talk with his usual intensity and enthusiasm. Churchill was enthralled. "We had not talked for half an hour before I felt myself in the presence of a man of the highest quality," he later recollected, and on the spot he invited Wingate to go Quebec with him. Their train would leave in an hour. Wingate agreed with alacrity but protested that he would like a chance to see his wife. That was no problem. She was already on the way from her highland home to meet Wingate in London. The police intercepted her train in Edinburgh and transferred her to the official train for an unexpected reunion with her husband and a surprise journey to Quebec. With a nicely human touch, Churchill commented, "They had a happy voyage together." He did not adduce as evidence for that remark that the Wingate's only child was born nine months later.

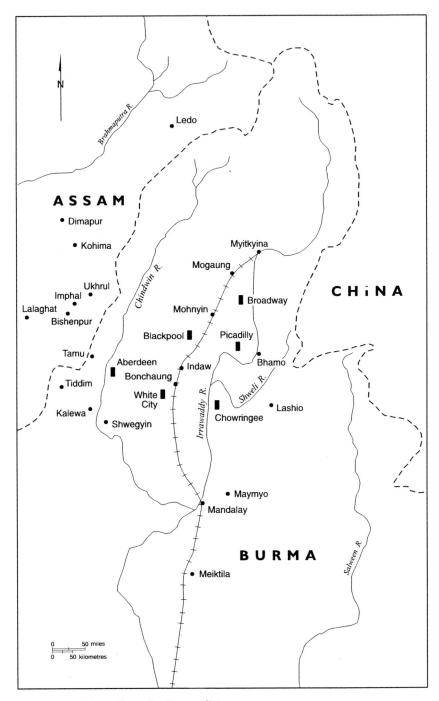

Map 7 — The Chindit Expeditions

There were matters of heavy moment to be discussed in the Citadel at Quebec, chiefly European concerns — should a second front across the Channel get precedence over the Italian campaign or would increased activity in Italy help by taking pressure off the second front? Mussolini had just been deposed and Italy was making strong overtures for peace. How did that play into the mix? As for the Far East, the American Admiral King was loudly insistent that naval action in the Pacific should take precedence over land action in Burma, while the American Army wanted action in northern Burma that would hasten the reopening of the Burma Road. Churchill wanted to skip Burma and start with Sumatra. Discussion on these contentious issues became so heated that the advisers were asked to withdraw and allow the principals a moment for quieter debate. Left alone, the great men came quickly to an agreement and were then ready to hear Wingate's proposal for action in Burma.

Before Wingate took the podium, Mountbatten asked leave to demonstrate a pet project he had in mind. Two large blocks of ice were wheeled into the conference room. One block, as Mountbatten explained, was ordinary ice, but the other was Pykrete, a frozen mixture of water and wood pulp. His proposal was that enormous slabs of Pykrete — named to honour Mr. Geoffrey Pyke, the scientist who developed the mixture — should be towed to the assault beaches of the Second Front and there serve as front-line refuelling stations for the fighter aircraft supporting the invasion. He even had a code name for the project, "Habakkuk," derived from Habakkuk 1:5, "Behold, ye among the heathens, and regard, and wonder marvellously: for I will work a work in your days, which ye will not believe, though it be told to you." Taking out a pistol, Mountbatten prepared to demonstrate the comparative strength of ice and Pykrete. Prudently the audience arranged itself behind him and he fired, first at the ordinary ice. It shattered and splintered, sending shards in all directions. Then he fired at the Pykrete. The block was completely undamaged, but the bullet bounced off and bounded about the room like an enraged hornet. The advisers still waiting behind the closed doors were startled to hear the shots. "My God," one wit quipped, "Now they are shooting at each other." Not all the spectators were convinced by Mountbatten's demonstration and though some experimentation followed on an isolated lake in Jasper, Alberta, nothing came of Habakkuk.[1]

After Mountbatten's display, Wingate took the stage with his plan to insert 26,000 troops into the guts of the enemy. He was forceful and eloquent in detailing how his long-range penetration groups were to infiltrate and how

---

[1] This incident has nothing to do with the Burma Campaign, but it has a Canadian connection, it shows Mountbatten's ever-active mind at work, and it is a good story.

they would harass the Japanese line-of-communication between Mandalay and Myitkyina, thus directly supporting Stilwell's offensive in the north and indirectly supporting Slim's planned offensive on the central front. The Combined Chiefs of Staff were all won over, the Americans particularly pleased that Wingate all but promised the reconquest of northern Burma and the reopening of the Burma Road.

Enthusiasm for the new Chindit expedition peaked when Mountbatten was named Supreme Allied Commander in South East Asia for he was recognized as a strong advocate of guerrilla operations and commando tactics. Churchill glossed over the fact that he was young, that he was a naval man coming to an air and land command, that his last two ships had been sunk beneath him and that his last commando venture, the Dieppe raid, had not been an unalloyed success. It was enough that he was energetic, enthusiastic, imaginative, and exceedingly well-connected.

For his part, Wingate could not help but be pleased with the promises he brought home from Quebec. Churchill had given him to understand that he would have priority treatment including the right to appeal directly to the Prime Minister's Office if he encountered road blocks as he developed his second expedition. The Americans promised him what amounted to his own private air force. He was to have transport planes for full supply by air and "cab rank" fighters and bombers that he could call upon for ground support as easily as one could whistle up a cab on the streets of Manhattan. Most importantly, the wounded would no longer have to be abandoned in the jungle; there would be light planes capable of landing in small rough clearings to evacuate them from the very field of battle. All these promises were fulfilled. A new unit was formed within the USAAF to serve the Chindits. Philip Cochran, already famous and bemedalled for his victories in North Africa and widely known in the United States as Flip Corkin, the hero of the comic strip "Terry and the Pirates," was named commander of the group. Casual, affable, and thoroughly capable, he was in many ways the exact opposite of Wingate. Cochran chose as his co-commander his quieter friend, Bob Alison. With such strong support and rich patronage, Wingate returned to India to train his second Chindit Expedition.

By the end of February the momentum of the Arakan campaign was firmly in favour of the British and by the beginning of March Wingate was ready to launch his second Chindit expedition. Whereas 3000 men and 1000 animals had gone in on the first Chindit penetration, there were to be 16,000 men and 3600 animals on this one. The same sort of training preceded it — demanding route marches, night schemes, river crossings, jungle deployment, bush craft, bivouac practice, patrolling, unarmed combat — but this time the troops were more carefully chosen and something new was added, practice in emplaning and deplaning from a glider, for this expedition, or at least the greater part of it, was to be introduced into the enemy's rear by air.

When Wingate pondered all that the 1943 experience had taught him about long range penetration, two problems fretted his mind. First, given the much greater size of this new expedition, could the RAF afford him air supply and tactical support in the massive quantities he would now need? He knew the answer to that question was NO. The second question was more difficult: How could he avoid that heart-rending situation that required a field commander to abandon his sick and wounded along the line of march? General Hap Arnold, the American Chief of Air Staff, answered both questions — he would provide transport planes for supply, bombers and fighters for tactical support, light planes for jungle rescue. Thus the 5318th Provisional Unit (Air), later renamed the 1st Air Commando in recognition of Mountbatten's previous commando activities, came into being. There was no establishment table for such a force, so the two commanders, Cochran and Allison, held long talks with Wingate and Mountbatten, then, assured of Hap Arnold's full support, dreamed up their own: 12 Mitchell bombers (B25s), 30 Mustang fighters (P51s), 25 Dakotas (C47s), and 150 light planes, Stinson L5 Sentinels and Vultee L1 Vigilants. A few Sikorsky helicopters were included. They had a range of only eighty miles, but here was a chance to test them in combat operations.

While they were gathering their fleet, Cochran and Allison became aware of gliders as an adjunct to air transport. At the time the USAAF was experimenting with huge cargo–carrying gliders — and so was the RCAF. In June 1943 S/L Fowler Gobeil, a sixteen-year veteran with the RCAF, teamed up with an RAF pilot to test the radical notion that a tug and glider train could be used to ferry freight across the Atlantic. S/L Gobeil flew the glider, while F/L W Longhurst, a Canadian in the RAF, captained the Dakota tow plane. In his crew were a New Zealand navigator and co-pilot, a Canadian wireless operator, and an RAF flight engineer. The flight was not uneventful. On the first day they met winds that so buffeted them that it took all the strength of S/L Gobeil and his co-pilot to control the glider. On the second day they discovered that one strand of the tow rope was dangerously frayed. On the third day they entered fog so thick that they could not see the tug and had to position themselves by the "angle of the dangle" of the tow rope.

Even when they reached England their troubles were not over. First they had to extricate themselves from an unexpected entanglement with barrage balloons, and then they had to circle while waiting for a newsreel camera plane sent to record their feat. Finally they gave up on the camera plane and touched down at Prestwick, 28 flying hours and 3500 miles after they had left Montreal. They had demonstrated two things — first, that a load of aircraft spares and vaccines for Russia could be delivered by glider train

across the Atlantic, and second, given the expense, the extreme danger
and the minimal pay load, it was a feat hardly worth duplicating. The Waco
Glider, christened "VooDoo," lived up to its name. On the flight that was to
take it to London to be displayed in the British National Museum "VooDoo"
crashed and was completely destroyed.

Cochran and Allison were probably not aware of this story when they
selected gliders for inclusion in their air force. What interested them was
the possibility of delivering heavy equipment for building airstrips and big
guns for artillery defence into the field of battle by air. When Mountbatten
heard that 150 gliders had been added to the transport section he and Hap
Arnold agreed that they should be used to fly the troops in.

On his way home from his London talks with Wingate, Cochran stopped
off in Ottawa long enough to become intrigued by a unique plane he
saw there. It was called the Noorduyn Norseman, a rugged, dependable
workhorse much favoured by the bush pilots of the Canadian North. It
could carry 2000 pounds of cargo on a single engine, land on a 2000 foot
strip and cruise at 160 mph. (The Air Commando pilots who flew it joked
that it rotated, cruised, climbed, descended and landed at 160 mph.) Back
in Washington, Cochran learned that the USAAF had already ordered 14
Norsemen, UC64's in USAAF nomenclature. He said he wanted them, and
he got twelve. Because they were a single engine aircraft and had the same
Wright engine as some of the advanced fighter trainers, Cochran recruited
fighter pilots to fly them. One of them registered his consternation – and
his conversion: "Here we were checking out in one of the ugliest airplanes
known to man after completing training in the sleekest aircraft in the
Air Corps inventory, the P-51. It wasn't long however, before we began to
appreciate why they had selected the UC-64 aircraft for the job that lay
ahead. It was one tough bird. It could haul four stretcher cases plus three or
four more wounded sitting on the floor." The pilots grew fond of their ugly
workhorses, giving them such names as "Grin and Bear It" and "Ramblin'
Wreck," and declaring stoutly "You can beat 'em up, but you can't keep 'em
down." The first plane to land at Broadway, the main Chindit airstrip in
Burma, was a Norseman with barbed wire for the perimeter and the second
was a Norseman bringing in Wingate for a visit. Repeatedly thereafter they
were to prove their worth, both in bringing in supplies and in ferrying out
wounded.

The addition of gliders to the flotilla ignited new ideas in Wingate's
fertile mind. If he could have heavy construction equipment, he could
make regular runways and receive regular supply flights. If he could have
artillery, he could defend the runways and the supply flights. Thus was
born the notion of static defended bases in place of the hit-and-run tactics
of his earlier expedition. With that ease of Old Testament reference that

seems inborn in senior British officers he reached back into Zechariah 9: 12, "Turn ye to the strong hold, ye prisoners of hope" and christened these defended bases "strongholds." He further decreed that the motto of the strongholds should be "No surrender," and for their protection he set up "floater" columns that were to operate outside the stronghold and act as the hammer to crush attackers against the anvil of the defence perimeter.

Now began an intense period of planning and practising. There were thousands of details to be attended to, moon schedules, weather considerations, mule loading, troop emplaning, weight calculations, loading tables, glider training, takeoff timetables, traffic control, dispersal orders, defence platoons, sector familiarization, water supplies, radio protocol. Nothing could be left to chance or improvisation. And yet in the end something was bound to go wrong and only improvisation could save the day.

With the planning as complete as it could be, the date for the actual fly-in was set. It was entrusted to Troop Carrier Command, a combined RAF and USAAF force, and given the code-name *Thursday*. In the weeks preceding the fly-in, a thorough air reconnaissance of the target areas had been made, each photo flight being disguised as a bombing or strafing mission. In the last fortnight Wingate absolutely forbade any flights in the area with the argument that nothing should be done to alert the enemy to their interest in it. As the day grew closer, the Air Commandos grew increasingly anxious. Surely it would be prudent to make one last check on the landing grounds? Daily they begged Cochran until on the very day of the departure he agreed to a secret foray across the clearings. There were two landing spots, one named Broadway in deference to the American contingent, the other Picadilly to honour the British contribution. The Mitchell bomber turned over Broadway and took its pictures. There was nothing untoward. But at Piccadilly something was wrong. Great teak logs lay patterned across the entire landing area. Frantically the Mitchell took its pictures and streaked for home. It was mid-afternoon when the pictures were developed and takeoff was scheduled for six o'clock. They came into the hands of Wingate, Slim, and Cochran just two hours before the fly-in was to begin.

For just a moment Wingate was furious that his strict injunction against photography had been disobeyed, then he realized how fortuitous that disobedience had been. Had the Picadilly landing gone ahead, all the gliders would have crashed. Still the big question loomed — was this sabotage, the work of the enemy, or merely teak foresters at work? If the decision was to avoid Picadilly and put everyone in on Broadway, was that just the decision the enemy was trying to force on them? Were the Japanese lurking in the shadows of Broadway and waiting for the Chindits to fly into their trap? Take-off time was now an hour away. A decision had to be made. The moon was right, the troops were sizzling with eagerness, months of planning and preparation waited on the word. It was now or never. And if it was never, the soundness of Wingate's theories would never be tested.

The leaders, Wingate, Cochran, Slim, anxiously scanned the pictures and debated what should be done. To this day there is hot and partisan debate as to whether Slim or Wingate made the final decision, but for us it is sufficient to know that the conclusion was that the show must go on and that all the troops would land at Broadway.

All was ready on the runways of Lalaghat. Long lines of nylon rope were laid out in neatly parallel rows, gliders were loaded with light bulldozers and graders, jeeps, generators, wireless equipment, anti-aircraft guns, ammunition, airfield lighting and all that planners could envision needful. Mule stalls or tiedowns had been installed, troops and animals carefully assigned and lined up to enter their designated aircraft, the troops more eagerly than the animals. Every load had been meticulously manifested, all weight distribution arranged. Thirty Dakotas and 52 Waco gliders were ready to take to the air. There was an hour's delay to rebrief the crews for landing on Broadway alone, and then the greatest armada of aircraft, gliders and troops that the war had thus far seen began its journey. It was still light when the take-off began, but the dust was so thick that each aircraft had to be preceded by a jeep speeding down the runway with an officer holding a flashlight to guide the pilot. The Dakotas throbbed upwards in circles over the drome, struggling to gain the 8000 feet of altitude that would enable them to clear the Chin Hills. Then they turned eastward toward the Chindwin.

The glider train had not crossed the Chindwin before the pilots in the tow planes and even more the pilots in the gliders realized that things were going wrong. The first planes were all double tows and it was soon evident that, no matter how well this strategy had worked in practice, it was not advisable with a full load over the Chin Hills. The gliders on a double tow could not see each other and were always in danger of colliding. At one moment they could be well above the tow plane and seconds later below it. Sometimes they were struggling along at the full stretch of their rope and then pitching forward to overtake their tow. Even the single tow gliders were having trouble. There were moments of smooth sailing and then severe pitching and yawing to the extent that the glider became unmanageable. Tow ropes began to break, gliders released in panic.

Major Faulkner, despite his conclusion that one would have to be a bit daft to be a Chindit, had volunteered again. It seemed, however, that he was doomed not to make the journey. He was assigned to glider P15, an unlucky start since the "P" meant the glider was intended for Picadilly. Then the pilot originally nominated to fly it in had been injured in a jeep accident. Finally, Jean, Brigadier Mike Calvert's pet pony, had inadvertently put her foot through the glider floor. The whole crew had to switch to a new glider at the last moment. (Except for Jean; she was downgraded to a Dakota.) They had scarcely cleared the Chindwin when the gyrations of the glider became uncontrollably violent. The pilot called one man, then two, then six, then everyone forward in an attempt to redistribute the weight and stabilize the trim. It didn't work. The tow rope whipped and snapped across the windscreen, the glider tried to loop, the glider pilot felt the tail was about to break off. He pulled the release and the glider dropped like a stone toward the jungle below.

They made a decent landing in a small clearing and while the glider commander, Colonel Peter Fleming, arranged the burning of the orders and ciphers, Major Faulkner reconnoitered the area. He found they had landed within a 100 yards of a well-used road along which ran a telephone line, signs of a Japanese encampment nearby. Hurriedly they took stock – six officers, seven British other ranks, one Indian other rank, ample arms and ammunition, three compasses, and K rations for eight days.[2] Fleming made two decisions; first, they would immediately go on half rations, and second, their best bet was to head west across the Chindwin and go back to their own lines. Because the tow plane had done the navigating, they were not at all sure of their whereabouts and they only had large scale maps. Still, they knew they wanted to go west and they headed in that direction or at least as nearly in that direction as the obdurate terrain would allow.

For the first day they followed a track in order to distance themselves at once from the wrecked glider but thereafter they crept through the jungle, Colonel Fleming leading with a recce group and Major Faulkner bringing up the rear. For eight days they marched on, carefully skirting around each native village and avoiding the well-worn trails. One day they circled behind an outpost manned by a lone Japanese soldier attending the call of nature. Fleming described the scene: "He was gazing intently towards the centre of the clearing and his buttocks offered, at 250 yards, a target which it required the strongest sense of duty to forgo."

On the eighth day they reached the Chindwin and saw before them a dispiriting sight, a half mile of brown water flowing between high banks, and no boats. Major Faulkner was not daunted. Under his direction they began to build an ingenious raft. He ordered that their eight packs be wrapped in three of their four groundsheets, with the K rations on the bottom for buoyancy. Then this bulk was encased in a bamboo frame

---

[2] K rations were the American emergency food packs. Made up in breakfast, lunch and dinner format each in a package a bit smaller than an ordinary brick, they contained a small tin of scrambled egg or processed meat, powdered coffee, sugar, a dried fruit bar, a few hard crackers, a small swatch of toilet paper and matches. They were in a box of heavy waxed cardboard that served also as a fire starter. At first the British (and Canadians) were enthusiastic about K rations, but after three days, enthusiasm waned markedly.

and covered with the fourth groundsheet. There had, however, been a miscalculation. The groundsheets let in water where they joined and the K rations were not buoyant. By now they had been three hours on a muddy strip of shore with a wide river before them and a 100 foot bank behind them. Along the top of the bank there ran a main line-of-communication path that was undoubtedly in enemy possession. Coolly they tried again and by dint of swimming, using their Mae Wests, and helping each other, they got across. One man was swept away and drowned, their only fatality. They lit a fire to dry their clothes, lift their spirits and warm their shivering naked bodies. In the morning, still not sure whether they were in enemy territory or not, they probed cautiously westward and stumbled into a patrol of the Seaforth Highlanders. On March 13, a week after leaving India, the group was back where they started from. In his report Colonel Fleming made special mention of Major Faulkner "who displayed throughout coolness, good judgment and resource."

Of the 54 gliders that took off, 8 broke away and landed in friendly territory so that the crews returned. Nine crashed in enemy territory; most of these troops were either killed or taken prisoner (or both). This inadvertent and unplanned random distribution of invading troops did however have one happy side effect in that it confused the enemy altogether about the where and why of the operation. Thirty-seven gliders did arrive on the clearing at Broadway, although "arrive" is a bit euphemistic. The photos that showed Broadway to be clear of logs did not show that the innocent looking smoothness of the clearing was crosshatched with troughs and ridges, the marks left by teak logs that had been dragged across its surface. The first glider landed safely. Lt. Colonel Walter Scott, commanding the King's Regiment, jumped out and sprayed the perimeter with his Tommy gun. There was no answering gunfire. Good. Their visit was not anticipated. One after the other the gliders lined up to land. But there were obstacles hidden in the tall elephant grass — teak logs, furrows where logs had been dragged, tree stumps. The following glider hit the furrows and ridges and immediately slewed to a stop. Nor could it be cleared from the flight path for it had lost its undercarriage. The third glider, carrying Brigadier Mike Calvert, came in steeply and too fast, but its excessive speed was its salvation. "Wreckage ahead!" shouted the co-pilot, and the pilot pulled up, jumped over the impediment and landed safely beyond it. The following gliders could not avoid collisions and soon the field was littered with their battered, .twisted frames. Calvert had no option but to send back to Wingate the fateful phrase "Soya link,"[3] the code that meant "Stop the flights." Wingate

---

[3] Soya link was a meatless sausage with a sawdust taste. It was much despised by the British troops.

received the transmission at two in the morning and he waited in wretched impatience till the better word, "Pork sausage," came six hours later and the fly-in could continue.

When all the news of that first day was gathered and assessed, the sum was that 30 men had died and 33 had been injured, but 500 soldiers had arrived safely, a sufficient number to clear a proper airfield and secure its edges. Airfield lighting was installed, signal stations brought into operation, air traffic control facilities arranged, and a day after the initial landing Broadway was receiving Dakotas at the rate of one every three or four minutes throughout the night. At the end of its first week of operation 9000 troops plus animals and munitions had been set down in the middle of the Burmese jungle without any interference from the Japanese.

In general throughout the war, relations between ground forces and air forces were marked by a raw edge of resentment that sometimes bordered on hostility. In Burma the two forces worked so closely together and with such appreciation for what the other was doing that there was no room for anything but mutual admiration. Invariably when a Dakota finished a drop and headed for home the crew would look down on the soldiers in the monsoon mud and say "Those poor bastards. Thank God we don't have to live through that." For their part the soldiers would look up and say "Thanks for the rations, but I wouldn't fly into that dirty black cloud and those mountain tops for all the tea in China." On this Chindit expedition the Army-Air Force connection was even closer, for the Dakotas flew in daily and the Light Plane Force lived with the Army day by day, sharing every danger and deprivation with their land-bound brothers. During training two gliders collided and four British soldiers were killed. Sensing the guilt and remorse that could seize the American glider pilots, the British sent them a note the next day: "Please be assured we will go with your boys any place, any time, anywhere." No. 1 Air Commando very much appreciated the gesture and they took their motto from its text: Any Time, Any Place, Any Where.

To ensure that this close cooperation continued, Wingate attached an air force officer to each column. Their job was to approve the dropping zones, supervise the drops and coordinate air support. To find his air liaison officers, Wingate sent a request to various RAF squadrons for volunteers for "a secret mission." Thirty-two of these volunteers were chosen, and thirteen of them were Canadians, among them Dave Bockus, Stickney Harris, Bill Kempling, John Knowles, and Eric Loken. Three other Canadians starred in Wingate's second expedition — Major Faulkner, who rejoined the Chindits once he had recovered from his walk-out from the crashed glider, Ian MacPherson, a young man from Regina who had joined a Gurkha regiment upon graduation from RMC, Kingston and who was especially chosen by Major Mike Calvert for the expedition, and Corporal Neil Turnbull, an RCAF radio technician from Leamington, Ontario, who was to be the column's radio operator. The adventures of these eight Canadians cover well the story of the Second Chindit Expedition.

Dave Bockus had scarcely been two months on 67 Squadron when the request came round for aircrew who were willing to volunteer for certain unspecified special duties. It sounded like adventure, and that appealed to Dave. Moreover, the offer promised immediate promotion to Flight Lieutenant. He applied and was attached for training to the King's Regiment (Liverpool), commanded by Colonel Walter Scott. As the March departure date approached, fate intervened — an unfortunate training accident left him with a broken ankle. The medical officer put a cast on it and delivered the verdict: "With that injury, you're unfit for jungle service." The cast wouldn't harden and Dave ripped it off. The doctor put on a second cast. It too wouldn't harden. Dave tore it off and hobbled away to find a second opinion. The doctor to whom he appealed was Major Faulkner. He found a sympathetic listener for not only were both from Belleville, Ontario, but Faulkner confessed that he too had once had a broken leg and had impatiently torn off the cast. Nevertheless his verdict echoed the previous doctor: "You can't go."

Disconsolate, and still hoping, Dave haunted the airfield on take-off day. He watched when Phil Cochran jumped up on the hood of a jeep and announced, "Fellows, we've got a better place to go!" but he realized it didn't apply to him. Even though he accepted that he was not going to be a Chindit, he couldn't leave the strip. He walked out to the flight line with Dick "Tex" Kuenstler, one of the American glider pilots. 'I'm gonna need help tonight," said Tex, "I wish you were going with me." "Well," said Dave, "Why don't I? What's your weight?" "Weight's no problem. Let's go!" And that's how Dave ended up in Burma despite the doctors' veto.

As they bumped through the dark turbulence over the Chin Hills, Tex grew uneasy. "Can you see the other glider?" he asked. "No," answered Dave, "but something's wrong because its towrope is across our windshield." Then they realized that the second glider was gone, down in the jungle. For Dave and Tex the flight went better on a single tow and an hour later they saw the bonfires of Broadway. The two had agreed that Tex would fly the glider and Dave's job would be to watch the ground and call out the height. "We're coming in too fast and too high," shouted Dave. "Get him to go round again." This they did, but still they landed hard. The undercarriage broke away and the wings were smashed; they, their mules, and their passengers stumbled out of the wreckage unhurt. Colonel Scott, the column commander was the first to greet them. He gaped when he saw Dave. "What the hell are you doing here?" Dave confessed he had stowed away, "I thought you could use some help." "Well, we could. But you're out of here tomorrow morning." It was two and a half months before Dave returned to India.

Those two and a half months were filled with adventure, beginning with the chaos of the first glider landings. Dave watched as one glider crashed on landing. In it the officer who had taken his place was killed. He saw a second glider overshoot and plunge into the jungle. The sound of the crash carried above all the turmoil on the strip. Surely a total write-off. But out of the jungle chuffed a jaunty little bulldozer. The glider had landed between the only two trees spaced to accommodate it and, though the wings had been sheared off, the bulldozer had been unharmed. That crash revealed another of the glider force's many tricks. Aware that in a rough landing, momentum would carry a heavy piece of equipment onward right through the pilot's compartment, the engineers had attached a rope to the back of the equipment so that its forward movement pulled the strap that allowed the nose compartment to fly up. The two pilots then sat high in the air while the bulldozer hurtled forward beneath them.

There was a particular irony connected with one of the crashes that night. After 18 months on Ceylon with 413 RCAF Squadron, Bob Lassiter, a schoolteacher from Chilliwack, BC, and his roommate, Stickney Harris from Chatham, NB, were getting restless. When the opportunity to go on a secret venture in Burma came round, they jumped at it. Stick was disgusted to learn that his column would walk in, while Bob was delighted to learn that he would go in by glider. Stick's adventures will be related later in our narrative; for the moment we will focus on Bob Lassiter. When Dave Bockus was taken off the mission with a broken ankle, Bob took his place. Bob Lassiter's aircraft was one of those that crashed that night and all on it were killed.

The build-up at Broadway continued apace. Immediately after the gliders were launched, a formation of 10 Norsemen set out loaded with supplies for the new garrison. Unfortunately they were not equipped for night flying and the pilots had been inadequately briefed so that in the darkness the formation lost cohesion. Some of the Norsemen turned back and then were forced by low fuel to land at a strange air strip, fortunately one held in friendly hands. Others aborted their mission and returned to base. Only two planes managed to find Broadway and drop their cargo, not an auspicious beginning for the Norseman flotilla. Next morning however the workhorse of the North redeemed itself. With better briefing and daylight to guide them, the Norsemen dropped supplies and brought in roll after roll of barbed wire, the first air supply for Broadway. On the second day a Norseman brought Wingate into Broadway for a visit.

Twenty-four hours after the Chindits first arrived, the jungle clearing was ready to welcome Dakotas and every night thereafter the lights were on and the transports lumbered in one after the other scant moments apart. Soon there were two landing strips defended by 25-pounder artillery and Bofors anti-aircraft guns with machine gun emplacements and barbed wire on the perimeter, just the stronghold Wingate had foreseen. To this point however the stronghold's defences had not been tested; the enemy was strangely reluctant to attack.

The operational intent of the Chindit force was to harass the Japanese line-of-communication between Mandalay and Myitkyina for the dual purpose of directly supporting Stilwell's offensive in the north and of indirectly supporting General Slim's planned offensive on the central front. To that end Colonel Scott and his column moved out of Broadway to blow bridges and rail lines, to ambush Japanese troops on jungle trails, to locate and destroy supply depots, to mark Japanese encampments for strategic air strikes, and even to establish a "permanent" block on the railway. Dave Bockus went with them to arrange landing spots for the light planes that would take out their wounded. He was particularly delighted by one of Colonel Scott's tricks. To lighten their load for an arduous trek through the jungle, they put their surplus explosives on a raft and sent it down the river with a carefully timed fuse. Word later came back to them that the trick had worked. The explosion had occurred right in front of a Japanese encampment and thoroughly confused the enemy.

On the whole however moments of fun were rare for an operational column away from the stronghold. If they moved down a jungle trail they had to expect an ambush around every turning. Moving overland meant crawling through damp entangled undergrowth on their bellies or hacking away iron-hard bamboo with their kukris. At times they went for two or three days without water, other times they walked through pounding rain for miles. Ammunition and explosives, food for themselves and for the mules fell from the sky as long as all the elements were propitious, but if they weren't, they went hungry. Despite all that, morale was high, in part because they believed in Wingate and in part because there was a great tingle of satisfaction in their absurdly audacious accomplishments, in blowing up a bridge 200 miles behind the enemy lines, in ambushing an unsuspecting enemy platoon on a jungle trail, in setting fire to a Japanese petrol dump. Every day the Chindit columns were giving the lie to the myth of the Japanese as elusive and invincible creatures of the forest.

While Colonel Scott and Dave Bockus were away, the Japanese had gathered to launch their long-expected attack on the Broadway stronghold. Corporal Neil "Doc" Turnbull remembers that attack. Turnbull had come out to India in October 1941, one of the many radar mechanics Canada supplied to the RAF in those early days. He was with a mobile radio unit on the Arakan front when the call came to join the Chindits. Actually, he wasn't exactly told where he was going, just posted with his crew and their equipment to Imphal for a "special assignment." "I was quite excited when I heard we were to fly with complete equipment to Imphal," Turnbull later recalled. "It sounded like something interesting and I had never been up in a plane before." They took off in the middle of the night and reached their destination at three in the morning. He remembers their arrival as "a kind of crazy business." Their plane overshot and landed up in the perimeter wire. They had to deplane by crawling along the fuselage and dropping off the tail to avoid the land mines. A squad of soldiers began to unload their equipment. A bit dazed Doc Turnbull turned to one of them, "Where are we?" "You're on Broadway. You're here to take our place. Our equipment has been bombed to bits." Turnbull found a protected corner and went to sleep. That night the Japanese launched their attack.

At first the young Canadian heard only rifle fire in the distance, then it got closer and the bullets ripped through the trees above his head. Then came the whomp of mortars and tremors that ran through the earth. The firing grew more intense and he could hear their own machine guns answering the Japanese. Turnbull worried about his equipment but he had been ordered to stay in the slit trenches and leave the fighting to the Gurkhas. Toward dawn the battle eased. "It had been quiet for about an hour," recalled Turnbull, "when I heard the colonel's rooster crowing. It sounded so normal and domestic and out of place I could hardly believe my ears." For two days the Japanese held part of Broadway, including the part where Doc's equipment rested. On the third day a strong counterattack backed up by dive bombers retook the strip and Turnbull regained his radio. It had been in enemy hands for three days but it was still serviceable. Doc Turnbull was soon on the air and he remained on the air until the Chindits were evacuated for he and his radio were the lifeline upon which the existence of Broadway depended.

The King's New Year's Day Honour List for January 1, 1945 announced the award of the British Empire Medal to Neil Turnbull. The citation that accompanied the announcement is unusually long and detailed:

> On the 19th March, 1944 this airman, who is a radar mechanic, landed at Broadway, Burma with a crew of four operators. He was instructed to place himself and his small crew and equipment at the disposal of an American Signals Corps Lieutenant and crew whose light warning set had been destroyed by fire as a result of an air raid. Sergeant Turnbull erected the new equipment two or three miles from the strip at the edge of a small jungle clearing, but at first the results were not up to standard. On 24th March the equipment was dismantled and moved to a new site. At midnight the enemy made a heavy attack on the site and the Gurkha guard was overwhelmed. Sergeant Turnbull and his crew were

forced to retire on 31ˢᵗ March. As soon as he was able to reconnoitre the
area and inspect the equipment, which had been damaged, he decided that
the chosen site was a good one from a technical point of view, afforded
good camouflage cover from the air, and was immediately adjacent to the
fortress, thereby ensuring greater protection from the enemy ground forces.
The American personnel, including the officer, had all left and Sergeant
Turnbull was required to work on his own initiative with his small crew.
By the 3ʳᵈ April all the faults had been cleared and the damage repaired.
The equipment was kept working throughout the daylight hours, being
manned by Sergeant Turnbull and three operators until 8ᵗʰ April when
more RAF radar operators arrived. Sergeant Turnbull was faced with a
very considerable responsibility throughout and the results that he achieved
were worthy of high praise.

It will be noticed that Neil is referred to as Sergeant Turnbull whereas he refers to himself as a Corporal. The explanation for this discrepancy lies in the more generous promotion policy of the RCAF as compared to the RAF. In the records of the RCAF Neil was a sergeant and was paid at that rate, but to conform to the establishment for his unit and to avoid arousing envy among his RAF colleagues, he had to continue being a corporal.

When the Japanese attacked Broadway, the American pilots and their light planes, because they were so necessary to the expedition, were evacuated at once. Two of the little planes, unserviceable and unable to fly, fell briefly into the enemy's hands. When the Japanese were driven off, these planes were recovered almost undamaged. Dave Bockus teamed up with another Canadian pilot, Eric Loken of Kelowna, BC, and, with the help of an RAF flight sergeant, salvaged the two planes. The two airmen, one a bomber pilot and the other a fighter pilot, had never flown a Sentinel L5, but that did not stop them. They tossed a coin to see who would fly their first salvaged plane. No one can now remember who won the toss but the aircraft flew, even though they had the airspeed indicator hooked up backwards. Soon, with a revolver on one hip and a water bottle on the other, they were busy servicing the outlying Chindit columns. Reconnaissance, casualty evacuation, supply drops, communication flights, they were ready for anything.

On one occasion they stripped their Sentinel of everything strippable, even down to a minimum of fuel, and flew out to rescue three downed light plane pilots. The rescued pilots threw a party that night and gave Eric and Dave each an American jungle hammock. That was no insignificant gift, for accommodation on Broadway was primitive. Eric and Dave had been living in a makeshift shelter crafted of glider wreckage and parachute cloth. With the jungle hammocks they were the envy of all the British officers. Slung between two trees, the hammock kept the occupant off the wet ground and free from snakes, ants, and rats. It also had a canvas cover to shed rain and a built-in mosquito netting.

Dave and Eric longed for a Canadian flag; people kept calling them Englishmen or Yanks.[4] The best they could do was to paste the front page of *Wings Abroad*, the newspaper published for RCAF personnel overseas, onto the side of their plane. Flying an unmarked aircraft that officially did not exist on missions that were unauthorized and unrecorded, Dave and Eric made a total of over 260 flights, supply drops, reconnaissance sorties, jungle rescues. Even today Dave has a vivid memory of one of those rescue missions.

Word came back to the stronghold that a patrol was surrounded and beset and that they would have to leave one of their wounded behind as they escaped. Dave knew the man and he radioed: "Can you hang on till we get there?" the word came back: "We can hold on for forty minutes." In just under forty minutes Dave and Erik landed their little plane in a field by the village. The men of the patrol dumped the wounded man in the back of the plane, tied him in, then fled into the jungle even as the enemy appeared at the end of the field. The little plane was hit three or four times as it sped down the paddy and skimmed over the heads of the Japanese soldiers. As they flew homeward, Dave turned to check his passenger. The wounded man was very pale, his eyes were closed and his breathing was shallow. Then Dave heard him speak; "Is that you, Dave?" "Yeah." "I knew you'd come for me." As Dave remembers it, there was a long silence and a choking feeling came over him, for the Chindit had said something that was best left unsaid.

On April 26, almost six weeks after Dave first arrived at Broadway, two American pilots asked him to go with them to bring out three passengers stranded on a small strip just over the border into China. Since Dave had been there before and they hadn't, he agreed to go. They found the strip, but scarcely had they landed than they discovered it was threatened by an enemy patrol. The first L1 got off with his passenger but Dave's L5, smaller and less powerful, crashed on the short, rough strip. The second L1 could take both the passengers, but that was all. "Sorry Dave, no room for you." All this activity had brought the enemy troops to the clearing and Dave dived into the jungle. He lurked nearby, knowing that hundreds of miles of unmapped, impenetrable geography separated him from home and he had no equipment except for a revolver, two hand grenades and his camera. Clearly his best chance for rescue was to be picked up here. He crouched and watched as the Japanese burned his plane, then found a more secure lair for the night.

[4] Bill Towill makes this mistake when in his book *A Chindit's Chronicle* he ascribes Eric's and Dave's exploits to "our own two attached RAF officers,"

Next morning Eric Loken came over in the other L5 but wisely decided against landing, especially since Dave, well aware that the Japanese patrols were still around, did not dare make any sign. He did sneak back for a quick picture of his burned-out plane then he joined some Chinese working in a poppy field. They brought him together with another lost soul, a British cavalry officer named Kennedy. The two spent the next night in a field worker's hut. Dave calls it an opium den, but every labourer's basha was an opium den since opium was the preferred currency of the area. Dave and Kennedy took turns sleeping and when one of the Chinese, a surly, unfriendly fellow, slipped out in the middle of the night, Kennedy became suspicious and suggested it would be advisable for them to slip out as well. They had heard of an American guerrilla outfit off to the northeast and they made their way toward it. Enemy patrols were frequent in this area. Once they hid so close to a Japanese encampment that they were able to steal some rice, a welcome theft, for the jungle provided very little sustenance. Kennedy says that one Japanese actually stared right at him for a moment and then turned away with a shrug.

They were shivering with cold and ravenously hungry when they finally found Pete Joost, the American guerrilla leader. Joost was one of those legendary figures to whom unimaginable adventures seem to come unbidden. He was actually Sherman B. Joost, erstwhile captain of the Princeton University Boxing team, urbane, cheerful and confidently competent in all manner of things. Here in China he was Area Commandant for an OSS Detachment[5] and a liaison officer with Cochran's No. 1 Air Commando. Dave was tempted to stay with Pete. The water was good up here in the mountains, there were no flies, no commanding officers to worry about, and, if you were a bit careful, you could always outwit the enemy. But duty called, and eventually Dave got a flight back to Broadway. Nine days after he set out for Sim'pa he was at work with his little L5 again.

As the monsoons increased, it became clear that the Chindits could not operate much longer. Dave flew Eric out to Ledo, all skin and bones and only half conscious. Dave too was suffering from malaria and dengue but he continued his work for there were still "casualties, casualties, casualties" to be picked up from "sweat-it-out strips." Somewhere around May 22 he flew his last rescue mission and was evacuated to India, two and a half months after Colonel Scott had ordered him to get out on the next plane. By July he was back with 67 Squadron flying Spitfires.

Even in the comparative quiet of the Squadron, Dave found life eventful. In mid-January 1945 he lost his engine while escorting a flight of bombers

[5] The OSS, the Office of Strategic Services, was an American behind-the-lines operation particularly interested in recruiting indigenous guerrilla troops. It was especially active in China and northern Burma.

and bailed out over the sea. His wing man had seen what had happened and radioed a mayday. Dave was drifting to shore in the dinghy when the rescue plane landed. Bob Day, the Canadian CO of 67 Squadron, stuck his head out and shouted: "What the hell are you doing sitting in that goddam thing? Don't you know we've got ops to fly?" Dave got out of the dinghy and went right back to flying. In the Air Force there were sometimes mutterings about "awards that are just handed out with the rations." Dave Bockus's DFC was not one of these.

While most of the Chindits were flown into Burma either in gliders or in Dakotas, Brigadier Bernard Fergusson's column elected (if that is the right word) to make the journey on foot. Two Canadian airmen, Stickney Harris and John Knowles, walked with them. In March 1940 Stick Harris was working in Chatham, New Brunswick. He had already applied for pilot training with the RCAF and been told he would have to wait. When a Mobile Recruiting Unit came to Chatham he decided he had waited long enough and signed up as a Wireless Operator/ Air Gunner. The recruiting officer assured him he could always remuster to pilot when his call came through. The call came four years later. By that time, Stick was in Burma and about to walk 200 miles behind the Japanese lines. It was no time to consider going back to Britain or Canada for pilot training. He would just keep being a wireless operator.

Stick's column left from Ledo and covered the first ninety miles by truck on the road that the U S Army Engineers were building to connect to the Burma Road at Bhamo. It wasn't much of a road yet, deep ruts in a foot of mud, but it was heaven compared to what was to come. The audacity of Fergusson's plan is startling — 400 miles on foot over jungle swamp, steep mountains, and angry rivers, and most of it through enemy-occupied territory. They left Ledo on February 4 and they did not cross the Chindwin until March 5, the day the other columns were preparing for the fly-in. Like all the Chindits, Stick was carrying more than seventy pounds on his back and other appurtenances hung variously about his person when he jumped from the truck and began the long trek. "We marched for an eternity over those Naga Hills." Stick recalls. "It wasn't so much the climbing as the descending. That played havoc with my knees." The steepness of the trail was appalling. On one march they only advanced one and a half miles but they ended a mile higher than they began — that's a gradient of 67%. Stick remembers slopes where they had to unload the mules, carry the mule packs to the top of the mountain, and then go back and push the mules up. Stumbling, slithering, sometimes even crawling on their knees, the column stretched out like an elastic over 65 miles. The first to arrive at the night's bivouac were fed and bedded down before the end of the column came in. And then Stick, as the leader of the wireless group, had to set up his radio, establish wireless communication through the crackle of static, code and send outgoing messages, receive and decode incoming messages. He got to sleep as the sun was coming up and the column was stirring for the next day's march.

Eventually they reached Aberdeen,[6] the stronghold they were to operate from, and Stick took up his duties, arranging for air drops, controlling the air traffic on the strip, and supervising the wireless communication with the base in India. All the flights came in at night and Strip remembers the unending stream of Dakotas and Norsemen landing in one direction and taking off in the other, each trying to break the record of an 18 minute turnaround. The strip was short, barely 600 yards long and had an awkward hill at one end; there were four or five Dakotas piled up in a heap of wreckage at the other end. The Japanese air force attacked and several troops were killed but it was the enemy soldiers sniping at them from the surrounding hills that they most feared. Brigadier Fergusson and his company moved out to begin the guerrilla operations they were there to do. In his book *The Wild Green Earth* he wrote: "To maintain communications with me, I left an RAF wireless set at Aberdeen under an amusing Canadian Air Force officer called Stick Harris." Commenting on that word "amusing," Stick says, "The Brigadier was a great guy. We used to laugh at his monocle at first, but we got used to it. He was full of fun in the Mess in our training days."

Stick remembers a platoon of West African troops coming into the stronghold: "They had their packs on their heads and their rifles and boots on top of their packs. It was said they could walk a mile with their boots on and another twenty when they took them off." He also remembers General Wingate asking him to arrange a flight back to India. "We can't fly you out today, sir. The ceiling is too low." "Get one of your light planes to fly me to the American strip at White City," snorted Wingate. "They will fly me out." Stick remembers that encounter very well for it was March 24, the day Wingate died in an air crash.

Stick did not last out the campaign. Before Fergusson returned he was ordered out by the Medical Officer because of his malaria. After convalescing in India he was repatriated to England and by the fall of 1944 he was back in Canada.

John Knowles too remembers the trek from Ledo to Aberdeen. John was an American, born in Manhattan, brought up in Brooklyn. The United States was not yet in the War when John, barely turned 18, took the train to Toronto and joined the RCAF. It was June 1941. In June 1943 he was flying Hurricanes with 146 RAF Squadron in Burma. When in December 1943 the call came round for volunteers for a long-range penetration group, he

[6] Brigadier Fergusson was from Aberdeen.

stepped forward. Two months later he jumped off a truck at the end of the Ledo Road, listened to a prayer service and a couple of rousing hymns led by General Orde Wingate and then began the wretched march across the Naga Hills. John remembers his pack as weighing a good deal more than 70 pounds: "After an air-supply drop it would take two men to lift your pack onto your back. You'd get on your knees so they could put it on you and then you would gradually straighten up." But it was the hills that did them in. For the troops they were invariably "them fuckin' hills." That is how John Knowles remembers them too: "We were pretty thoroughly exhausted physically. It was, above all, the three-week slog through the hills that did it. Having carried up to 100 pounds through 400 miles of the worst conceivable terrain, we were walking skeletons, without reserve energy and subject to hallucinations." John kept hearing an orchestra playing one tune over and over. Ironically the tune was "I'll walk beside you."

Soon after the column reached its area John was ordered to go back to the Brigade HQ and go to a certain basha. Within he came face to face with Orde Wingate himself. After a few curt "pleasantries," Wingate pointed to a huge map that covered the floor like a carpet and asked "Where are we?" John asked for permission to get down on his hands and knees. "Never mind!" snapped Wingate. "We're here." Then he ordered John to reconnoitre a marked area and ascertain if it was suitable for a light plane landing strip. The area was suitable and soon Aberdeen had its first landing strip. While Stick, the amusing Canadian, was left behind with the wireless, John moved out with Fergusson and the column to undertake the mission that was assigned to them, the capture of Indaw, an all-weather air strip and a central Japanese supply point. Wingate wanted the attack to go in right away so, tired as they were, they set off to butt their way through fifty miles of lantana scrub and spiny bamboo.

On March 26, they found a good spot for an ambush, a small hill whose face sloped gently down and ended in a three-foot drop onto the road. Here they dug in and waited. A Japanese staff car came by. It could be a high ranking officer carrying battle plans and troop dispositions, or it could be a decoy to tempt them to reveal themselves. They let it pass. At 2:30 in the morning a convoy came, twenty-five or thirty trucks crammed with soldiers. Flame throwers at either end of the 1000 yard long ambush flared, trucks accordioned into one another, screaming Japanese soldiers fell and jumped onto the road. Aware that the attack was coming from the slope, they ran into the scrub on the lower side, and straight into the minefield Fergusson's sappers had prepared for them. John Knowles heard Japanese voices below him trying to organize and regroup. He dropped a grenade into their midst — and nothing happened. The satisfying *whump* of his companion's grenade somewhat compensated. The fighting abated and

John heard one of the Chindits further down the slope crying for help and crawled down to rescue him. The soldier was heavier than John reckoned. Half dragging, half carrying his comrade, he struggled up the hill, almost unaware of the rifle and machine gun fire that beat angrily around him. At the top he tried to comfort the wounded man, but it was no use. He died a short time later.

The ambush had been successful. The Chindits estimated the enemy dead and gathered what intelligence they could from the wreckage of the trucks. From the paymaster's vehicle they grabbed thick bundles of worthless "Government of Japan" paper currency and threw them gleefully into the air. Then they tended their wounded, buried their six dead, and set off to renew the attack on Indaw. They later learned that the Japanese had exhumed the British dead, strung them up by their ankles, and used them for bayonet practice.

The battle for Indaw did not go well. Although Fergusson had marched in without alarming the enemy, another Chindit column had moved through the area just the week previous aiming at a different objective. To disguise their intentions and mislead the enemy they had told the locals they were headed for Indaw. Thus the town was prepared and reinforced when Fergusson's attack went in. About this time news of Wingate's death came to the Column. It was unthinkable! Wingate was not merely the leader of the whole operation, he was its messiah, its spiritual embodiment. John's reaction echoed that of many Chindits: "We had tremendous faith in him. You just knew that as long as he was there everything was going to be fine and when we heard he'd been killed we thought 'Oh God, what's going to happen to us?'"

After a few more weeks the authorities back in India realized that Fergusson's men were at the point of collapse and in mid-May they were flown out from Broadway. John went back to England by ship and eventually back to Canada and to civvie street. But many things had changed for John Knowles. The Chindit from Brooklyn had become a Canadian citizen even before the war ended. And the Air Force Flight Lieutenant had developed an affection for the British Army: "I really loved my regiment, The Queen's, Second of Foot in the British Army Order of Battle — notwithstanding the fact that our battle honours included burning the White House in the War of 1812." After the war, John joined the Canadian Foreign Service and for a time even served as Canadian Consul and Trade Commissioner in Chicago.

It is almost a miracle that Bill Kempling ended up as a Chindit in central Burma. As an eight year old in Grimsby, Ontario he contracted a severe case of polio and was left with a twisted leg. At the doctor's one day he was intrigued by a cage of squirrels at the bottom of the garden. "Billy," said the doctor, "when you can walk to that cage, I'll let you feed the squirrels." With endless hours of massage and exercise and with sheer grit, Bill walked down and fed the squirrels. Polio struck the Mustard family in the house next door and they were quarantined; no one was allowed in or out. A knock came at the door and there stood Billy Kempling. "I've had polio, Mrs. Mustard. I can run errands for you." The Mustard house became his second home. Bill left school at the age of 16 and took a job in a knitting mill at 9½ cents an hour to help his family. When the war came he joined the Air Force. During training he worked twice as hard as the other recruits so he could graduate with his Wireless Operator/Air Gunner wing and with a high school diploma.

Bill's first operational flying was on the Murmansk run, escorting shipping around the tip of Norway and into the icy Russian port. Then he spent a short time in Palestine keeping the Nazis and the Zionist guerrillas at bay. In 1943 he was posted to an internal ferry squadron at Karachi. It was not an exciting job and he and his roommate often talked of looking for something livelier. One night he came home from another routine flight to find a merry party in the Mess. "What are we celebrating?" he asked. The answer was surprising: "Two crazy guys have volunteered for a secret mission, and you're one of them."

Bill Kempling never said much about his time with the Chindits in Burma, but he did have vivid memories of the walk out. Unlike the Chindits on the First Expedition, most of the Second Expedition Chindits were flown out from Broadway or from the other strongholds, but Bill, ordered to lead one section, put his wounded and seriously sick on the last plane out and then, with 35 others, began the trek home on foot. Bill claims the journey took six months. The monsoon was in full force so that it was either raining in endless deluge or so hot and humid they could scarcely breathe. For a time they walked at night and slept during the day, then it didn't seem to matter and they just walked. Walked, walked, walked. Up one hill and down again, then up the next hill and down again. One foot after the other, eyes on the ground, seeing nothing but the heels of the guy ahead, Bill separated his mind from his body and tried to let his body lift one foot and put it down while his mind did math problems or thought of good things to eat. He had malaria and dysentery. He just took off his pants and walked on. The Air Force tried to drop supplies but usually could not find his little troop and so they went hungry. When they came to a village they would lurk and watch to gauge whether it was safe to enter. If they entered they sometimes got food and sometimes were quickly chased away by villagers who feared, with good reason, that the Japanese would kill them if they helped the British.

One day in near-delirium Bill thought he heard Bing Crosby singing and feared that he had lost his mind. Around the next turn in the jungle track they came upon a small village and an old tribesman winding up an ancient gramophone he had inherited from a missionary. Some of the men gave up and just quit or even shot themselves. Bill understood that: "I tried to encourage them, but our case looked pretty hopeless and dysentery is a very depressing disease." Others were drowned crossing spated rivers, others just simply died. "It always bothered me," Bill said, "why some committed suicide and others didn't. Some would appear to be all right mentally and then you'd hear a gunshot and he'd blown his brains out." Feebly, he tried to make a joke out of what is obviously a dark memory within him: "I buried so many people, I thought I'd be a mortician when I got home." Of the 35 men who started together, only six reached India. Bill weighed 160 pounds when the trek began. He weighed 120 when it ended.

Bill entered federal politics after the war and for twenty-one years he was the Conservative member for Burlington, twenty-one years with an unblemished record of honest, conscientious public service. For a time he was party whip in the Mulroney government. "Was that a hard job?" some one asked. Bill thought for a moment, remembering the walk out, and then he grinned: "Let's just say that Question Period was a yawn after that." In Burma the column had captured two badly wounded Japanese soldiers. Bill tended them and one, in his last moment, gave Bill a set of chopsticks in a leather case and his personal flag, the Japanese Red Sun flag signed by friends and relatives. Many years later, when Bill accompanied a Canadian Trade Mission to Tokyo, he took the souvenirs of Burma with him for he had always harboured the notion of some day returning the flag to the dead man's family. As a result of front page publicity in the Tokyo papers, the man's sister was found. Before a formidable battery of Japanese microphones Bill returned the flag to a tearful woman. As grateful as she was to have the flag, she was even more grateful to learn that her brother had died on the battlefield for his Emperor.

Wingate's original intention for his Chindit columns was that they should haunt the enemy's rear, harassing lines of communication and supply and then disappearing into the jungle, all in support of a main offensive being fought in the traditional way. This corresponded with Slim's understanding of their role. Once Wingate was seized by the stronghold concept however, he could not let go. More troops, more support, grander objectives, there was no end to his demands, and all backed up by threats of a direct appeal to Churchill and Roosevelt. It seemed that in Wingate's mind, the concept of long-range penetration had become reversed. Rather than harassing the enemy's rear to support the main offensive, the Chindits were the main offensive and action elsewhere was supporting them. Eventually General Slim balked and called his bluff. When Wingate again uttered his threat to contact Churchill directly, Slim pushed a message pad across the desk.

Wingate reneged. But he already had a far more extensive behind-the-lines operation than had originally been conceived. At various times and for varying periods there were four strongholds complete with air strips, a forward headquarters, a defence platoon, support troops, and its complement of American light planes. Each was given a code name —Broadway, Aberdeen, Chowringhee, White City. The expedition was making logistical demands that the rear echelons found almost unbearable.

Still Wingate made another demand. The strongholds were being attacked by enemy bombers and strafed by enemy fighters. He asked for, and got, a detachment of RAF Spitfires stationed at Broadway and a detachment of Hurricanes stationed at Aberdeen. John Knowles remembers the two Hurricanes at Aberdeen, both of which simply disappeared on their first flight: "I have often wondered if, when ordered to supply two Hurricanes for these operations, some very clever bastard saw it as an opportunity to get rid of a couple of clapped-out old bangers. Both Gilly and the squadron leader were top quality pilots — it had to be the machines. I could only hope they would not send in yet another one and order me to fly it." The authorities rethought the whole exercise and withdrew the detachment.

Flight Lieutenant Bob Day, the pilot from Victoria who had shot down an Oscar over the Arakan in February, led a second detachment into Broadway on March 13, but this time they had Spitfires. Even before they could find their billets, the Japanese fighter-bombers came in. The Spitfires had the advantage of surprise — the enemy had no inkling that there were fighters on the strip and Bob and his comrades tore into them with relish. As Bob tells the story: "I got a squirt at one and then went down after another one and saw flashes of cannon strike on his cockpit. Something fell from him. It may have been part of the wing. Then he rolled down in a spin with flames coming out of him, and I saw him hit the ground." The detachment's score for that day was three Oscars destroyed, one probable and six damaged. They lost one Spitfire.

When the detachment did have time to seek their billets, they found there were none. They simply draped mosquito nets over the wings of their aircraft and bedded down within. There was a small stream nearby for water and along its banks signs which read, in sequence with the water's flow: "Men drinking," "Men washing," "Mules drinking," "Mules washing," and finally, "Socks washing." For two days Day and his pilots camped out happily at Broadway but on March 17 the tables were turned and the Japanese surprised the RAF. The light radar station at Broadway had been knocked out so the attack came without warning. Three Spitfires were destroyed on the ground and a fourth before it could get to height. The remnants of the detachment were withdrawn the next day. Bob Day had come to Broadway as a Flight Lieutenant; he left as a Squadron Leader. After a tour of staff duty he was appointed Commanding Officer of 67 Squadron. He was credited with 1½ victories in the Imphal fighting and two more in later encounters. With a total of 5½ enemy planes shot down, Bob Day was awarded the DFC and, along with Tex Barrick, recognized as a Canadian air ace in Burma.

While the tow planes and gliders involved in the Operation *Thursday* fly-in on March 5 were all USAAF, there were 12 RAF aircraft assigned to drop supplies that first night. By the time Operation *Thursday* was finished a week later 9000 men, 1350 animals and 250 tons of supplies had been brought in over the heads of the Japanese. A total of 660 sorties had been flown, 329 by the USAAF and 331 by the RAF. Joe Curtiss, the 194 Squadron pilot from Alberta who had nursed his plane home on one engine over the Arakan, had done more than his share. Joe's log book reveals the tempo of their flying: on March 7 they took off at 2 in the morning and got home at 6; on March 8 they took off at 5:30 in the evening and got home at 9, then took off again about two hours later and got home at 2 am on March 9. That same day they took off again at 8 pm for a three hour flight and just before midnight they began another flight that got them home at 2 o'clock in the morning of March 10. At seven that evening they set out again and returned about three hours later. Over the four days March 7 to 10, Joe and his crew flew a total of 17 hours, all by night, all over enemy territory, in a loaded, lumbering unarmed aircraft that had a theoretical top speed of 220 mph. They had delivered 71 troops with their equipment and 15 mules.

No flight over enemy territory is uneventful, but for Joe Curtiss and his crew one sortie will always be remembered. Halfway to Broadway, one of the mules went berserk, kicking the floor and walls, frightening the other animals and threatening the safety of the plane. There was nothing for it but to shoot it. The Chindits didn't want a dead mule, so Joe brought it back. Ken Moses, the crewman for the Curtiss aircraft, tells what happened when he went to the dispersal next morning to service it:

> On this particular morning one of the lads said, "Ken, your aircraft has one hell of an oil leak from the hydraulics – it's running down the belly." I jumped off the flight 'gharri' and walked over to "C" Charlie. I looked at the oil leak, rubbed my hand in it and realized it was not oil but blood. I opened the door and looked in — there was a dead mule lying on the floor with half its head shot away. We borrowed the 'gharri' and tied a rope to the coconut matting and towed the mule down to the fuselage door. As it dropped out of the door, a fountain of blood spurted up. We towed it to the edge of the dispersal where vultures and kite hawks had all the bones clean by next day. Our problem had just begun — we had to take up the floor panels and clean the whole fuselage with Jeyes fluid and obtain a new mat from the Indian Army Service Corps. Also, whoever fired the bullets did a good job — they went through the

fuselage roof, sides and floor — the latter ones just shaving the rudder cable. The aircrew could not have known how close they were to disaster. All the bullet holes had to be repaired to the appropriate Air Ministry standard but we made it in time for our Dak 'C' Charlie to fly on ops that evening.

Joe and his crew were always very grateful to the ground crew for the good work they did. The events of this day gave them even more cause for gratitude.

Of all the Chindit strips Joe and his crew visited, Aberdeen, the one established by Bernard Fergusson near the end of the campaign, was the most challenging. It was short, not more than 600 yards long, and, because of the mountains that surrounded it, landings were made in one direction and take offs in the opposite direction. This was an awkward arrangement, and all the more so since all landings were made at night. In consequence, it was common for planes to be stacked above the strip waiting to be called down. Thus it happened that Frankie Bell, the popular Canadian flight commander with 194 Squadron, was hovering above Aberdeen when a Japanese night fighter attacked, killing two of his passengers and knocking out both of his engines. A skilled and unflappable pilot, Frankie called for immediate clearance, and coolly set about making a dead stick landing in the dark onto a 600 yard strip 6500 feet below him. His successful landing was the culmination of a masterful piece of flying. Joe and his crew brought in a load of mules and troops at three o'clock that morning and took Frankie and his crew back to base. When Aberdeen was abandoned at the beginning of May, the wreckage of some 25 Dakotas lay scattered about the strip, sad testimony to the bravery and determination of the transport crews that made the Chindit expedition possible.

While one quarter of the air force liaison officers with the Chindits were Canadians, Canadians in the Army were a rarity. Still, there was at least one Canadian with Mike Calvert at Broadway, Ian Edgar MacPherson from Regina. One of three sons born to a prominent Regina family, Ian had a happy prairie boyhood. He made his own sailboat and sailed it at the family cottage, played football for Central Collegiate, became a proficient piper and, having switched from hockey to figure skating, became sufficiently accomplished in that art to compete in local skating competitions. In 1938 he entered Royal Military College, Kingston. When war broke out, the four year course was shortened to two and Ian graduated in 1940 with a "War Certificate." He had read *Mother India* and other books about Nepal and Kashmir and the North West Frontier so he elected to be commissioned into the Indian Army. The ship that was to take him from England to India was torpedoed off the coast of Ireland. Ian suffered a severe gash on the head, but even more devastating was the loss of his bagpipes. He was rescued from a lifeboat and taken back to England to try again, this time without further difficulty.

Assigned to the 1st Battalion, 7th Gurkha Rifles, he quickly learned Gurkhali and developed a close affinity with and a lasting affection for the brave Nepalese soldiers of the regiment. They were transferred to Burma when the Japanese invaded and throughout the whole of the long retreat, the 1/7 Gurkhas were in the thick of the fight. On April 12, 1942 the War Diary records that "The tanks from a platoon of A company, led by Captain I. E. MacPherson with great gallantry, now made a fine advance into the village. Large numbers of enemy were flushed by Tommy guns and bombs. They forced their way right through the village, driving the superior numbers of enemy in front of them." In May he was sent with two companies of Gurkhas to join and take charge of a British commando party to protect the retreat across the Chindwin. The War Diary adds an ominous note: "They were ferried part of the way in a convoy of tugs and will have to make their own way back and it is not known where they will rejoin us." Hearing sounds of battle ahead of them, Ian scented action and led his troops toward it. The skirmish that followed was fierce, the losses on both sides were heavy, but Ian did succeed in scattering the enemy forces and eventually rejoining his regiment.

It seems that whenever a river was to be crossed, the 1/7 Gurkhas were called into play. At the Bilin they gave the Japanese the sort of resistance they had not yet met in the campaign. They were put out on the perimeter to protect the gathering point for the ill-fated Sittang crossing. At the Ava Bridge just below Mandalay Ian's Gurkha Regiment provided the rear guard that held off the enemy till the crossing was complete. Much the same happened again when the retreating army crossed the Chindwin at Shwegyin. Each of these encounters was ferocious and costly in terms of lives lost. When, at the end of the retreat, the 1/7 Gurkha Rifles marched into Imphal they numbered only 300 men out of a normal battalion strength of 900. At one point, all the senior officers had been killed and Ian MacPherson was the Commanding Officer. He was 22 years old, an acting Lt. Colonel, and had been mentioned in dispatches.

At some point in this adventure-filled life, Ian had a moment that took him back from Burma all the way to Regina. Somewhere in the middle of Burma he encountered Jack McGillivray, a friend from Regina, now a doctor in the Indian Medical Service. As they talked, one of Ian's Gurkha officers approached with a bottle he found in an abandoned house. Handing it to Ian, he asked, "Is this whiskey?" Ian glanced at the label. "No, it's not." The Gurkha lost interest, shrugged, and walked away. Ian and Jack sat on the bank of the stream, talked about their home town, and finished the sherry between them.

When the first Chindit expedition went in, Ian MacPherson applied to go but was rejected because he was doing uniquely important work with V Force. This was an irregular and clandestine network operating very far forward or even behind enemy lines. An Indian or British Army officer was selected to head the small encampment but its strength was in the recruitment of forest officers or missionaries who knew the region, knew the people, and knew the language. They could for example persuade coolie platoons who worked for the Japanese to reveal all they knew about troop dispositions and movements. Sometimes the informants worked for both sides, but that was all right since, as Slim slyly noted, the British offered better pay and better treatment and therefore got the better information. Because the activity of V Force developed an intelligence network that delivered information that was otherwise very hard to come by, Ian could not be spared for the 1943 Chindit campaign. For his work with V Force he was again mentioned in dispatches.

Major Mike Calvert came to know and admire the young Canadian during the retreat. When he was forming his 77 Brigade for the operation at Broadway, he determined that his Headquarters Company would be an elite outfit, the very best that courage, determination, training and discipline could deliver. In his book *Prisoners of Hope* he reiterates that conviction and then he adds: "They had a wonderful young Canadian Gurkha officer who had fought with me in 1942, and whom I had especially asked for and got. This officer, Ian MacPherson, was one of the finest men I have met. Skillful, fearless, quiet, with tremendous energy and endurance, he was a proud and worthy soldier."

When Calvert moved from Broadway to establish what later came to be known, because of the many parachutes draped over the trees in the area, as White City, Ian's Headquarters Defence company was given the place of honour, the defence of Observation Post Hill. It was also the place of prominence and the enemy mortar attacks that started each evening at 5 for the next week concentrated on it. Fortunately the enemy's mortar attacks were less lethal than the defenders' grenade defences and when the week-long series of assaults ended, the barbed wire was hung with decaying Japanese corpses. "We don't have to navigate to White City," the gallant light plane pilots joked. "We just follow the smell."

Even as the siege of White City continued, Calvert moved out to get round his attackers and get at them from behind. The defence company under Ian MacPherson went with him. Repeatedly, as they prowled through the jungle to get in position behind the enemy, Calvert sent Ian and his men out to "scupper" this or that pocket of resistance. On one occasion they came back and Ian reported he had himself killed seven of the enemy. The main action began when the column found the enemy well dug in behind a thick hedge of lantana scrub, a twining, tangling vine-like bush that clutched at clothing with prehensile insidiousness. There was no way they could penetrate the lantana and they went to ground in front of it. The Japanese laid down a murderous fusillade of machine gun fire and Calvert and his men could do little but lie there and endure it. Calvert called for an air strike, giving the Mustang fighters very explicit instructions, for the two forces were scarcely 50 yards apart. The air strike was delivered precisely where it was needed and as soon as it was over the British and Gurkhas stormed in with rifle, bayonet and kukri. The fighting that followed was fierce and furious but the Japanese casualties were heavy and the enemy broke and ran.

After the battle, Calvert asked about Ian. "He's dead," replied his brigade major. "He can't be," burst out Calvert. "He is. I saw him shot through the forehead," came the reply. Half crazed with the impact of that news, Calvert turned to go back into the battle to see for himself. "You can't go back in there. You'll get killed. Your place is here with the brigade." "I don't believe Ian is dead I've got to see," said Calvert. The brigade major pulled out his revolver and stuck it in Calvert's stomach and, with a cold earnestness, declared "I'll shoot you if you go back. I was with him when he was killed."

There can be no better epitaph for Ian MacPherson than that written by Calvert himself in *Prisoners of Hope:*

> *Ian had a wonderful end to his career. He, with his company, must have accounted for forty to fifty Japs that day. He was a slim, fey, quiet, almost lonely chap who lived for his Gurkhas and for soldiering. He would have been well decorated in 1942 if all his company officers had not been killed. His company commander told me that Ian was his best officer; Ian had scuppered a Jap machine gun by himself, running across open paddy to do it. Later in 1942, Ian, cut off as all our particular force was, chose to return through the Jap H. Q. near Shwegyin, causing havoc as he did so. His N.C.O's and men loved him, and his subahdar [Gurkha officer] was desolate for days after. One of the bravest and most carefree soldiers I ever met had been killed, but he must have taken at least a dozen Japs with him."*

In the Fall of 1944 Ian's father in Regina received two letters. The first was from Major General Lentaigne, the man who took over command of the Chindits after Wingate's death. It is an appreciative letter, but it is impersonal and in a sense official. All commanders tried to write to the families of officers who were killed serving under them. The second letter is quite different. It is from Mike Calvert, it is almost two pages long, and it is far more than a "duty" letter:

> *After ten days of attack by a Jap mixed Brigade I went out with a striking force to get them in the rear. After five days hard fighting we*

*had overrun their H.Q. and guns and had sandwiched about 2000
men between us and the block. En route I heard Japs talking in the
jungle close at hand and I sent Ian with a platoon quickly at them.
He overran them killing about twenty of which he himself killed seven.
He got a flesh wound in the arm. He carried on. The Japs later reacted
and put in a very strong counterattack. Ian was all over the place. As
we all said it was his day and he was at the top of his form. I saw
him very shortly before he was killed, and my Brigade Major was with
them then. We [censor deleted] casualties and I had to withdraw some
distance, only to find later that the Japs had also withdrawn. We went
back to bury the dead and collect the few wounded we had been unable
to carry out. Your son was buried there. I knew him well and his death
was a great personal loss to me, and, especially at the time when we
were all excessively tired, affected me most strongly. He was well liked
by all members of the Brigade and his Gurkhas would do anything for
him. After that attack of ours the Japs never attacked [the Block] again
and withdrew in haste. Our method of attack should shorten the war
out here by years and I hope it may be some consolation to you that your
son has so greatly assisted in this …. Please don't bother to answer this.
I am not very good at writing letters.*

    Yours sincerely,

    "J.M. Calvert"

Among all the audacious moves of the Chindits, White City must rank
high, for with it Calvert put a block across the railway *and* the road between
Indaw and Myitkyina[7] and held it for six weeks. The consequent inter-
ruption of their line of supply and communication to Northern Burma
infuriated the Japanese and it is no wonder that they had attacked it with
such determination and vigour. The success of the action in which Ian
MacPherson was killed ended the attacks on White City, but it also bid fair
to end the staying power of Calvert's 77 Brigade. Indeed, all of the Chindits
were now on the verge of exhaustion. Wingate had estimated that, given
the rough living conditions, the tension of being in enemy territory, the
inability to draw back for even a week of rest, the battle and constant threat
of battle, and the inadequate rations and medical care, no long-range
penetration force should serve longer than three months. Now, as May
drew to its end, the Special Force was feeling that it too was drawing to an
end. Moreover, the monsoons were already threatening. Jungle life would
then be hellish, and all attempts to move along jungle trails and up steep
mountain pitches even more hellish, The Dakota strips in the strongholds
could not be converted to all-weather and air dropping from a sky filled

---

[7] Pronounced Mitcheenuh, with the accent on the middle syllable.

with monsoon clouds was altogether unreliable. It was time for Chindit II to be withdrawn.

It was perhaps more than time for the Chindits to be evacuated. Casualties and illness, in particular malaria, scrub typhus and trench foot, had reduced many of the units by more than fifty per cent, and fifty per cent of those who were left were not fully fit for battle. But by mid-May they had fought their way so far north that they were into the Northern Combat Area and Slim handed them over to Stilwell. For the Chindits this proved to be an unhappy move.

At this point we must briefly go back to the Quebec Conference and pick up a portion of history that we have to this moment overlooked. When Roosevelt and Churchill accepted the notion of Long Range Penetration Groups they also accepted the notion of a smaller parallel American force to give the project an American flavour. This group, originally called *Gallahad,* trained with the Chindits and went in with the Chindits. As was usual with an American force, provision was made to transmit news of their activities to the folks back home and soon it was well known that Colonel Merrill and his "Marauders" were accomplishing heroic deeds behind the Japanese lines. Three thousand strong and "the only American infantry unit operationally active between Italy and New Guinea," they had marched 600 miles behind enemy lines, taken part in five major engagements and seventeen skirmishes, and won a well-deserved reputation for valour and determination. But now, at the end of April, they were as worn out and broken, as decimated and dispirited as the Chindits, and were desperately looking forward to the evacuation that had been promised to them. Stilwell, alas, had other plans.

Among the objectives Stilwell had agreed to take on was the capture of Myitkyina, the railhead, airstrip and central Japanese supply depot for Northern Burma and consequently an important target. The opinion of the British planners was that it could not be taken or, if it was, could not be held and Stilwell therefore determined to take it and to hold it. He had Chinese troops he could send to do the job, but he knew they would not do it unless they were spearheaded by an American group. The Marauders, weak, weary, mightily understrength, were nominated for that role. On May 16 they were within striking distance of the airstrip and they bivouacked for the night, resting and priming themselves for the battle next day. On the morning of May 17 they took over the strip almost without firing a shot. Stilwell was beside himself. In bold capitals he wrote in his diary: WILL THIS BURN UP THE LIMEYS!

His elation was short lived. Although transports flew in next day, they brought reinforcements and anti aircraft guns while the need was for food and ammunition. Moreover, though he held the strip, Stilwell did not hold the town, and over the next few days all efforts to take it were in vain. The Marauders, who by now had every right to be evacuated, were instead ordered to take Myitkyina. This is the point at which hatred of Stilwell reached its height and the point at which the legend gained currency of a Marauder cursing himself that he had Stilwell in his sights and didn't pull the trigger. Colonel Merrill suffered another heart attack and was flown out. Because of illness or utter exhaustion, other members of his force were being evacuated at the rate of 100 a day. By the end of May only 200 of the original force of 3000 Marauders were considered fit to carry on. Eventually even Stilwell had to concede that the Marauders were finished. He also had to concede that, until he could take the town, his victory at Myitkyina was a hollow one for Japanese artillery still covered the strip. He now ordered the Chindits to complete his conquest.

Preparatory to the taking of Myitkyina, he asked Calvert and his Chindit column to occupy Mogaung, a largish town on the railway just to the south. They were as worn out and exhausted as the Marauders, but they answered the call. For a week they fought their way northward to reach Mogaung and for four long weeks they besieged the town. Mogaung was an important junction and was therefore strongly held and heavily bunkered. A regiment of Chinese accompanied by an American Lieutenant Colonel as liaison officer joined the Chindit besiegers and was assigned a portion of the perimeter. After days of probing and pushing, of night assaults, mortar and artillery barrages, prolonged and accurate air strikes, the Chindits made their move. The fighting was close and furious as the Gurkhas and British slowly, street by street and house by house, moved through the town. Casualties were heavy. Calvert went over to the Chinese sector and asked for support but was told the regiment had no orders. He seized one of their Bren guns and demonstrated that he wanted covering fire. They grinned but did nothing. Calvert went back and led his Chindits forward till at last, on June 26, Mogaung was theirs, the first town in Burma to be recaptured.

That night Calvert was astounded to hear the BBC news announce that a Chinese-American force had retaken Mogaung. He messaged Stilwell: "Since you have taken Mogaung, we will proceed to take umbrage." Myth has it that Stilwell's staff then spent half an hour scouring the map to find umbrage. What is not myth is that the Chinese commander, on hearing of the news, came to Calvert's HQ and, in front of the American officer who had wirelessed the report to Stilwell, apologized for the announcement and said: "If anyone has taken Mogaung it is your brigade and we all admire the bravery of your soldiers." Calvert concludes the story: "He said this with great dignity, looking me in the eyes as we both stood there; then he bowed, saluted, and left."

The retaking of Mogaung had cost Calvert dearly — 250 dead and over 500 wounded, one third of his column. 77 Brigade was now truly finished and ready for evacuation. Throughout the Mogaung affair and even before, Stilwell's constant song had been that the British were cowards and would not fight. Before he left Burma, Calvert got a chance to meet Stilwell and tell of his Chindits' exploits. There was good reason to expect that it would be an awkward adversarial confrontation. Stilwell opened the meeting: "I've been wanting to meet you. You sent some pretty strong signals." "Sir," replied Calvert, "You should have seen the ones my brigade major wouldn't let me send." Stilwell roared with laughter, then listened carefully to Calvert's story of his four months behind enemy lines. In the end Stilwell wrote out citations for Silver Stars to be awarded to men of the 77 Brigade, including one for Calvert.

The peace Stilwell had made with Calvert by no means mitigated his anti-British proclivities. Myitkyina town was still to be taken. Having completely abraded the starch from Merrill's Marauders and from Calvert's 77 Brigade, he asked another Chindit column, Morris Force, to do the job even as he castigated them as cowards who would not fight. Morris Force, under Colonel "Jumbo" Morris, and Dah Force, under Lt. Col. "Fish" Herring had been brought in by glider in March to Chowringhee, a clearing east of the Irrawaddy. The two columns were to act in concert, Morris Force stirring up trouble along the road from Ledo and Bhamo to Myitkyina and Dah Force recruiting Kachin levies to back them up. Scarcely had "Fish" Herring begun operating than he felt the need for a medical officer. Major Faulkner, after having survived the crash of Glider P15 and the walk out, was "sitting on his behind" in India when Herring's frantic appeal came in. It was in his nature to accept challenges and he arrived at Chowringhee on March 27 to walk again with a Chindit column. Headquarters promised that they would drop the medical supplies he had had no time to collect himself, but they never did. Even without them, he was appreciated. In his report after the expedition ended, Herring wrote: "Of all the Medical Officers I know, I could have wished for no better than Faulkner. His presence made a great difference to the spirits of the BOR's (British Other Ranks) who were feeling a little depressed".

From mid–April on, Faulkner became Senior Medical Officer to Morris Force and he was with them when they were ordered to make their way north to assist in the taking of Myitkyina. Like all the Chindit columns, Morris Force was in sorry state even before it began the northward trek; it was much sorrier when it ended. Their route required that they cross the Shweli and then the Irrawaddy and they had no equipment for such crossings. The Brigadier ordered that they dig in as they waited for a drop and they had nothing to dig with. When the drop did come, the clearing was small and the recognition fires close together. The Brigadier ordered that they be set as regulations required. In consequence the fires were located well beyond the limits of the clearing and the bulk of the drop was lost in the jungle. One moonlit night they toiled for three hours 4500 feet up a steep, barren hillside. The temperature at the top was below freezing; during the day it had been over 100 degrees Fahrenheit in the valley. The Force skirmished with Japanese patrols and even captured a small village. A Gurkha, wounded in the stomach and holding his guts in with hands, cursed loudly at his fate. "As long as he's cursing, he'll live," said Doc Faulkner as he put him on the bamboo operating table and sewed him up. When Morris Force arrived before Myitkyina Major Faulkner estimated 60% of them were absolutely unfit for further combat and 40% were capable of limited operations only. By this time, he himself was unfit for further service. Despite taking three mepacrine tablets a day, he could not control his malaria, and in mid-July he was evacuated. In his diary he wrote: "So ended an experience that I will, under no circumstances, repeat." Major Faulkner returned to Belleville and took up his medical practice. He died in 1955 at age 47; there is no question but the Chindit experience hastened his death.

Stilwell, in part because he was unaware of the Chindits' plight and in part because he considered all Limeys malingerers, did not hesitate to conscript Morris Force into his Myitkyina Task Force and order them to take the town. They tried, and with some success, but in truth they were thoroughly worn out. Myitkyina was finally taken by Stilwell's Chinese on August 3, two and a half months after the first triumphant announcement of its capture. By that time what was left of the Chindits and of Merrill's Marauders was back in India.

The return of the Chindits was not a pretty sight. They had been put under Stilwell's command and he had used them as orthodox army units in pitched battles and thus deprived them of the jungle mobility that was their greatest strength. Moreover because he had insisted on using them well beyond their "best before" date, they had been kept in the field long after they should have been relieved. Corporal "Doc" Turnbull remembers seeing a patrol come back so hollow-eyed and gaunt that the leader marched straight into a barbed wire fence without seeming to see it. The rest of the patrol bumped into him and then all just stood there, unable to comprehend where they were or what had happened. One commander asked that his whole force be medically examined. Of a total of 2200 men, only 218 were classified fit for further active service. Every one was suffering from malarial fever and amoebic dysentery combined with a host of other infirmities and diseases: dengue fever, typhus, foot rot, trench mouth, leech ulcers, septic sores. The average weight loss was between thirty-five and forty pounds. In preparation for the march out to the evacuation point, the medical officer again examined the whole column. Some men could manage the march, some men could manage it with help, some thirty men lay more than half dead on litters. The Medical Officer shook his head. Nothing could be done for them. There is no record of who stayed behind to commit the act of mercy that ensured they did not fall into enemy hands after the column had marched out.

The withdrawal was perhaps the low point of the Chindit endeavour, but there had been high points as well. The importance of Operation *Thursday,* the fly-in, should not be underestimated, for it was a daring affront to Japanese commanders and an excellent learning ground for planners in Europe about to launch Operation *Overlord.* The whole of the Chindit expedition was a model of Army-Air Force cooperation. American pilots with their light planes showed, not only how to cooperate with ground forces, but how important that sort of cooperation is. The rapport that grew up between soldiers and airmen when they lived and worked so closely together became a bond of mutual gratitude that lasted throughout their lives. Ground forces came to rely upon their airborne brothers to come to their aid whenever they put down smoke and called for an air strike. They looked upward and blessed the "quartermaster wallah" in the sky when food, ammunition, clothing, and every other need was delivered to them. In this regard we take one more look at the log for Joe Curtiss and his crew. In the four days from March 7 to 10 they made six trips to the Chindit area, either Broadway or Chowringhee, and delivered 75 men, 15 mules, and a wireless station. They then continued to fly in supplies, whatever the weather, however awkward and dangerous the dropping zones. No other action throughout the War brought air and ground forces so closely together.

For the men who took part in Chindit II the experience seemed to have a lifelong effect. Philip Cochran was by nature a casual and practical man, not given to poetic utterances and flowery speech, but in his last briefing for the men of No. 1 Air Commando he struck a different tone: "Nothing you have ever done, nothing you're ever going to do, counts now — only the next few hours. Tonight you are going to find your souls." Wingate also made a final speech to the men of the Chindit force, but the officers were excluded and no one knows now what he said. It is likely that he spoke in the same vein, for the soldiers came out looking like men who had been transfigured. Even to this day, when the Chindit Old Comrades Association gathers in Britain or the First Air Commando Association in the United States, they seem to speak a language the rest of the world does not know. John Knowles expressed this apartness most eloquently: "Something had burned into our souls that made it possible for us to bear the burden, and which somehow set us just a little bit apart from everybody else, but would still take years to mature into the knowledge that, like the anointed members of some strange priesthood, we were once and forever, Chindits."

The Chindit foray had its effect on the Burma Campaign as well. From the outset, General Slim had his doubts about Wingate and his project. He was willing to accept the notion of long-range penetration, but in his estimation the first Chindit campaign had not been worth the cost and the second, very much bigger and more costly, was even more suspect. Moreover, he was sceptical of Wingate as a leader and as a planner. Still, the man had the ear of important people and for Slim playing along was therefore bound to be more profitable than trying to hold back. In the end, he had to concede that, even though the cost was high, the game had probably been worth the candle. First, the activity of the Chindits along the Mandalay-Myitkyina line of communication and later in direct support of Stilwell at Mogaung and Myitkyina had been significantly helpful in freeing the whole of northern Burma and reopening the route to China. Second, the confusion and concern they caused the Japanese was at least partly responsible for some Japanese forces being diverted away from the Chindwin and the Assam front. Slim was nevertheless glad he had not dug any deeper into his reserves to reinforce the Chindits. He needed all the force he could muster back at Imphal.

When all the bills are added up and all accounts are paid, Stilwell was the one who paid the biggest price. He lost credibility with the British by his premature announcement of the taking of Myitkyina and a certain stigma attached to him for his shameful abuse of the Marauders. He had staked everything on retaking Northern Burma and reopening the road, but the road never did deliver sufficient matériel to make it worthwhile. Chennault had staked everything on a theory of conquering Japan through long range bombing and he demanded priority on the Hump flights for his supplies. Chiang Kai-shek, already disposed against Stilwell, sided with Chennault, and Stilwell was ordered back to America.

IMPHAL AND KOHIMA

THE FIRST Chindit expedition had demonstrated to Mutaguchi, the Japanese general in command of the Burma Area Army, the feasibility of moving troops through the jungle and mountains of Northern Burma by animal transport. He drew from that insight two conclusions: one, that he too could move in that manner and, two, that his defence line from Myitkyina through Mogaung to Kalewa was vulnerable. What he overlooked, however, was that whatever success the Chindit expedition had was due to air superiority and air supply, and he had neither. Nevertheless he resolved to push forward at least to the Chindwin, or, even better, to the western edge of Assam since there he could cover the Allies' main points of supply, Dimapur, the railhead in the north, and Chittagong, the port in the south. Subhas Chandra Bose, who had been plotting a Free India movement in Berlin, was brought back by submarine to head a Provisional Government of Free India and to take command of the Indian National Army. Fired by Chandra Bose's readiness to join his Army to Mutaguchi's and by his enthusiastic accounts of all Bengal ready to rise in revolution, Mutaguchi began to dream of riding in triumph through the streets of Delhi on his white charger. Cooler heads prevailed however and the plan finally accepted in Tokyo was more modest, the occupation of Imphal and Kohima, a move that would ensure that the main launching points for a British offensive would be in their hands. This became known as *U-Go*, the counterpart to *Ha-Go*, the initiative that had already been launched in the Arakan and had resulted in the encirclement of the Admin Box. The newly completed Bangkok-to-Burma railway brought two and a half new divisions in for the offensive. It was to start at the beginning of March 1944.

The Allies' plan was more modest: the Arakan offensive (which opened at the end of November 1943), Wingate's and Stilwell's (in early March), and

Slim's drive from Assam (planned for late March).

As General Slim notes in his book *Defeat into Victory*, there is nothing quite as disconcerting for a commander as to be attacked just as he has one foot raised to plunge into attack himself. Fortunately captured documents, marked maps and even operation orders had fallen into Slim's hands and given him advance notice of the enemy's intentions and time to plot a counter move. The Allied division that was already southeast of Imphal and preparing to advance would stay there as a first defence for the time being and then fall back to join the Imphal garrison. The divisions already engaging the enemy in the Arakan would continue to keep the Japanese occupied on that front. The rest of his Army he would concentrate on the Imphal plain to meet the foe in the open, on the level, face to face and toe to toe, for one full, final, and decisive encounter. If and when reinforcements were needed, he could recall the troops from the forward area and from the Arakan. The Imphal battle would be the ultimate test of the two armies that he had been yearning for since it had been denied him in lower Burma in 1942. Given his superior numbers, his shorter supply line, and his domination of the air, Slim had every reason to expect a victory.

On March 6, the very day No. 1 Air Commando gliders were taking the Chindits into Burma, Mutaguchi's army launched itself across the Chindwin on a 100 mile wide front with the intention of cutting the road from Dimapur, the railhead for the Imphal valley, and then of besieging and occupying Imphal itself. Their orders were to "advance through the hills like a ball of fire," and this they began to do. It is difficult to give a complete chronologically coherent picture of the attack on Imphal, for the assault did not advance uniformly on a broad front. Rather, like a forest fire, spots of conflagration sprang up in one sector and then jumped to a different area as though carried by the wind. In fierce screaming attacks that ended in bloody hand-to-hand engagements, sword against kukri, the Japanese troops cut off isolated forward posts arrayed defensively around Imphal, first Tamu to the southeast, then Ukhrul and Kohima to the northeast, and then Tiddim, due south of Imphal. Tamu and Tiddim were overrun, but the garrisons fell back on Imphal in accordance with Slim's plan. Kohima however was a different case. Here there was no question of falling back. Kohima had to be held, not merely for defence of Imphal, but because it was indispensable for the protection of Dimapur and the defence of India.

Before the war, Kohima was a small and unknown administrative town occupying a series of ridges along the all-weather road from Dimapur to Imphal (*see map p. 64*). On one ridge the District Commissioner had his neat little bungalow with a roof of red tile, a pleasant garden, and a tennis court. Other administrative offices and warehouses stretched for five miles along the road, while a sizeable Naga village occupied a slightly higher ridge to the north. From the height of the village one looked out in all directions on an unending series of mountain ridges and valleys, all thickly clad in jungle growth. Remote and isolated in time of peace, Kohima was soon to emerge in time of war as one of the most hotly fought for areas in the whole of the Burma campaign, for it stood at the height of the pass on the supply road from Dimapur, the life line to Imphal. Even more threatening however, was the real possibility of the Japanese moving on from Kohima to take Dimapur itself, for the railway that passed through Dimapur served not only Imphal, but Ledo as well, the supply base for every item that flew over the Hump and into China. Kohima had only a scratch garrison, and Dimapur had no garrison troops at all. General Slim sent in what reserves he could scrape up, a battalion of the Royal West Kent Regiment to Kohima and an untried division from India for Dimapur, and hoped the jungle and the mountains would supplement the little defence he could provide. He was surprised at how quickly and how strongly the Japanese moved against the village; at the end of March the three thousand troops in Kohima, and that includes a great many non-combatants, were surrounded by a force of 15,000 Japanese attackers.

The siege that followed lasted sixteen days. For ferocity and intensity, for individual acts of bravery and resistance beyond enduring, it is unmatched in the annals of war. All day long, day after day, the enemy's mortars and artillery shells fell on the ridge like rain, slaking only momentarily when an RAF air strike came. Soldiers lived in slit trenches beneath the cease-less whine of bullets and crump of mortars. The wounded, 300 of them and their numbers growing daily, lay helpless in scrape-outs and were re-wounded and killed. Doctors in a makeshift hospital bunker did what they could for their patients while the noise and threat of battle surged all round them. Cooks crept along the perimeter ladling food from their dixies (large metal containers) into mess tins for men who could not for an instant relax. The Dakotas defied enemy machine gun and rifle fire to drop food, ammunition, supplies, and even water, for early in the siege the only water point fell to the enemy. At night the Japanese alternated large, determined frontal attacks with small "jitter" raids, infiltrations carried out sometimes with screaming charges, sometimes in silent insinuations meant to unnerve the defenders and deprive them of sleep. Men staring out at the darkness till their eyes grew tired saw shadows move and figures crawling forward where there was nothing, or they crouched in their trenches and heard nothing till the enemy was upon them. The enemy tried tricks with them, crying out in English for help, or pretending to be a friendly platoon returning from a patrol. And sometimes it worked, as when a sleeping Tommy or sepoy woke in his slit trench to find he was sharing it with a Jap.

Each day the Japanese line drew tighter around the besieged defenders until what had begun as an encampment strung out along the road for five miles ended as a stoutly defended rectangle a bare 350 yards on each side. At the end, the Japanese were holding one end of the tennis court and the British the other, each lobbing grenades across like tennis balls. Hand to hand encounters became commonplace. The Japanese got into the bakery; from there they could fire into the backs of the defenders and then duck into the tandoori ovens for protection. Lance Corporal John Harman, a burly North Country man of 19, killed the crew manning the machine gun that protected the bakery, then ran forward, seized the machine gun and ran back holding it over his head in triumph. He dashed into the bakery, lifted the heavy iron lids of the ovens and dropped a grenade into each. Picking up two wounded Japanese, he brought them back to his section, one under each arm. For this action and for a like action the next day, wherein he was killed, he received the Victoria Cross. A sergeant major who had been blinded by his wounds continued to urge his men on, led round by one of his privates. A sepoy with an empty magazine swung his rifle round and bashed his attacker with the butt of it. With each passing day the pre-monsoon rains grew stronger and the strength of the garrison grew weaker. Their only consolation was that the enemy losses were greater than theirs and the enemy's supply problem even more acute.

They also knew that they had friends on the outside fighting for them. A British artillery regiment fought its way to the top of a nearby mountain and directed precise fire onto the enemy lines. That helped control the attacks, but the Japanese, who always dug in like ferrets, had by now had time to construct in the parts of the village they held the same kind of impregnable bunkers they had made in the Arakan. During the night the British brought tanks as far forward along the road as they could, then used a bulldozer at the top to winch them straight up the hillside. The bunkers fell to the direct fire of the tank guns followed up by flame throwers. The Japanese were shot as they fled. Not one surrendered.

When, on May 13, the siege of Kohima was lifted, the defenders were so spent they scarcely realized that help had arrived. For sixteen days they had fought unceasingly, slept on the ground for a few stolen moments, eaten even as they fought, and never washed or changed their clothes. All that remained of the colonial buildings was a few bullet-pocked walls and piles of rubble. Every tree stood as a gaunt skeleton completely stripped of leaves. The Naga village was demolished, the lawns and gardens were a black mass of churned up earth, looking for all the world like the aftermath of the Somme in World War I. But the small, gallant force at Kohima had held for sixteen days against unrelenting attacks from the most fanatic and determined besiegers one could imagine. The road to Dimapur was now open. There was another two months of fierce fighting in the area south of Kohima before the road to Imphal was clear, but in Kohima itself the garrison had triumphed. On the Kohima Ridge the British Second Division erected a slab of native stone and carved on it one of the most moving epitaphs of the War:

> *When you go home*
> *Tell them of us and say,*
> *For your tomorrow*
> *We gave our today.*

All the bravery and tenacity of the ground forces in Kohima would have been futile without the support of the Air Force, in particular the transport squadrons who brought the Army everything it needed. There was no place to land, but with parachutes or in free fall drops, the Dakotas delivered rations, ammunition, barbed wire, clothing, medical supplies, and mail. When the enemy overran the water point, water rained down, either in barrels with parachutes, or, experimentally, in partially filled rubber tubes. The monsoons were approaching but the flights had to be continued whatever the weather. 194 Squadron, now one of the most experienced and dependable of the transport squadrons, was called upon to do double duty, supplying the Chindits and the forces at Kohima. Almost half of the aircrew on the Squadron were Canadians and it was inevitable that there should be casualties. Burton Christie was a twenty-two year old pilot from Toronto when he set out to deliver much needed supplies to the Kohima mountain top. In a letter to the family, his Commanding Officer tells of that last flight:

> *Burton was engaged on a hazardous supply dropping assignment*
> *to the Army, an operation that necessitated his flying through very*
> *adverse weather over wild and mountainous terrain. By sheer tenacity*
> *and courage he completed his task, but he was unable to see his way*
> *out of the valley into which he had dropped his vital supplies due to*
> *the very low clouds and crashed into a hillside. Your son's funeral was*
> *conducted in the field but owing to war operations it was not possible*
> *to accord him full service honours. He is buried deep in the heart of*
> *Burma in a small cemetery made by British troops. When Burma is*
> *eventually recaptured this cemetery will come under the care of the Impe-*
> *rial War Graves Commission which will erect a permanent memorial*
> *on the site.*

A similar letter was sent to the families of the men who were killed with him, Charlie Tattrie of Vancouver and George Hansford of Brantford, Ontario.

The stout defence at Kohima had forestalled what could have been a major catastrophe for the defence of India, the fall of Dimapur. Equally important however was the fact that it occupied a good many Japanese troops who would otherwise have been available for the attack on Imphal 85 miles straight down the road.

Imphal, once the central market town of the Assamese province of Manipur, was now the central forward base for the Fourteenth Army. It lay at an elevation of 2500 feet in the middle of a flat plain about 20 miles wide and 60 miles long; all around it the mountains rose quickly to 7000 feet with spot heights over 9000. Whether it was to be the base for the Fourteenth Army's advance into Burma or for the fight against a Japanese advance into India, it was obviously going to be an important supply point and it had been stocked with matériel of war sufficient to last at least a month. One hundred and fifty-five thousand Allied troops were massed in and around the town, even after 25,000 non-combatants had been evacuated in anticipation of a siege. Slim had alerted his RAF and USAAF partners to the possible need of air supply on the order of 540 tons per day.

The Japanese commander sent his men off to Imphal with stirring rhetoric, and a touch of foreboding, telling them they could expect certain victory, and almost complete annihilation. Afire with valour and dominated by one thought only — to annihilate the enemy, they must regard death as something lighter than a feather as they tackled the task of capturing Imphal. Mutaguchi expected the task to be completed by April 29. Once again the Japanese arrogantly overestimated the puissance of their own troops and contemptuously underestimated the tenacity of the British. From every direction, the invaders set their sights on Imphal and scratched their way toward it — from Tiddim in the south, Tamu in the southeast, Ukhrul in the northeast, Kohima in the north, and even along the small jungle track that led from Silchar in the west, the Japanese fought toward Imphal *(see map p. 64)*. Slim's strategy was to make his stand on the Imphal plain, but it also included a bloody defence along the way. Thus even as his troops dropped back from Tiddim and Tamu, they fought fiercely for every inch of the road, just as they did on the track from Ukhrul and the highway from Kohima. Typical was the battle along the Silchar track.

The track was just a jungle path with numerous swinging bridges over steep narrow gorges but it had served as a route of retreat for the civilians during the 1942 flight from Rangoon, and at the end of it the town of Silchar gave access to the railway and the larger towns of Comilla and Chittagong. The Japanese, having swung all the way around the north side of Imphal, now turned south to seize the Silchar track. Repeatedly they occupied a portion of the track and next day the Indian troops launched a vicious attack and took it back. On April 13 Japanese suicide bombers blew one of the swinging bridges and cut the road, but still the fight went on. Each side ambushed the other on the gloomy jungle paths until this little corner of the campaign became a war of attrition. Slowly, according to plan, the British fell back onto Imphal. Both sides had suffered heavy losses, but Japanese losses were heavier, and, for the first time, Japanese deserters fell into British hands. Having been captured by the enemy they were as good as dead to their families at home and therefore had no compunction about talking freely of regiments that had begun with three thousand men and ended up with eight hundred. Despite these losses, the Japanese clung stubbornly to the track and worked their way eastward along it to the village of Bishenpur, just eighteen miles south of the town of Imphal.

At this point, the Japanese commander saw an opportunity. By joining his eastward push along the Silchar track to his northward push up the Tiddim Road, he could take Bishenpur and open the southern gate to Imphal. What followed was another of those vicious, bloody encounters which characterized every meeting of the Japanese and the British in the Burma campaign. British troops set a block across the road and ambushed three enemy tanks and eleven lorries filled with troops. The Japanese retaliated by hurling themselves furiously at the block over and over again for five days in a row. RAF Hurribombers joined the fray, but unfortunately attacked their own troops. Bishenpur Hill was carpeted with dead, decaying bodies, mules and men together, and the sickly stench of putrefying flesh infected the air. An attempt to burn the corpses only made it worse and bulldozers had to be used to sanitize the area. In one sentence General Slim, in his book *Defeat into Victory,* captures the absolute determination of the enemy in the face of what any other army would consider utter hopelessness: "There can be few examples in history of a force as reduced, battered, and exhausted delivering such furious assaults, not with the object of extricating itself, but to achieve its original offensive intention."

The vital avenue for the eventual relief of Imphal was the road leading down from Kohima. With the Kohima siege lifted, the supply route from Dimapur was open again, but of course, only to Kohima. From that point on it was still in enemy hands, as it had been since March 29. Mountbatten ordered that it should be opened not later than mid-July. Slim began that task by sending his troops northeast toward the little village of Ukhrul with the double objective of thwarting a Japanese advance from that direction and of cutting the supply route for the enemy holding the Kohima-Imphal road. All the way along the track to Ukhrul the Allied soldiers fought to gain a mile and then were pushed back for half a mile. The Japanese resisted and counterattacked but lost heavily, so that in the end the British troops prevailed.

The Japanese who had been holding the Kohima-Imphal road were now cut off and ought to have been an easy prey for the British troops fighting down from Kohima, but against the Japanese army, nothing was easy. Nowhere are the mountains that surround the Imphal plain as steeply pitched and as closely crowded as in this northeast sector. For its first twenty miles the road south from Kohima wriggles like a snake through nine thousand foot peaks in its attempt to find a track to the valley. The Japanese had had their orders: "Continue in the task till all your ammunition is expended, till all your strength is exhausted. If your hands are broken, fight with your feet. If your hands and feet are broken, use your teeth. If there is no breath left in your body, fight with your ghost." And that is what they did. The Allies had to battle for every inch of the winding, twisting road and they marked every mile with dead and wounded Japanese soldiers. Mutaguchi had declared that Imphal would be his by April 29, instead, on June 22 Slim could declare that the road to Imphal was open again.

This was the siege of Imphal. Not an established perimeter defended and fought for in a series of nightly attacks, but thrust and counter-thrust along the five avenues that aimed at the town, the Silchar track, the Tiddim road, the Tamu-Palel road, the track from Ukhrul, and the Kohima road. Military writers biased in this direction or predisposed to favour this commander have seen the Bishenpur battle or the action around Palel, the fight for Ukhrul or the onslaught from Kohima as the turning point of the siege of Imphal. In truth, it was exhaustion, starvation, malaria, overstretched supply lines, and lack of air support along with the unexpected stubbornness of the British defence that turned the tide of battle on all these fronts and worked the failure of the Japanese attack. On July 5 the Japanese Area Command acknowledged that failure and cancelled the *U-Go* operation. Mutaguchi, the proud general who, as a regimental commander, had started the Sino-Japanese war in 1937, who had planned the Imphal assault, and who dreamed of riding in glory down the streets of Delhi, was recalled to Tokyo for staff duties and for ignominy. Subhas Chandra Bose had seen a good part of his Indian National Army go into battle in the Palel area and then scatter and defect to the British. The casualties had been heavy for both sides, but far heavier for the Japanese. Kohima had cost the British 4000 troops killed and wounded and Imphal a further 12,700 (remembering that the bulk of these were sepoys and Gurkhas). On the Japanese side the best estimate is that 5700 were lost at Kohima and 58,000 at Imphal. The Imphal-Kohima battle was for Japan the greatest defeat her army ever suffered and for General Slim it was the victory he had so ardently yearned for.

Most of the Canadians involved in the Kohima-Imphal battle were with the RAF, but there were others. Major Taylor, the Toronto surgeon who had led his section on the retreat from Maymyo, was still in the Imphal area. After a time in hospital to recover from malaria and dysentery and a period of convalescent leave, he was posted back to Imphal to take charge of 41

Indian General Hospital. It was located at Kanglatongbi, a small village on the Kohima road about fifteen miles north of Imphal. During the 1943 hiatus it grew to be a 1000 bed facility with well-built bashas gradually replacing the original tents. For a time things were relatively quiet, except for the occasional air raid and the day when the Naga hillmen, burning scrub brush in the neighbourhood, set half the wards on fire. All that changed on March 29, 1944 when the Japanese cut the Kohima road. Taylor's hospital was given two days to evacuate into the "Box" at Imphal and set up next to the main airstrip.

Here conditions were far from ideal. Their only protection was old leaky tentage, the land underfoot was swampy, a brook even ran between the wards and the living area, and enemy planes that attacked the airstrip invariably ended their sortie with a playful strafing of the hospital tents off the end of the runway. And then the rains came. The canvas floor of the operating theatre was soon a slosh of stinking mud, groundsheets were strung over the operating tables to keep the patients dry. Robert Street, an operating theatre technician from Birmingham, describes his day:

> The theatre was like a butcher's shop and every case needed major surgery: arms off, legs off, sometimes both; bayonet wounds, bullet wounds, horrendous burns and lots of head injuries. It went on and on, every day and every night.
>
> They brought the bodies to the operating table and then we started. Many a time we got half way through a repair job and found the patient had died. That is when you had to be very hard and just move to the next table and start all over again.

Even when the long day in the operating tent was over, the incessant monsoon rain and the primitive living conditions offered little rest or comfort. In his diary Taylor tried to lighten life with a little poem:

> Oh, to be in Assam
> Now that May is there,
> For whoever walks in Assam
> Finds some morning unaware
> That his bed's soaked through with the driving rain
> And his boots are floating down the drain
> And the floor of his tent's a miry stain
> In Assam now.

As the fierceness of the fighting grew, there was little time for writing poetry. There was so much to be done, so many wounded to be operated on. Len Thornton of Birmingham, England, a medical orderly with the 41 Indian General Hospital, remembers those intense days: "The Operating Room was going full blast day and night in a medium size tent with tarpaulin on the floor, no electric, all the Ops were done with the aid of small oil lamps and one Tilly lamp that worked sometimes. All the sterilizers were heated with primus stoves and all the cutting instruments kept in Lysol. The sergeant in the operating theatre was ill and I took over and assisted in Major Taylor's surgery. He was a very quiet man, very efficient, but he looked very pale and I could see he was not well. The last few months had taken their toll."[1] They had indeed, and Major Taylor was sent out on sick leave even before the siege had ended.

For his part in the Burma campaign, Major Taylor was mentioned in dispatches and later awarded the Order of the British Empire. The citation notes his "gallant and distinguished service," and specifically states that many hundreds of survivors owed their lives to his medical skill and his devotion to his duty. After the War he served for a short time on the North West Frontier but very soon was picked to become Surgeon to the Viceroy, a prestigious appointment that brought with it a large house in the viceregal compound and invitations to many magnificent occasions. When India gained her independence Colonel Taylor was named Surgeon to the Governor General of India. When, in the turmoil that followed independence and partition, Gandhi was assassinated, Colonel Taylor attended the funeral.

Group Captain Seton Broughall, whom we last saw leading the thin remnants of the RAF out of Burma in March of 1942, was now the Officer Commanding the RAF Wing at Imphal. He was 46 years old, but still a favourite with the pilots, though perhaps better known for his popularity in the Mess than for his tactical leadership. T. Meyer, an RAF pilot at Imphal, remembers Seton Broughall as "a good friend to all the chaps, and despite the fact that he was much, much older than everybody else, he generally got on well with us. We gave him a sort of youthful outlook which was fairly rare in an officer of such seniority." Another RAF pilot, H. Bishop calls the Group Captain "A colourful Canadian," and adds: "At Imphal ... we could get him to sing the famous old tune – 'Take the conrod out of my backbone, Take the piston out of my brain, Take the sparkplugs out of my kidneys, And assemble the engine again.' He had a voice like a file, but it was worth listening to." Atholl Sutherland Brown, a Beaufighter pilot from Vancouver, also remembers Seton: "Seton Broughall seemed quite British to me although somehow I knew that he was a Canadian who had stayed in the RAF since the Great War. Although he was the Station Commander he was very informal and also friendly to us. He was reputed to be still flying a Tiger Moth although his vision was poor. I was told he landed looking sideways at the trees to judge his height above the deck."

---

[1] In a letter to the author.

Norman Franks in *The Air Battle of Imphal* gives us the memory of a rigger of 607 Squadron:

> *One morning I was carrying a motor generator on my shoulder and hurrying to replace one in a Spit where a bullet had gone right through the generator. I met an (English) Indian Army brigadier. He was not satisfied with my 'Good morning,' and insisted that I put the geni down, salute him, and then pick it up again. I treated this with the contempt it deserved and carried on with the job. He insisted I be put under arrest. The final result was the Group Captain came from HQ, told the Brig that when he was on an airfield, he was under RAF rules, and then he said, 'The buggers don't even salute me!'*

Although the Group Captain is not identified, it is safe to assume it was Seton Broughall since he was the Station Commander at the time. Certainly, it is very much in character.

All this sounds somewhat insouciant, but the fact is that, as Commander of 170 Wing, Seton had nine fighter squadrons in his charge, no insignificant responsibility. There was in this man a capable senior officer as well as a jolly companion in the Mess.

These are the two sides of him that Ken Hemmingway extols when he dedicates his book *Wings Over Burma* to him and describes him as "the shrewd, sincerely popular Group Commander, coiner of the current greeting, 'Have a snort'" and as "the Group Captain who ably bore a great responsibility throughout the campaign." That seems to sum up Seton Broughall quite fairly.

For most of 1943 Seton's squadrons had a relatively quiet time at Imphal. There were a few aggressive sorties aimed at trains and road convoys, and of course the intense air supply action associated with the Chindit I expedition, but there was also time for duck shooting on the lake below Imphal and visits by the Viceroy, Lord Wavell, and the Supremo, Louis Mountbatten. When the Chindits returned, both Wingate and Bernard Fergusson dropped in to lecture the aircrew on jungle survival. All that changed with the explosion of activity that came with the new year — Arakan II, Chindit II, and then the siege of Imphal.

In the air war that accompanied and followed the siege of Imphal the relative strengths of the Allied and enemy forces greatly influenced the outcome. The *bushido* spirit that inspired Japan's soldiers to fight with such fatalistic determination also enflamed her airmen, and led to an expensive and extravagant expenditure of trained aircrew and to their willingness to forego such rudimentary survival equipment as armoured back-plates and self-sealing gas tanks. The Japanese homeland was unable to produce the men or the planes in the quantity this profligate use required. To protect their dwindling air strength, the Japanese air force sequestered its squadrons in Malaya and brought them forward only for irregular, erratic raids.

There was no thought of having a "cab rank" fighter force readily available for immediate ground support.

By contrast, the Allied air superiority which had begun with the arrival of the Spitfire was now enhanced by the advent of Mosquitoes, Thunderbolts and Liberators, as well as American long range fighters, Mustangs and Lightnings. General Slim and Air Marshal Sir John Baldwin lived and worked together to ensure the utmost cooperation of the two forces. The advantages of that cooperation were demonstrated even before the siege began when Slim realized, somewhat belatedly, that reinforcements for the defence of Imphal would have to be brought up from the Arakan front. Mountbatten, scarcely recovered from a severe eye injury, begged 20 Commandos from the Hump route to augment the Dakotas he already had. What followed was, if not a miracle, at least a model of logistical planning and army-air force cooperation. At the Arakan airfield, a plane-load of troops stood ready at a precise spot along the strip. An aircraft swooped down, stopped at that spot, loaded its quota, and soared off again without even stopping its motors. Ninety minutes later it disgorged its passengers with the same dispatch at Imphal and headed back to the Arakan. So efficient was the operation that a field artillery company was drawn from the Arakan battle one day and was in action on the Imphal front two days later. In all, 20 Commandos and 25 Dakotas flew 758 sorties to airlift a full division with all its equipment, including guns, from the Arakan to Imphal in nine days.

Throughout the siege, the availability of sufficient air transport was an absolute requirement. Thus, when the time came for the Commandos Mountbatten had borrowed to be returned to the Hump, 79 Dakotas were flown in from the Italian front to supplement the resources of the four transport squadrons now working in the Imphal area. Even with this addition, the need was scarcely met. In the Arakan air transport was required to supply the West African forces in the Kaladan Valley and to redeploy troops and evacuate casualties from the Buthidaung region. Behind the enemy lines the Chindits were still on full air supply, and during the siege Kohima and Imphal were requiring at least 540 tons of ammunition and supplies each day. Like all the men of 194 Squadron, Joe Curtiss and his crew were kept busy day and night. In the move of 5 Division from the Arakan to Imphal, they flew up to eight hours a day for four days straight, transporting men, mules, heavy guns, ammunition and jeeps. On 24 March, they made their last two flights connected with the 5 Division move, then ended the day by bringing men and guns from India into Imphal and taking a fighter squadron back to India for relocation.

When the move of 5 Division was over, they reverted to flying supplies into Imphal and flying casualties out. As it was at the Admin Box and with the Chindits, so it was at Imphal and Kohima, only air supply made victory possible. The one difference was that at Kohima everything had to be dropped whereas landing was always possible at Imphal. Every thing needful for the campaign came "down the chimney." On one trip Joe Curtiss and his crew defied inclement weather and the enemy's guns to bring 25 barrels of rum into Imphal. Who can say how necessary this cargo was to the final victory? As well as the Imphal commitment, they were still flying mules and troops into the Chindit strips and bringing out casualties.

Throughout all this, the Curtiss crew had flown one aircraft, "C" Charlie, and they looked upon it as their own, secure in the faith that it would never let them down. On the morning of April 9 they delivered a load of bombs to Palel, an all-weather strip south of Imphal now under heavy attack by the Japanese. For the return flight, they took on the equipment and 22 ground personnel of a fighter squadron that was being relocated further back. Douglas Williams, in his admirable little history of 194 Squadron, tells what happened next:

> We proceeded on a normal take-off when, at the point of becoming airborne, we encountered a terrifying gusty cross wind which suddenly blew across the valley; as one wing dipped dangerously our pilot Joe Curtiss with great presence of mind thumped the throttles back injuring his wrist. He abandoned the take-off and with great skill managed to level the Dak as we bounced heavily back on to the runway. The oleo legs collapsed – I think we hit a ditch – and I opened the door leading from the wireless cabin and called to the passengers to disembark calmly. This they did in an orderly way, very praiseworthy. We all sat on the ground, pretty dazed, the Hurricane ground crews and ourselves. Joe Curtiss, Ian Darnley, Jimmy Howe and myself were greatly upset at the state of our beloved "C" Charlie which was a write-off. A Dakota that had served us so wonderfully well on most of our operational trips into Burma, it was just like losing a home.

Things were never quite the same for the Curtiss crew after the loss of "C" Charlie, but there were other aircraft and many more loads to haul. They just kept working till their tour was over. After the war, Joe continued flying in Europe with 435 RCAF Squadron. In October 1945 when he was recommended for the Air Force Cross, it was noted that he had flown over 1500 operational hours, 300 of them in the previous six months. When the AFC was awarded in January 1946 he was cited as "an exceptional Captain, often called upon to fly the most important personages and freight through the worst weather." It was because of the work of the Curtiss crew, and all the transport squadron crews that Mountbatten declared that the Dakota was the most powerful weapon in his arsenal of war.

Canadians were heavily involved in the air supply work. In June 1944 there were more than 50 Canadians flying with 194 Squadron, about one third of the total aircrew, and they acquitted themselves well. Jim Baillie, from Toronto, was a navigator with 194. His pilot was Murray Rice from Essex, Ontario and the co-pilot was John Cox from Oakville, Ontario. On June 14, 1945 they were caught in vicious monsoon turbulence and crashed just south of Myingyan air strip near Mandalay. Jim was knocked unconscious; when he came to, the entire plane was a red fury of fuel-fed flames, his legs were entangled in the static lines, and his clothing was on fire. Shaking off the pain of a broken cheekbone and concussion, he struggled to drag himself and two Indian army kickers free of the wreckage. Then he heard a scream from the burning plane and he stumbled back into the fuselage to pull out Jock Smith, their RAF wireless operator. Jim Baillie was awarded the George Medal for what he did that day.

At this time, the pilots of a fighter squadron stationed at Palel took off to attack the Japanese that were pressing so hard against Kohima. Among these pilots was Jimmy Whalen from Vancouver. Before he arrived in Burma he had already shot down three enemy aircraft over Northern Europe and before he arrived at Palel he had shot down three more in the Easter Sunday fighting over Ceylon. Now he was a flight commander involved in air support for the ground forces defending Imphal and Kohima. One Japanese bunker was particularly obstinate. The squadron had gone for it repeatedly but it had repulsed their best efforts with murderous flak. Jimmy thought he had a plan for blasting it and asked the squadron leader to let him have another go at it. With reservations and considerable reluctance, the CO consented, but with the caution: "OK, one more shot and that's the last. But you only do it once, then go on through and out." On the morning of April 18 Jimmie flew down the Kohima-Imphal Road to a point 18 miles south of Kohima and got right down on the deck to deliver his 500 pound bomb directly into the bunker. Heavy ground fire crashed all around him. He rolled over on his back, corrected, then dove over a ridge and out of sight. He was killed instantly in the crash. His body was buried at the site, then later exhumed and reburied at the Kohima Cemetery. Jimmy Whalen was only 22 when he died, but already he had fought in two theatres and been credited with six enemy planes destroyed. He was subsequently awarded the DFC. In 1996 Joe Smith of West Midlands, England wrote his epitaph: "I especially have happy memories of Flt. Lt. Jim Whalen who was shot down and killed over Kohima in April 1944 flying a Hurricane with 34 Squadron. I still have a pair of his flying goggles, the bravest of the brave."

In September 1943 Bud Walker's photo reconnaissance squadron was moved from the Arakan to Imphal in anticipation of the coming action. William Arthur Walker was born in 1919 in Dundas, Ontario. When he finished high school, he took a long bike tour around southern Ontario before settling into a job with Dofasco. In 1941 he joined the RCAF but postponed his call-up so that he could marry his high-school sweetheart. Immediately after the wedding, he began his training, and Dorothy, known to everyone as Dolly, followed him from station to station. When his ship sailed out of Halifax harbour, Dolly stood on the point to wave goodbye.

In England Bud was given specialized training in army cooperation and ciné photography. It was on that course that he first fell in with Charlie Watt from Toronto. They became fast friends and stayed together to the end. On October 26, 1942 they boarded the *Stirling Castle* and began an extended sea voyage that took them westward to the coast of Canada, south to Brazil for a refuelling stop, eastward to South Africa and finally into the harbour of Bombay. After further training, Bud and Charlie and a new Canadian friend, Bert Madill of Edmonton, joined 28 RAF Squadron and began operating at Maungdaw in support of the first Arakan operation. In October 1943 they were transferred from the Arakan to the Palel strip in the Imphal sector.

Air reconnaissance was particularly important in the Burma campaign since there was little opportunity to infiltrate informers into the area, and the heavy jungle umbrella concealed most troop movements and supply lines and depots. The Japanese were skilled at high level reconnaissance, not least because their Mitsubishi Ki46, known as Dinah to the RAF, could fly faster and further than any Allied aircraft until the Spitfire and Mosquito arrived. But for peeking into the jungle and penetrating its cover, the old Hurricane flying at a height of only 50 to 100 feet and using the sharp eyes of trained pilots and the prying lenses of high speed cameras proved especially adept. Moreover, there was an immediacy to their operational method that served well in the Burma campaign. The recce pilot could spot a worn trail leading to an innocent-looking jungle hut and attack it at once if he had reason to suspect it contained enemy troops or a stock of ammunition. He could keep the rear echelons informed of the whereabouts of both Allied and enemy columns, or take a picture of a gun emplacement in the morning and drop it to a forward unit in the afternoon.

That is the sort of thing Bud Walker and Charlie Watt were doing at Palel. In November 1943 Walker flew 28 operational hours, on average a two-hour sortie every second day. After one such sortie, Bud noted in his diary: "much enemy movement, bullock carts and lorries on the east bank of the Chindwin." On another occasion they fired on a large herd of cattle that the Japanese had gathered as rations on the hoof. It was this sort of surveillance that warned General Slim of the coming attack on Imphal.

Charlie, Bert and Bud shared a basha with two other friends. They slept on the usual Indian *charpoy,* a bed of rope strung across a wooden frame, improvised their own shower arrangement by punching holes in a ration tin and stringing it up on a bamboo pole, and took care to shake the scorpions

out of their shoes each morning before they put them on. Bud's passion for
soccer earned him the nickname "Sam," a sobriquet borrowed from some
forgotten British football star. They adopted two kittens and in his next
letter Bud told Dolly they were called Hurri and Cane, a coy hint as to what
aircraft they were flying. Mountbatten visited the squadron and gave them
a rousing address. An RCAF Welfare Officer visited and promised to look
into the question of delayed promotions.

Throughout the first months of 1944 Charlie and Bud flew almost every
day in their search for enemy concentrations and hidden supply dumps.
Rarely was there even a hint of enemy air action. On the morning of 12
March Charlie and Bud took off on a tactical reconnaissance to look for
an enemy column threatening the British forward post. March 12 was one
of the rare days when the Japanese Air Force was abroad and Charlie saw
the two enemy aircraft streaking down on them out of the sun. "I tried to
call Bud," he said later, "but it was too late." Bud Walker bailed out, but
he did not survive. His body was never found. Only an inscription on the
Singapore War Memorial marks his memory, that and the shrine, a cross
and a picture, that Dolly Walker keeps by her bed. She never remarried.

Charlie Watt continued to fly with 28 Squadron. In February 1945 while
on an army cooperation sortie he encountered two Japanese fighters. His
one short burst set one of them afire. It slewed into the second plane and
they both went down. Charlie Watt got a DFC for that action.

Palel features often in the air defence of Imphal since it was the furthest
forward of the six airfields in the Imphal valley and therefore closest to the
action. Everyone was well aware that the enemy were pressing closely, and
precautions were taken. Enemy aircraft could come over at any moment,
Japanese guns and mortars pounded the strip daily. At night the aircraft
were moved off the strip and into a "box," simply a rough earth embankment. After the first enemy air raids, the squadron personnel also moved
into the box, digging deep trenches and covering them with sacking or
corrugated iron. Each night at dusk a perimeter check was made to ensure
that the enemy had not infiltrated and then the guards were mounted. Everyone took a turn at guard duty. The latrines were outside the box and woe
betide the airman who had to make a midnight visit and had forgotten the
password. The rations were adequate but not appetizing — bully beef and
dehydrated vegetables. There was rarely beer, but there was always tea.

When the battle in the Arakan abated and the fight for Imphal began,
Verne Butler and Lorne LeCraw were transferred to the Palel strip. Though
they were now flying Spitfire VIIs, they still preferred to get above the
enemy and fall down upon him from a height. There wasn't time for that
today. At a scant 1000 feet Verne got on the tail of an invader and gave it two
short bursts. Out of the corner of his eye he saw it go down trailing smoke,

but he did not see the enemy aircraft on his tail. It fired and Verne went down. His aircraft crashed just three miles from the Palel strip but his body was never found. This happened on March 12, 1944, just three days short of a year after his close friend Bing De Cruyenaere had been killed over the Arakan. Owen Hearn wrote a little book for Verne, just as he had for Bing, but it has not been possible to find a copy.

Credit for the eventual triumph at Imphal goes not to the Army or to the Air Force, but to the Army and the Air Force working together. Forced to live and fight side by side, each could see at once how the other sacrificed and suffered, how each fought and persevered. In these circumstances there was no room for inter-service rivalry. Rank differences too disappeared. Officers and men lived under the same conditions, ate the same food. So closely gathered were the edges of the battle that ground crew could often bomb up the Hurricanes and then watch them fly off and drop those bombs on the nearby ridge. Conversely, Bud Walker's diary records that on one day when the weather washed out flying, he stood guard from 3:30 am to 6:00 "to give the erks a rest."[2]

Having acknowledged that every man, whatever his rank or his arm of service, was a necessary member of the team, it is still appropriate to give special recognition to the Dakotas and Commandos of the transport squadrons, if only because the importance of their role is not always appreciated. After the siege was over, General Sir George Giffard, Commander-in-Chief in Burma, was unequivocal: "Had we not had air supply, we should have lost the Imphal Plain." It is fortunate almost beyond credence that the Japanese Air Force did not recognize the vulnerability of the airborne supply line and concentrate their meagre air power on the unarmed transports. As it was, air supply was only just able to keep the battle going. At the height of the siege rations were cut to 50% and at times the supply of this or that specie of ammunition was dangerously low. The first convoy to enter Imphal when the road was cleared brought in a bottle of beer for every man and an ample supply of fresh potatoes. After a prolonged diet of dehydrated potatoes and bully beef, the fresh potatoes were appreciated more than the beer.

With the siege of Imphal lifted and the road from Dimapur open again, Slim turned to a policy of hot pursuit, determined to exploit his recent victory to the full. Normally a general could expect that a battered and disarrayed army would draw back to regroup, but the Japanese army rarely fell back easily. Expelling the enemy from the west side of the Chindwin turned into a series of bitter battles against strong pockets of stubborn resistance scattered throughout the mountains of Assam. It was campaigning at its hardest, and made all the harder by the advent of the monsoon. Five hundred

---

[2] Erks – RAF slang for groundcrew.

inches of rain fell on Assam in this 1944 monsoon season. For three weeks rain fell without stopping at the rate of five inches per day. Soldiers slogged through mud to their knees. At one point the Tiddim Road climbed 3000 feet in seven miles through a series of thirty-eight switchbacks. Now the road surface was six inches of mud. In places the roadbed was washed away and in other places mud slides completely covered it.

Wheeled traffic was stalled and troops slithered and slid up it as best they could. And all the while the bitter, unrelenting fighting continued. When the British troops entered Tamu they walked along streets lined with smouldering ruins of bamboo bashas, twisted sheets of corrugated iron, and the mud-clumped bodies of 550 Japanese soldiers. Only one thing lightened the Allied soldiers' march — they were winning, they were advancing. The map that traced the retreat of 1942 was now unrolling in reverse and names that signified humiliation and defeat two and a half years ago — Kalemyo, Kalewa — were now revived in memory as sites of victory.

In his push to the Chindwin, Slim was once again helped by willing air support and once again Canadians were prominent in that work. Bruce Pinch's air force story began in 1941 when he and his chum decided to quit their job in a Red Lake gold mine and join the Army. The recruiters in Toronto suggested they would do well as army cooks. Bruce and his chum walked out in disgust and solaced themselves with a few bottles of beer. An RCAF corporal joined them, heard their tale, and upon learning that they both had senior matriculation, invited them to visit him at the Air Force recruiting office next morning. The upshot of that visit was that Bruce Pinch joined the RCAF, not as a cook, but as pilot. Shortly he was told he would leave on the morrow to begin his training. Elated, he went out to celebrate, got a bit too happy, got into a fight with the Duty Officer and ended up under arrest in the Guard House. Next morning the Depot Commandant himself came in and called his name. Pinch stood at attention before him, expecting the worst. "Pinch, are you sober," he asked. "Yes, Sir," replied Bruce. "Then get the hell out of here," and Bruce's skin and his air force career were saved.

After training in Canada and in Britain, Bruce flew a sleek blue Spitfire out to India, chronicling as he flew the high lights of his flight. In Gibraltar he enjoyed the steak and eggs, in Algiers, the pretty girls. His logbook records that Marble Arch (wherever that is) was a "hell of a dump," and that in Cairo their aircraft conveniently went unserviceable to give them an opportunity to view the pyramids. Besides, Cairo had "good beer." Twice he had to make a forced landing. On one occasion that meant spending the night alone beside his aircraft in the desert while he waited for help. The logbook chronicle ends with their arrival in Calcutta and the succinct entry: "They were glad to see us."

Arrived at the squadron, Bruce was disgusted to learn that he would have to give up his Spitfire and settle for a Curtis Mohawk, a short, fat little fighter that was already obsolete in the more privileged arenas of war. By the time he began operational flying however, on March 23, 1943, he had made his peace with his new plane. In August 1943 the squadron was based at Comilla and operating in the Chindwin area. This was a quiet moment on the Assam front; in December he flew only thirteen operational hours. His logbook comments are suitably laconic. He "shot up sampans on the Chindwin," and he took part in a search for a downed Hurricane. His log-book comment is succinct: "Found the pilot sitting on a hill. He was OK." In November he "killed some mules" near Kalemyo. Three times he records that control scrambled him onto a Japanese reconnaissance plane and he was unable to find it. On November 9 it happened again. This time he saw the Dinah, got within half a mile of it, then it spotted him and glided away. In his logbook Bruce vented his frustration: "Scrambled after Jap recce plane. Spotted it at 27,000 feet but could not catch it. We want Spitfires!" In January 1944 his wish was granted. The squadron was taken off operations to convert to Spitfires.

In August 1944, just as the Army was lifting the Imphal siege and begin-ning to fight toward the Chindwin, Bruce's squadron moved onto the Palel strip and began to operate in support of the Fourteenth Army's advance to the Chindwin. This was the monsoon season and, while Mountbatten might confidently proclaim that the Army would fight right through, there were many days when Spitfires dared not take to the air. Repeatedly Bruce's logbook shows him making a weather reconnaissance or being recalled because of duff weather. When they can fly he briefly records that he "destroyed one motor transport," or "shot up some Japs," or "shot up small boats." In between there were tedious trips escorting Dakotas on supply dropping missions. These sorties were a trial because the Dakotas were too slow and all the Spitfire could do was stooge above them in circles as an umbrella. In October the action became more heated. Twice they were scrambled to meet incoming Japanese reconnaissance planes, their chance to show what the Spitfire could do. It proved itself on the first scramble when one of Bruce's mates shot down a Dinah. On the second encounter, the Dinahs shot down one of their aircraft, but the encounter seemed to discourage the enemy, for there were no more reconnaissance flights over their area. On October 16, while strafing at Shwebo, well forward of Slim's line of advance, Bruce's canopy was pierced by a shot from the ground. It probably had nothing to do with that ill omen that he was posted the next day to the Headquarters Command Squadron at Comilla.

His job here was flying light planes, Tiger Moths and L5's, on Line of Communication work and casualty evacuation. It also meant switching from the Chindwin front to the Arakan area and it meant a more active flying life. On the Spitfire squadron he did well to get in twenty hours a month. Here he flew forty hours even though his longest flight lasted only an hour and forty minutes. Often he was asked simply to fly a Colonel to Chittagong, a Brigadier to Razabil, or a radar corporal to Maungdaw, but Bruce remembers the casualty evacuation flights as being "more dangerous than anything on operations." A make-shift door could be opened along the fuselage behind the cockpit and one stretcher inserted. Then Bruce would take off on a strip that was always too short and often very rough.

Bruce's logbook has a short one-line entry for January 4, 1945 where he records a three hour flight from Comilla to Akyab Main Strip and return. His passenger was an unnamed British Army Captain, and the entry concludes with a terse comment: "The first." Bruce Pinch was not a man to waste words, but what he is telling us here is that he and the unnamed captain have single-handed taken Akyab, the airstrip and seaport that four divisions have been fighting for. In *Defeat into Victory*, Field Marshal Slim relates the event thus: "On January 2, 1945 an artillery officer flying over the island in a light aeroplane, seeing the local inhabitants making friendly signs, boldly landed on the airstrip and single-handed captured Akyab — the last Japanese battalion had pulled out forty-eight hours earlier." There is a discrepancy in the dates, of course, but it seems Slim has erred here. On January 4, the very day Bruce landed there, Mountbatten signed the plan for taking the place, something he would not be doing if it had been taken two days earlier.

In May 1945 Bruce bid farewell to India and sailed off to Britain. In London he checked in at RCAF Headquarters to get some money, and found that as far as they were concerned, R112806, Warrant Officer Bruce Pinch did not exist. There was no record of him, and certainly no pay account. Then one of the clerks had an idea: "Perhaps you've been commissioned." And he had. Bruce drew a portion of his back pay sufficient to ensure a decent celebration of his promotion before he caught a ship back to Canada.

Bert Madill of Edmonton was also involved in the action in the aftermath of Imphal. As a seventeen year old living on a mink ranch on the outskirts of Edmonton he had volunteered for the RCAF and been rejected because of his age. Impatiently he waited out a year and tried again. Bert arrived in Bombay December 18, 1942 after having spent two months cruising the world's oceans with Charlie Watt and Bud Walker on the *Stirling Castle*. He was also posted with them to the photo reconnaissance squadron at Imphal but just before the siege began he was transferred to a squadron that was converting to Thunderbolts. At the end of December 1944 Bert and his Thunderbolt were back on operations in the Imphal area. The Republic

Thunderbolt is a massive machine, a single-engine fighter with the temperament and the power of a tank. Most of his missions were bombing and strafing in close support of ground action. "For this type of work," Bert remarks, "the T-bolt provided an unbeatable, stable platform, and the eight .50 calibre guns were hard to beat — a formidable weapon!" It was also superb as a dive bomber. Bert delighted in climbing to 10,000 feet with a 500 pound bomb under each wing, then rolling over and hurtling the mass of his Thunderbolt down at better than 500 mph. At 4000 feet he would release and begin his pullout, levelling out and screeching across the target area at 1000 feet. To the enemy below it was a terrifying tactic. For Bert, once he had mastered it, it gave excellent accuracy to his bombing.

Like Bruce Pinch, he did his share of escort duty, escort for Dakotas on their supply dropping missions or, since the Thunderbolt had a range of just over 1000 miles, escort for Liberators on bombing missions. The squadron experimented with a new bomb, a 500 pound explosive with a six to eight inch spike on its nose. Bert developed a feeling for this device and found it just the thing for nailing a tank, a train, or a river boat. He even tried it on the forty foot defence wall around Fort Dufferin at Mandalay. In the Mess his enthusiasm for it gave him his squadron nickname, Spike. But there was one target Bert would not attack, an elephant. "The Japanese used them extensively, and they could carry the equivalent load of a three-ton truck. We were told to attack and kill them behind enemy lines, but that was one military order I categorically refused to obey," Bert wrote later. "I could never see the elephant as bearing any responsibility for the fracas we were engaged in."

When the push forward from Imphal began in June 1944 there were eleven RAF fighter squadrons stationed on the six airfields in the area. Eighty of the pilots were Canadians, about one quarter of the total. The exploits of Bud Walker, Charlie Watt, Bert Madill, Verne Butler, Lorne LeCraw, and Bruce Pinch are representative of what these Canadian with their Spitfires, Hurricanes, and Thunderbolts did in offering close support to Slim's advance.

Atholl Sutherland Brown from Victoria played a slightly different role. After two years of training and waiting in Canada and Britain, he was posted to India and to 177 RAF Squadron. They were flying Beaufighters, twin engined fighter-bombers with a reputation for stealth, especially at night, a top speed of 330 mph, an endurance of four hours, and a range of 1500 miles. Moreover they were heavily armed and adaptable to various conformations of weaponry, including rockets and bombs. Their usual and preferred role was in the interdiction of lines of communication — road convoys, river barges, trains and locomotives. The enemy had quickly become wary of these dangerous aircraft that could swoop silently down and blow up troop formations and truck loads of supplies headed for the front, and took to travelling by night, hiding their lorries, engines and motor launches under cunningly camouflaged shelters by day. On one of Atholl's first operational sorties he flew as No. 2 to Joe Van Nes, another Canadian and a veteran on Beaufighters in Burma. Joe was especially renowned for his ability to spy out locomotives no matter how well they were hidden or disguised. On this patrol they flew to Mandalay, then track-crawled up to Lashio, the western terminus of the Burma Road. Before they returned they had accounted for two freight trains and two lorries. Throughout May, Atholl completed seven sorties and every sortie meant more discomfort and inconvenience for the enemy; at the end of the month his total was five locomotives and thirteen lorries. "Damage to locomotives looked spectacular," Atholl remembers, "as they erupted like geysers, but they were often repaired in a week or so." They had little to fear from enemy air attacks on these patrols but flak was frequent and often intense. Their speed and their stealth were their protection and kept the damage and casualty rate down.

For two weeks in August Atholl moved with a detachment from his Squadron to the Tulihal strip at Imphal. Despite monsoon weather that wiped out flying for five days, Atholl and his navigator — the Beaufighter carried a crew of two — completed seven sorties, strafing and bombing the roads and the railway between the Chindwin and the Irrawaddy. Often the only target they found was a single lorry or a small bridge; the patrol when they shot up a moving train and a convoy of lorries was counted a real success. The last four months of 1944, and the last four months of Atholl's tour, were particularly intense. In an article entitled "Indian Days and Burmese Nights" in the journal *Canadian Military History*, Atholl matter-of-factly catalogues the score of his 58 sorties:

> We caused, or shared in, the following damage to the Japanese-run
> transportation network and other targets: 9 locomotives under steam
> and six goods trains damaged, 30 lorries, 3 staff cars, 2 bulldozers and
> a gasoline lorry destroyed. We also damaged some 30 other lorries. We
> attacked 3 coastal freighters and two oil barges, rocketed several bridges,
> set an oil pipeline on fire and destroyed a cache of oil drums.

Atholl finished his tour on December 28, 1944. He was awarded the DFC in 1945. In his retirement years he wrote a well-received history of 177 Squadron, *Silently into the Midst of Things*.

It was with this calibre of support from the Canadians and other members of the RAF that Slim and the XIV Army were encouraged and enabled to succeed in the hot pursuit that followed the success of Imphal and Kohima and eventually opened the road back to Rangoon. The first phase of the "road-back" initiative finished in mid-December when the Royal Engineers slung an 1154 foot bridge across the Chindwin, the longest Bailey bridge in the world and the culmination of the Kohima-Imphal battle. It had cost the British forces 40,000 men, killed and wounded. But 50,000 Japanese were dead on the battlefield, and it is estimated another 25,000 died of wounds. If one adds the casualties of Stilwell's Northern Combat Area Command, the Japanese army had lost a total of over 90,000 men during the *U-Go* operation. Knowing all this, Slim began to plan for the retaking of Mandalay and even began to scheme of going beyond that and heading for Rangoon.

XIII

THE CANADIAN OFFICER PARTY

A LETTER to *Dekho*, the magazine of the Burma Star Association in Britain, asking for information about Canadians with the British or Indian Army in the Burma Campaign, evoked the following response from David York of Croydon:

> *I served in 5/57 Battery, 28ᵗʰ (Jungle) Field Regiment, Royal Artillery and recall the following brief encounter in the Imphal siege. As a Gunner Wireless Operator I frequently found myself on the Forward Observation Post with the Observation Officer and an Observation Post Assistant. On one such occasion — I believe we were in the Litan Valley — we were accompanied by a young Canadian Artillery officer, with us to learn the ropes on such operations. I can recall no name or rank and he was with us for the duration of the patrol, probably no more than five days. One item does stick in my mind is that his personal weapons included a very light carbine rifle which, when compared with our heavy .303 Enfield rifles, was something to behold!*

This was a puzzling communication, for there was no record of Canadian Army personnel in Burma. With the next mail came a similar letter from Ross Stuart of Stirling, Scotland and the mystery deepened:

> *Whilst guarding a trail in Burma about December 1944, a Canadian captain from the Princess Pat's Canadian Light Infantry, our sister regiment, came in sight and asked if we were the Royal Scots and, on my replying in the affirmative and getting a replacement, I took him to our Adjutant. On the way I told him he was the first Canadian I had seen since North Africa. He told me he had been in London 10 days ago and he and a colleague, who had gone to the Queen's Own Cameron Highlanders, had been sent to evaluate the situation in order that a whole Canadian division would be uplifted from Italy and be sent straight into Burma.*

Here was evidence of three Canadian officers coming directly from the European theatre to Burma, yet no hint of how they got there or what power had sent them. An enquiry to the Directorate of History of the Department of National Defence brought a sceptical response: there was no indication whatsoever that Canadian troops were ever sent to Burma during World War II.[1] The historians were confident in that reply since it was well known that Mackenzie King was adamantly opposed to any Canadians being involved in Britain's fight to regain her empire. In recording a discussion with the War Committee in his diary he wrote: "I held very strongly to the view that no government in Canada would send its men to India, Burma or Singapore ... and hope to get through a general election successfully. ... Our people, I know, would never agree to paying out taxes for Canadian troops to fight, whether in the air or at sea or on land for the protection of India or the recovery of Burma or Singapore." Despite this, Stacey in his official history of the Canadian Army notes that one rumour — among many then current — was that the First Canadian Corps was to be withdrawn from the Mediterranean Area and sent to Burma.

Unit records corroborated the anecdotal evidence. The War Diary of the Queen's Own Camerons of Canada showed that the regiment had tested and accepted the light-weight Winchester carbine in November 1944. The War Diary of the British Camerons throughout August 1944 notes that "Captain J. S. Mulholland, Q. O. Cam. H. of Canada is attached to the battalion for training." Moreover, Peter Grant, in his book *A Highlander Goes to War*, mentions the visit: "We were kept amused at this time by the arrival of a Canadian officer, Jim Mulholland, who was a member of the Cameron Highlanders of Canada, and who had been present at the Dieppe raid where so many of his countrymen died. He was an expert on regimental history and never missed a chance of going on a patrol or a reconnaissance."

It was almost a year before the mystery began to unravel. In December 2000 Mary Anne Kinloch of Victoria sent the author copies of all the letters her father, Major William Bramley-Moore, had written home when he went to India and Burma with a group of Canadians. A week later, Major General George Spencer of Chester Basin, Nova Scotia revealed himself as the senior officer of the Canadian Officer Party and the man who could tell the whole story.

The story begins in August 1941 when General Crerar sent General McNaughton a short memo: "Have been considering the feasibility and desirability of attaching limited number of highly qualified Canadian

---

[1] This opinion is a slip in institutional memory. Colonel C. P. Stacey in *Six Years of War*, the first volume of his *Official History of the Canadian Army in the Second World War*, had briefly mentioned the Canadian Officer Party in Burma (p. 509).

officers as observers with British Armies operating outside U.K. These would report on operations, training, administration and also on equipment manufactured in Canada. Proportion of these to be nominated by you from officers overseas. Desire your comments this proposal and any suggestions concerning implementation." The policy that eventually grew from this suggestion resulted in Canadian observers being attached to the British Army in Tunisia, the Australian Army in Australia and New Guinea, and the American Army in the Pacific. It also accounted for the Canadian Officer Party in Burma.

McNaughton's thinking was that the observers were not to be senior officers who experienced the war at command and headquarters level, but captains and majors who would have direct contact with the enemy, though he did allow for "a sprinkling of Lt. Colonels with Staff College qualifications." Nor was it to be a "Cook's Tour" for a group of mere observers. Canadian staff officers were to take over staff appointments and carry out duties in full. All officers were to have European battle experience and were to go to units and formations that were in contact with the enemy. To broaden the experience, the group was to include officers from various army corps, infantry, artillery, armoured, signals, engineers, and medical. On January 19, 1944 approval was given for twenty Canadian officers from Europe to go to SEAC and twenty Canadian officers from Canada to go to the South West Pacific for service with Australian and American units. The Initiating Order stated that the expectation was that "the information and knowledge gained will be of great benefit to any future operations in which the Canadian Army may participate in this theatre (SEAC) or elsewhere in the Far East." Then came a cautionary rider: "This does not imply any decision as to future Canadian involvement in these theatres."

The nominal role of the five staff officers and eighteen company commanders selected for the SEAC party reflected McNaughton's thinking:

Lt-Col G. H. Spencer, Royal Canadian Engineers
Lt-Col P. R. Bingham, Canadian Infantry Corps
Major C. H. Cook, Canadian Infantry Corps
Major A. A. Duncanson, Canadian Infantry Corps
    (Royal Cdn Regiment)
Major W. Bramley-Moore, Royal Canadian Army
    Medical Corps
Major C. P. Keeley, Canadian Infantry Corps
Major H. D. P. Tighe, MC, Canadian Infantry Corps
Major J. S. Mulholland, Canadian Infantry Corps
    (Cameron Highlanders)
Major E. G. F. Anderson, Royal Cdn Corps of Signals
Major H. A. Farthing, Royal Cdn Artillery

Major C. V. B. Corbet, Canadian Infantry Corps
Captain J. G. W. Turney, Royal Cdn Corps of Signals
Captain F. G. Henderson, Royal Cdn Army Service Corps
Captain A. P. Boswell, Canadian Infantry Corps
Captain J. M. Patton, GC, Royal Cdn Engineers
Captain P. A. Ballachy, Canadian Infantry Corps
      (Royal Hamilton Light Infantry)
Captain E. H. A. Carson, Royal Cdn Artillery
Captain W. H. Law, Canadian Armoured Corps
Captain G. P. Knifton, Canadian Infantry Corps
      (Algoma Regiment)
Captain W. R. Berwick, Canadian Infantry Corps
      (S. Saskatchewan Regiment)
Captain M. N. Bow, Canadian Infantry Corps
      (Calgary Highlanders)
Lieut. F. K. Trites, Canadian Infantry Corps
Lieut. V. H. Zala, Canadian Infantry Corps

The group left England by ship in early June. Although the southern half of Italy was now in Allied hands and they were able to take the Mediterranean-Suez route, they were nevertheless thirty-two days in transit and the final arrival in Bombay was a relief. Still, the sea voyage had its high points. The Canadians entered two teams in the deck-hockey competition and were eliminated almost before they started. They did better in the tug-o-war. In the semi-finals they found themselves confronting a team from DEMS (Duration of Emergency Merchant Seamen), burly, brawny men with forearms "the size of other people's thighs." Undaunted, the Canadians put their all into the contest and won the first pull. After a long sweating and straining, tugging and struggling, they lost the second by scant inches. Worn out by that effort, they lost the third. They took comfort in the fact that the DEMS team then went on to defeat the other finalist with no trouble at all and in the awareness that they could now turn their attention to the three hundred females on board. According to Major Pat Keeley, the Canadians "corralled all the good-looking ones." Perhaps the heat of the Red Sea passage quieted even that sport. The midday temperature on the boat deck was reported to be 110° F in the shade.

The reception the party received at Bombay almost overwhelmed them. They were whisked off the boat and through customs as privileged travellers. A Brigadier made a special trip from New Delhi to bring personal greetings from Lord Mountbatten, and then they were taken by private auto to their various billets. The two Colonels, George Spencer and Peter Bingham, were accommodated with the Area Commander and his charming wife who, on their first night in India, took them to dinner at the Taj, the most sumptuous hotel in Bombay. On the second evening they were taken to the Royal Bombay Yatch Club — according to Peter Bingham, "the most exclusive club in India." The short stay in Bombay was marred by incessant rain, since it was the height of the monsoon season. They took time to do some shopping and fill in what was missing from their tropical kit, in particular, a tin trunk to keep clothing at least a little bit dry. And they took time to see some of the sights of this strange land. William Bramley-Moore delighted to report to his nine year old daughter, "Helen, I've seen camels on the desert, Arabs, bullocks drawing all kinds of loads, people with parcels on their heads, veiled women, sacred cows, big monkeys with little monkeys on their backs, and all sorts of funny things."

After the sojourn in Bombay, the plan was that the officers were to visit training formations and units associated with their arm of service. For some, this part of the plan seems not to have gone as well as had been hoped. Bramley-Moore and Pat Keeley spent a lot of time playing rummy in the rain and complaining about the lack of mail from home. On the other hand, George Spencer was given a busy month of indoctrination and acclimatization, including a short course in Urdu, familiarization with the various religious and dietary observances of Indian, Sikh, and Gurkha troops, and an introduction to jungle operations. At the end of this part of the visit, the party gathered in Calcutta. They stayed in Canada House, a hostel run by the Canadian Legion for Canadians on leave and not comparable to the treatment they were accorded in Bombay. However, the Women's Volunteer Service took them over and made sure they were well entertained. In any event, their stay here was short; Bramley-Moore had time for a scant half hour meeting with Doug Haddow, his cousin from Edmonton now with a radar station in India. Then they went off to Burma to join front-line formations and units, and to begin the action that was the whole purpose of their SEAC sojourn.

After his crash course in Urdu and the cultures of India, George Spencer found himself posted to an East African Division. The common language was Swahili and there wasn't a Jain, a Brahmin, a Hindu, or a Parsi in the camp. The Division was without a chief administrative staff officer and George was asked to take over the position. Fortunately the Headquarters functioned in English. It was mid-August 1944, scarcely a month after the siege of Imphal was lifted. Slim was pursuing the fleeing Japanese toward the Chindwin and the division George Spencer was assigned to was given the task of pushing the enemy down the Kabaw Valley. Spencer was a well-trained and very experienced engineer, but nothing in his training or experience had prepared him for the Kabaw Valley in the monsoon rain. The "road" was a jungle track that had to be cleared, widened, drained, and surfaced with a corduroy of logs before it was fit for even a jeep. He had never before thought of mules as a preferred mode of conveyance, and elephants, he thought, had gone out with Hannibal. In the Burma jungle both, he discovered, were indispensable. "These factors," Colonel Spencer matter-of-factly remarked, "abetted by a tenacious enemy, slowed the rate of advance."

As chief administrative staff officer for the Division, George found one of his priority tasks was to devise a standard operating procedure for daily and weekly supply drops so as to facilitate planning and reduce signal traffic. He was also responsible for drawing up procedures for selecting and establishing dropping zones and for collecting, storing, and distributing air-dropped supplies. Air supply, mule transport, jungle tracks, monsoon rains, precipitous mountains — all these things were challenges George Spencer had never before imagined. He dug into them with a will. When the regular administrative staff officer was invalided out, he took over completely. "I am very pleased with my lot," he wrote to his superiors in London, "the work is intensely interesting and I have been working at 'intensive' rates."

Major Bramley-Moore's Burma assignment took him to a tent on top of a 5000 foot hill south of Imphal. In a letter home he mentions that the Japs were recently here, but he quickly reassures his wife that "they are now well south of here and still running."

He was in charge of part of a field ambulance manned almost entirely by Indian troops. The best part of his command, however, was that it included 36 mules! The ambulance marched forward with the advancing army, one day climbing 2000 feet in two miles to clear a 6500 foot mountain. Three mules fell over the cliff and Bramley-Moore had to go down to cut them free of their packs. He was surprised that they got up, shook themselves, and then scrambled back up the slope unhurt. The men chatter away in Urdu or Hindustani and Bramley-Moore in English, but eventually they all understand one another. In some ways, it was frustrating to be dependent upon air supply. Their mountain–top camp was usually in cloud and the rare supply plane that got in brought rations and petrol, whereas they desperately need blankets and tarpaulins. Since their only transport was mules, the petrol was useful only for lighting fires.

The British Army did its best to put the Canadians into interesting and responsible positions. Peter Bingham, attached to an infantry regiment in the Tiddim Road area, was sent on a special operation to outflank the Japanese who were trying to block their advance. In a letter to Canadian Military Headquarters in London, he described the patrol: "It was a wonderful experience over hellish country, climbing two ridges of 4000 feet and one of 6000, both covered with thick jungle and all by means of a goat track that was never wider than four feet. The rate of advance was about a mile an hour with good going, and less off the track. It took four days to get behind the enemy and one to push him off." Even though they had to subsist on mule meat for three or four days, Colonel Bingham's enthusiasm shines through in his account. He gleefully reports that he has been promised the job of second-in-command of a Brigade "that is in for a lot of fun in the near future."

Major Andrew Duncanson of the Royal Regiment of Canada began his SEAC sojourn with three day train trip in "a beautifully appointed air-conditioned coach" and then a seven-hour wait on "the dirtiest, hottest, most fly-ridden station platform I have ever seen" to spend a few days at a Technical Training Centre. Then he was posted to the Fourth battalion of the Royal West Kent Regiment just as they were about to begin pursuing the Japanese down the Tiddim Road. Andy felt he was really into the midst of the Burma campaign when he was welcomed by Colonel Dan Laverty, the hero of the Kohima siege. Four days later he was sent to A Company "to be acting 2 i/c (second-in-command), to observe, and to make myself generally useful." It was a fortuitous appointment. A Punjab Regiment was going forward to confront the enemy at Milestone (Ms) 86 on the Tiddim Road and A Company of the West Kents was ordered to beat its way over mountains and valleys, through rivers and jungle, and to come in behind the confrontation. At 0700 hours on 24 August they set off, with Andy in charge of the mules.

Only a mile along the way, the track became "unmuleable," and Andy and his engineers worked till midnight to improve it. "Most uncomfortable," Andy's diary notes, "Rain and midges very bad." Next day the platoon backtracked and tried a different route. Six mules fell over the "khud" (cliff) and it took four hours to get them back on their feet. Ahead of them, the muddy track climbed 2000 feet in one mile and it took another four hours for the column to reach the top. On the third and fourth days they repeatedly brushed with the enemy or ambushed his patrols. The supply planes circled but did not drop because of the enemy action so Andy's platoon had to eat emergency rations. But their spirits were high, for in each encounter the enemy's casualties exceeded theirs. At the end of the month they were hovering just beneath the mountain that was their objective while the tanks and artillery blasted the enemy position. When the barrage lifted, they stormed the top and found the Japanese had withdrawn.

Andy and his company fell in with another company of the West Kents that was under the command of another Canadian exchange officer, Captain Berwick of the South Saskatchewan Regiment, and they struck out for the Tiddim Road. The first tank they met on the road was commanded by Captain Law of the Canadian Armoured Corp.

Briefly, the Battalion rested and took stock. They had started at Ms 77 and they had reached Ms 96, nineteen miles in seven days. Considering the weather, the terrain, and the enemy action, it was an acceptable advance.

They had counted 59 enemy dead while their own losses were two killed and 26 wounded, but it was disconcerting that 70 soldiers had been evacuated with malaria and other illnesses despite strict hygiene discipline. The Battalion continued its advance next day and accounted for twelve more enemy soldiers. They also came upon thirty enemy dead in an abandoned First Aid Post, a sure sign of the trend of the battle. Increasingly Japanese stores and equipment fell into their hands. Andy personally found several bags and boxes of unopened mail hastily abandoned in the elephant grass along the roadside.

The West Kents took up the advance toward Tiddim. They fought the rain, the mud, the steep mountain slopes, the torrents of water in the chaungs, midges and mosquitoes, and of course, the enemy. Because they were now completely on air supply, they got mail and a few amenities. Andy's diary notes with particular satisfaction that his ration of whiskey consisted of one bottle of Canadian Club. On October 31 they reached a small village on the banks of the Manipur river 20 miles south of Tiddim. Briefly the Brigade concentrated here and the Headman of the tiny village gave a party to celebrate the eviction of the Japanese and the return of the "government." The singing and dancing and the *zhu* drinking (rice beer) went on till 2 in the morning. Andy didn't stay for the whole party, but he took home with him a translation of the songs the villagers had sung:

> *The enemy wanted to rule the whole world, but the English govern-*
> *ment and we drove them all out so they cannot rule even one district.*
> *This enemy is not only the Chins' enemy but of the whole world. They*
> *came to spoil our Chin Hills by using fire on our houses, but we drove*
> *them out. They cannot burn our houses and we are still alive, by our*
> *own efforts, with the help of the government.*

The sentiments expressed in the song were not untypical of the hill tribes as the British returned — pride in their tribe and happiness that the "government" was back. One native village, when asked why they celebrated the return of the British answered that "at least the smallpox vaccinations would be resumed."

On November 21 the West Kents got the word that the Fifth Division was being withdrawn. They were then thirty miles beyond Tiddim and Andy calculated that, after the first off-road operation to get behind the action, the Battalion had managed an average advance of 8 miles per day, a more than creditable achievement.

Andy Duncanson's personal achievements with the West Kents were also creditable. In reporting on Andy's service with the Battalion, the Commanding Officer wrote: "This officer was a great help to the Battalion and commanded a company during one phase of the ops in action. A sound, pleasant personality and not afraid of hard work or accepting responsibility." To this commendation the Brigadier added: "This officer has done me well. I feel sure that a course at Staff College will not only benefit Duncanson, but any formation he may subsequently join." The Army was in Andy Duncanson's blood — his father was a colonel back in Canada — and he delighted at the idea of Staff College, but army life did not appeal to his wife, and in deference to her objections, he reluctantly turned his back on the opportunity that his service in Burma had provided.

Many of the Canadian officers in Burma encountered critical moments. Captain Law, the tank commander Berwick and Duncanson had met on the Tiddim Road, was captured by the Japanese but managed to escape and rejoin his unit the same night. Captain Henderson, a Royal Canadian Army Service Corps officer, was made Divisional Transport Officer. Major Farthing fought in the Litan Valley, just south of Ukhrul, with the 28th Jungle Field Regiment, Royal Artillery. All these officers were in action on the push to the Chindwin. Others, including Keeley, Bow, Boswell, Knifton, Trites, and Zala, had been posted to the Arakan front. Captain Bow was reported to be doing very well as second in command of a company there, and even, for a time, as Commanding Officer of the battalion. Lieutenant Trites was wounded in the chest and head in the attack on Goppe Bazaar. The British commander visited him in hospital and reported him "very cheerful and getting along well."

In short, the Canadian officers were getting just the sort of experience they had come to Burma for. They were meeting the enemy and learning his ways, they were experiencing monsoon weather and prickly heat, and they were testing their stamina against an inhospitable terrain. Moreover, they were proving themselves. In his informal reports to Canadian Military Headquarters Colonel Spencer passed along the comments and compliments he had received. In September he wrote: "All reports I have had about and from our officers out here are most encouraging and they are doing splendidly." Next month he added: "I have received most encouraging reports of the activities of our officers. The Corps Commander commented the other day on the cheerfulness and keenness of the Canadians."

As for the officers themselves, they had complaints at first. There was the uncertainty about the communication line between themselves and London. Were they forgotten? Would acting ranks be confirmed? And what had happened to their mail? Bramley-Moore had no mail between June 8 and September 8. It turned out, they had been told to have mail addressed care of the Base Post Office, Bombay, but no such unit existed. More vexing was the question of expenses. It was not until George Spencer wrote a detailed account of the out-of-pocket expenses each officer had incurred that a satisfactory settlement was made. For all the officers, however, once they got into action, all these worries seemed unimportant and the consensus was that the Canadian Army could easily manage the jungle and the Japanese. As Pat Keeley wrote "So far I have seen nothing to make me change my opinion that, given a couple of months acclimatization and getting used to the jungle, our lads could do a grand job out here. Personally, I think it would be 'right up their alley' for a good number of them." It is interesting to note that a similar conclusion was reached by the officer party to the South Pacific. Under the headline "Canadians Suited for Jungle War," a small article in the *Toronto Globe and Mail* for December 16, 1944 reads as follows:

> *Western Canadian bushmen would make good soldiers for the jungle war against the Japanese, Lt. Col. Harry F. Cotton of Winnipeg, commander of a group of Canadian officers who went to the South Pacific for training, said today in an interview on his return here. "The battle of the jungle is the battle of the trails," he added, "and Western Canadian bushmen would be good at that sort of fighting."*

When the time came for the Canadian Officer Party to withdraw, Lt. Col. Spencer gathered the whole group in New Delhi for a debriefing session. Then they were given a short sight-seeing tour of India. This too was to be part of their indoctrination, intended to give them a brief introduction to the history and geography of the Indian sub-continent. One group, for example, was sent to Peshawar, the Khyber Pass and the North West Frontier. Colonel Spencer submitted his official *Consolidated Report of Canadian Army Officers attached to South East Asia Command from 11 June 1944 to 17 January 1945,* a straightforward, well-written analysis of the Japanese as jungle fighters and of Canadian soldiers as potentially effective opponents. In it Spencer stressed the tenacity and foolhardy bravery of the foe, the intractable nature of the terrain, the peculiarities of air supply, and the need for special attention to hygiene and medical concerns. He also emphasized the excellent cooperation the Canadian Officer Party had enjoyed and noted that all officers had held staff or command positions and all had acquitted themselves nobly. This last point he underlined by passing on the recommendation that two of the officers be sent on staff courses. His conclusion was that, given two or three months training and acclimatization, the Canadian Army could perform well against the Japanese in the jungle or elsewhere.

In mid-January 1945 the Canadians left India for Britain, taking with them knowledge and experience that made them unique among their peers. It was intended that they should communicate that knowledge and experience to the members of the Canadian Army Pacific Force and some were indeed serving that purpose when the dropping of the A-bomb made it all unnecessary.

XIV

435 AND 436 SQUADRONS, RCAF

MAJOR GENERAL Julian Thompson, writing in *The Lifeblood of War*, emphatically states the case for air supply on the Burma Front: "If the war in the Mediterranean was difficult logistically, that in South East Asia was infinitely more so. Indeed, it is hard to find any theatre of war which posed so many logistic conundrums or where supply played such a dominating part in deciding the outcome, on both sides." In the Imphal siege Slim had tested the truth of this judgment. Only by asking the Air Force to fly beyond safe limits had he been able to ensure delivery of the supplies he absolutely had to have each day. Now that the siege was lifted and the pursuit to the Chindwin was fully launched, the need was for more, not less, and it is in this context that one comprehends his concern upon hearing a great flight of Dakotas leaving the station on the morning of December 10, 1944:

> I knew loaded aircraft were due to leave for 33 Corps later in the morning, but I was surprised at this early start. I sent somebody to discover what it was all about. To my consternation, I learnt that, without warning, three squadrons of American Dakotas (seventy-five aircraft), allotted to Fourteenth Army maintenance, had been suddenly ordered to China. ... The noise of their engines was the first intimation anyone in Fourteenth Army had of the administrative crisis now bursting upon us.

It was fortuitous that two all-Canadian Dakota squadrons were waiting in the wings ready to dash onto the stage and rescue the bewildered general. 413 Squadron, Canada's contribution to coastal patrol in the Burma Campaign, had done a wonderful job in saving Ceylon, but the Japanese Navy was now virtually inactive and 413 was about to be thanked and sent home. If Canada were to promise another fighter squadron or another bomber squadron, it would be welcome but not absolutely indispensable. Two Canadian transport squadrons, on the other hand, were a *sine qua non* for Slim's push to the Chindwin and beyond. That is why Air Chief Marshal Sir Richard Peirse, Allied Air Commander-in-Chief wrote emphatically to the Vice Chief of the Air Staff in London on August 5, 1944 that "operations this coming winter depend entirely on the prompt arrival of 435 and 436 RCAF Transport Squadrons and their being operationally ready during October and December respectively."

They were not going to be quite so prompt as Peirse wanted. RCAF personnel for the two squadrons did not begin to gather in Gujrat, India until October 1944. Scarcely had the bare bones of a squadron appeared before the Canadian Government began to clamour for their recall. On November 9 Air Commodore Plant wrote to inform Air Marshal Leckie that "we have requested that Air Ministry withdraw our two Transport Squadrons from that theatre as soon as possible." So frequent and so persistent were these clamours that Air Marshal Leckie protested to the Canadian Minister of National Defence: "I deprecate any further pressure on our part at the present time as the withdrawal of the squadrons would unquestionably seriously jeopardize the operation now in hand." Still Ottawa insisted upon the return of the two squadrons, until finally, Sir Douglas Evill, Vice Chief of the Air Staff, wrote a rather petulant memorandum (in June 1945) saying, in effect, "Quit bothering me," and adding "There is still an acute shortage of air transport in SEA where the forces in Burma are still mainly dependent upon air supply." This muted, but did not end, the Canadian government's badgering.

Along with Ottawa's inability to understand the important role of 435 and 436 Squadrons in Burma went the misconception, harboured not merely by the Government but by the upper echelons of the RCAF as well, that transport flying in SEAC was as restful as a holiday at a luxury spa. Thus the advice given by the brass in Canada regarding the formation of the squadrons was that aircrew should be drawn from ex-operational crews, especially from Bomber Command "to reward air crew for completing an operationally dangerous tour." Flying an unarmed and unarmoured Dakota up to and into hostile territory through monsoon clouds and over unforgiving jungle and mountains was perhaps not as dangerous as taking a bomber over Hamburg, but it was not simply a stroll in the park.

Unaware of all that was going on behind the scene, the crews for 435 and 436 began to gather. The RAF had insisted that all the Canadians posted to these squadrons should be experienced and seasoned crews. The RCAF sent what it could. Some did indeed come from RAF transport squadrons that were active in Burma, but others came from two bomber reconnaissance squadrons that were being disbanded on the West Coast of Canada and others straight from the first course of the brand new Transport Operational Training Unit at Comox, BC. They gathered at Chaklala for six weeks of training and acclimatization — low flying, glider towing, glider pickup, formation flying. In November 1944 they were organized into two squadrons, 435 and 436, and moved to Gujrat.

Gujrat was a big station built as a permanent base but unused for some time. The billets were mud huts that reeked of mould and dampness. Apart from that, life at Gujrat, if not good was at least fascinatingly different from anything a squadron of Canadians had ever met before. For 45 rupees per month (fifteen dollars) a group of officers could hire a bearer who made beds, swept the floor, shone shoes, arranged for the "beasti wallah" to bring bath and shaving water and for the "dhobi wallah" to do the laundry. On the way to breakfast one could buy a banana or orange to augment the mess meals. Fruit that was peeled before consumption was taken to be acceptable. Other fruits the fruit wallah dipped in *pinki pani,* a potassium permanganate solution, before handing it over. Since no one knew the strength or age of the solution, the efficacy of this precaution was doubtful. The "char wallah" carried his boiler and supplies on a pole across his shoulder and sold tea and cakes all around the station. Tropical issue clothing was ghastly but the tailor could measure an airman for slacks and a bush jacket and deliver it the next day. All the messing facilities on the station were contracted out to a *babu,* a big shot, who in turn contracted them out to little shots. It was one of the duties of the orderly officer to visit the airmen's canteen, take a portion of chips from the delivery counter, and check its weight to ensure that the babu was not cheating the unsuspecting Canadian airmen.

After moving to Gujrat, the two squadrons added paratroop dropping to their repertoire. The wireless operator/air gunners took a course to qualify as jumpmasters. Their task was to ensure that each "stick" of ten paratroopers went out in short order and in even rhythm, and an important part of their training included making a jump themselves. In this part of their operations they trained with a regiment of Gurkhas, those affable men from Nepal who had won such a reputation for bravery in the First World War and enhanced it in the Second. The climax of the training was a mass paratroop drop, both squadrons taking off in formation and flying in formation. It was a simulation of the real thing and high-ranking officers of the Air Force and the Army were on hand to see if these two colonial squadrons could do the job properly.

It was still dark at 4:30 in the morning when the crews crawled into the buses and headed for the drome. The Gurkhas were already in the aircraft. The pilots did their cockpit check and run-up, gave "thumbs up" to the crewmen to pull the chocks and taxied out for take-off. They were to cruise at five thousand feet to two turning points, then head for the dropping zone in order to begin the drop precisely at 10 o'clock. Holding fifty planes in tight formation while making a turn is difficult, and the first turn was sloppy. The second was a bit better. Now on the approach to the dropping zone, the formation had to slow down and let down to 750 feet. At the appropriate moment, each pilot switched on the green light over the back door. The jumpmaster grabbed the arm of the first Gurkha, shouted "Go!" and literally threw him out the door. In short order all the troops were out. The crew checked their watches; they were twenty seconds late.

In three minutes the two squadrons had dropped seven hundred and fifty fully equipped paratroopers into an area less than ten acres in extent and within seconds of the designated hour. The high-ranking officers were impressed and the squadrons were judged ready to take their place at the front. They were to be the answer to the fervent prayer Slim had uttered that morning when the American Dakotas roared off to China.

Squadron Leader Bill Irving was the Protestant padre for the squadrons. He was looked up to because he had already done a tour as a navigator and been awarded the DFC. As was appropriate on a transport squadron he used a petrol drum for an altar when he held a drumhead service. Christmas was approaching and he was practising carols with a small volunteer choir when the word came that 435 Squadron was moving to the front. The choir never did finish learning the descant to "The First Noel." On December 20, 1944, 435 Squadron, with the help of 436 Squadron, flew itself forward to Imphal.

The move itself was a first for the area, forty aircraft moving a full transport squadron with all its kit and equipment across half a continent in 24 hours. One aircraft lost an engine shortly after takeoff. It was at 5000 feet and fifty miles from Gujrat. There was no thought of bailing out for they carried parachutes only for the crew. The pilot turned around and headed back. He ordered his passengers to jettison kit, first government equipment, then personal kit. With his load lightened he scraped into Gujrat and lined up on the murky line of acetylene lamps that pretended to represent runway lighting. Unfortunately he lined up on the wrong side of them, ploughed into a monsoon ditch and slid along it till he hit the embankment at the end. The aircraft was a write-off but apart from bumps and bruises, one broken ankle, and one broken wrist, the human cargo survived the crash. That was the only misfortune of the move, that and one instance of airborne infection. On the aircraft on which F/L Jim Barnard, 435's medical officer, was riding one officer said "Doc, I feel lousy." Jim listened to his symptoms — tiredness, nausea, loss of appetite, dark urine, light stools. He took him to the open door of the Dak and looked at his eyes. The whites were definitely

yellow. That was the 28th case of jaundice Jim had seen since arriving at
Gujrat, but the only one he diagnosed at 10,000 feet.[1]

At Imphal, the airstrip at Tulihal was to be 435's new home. It was not
much of a home. There were a few empty bashas with bare earth floors and
a metal plate set on bricks for a kitchen. The Operational Record Book
dryly notes: "Apart from the fact that there was no moon, no quarters and
no food, few difficulties were encountered." There was also no water, no
tools or equipment, and no spares. However, there were aircraft; there was
a strip; and there was a job to be done.

When 435 landed at Tulihal in December of 1944 the runway had a dust-
free all-weather surface and was outsize in all dimensions. The story was
that the American who had previously occupied the strip had asked that it
be surfaced to solve the dust problem and that it be at least 150 by 6000.
Since the Americans worked in feet and the British in yards, the runway
ended up being three times the required size.

As for the surfacing, it was a wonder-product made by impregnating heavy
hessian cloth with a bitumous substance that gave the cloth waterproofing,
flexibility, and durability. With this product an all-weather landing strip
could be built cheaply in one or two days so that tactical air forces could
keep pace with an advancing army. The Americans used pierced metal
plates, but they were noisy, heavy, unstable, expensive and only "waterproof"
if the heavy monsoons rains could be drained away. In Britain, Brigadier
D. H. Storms, a Toronto engineer who had joined the Royal Canadian
Engineers when war broke out, watched the engineers experimenting with
various coverings and concluded they were "not worth a damn." Naturally,
he was challenged to do better. He asked his colleague in Toronto, Charles
Baskine, a Russian oil technician who had emigrated to Canada, to come
to Britain to help him. They took over a whole roofing plant in London
with their experiments and soon had a product. To test their invention, a
French-Canadian company of Royal Canadian Engineers was given the job
of making an operational airstrip in one day. In light drizzle and before an
austere assemblage of red-tabbed engineers a flight of fighters came in to
test it. The first four planes landed easily, but the fifth opened a gap and
the following planes greatly enlarged the hole. The strip had been laid in
the rain and the seams were not perfectly sealed. "The operation was a
success, but the patient nearly died," recalled Brigadier Storms, but in fact
the experts saw what the trouble was and that it could easily be corrected,
and bithess was born. It was a boon to the Army, especially in Burma. Fourteenth Army engineers spread it over the road to Tamu, a road that would

---

[1] Dr. Barnard attributed all 28 cases to the "filth, flies, and fecal contamination" of the Transit
Camp at Karachi. Once the Canadians had their own kitchens, there was no more jaundice.

otherwise be a bottomless quagmire of mud, and Slim gloated: "For over a hundred miles this novel surface proved able to take a thousand vehicles a day when the monsoon came." One authority has said that the development of bithess by Brigadier Storms, his fellow Canadian army engineers, and a Russian civilian had a greater influence on the course of the war than the development of the V2 rocket.

As for the Tulihal strip, the siege was at its height when it was to be surfaced so the bithess had to be flown in, 368 tons of it from Calcutta in one week. When 435 Squadron arrived the runway had already been well broken in and only a sign at the entrance warned, in Urdu and in English, of the fragile nature of its membrane:

ASTI GUMAO.
JOR SE BRAKE MAT MARO.
CORNER SLOWLY.
AVOID FIERCE BRAKING.

The haste with which the squadron was thrown into operations under-lines how urgently it was needed. We arrived at Tulihal on December 20, and my log book shows I flew two sorties the next day. They were short, just over two hours each. We flew in formation, and we were told we had an umbrella escort, that is, fighters at height patrolling our track, but we never saw them. We were apprehensive, of course, for we had also been told that the enemy would know of our arrival and would probably come over to shake us up a bit, but we didn't see them either. It was a lovely bright day. We climbed to 8000 feet to clear the mountain range that lay to the east of our drome, then let down and flew 200 feet above miles of mountains covered with fluffy puffs of green foliage. When we took, off my navigator had given me a course; now he stood between the two pilots' seats with his map in his hand. How could he know where we were? Everything looked the same all around and in every direction. Our first trip was a landing; the strip, just a clearing in the jungle, looked too narrow for a Dakota and even if it was long enough for a landing, was it really long enough for a take-off? Surprisingly, both the landing and the take-off went well.

The second sortie was a drop. Again we flew up over the mountains and then down across the jungle. Somehow Pete Wasylyshyn, my navigator, found that wee jungle clearing with the recognition markings NR. We flew without doors and as we neared the dropping zone (DZ) the crew and kickers piled the cargo opening with as many bags and packages as it could accommodate. I tried to gauge the wind and estimate the lead-time to drop our supplies right on the DZ. There was a green and a red light and a bell by the cargo door. Approaching the DZ, I turned on the red warning light. When I estimated it was time to kick out the stuff, I turned on the green light and the bell, and when we were beyond the dropping range, I turned them off and banked steeply to see where our drop had gone. We estimated our corrections and we came round again and did it all a second time. It could take up to ten circuits to put out the whole three to three and a half tons of supplies.

The squadron was divided into A and B Flights; each flew one day and took the next day off. During the last ten days of 1944 my crew and I flew twelve sorties for a total of 27 operational hours, an average of just over five hours per day (since we flew only every second day). At that rate we could calculate that we would finish our tour of 500 hours in just 100 flying days or 200 calendar days, that is, six to seven months. The rate however changed quickly. In our second week of operations we flew 28 hours and 45 minutes; that included one day when we flew four sorties and logged a total of ten hours and twenty minutes. The tour changed too. Very shortly after we began operating it was lengthened to 700 hours. The increased intensity of our flying and the lengthening of the tour were both indicative of the Army's successes on the ground beneath us. As Slim and his forces rushed to the Chindwin, our trips got longer, and as his tanks and guns used up their ammunition and petrol, our trips became more frequent. If the army could do it, we could do it. Let them race forward as fast as they could, we were ready to keep pace. That was the spirit which prevailed in both the Canadian squadrons as the campaign gained in momentum.

The early days of operational flying involved a very steep learning curve and a good deal of on-the-job training. The close formation flying and precision dropping that had been prized at Gujrat was quickly forgotten. Each aircraft went out on its own, found the DZ, made its drop, and returned for a second, and third, and fourth load as quickly as possible. Eighteen and nineteen hour days were not unusual. At first the trips were short and well behind the lines, a landing at Tiddim at the extreme end of the Imphal valley or a drop on the steep mountainside at Fort White. Within a week we were flying farther forward, dropping or landing at villages on the Chindwin, places with unpronounceable names like Taukyan, Indiangale, Kawlin, Kalewa, Kalemyo. On January 9, and again on the 11th we dropped at a DZ at Shwebo, almost on the banks of the Irrawaddy. On January 12, F/L Herb Coons led five aircraft from B Flight into that same DZ and into a hornet's nest of enemy aircraft.

Herb was a very experienced airman. As a navigator with Coastal Command in Britain, he had twice been forced down at sea, had fought a fire in the bomb room, and had been attacked by enemy aircraft on three separate occasions. For this he was awarded the DFC. He then remustered to pilot and eventually came to 435 as Flight Commander. This day, on the drop at Shwebo, he took the precaution of asking his wireless operator, W/0 Buckmaster, to get up in the astrodome and watch for enemy aircraft. When the Oscars came, Buckmaster saw them and alerted the crew. Herb warned the other aircraft in the circuit and then took the only defensive measure a Dakota can take, he got down on the deck to protect his belly and prepared to outguess and out-turn the attacker. From the astrodome, Buckmaster called out the range: "1000 yards . . . 500 yards," and at the moment he judged the Japanese pilot was locked on —"Now!" Herb slewed the aircraft around in the sharpest, flattest turn he could manage. The Japanese pilot, unable to turn in time, screamed past, then made a smart stall-turn and came again. Again Buckmaster shouted "Now!" and Herb again turned into the attack and eluded his attacker. Four times they played this deadly game. On the fifth attack Herb got too low. His wing tip hit a tree. The Nip, now out of ammunition, did not follow as Herb opened his throttles and turned for home. His aircraft was punctured, but there was only one casualty. Corporal A. M. White, a ground crew member of the squadron who had gone along as a kicker, that is, one who pushes the cargo out the door, was shot in the chest. The crew gave him morphia and alerted base that they were coming home with a damaged aircraft and a wounded airman.

Cpl. White's life was saved by a miracle. "When I examined the Corporal's wound," Jim Barnard, the Squadron medical officer wrote in his diary, "I couldn't believe my eyes. The point of entrance showed that a small calibre bullet had hit him in the front just over the heart. The larger exit hole was just below the tip of his left shoulder blade behind. A straight line between the two would have meant a punctured heart and lung (near the point where the big vessels are)." Luckily, the bullet had tracked round the ribs beneath the skin and come out the back. White was back on the squadron after just ten days in the military hospital.

Other 435 aircraft in the Shwebo circuit that morning were not as lucky. Ken Ramsay and his crew didn't have a chance. The Japanese pilot pounced on them without warning. In an instant the plane was on fire and plunging to the ground. Yet in that instant Ken thought of his crew and rang the bail-out bell. Aware that the safest place to be when a Dakota crashed was in the toilet, he shouted "Get to the back!" His co-pilot, A. L. Thompson, ran through the fuselage and hurled himself into the john. When the aircraft crashed, its spine broke just in front of the bulkhead and Thompson was thrown clear. He suffered a crushed skull and badly fractured limbs. Ken Ramsay and the rest of the crew, navigator Dave MacKinnon from Toronto and wireless operator Edward Williams from Garden Head, Saskatchewan, were killed. So too were the two airmen who went along as kickers, Kenneth Scott from Pakenham, Ontario and Robert Prosser from Ottawa. Scott was nineteen years old and Prosser was twenty.

Bob Simpson, the Squadron's only RAF skipper, was the pilot of the third aircraft to be attacked. He was into his second run over the DZ when he saw the Japanese fighter coming at him. There was nothing he could do. The enemy's fire tore into the fuselage, into his cargo of ammunition, and into the crew. Trevor Jordan-Knox, the co-pilot, D. G. Cotter, the wireless operator, R. G. Evans, a member of the ground crew who had come as kicker, A. E. "Fearless" Foster, who had just come along for the ride, and Bob himself were all severely wounded. The navigator, Lynn Dumont, beat at the flames with his hands and thus he too ended up in hospital as a casualty. Wounded as he was, Bob found a spot to make a wheels-up landing and then he and Lynn carried the others clear of the burning plane. While their cargo of ammunition exploded, they did what they could to make Dave Cotter comfortable. They could not, however, save his life. He died later in hospital.

A fourth 435 aircraft, piloted by F/L Duncan, was attacked as it approached the DZ. Duncan immediately corkscrewed down onto the deck and set out for base as fast as he could go. The enemy fighter had probably exhausted his ammunition, for Duncan was not pursued. At the same time, Bill Rodgers was nearing the attack area when he heard Herb Coons' warning. Catching sight of Simpson's burning aircraft, he landed as close to it as he could and he and his crew set out for the crash site. They carried the seriously wounded members of Simpson's crew for two miles till they found a road where transport could bring them to medical attention.

For their coolness and bravery in the face of extreme danger, Bob Simpson was awarded the DFC and Herb Coons a bar to his DFC, both well deserved awards. For the Squadron as a whole, this January 12 encounter with the enemy was a rude and abrupt awakening to the reality of war. Six squadron members had been killed, five wounded, two aircraft shot down, and one badly damaged. The effect of this combat shock, however, was not to intimidate the squadron, but rather the opposite. They were now determined to do their utmost to show this foe defiance by putting all the arms and ammunition they could into the hands of the front line troops. 435 had found its motto: *Certi Provehendi*, "Determined to Deliver."

The Army men who were waiting for their heaven-sent supplies watched in helpless rage as the Dakotas were attacked. Lt. Col. Rex King-Clark, Commanding the Manchester Regiment, wrote in his diary:

> *A covey of OSCARS came over about 0900 hrs and attacked the Dakotas which were overhead at the time supply dropping. Unfortunately without fighter cover. I think at least two were shot down. The Thunderbolts arrived just too late. Felt very angry. Poor bloody Dakotas it must be hell for them under the circumstances. Someone wants the sack for not having a forward fighter strip.*

The major in charge of the ground defences at the DZ echoed King-Clark's feelings and sent a note of appreciation to the Squadron:

*It was terrible to watch. Your boys had been supplying us for several
weeks. They made a damn good job of it, and we'd come to feel they
were our special friends.... It was maddening to see those Japs go for
the helpless Dakotas. ...*

*After it was all over a Sikh sepoy came up to me and said: "Sahib, if
Canadian Sahibs must lose their lives to bring us food, then perhaps
we can go on half rations." At the time he made the suggestion, we were
already on half rations.*

Within the Squadron there were repercussions from the Shwebo action.
The CO, Wing Commander Tom Harnett, had put a "Prune Board"[2] up
outside the Operations tent on which to record any silly mistakes the
aircrew made. When Herb Coons found his name on it for some inconsequential offence, he smashed the board. The CO then posted him from the
Squadron. Because Herb was popular among the aircrew and a hero to the
younger pilots there was considerable resentment at his leaving.

For the next two weeks the Squadron avoided the threat of enemy action
by flying mainly at night. Taking off at midnight, the crews turned off the
navigation lights and set course in the moonlight for Onbauk, a small
rough strip closely hedged on both sides by thick jungle. The strip was short
and that meant touching down as soon as one cleared the teak trees on the
approach. Pilots were allowed to use landing lights for the approach and
landing or they could rely altogether on the three bonfires on each side of
the narrow strip. At the end of the strip was the unloading area with one
larger fire in the middle of it. Here a sepoy gave them wonderful hot cocoa
while the load was taken off. Unfortunately one plane landed long and, to
avoid crashing into the jungle, groundlooped over the fire and over the
sepoy who made the cocoa. Altogether these night flights were chancy, and
everyone flew a bit easier when fighters were laid on for protection and the
squadron could revert to daytime deliveries.

On January 14, 1945 Slim established his first bridgehead across the
Irrawaddy, a small penetration by a Gurkha battalion at Singu, about 40
miles north of Mandalay. Frank Smith from Vancouver, one of the first to
drop to the bridgehead, found that, however he tackled the DZ, he would
have to fly over the Japanese lines. He made his first three circuits, collecting a bit of small arms fire each time. On the third circuit, Nick Jarjour, a
ground crew kicker, was wounded in the foot and the arm. Frank tried to
continue the drop, but it was evident that Nick needed attention. He flew
to Shwebo, got Nick to a hospital, then flew back to finish his drop. Realiz-

---

[2] Named for P/O Prune, a legendary but fictional RAF pilot, famous for his maladroit flying.
Anyone mentioned on the Prune Board was awarded The Highly Derogatory Order of the
Irremovable Finger.

ing that it was sensible to avoid the DZ, he put the rest of his load off on the river bank. As for Nick, because he was swarthy and well-tanned, the British medical attendant asked, "Does this sergeant go to the British or Indian ward?" That question was quickly answered and Nick found himself under the tender ministrations of the sisters of the Queen Alexandria Imperial Nursing Order. He revelled in the care and attention that was lavished on him, saying later, "There was nothing like it in the world." After the war, he tried to get names and addresses so he could thank the good sisters but the British authorities would reveal nothing.

For the rest of the month of January, 435 continued to supply the bridge-head. All sorties had to be flown in daylight and each sortie drew ground fire. Bill Rodgers and his crew were into their fourth circuit over the DZ when the ground fire became intensive. Trying to ease the tension with a joke, Bill asked his co-pilot, by coincidence also Bill Rodgers, "Do you think your girlfriend would approve of you sitting up here like this?" The joke fell a bit flat as the bullets flew about them and repeatedly struck the aircraft. By this time Bill began to suspect that some vital parts of the aircraft had been damaged and when a bullet passed through navigator Glen Line-ham's shirt, though without drawing blood, they headed back to base. The remainder of their load was switched to another aircraft and they returned to the bridgehead only to find that the DZ markings had disappeared. They finished the drop on the river bank and turned for home. The mechanics working on their first aircraft greeted them with an excited exclamation: "You guys don't know how lucky you were!" A main hydraulic line had been cut and critical control cables were all but severed. Shortly thereafter the Commanding Officer of the 9th Gurkha Rifles sent a message of gratitude and commendation to the crew "who continued their dropping despite the enemy action they encountered. Their efforts were greatly appreciated by all ranks."

While this was happening to 435, 436 was still back in Gujrat waiting impa-tiently for orders to move to the front. There was nothing to do, grumbled the scribe of the Operations Record Book, "but to sit back and invent com-pletely unsubstantiated rumours which circulate at a truly amazing rate of speed." Finally the long-awaited orders arrived and during the second week of January, 436 Squadron began to move to Kangla, a dirt strip eight miles north of Imphal village. Preparations for their arrival were even less advanced than they had been for 435 but the Squadron ignored all handicaps and on January 15, seven 436 aircraft flew seventeen sorties and delivered 59 tons of supplies to Shwebo. That was a proud beginning and it set the tone for the Squadron's performance throughout its Burma service. The RAF had suggested a quota of 2500 operational hours per squadron per month. 436 decided to ignore the suggestion and strive for 4000.

Shortly after 436 began operating they got a foretaste of monsoon adventures. Early on the morning of February 7, S/L Dick Denison, one of the Squadron's flight commanders, set out to do his day's duty. Ernest "Bud" Lee was his co-pilot, Bill Lindsay his navigator, and T. F. Laffey, an Australian, his wireless operator. L. J. Van Nes, a crewman, went along to help with the kicking out. By 10 o'clock they had finished their first sortie and were ready to begin their second, moving a Spitfire squadron to a forward strip. They made four lifts in that move and just at dusk they set out for home. As the twilight faded and the darkness fell, Dick climbed to 8500 feet to clear the mountains. There should be no trouble. He had fuel for at least three hours and the radio beacon would show them the way. As they flew on, the air became more turbulent and a solid layer of cloud formed beneath them. In turn they tried all three radio beacons around Imphal — Imphal Main, Tulihal, and Kangla, their home base. Sometimes the radio compass fluttered vaguely, but there was no reliable indication of where they were. The question was, were they clear of the mountains and over the valley? And if they were over the valley, and if they let down through the cloud, would they find sufficient ceiling to allow them to track crawl home? Without a certain fix on their position, none of these questions could be answered. And no matter what Laffey did with his radio or his radar, he could not get a fix.

At nine thirty, after fumbling around in the cloud and the dark for three hours, the port engine failed. Only with difficulty could Dick hold height, and to add to their discomfiture, fuel was running low. In desperation, they got out their chutes and prepared to jump. Laffey had jumped before and he gave them a brief lesson on how to land. They listened attentively, then one by one they stepped into the darkness. Dick Denison steadied the plane while the others got out, then he struggled to the back, got his chute and followed them. The consequence was that he landed in the middle of the river and made his way to one bank and they were on the other. After a cold and uncomfortable night, a hospitable native took Dick to the village of Homalin where he was welcomed by the rest of his crew and by a surprised British Army detachment. Very soon, a flight of light planes flew in and ferried them back to Kangla. The next day, Dick Denison gathered the aircrew of 436 and led a discussion on how to survive a crisis in the Burmese skies.

After its January 12 attack, the Japanese Air Force rarely bothered the air supply planes, but as May approached, a far more dangerous enemy threatened, the winds and rain of the monsoons. From mid-May till October dark, menacing monsoon clouds filled the sky, not in placid stratus layers, but in towering, tumbling, boiling cumulus thrusts. The crews joked about the weather report, "Ten tenths cloud with intermingled mountain tops," but it was no joking matter. The Dakota is a steady, sturdy aircraft that can handle

Air Supply

Air delivery — 435 Squadron dropping supplies over Tiddim. *Courtesy DND, Canada.*

Dropping over Mandalay Hill.

The author (left) and Cpl. White (USAAF) and downed enemy fighter at Toungoo.

Bath Night

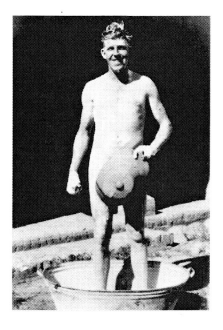

Left to right: On 436 Squadron at Kangla, you shower with a friend (to man the pump). Ivan Hansen at Camp Pizpur. Bruce Pinch demonstrates the proper use of government-issued topi. Art Adams gets a back scrub from Charlie Kewan. Stan Johns in regulation field bathtub.

Squadron Life

John Sokulsky looks on as Naga hillmen celebrate VE Day.

Manipuri dancers entertain in the 435 Squadron Officers Mess.

A 435 (Chinthe) Squadron wireless operator admires a huge replica of the Squadron's emblem.

Operation Dracula

Canadian jumpmasters are briefed for the para-drop on Rangoon.

Canadian armourers adjust pararacks for Dracula.

The drop on Elephant Point, "the only perfect paratroop drop of the whole war."

Burma Bombers

Coy's Boys: (left to right) Ted Stearns, George McGregor, Jim Noble, Charlie Campbell, Fred McDonald, Art Coy, Curley Despres, "Yank" Palumbo, Ray Jorgenson.

John Dey's "T" for Tommy Liberator lies like a deflated balloon 100 miles short of its base.

In a self-portrait, Harry Ho in jungle kit stands beneath the Liberator that dropped him behind the lines in Malaya.

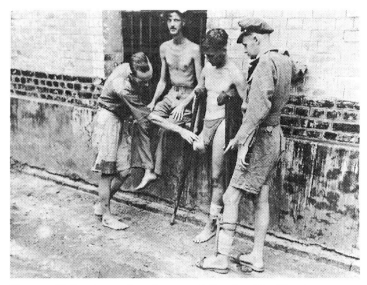

Norman McLeod examines the amputation he did without anaesthetic. *Courtesy IWM, London.*

Herb Ivens, John Joseph Yanoto and Keith Cuddy freed from Rangoon Jail and on their way home.

Action at Shwebo and Toungoo

R.W. Bradford depicts aircraft of 435 Squadron attacked by Japanese fighters at Shwebo, January 12, 1945. Two Dakotas were lost, one damaged, six Canadians killed. *Courtesy 435-436 Burma Squadron Assn.*

Dakotas of 436 Squadron experience ground fire while trying to re-supply clandestines behind the lines at Toungoo. *Courtesy 435-436 Burma Squadron Assn.*

Building Roads

Originally two roads led from Imphal to central Burma and beyond. The Tiddim Road (right) became a morass of mud during the monsoon and was soon abandoned. The road from Tamu through the Kabaw Valley (below) was "paved" with bithess, a product of Canadian ingenuity, and served throughout the campaign as the main land connection to the front.

ordinary turbulence with ease. But monsoon turbulence is not ordinary. There is no pattern to the buffeting; it takes all of a pilot's strength and vigilance to maintain even the semblance of controlled flight. Holding a course within ten degrees is out of the question.

Faced with a solid line of cloud, pilots flew as much as sixty miles out of their way seeking a light spot that promised safer passage. Nearing the DZ, one searched for a small hole and dropped through it, hoping for a recognizable feature that would pinpoint his position, and even more, hoping for a ceiling of sufficient height to allow some manoeuvring. Once the drop was made, the pilot spiralled tightly upward to gain height and clear the hills, all the time aware that if he did find some way through the squalls, he faced the same problem in getting down at the other end. Ted Harris has a vivid memory of that ordeal.

Sometime in mid-June, Ted, his pilot Ernie Bingham, co-pilot Buck Tamblyn, and wireless operator Jack Card returned from a drop to find storm clouds piled high over Imphal Valley and the mountains around it. There was no hope of crawling under the clouds so they climbed over them, climbed laboriously to 17,000 feet before a lead opened up between two huge cumulus heads and let them through. Without oxygen, they felt distinctly light-headed, but they didn't plan on staying there long. A small uncertain glimpse of the ground gave Ted and Buck a chance to pinpoint their position. "We're in the valley and north of base, I think," Ted reported. "You better be right," Ernie replied, "because Jack says this stuff is right down on the deck." They let down in a tight spiral, occasionally losing their hole and then coming into it again. The lower they got, the heavier the pelting rain and the greater the tension. It seemed a long way down. Maybe this stuff *was* right down on the deck. Finally, they broke through, two hundred feet above the road that lead south to Tulihal. Together, Ted and Buck map-read their way along the road, trying to give Ernie at least a few seconds warning of an upcoming swerve that the road made to avoid one of the many small hills that jutted abruptly up in the mist and dripping rag of cloud. Suddenly, there was the strip, right in front of them, and Ernie set the good old Dak down, just like that. "When we rolled to a stop," says Ted, "I can remember Ernie cussing (unusual for Ernie), throwing up his hands, and saying, 'I'll never do that again as long as I live'."

The dangers of monsoon flying were compounded by the huge ugly black cumulonimbus clouds that were often embedded among the cumulus. Any aircraft in a CuNim cloud is like a toy in the hands of a giant. In sane regions, a pilot is warned never to fly into a CuNim. In Burma, where delivery was imperative and CuNim clouds ubiquitous, we didn't have that option. There is probably no Burma air supply pilot who does not have a hair-raising tale of having blundered into a CuNim. The pilot knows when he has entered a CuNim by the much intensified buffeting, the darkness, the solid deluge of rain, and above all by the violence of up and down winds at velocities of up to 200 miles an hour. My own struggle with a CuNim began when we met a solid bank of dark cloud along our flight path. A small break of lighter greyness tempted us on. The rolling cloud darkened, the hole closed behind us, and rain pelted down so thick the windshield wipers were useless. There was a sudden feeling that we were alone in the world, that nothing existed but our pitiful aircraft in this seething mass of black cloud. We could no longer see the wing tips, just a faint glow of colour from the navigation lights; even the motors were only an indistinct blur. The sky darkened to blackness and the aircraft pitched and rolled uncontrollably. A vicious wind caught us and threw us upward, how high I cannot say. Then just as suddenly a downdraft seized us and plunged us toward the mountains below. The climb-and-glide indicator was useless, the altimeter was unwinding like a clock gone mad. I've no idea what the airspeed was doing. Chas Swift, my RAF co-pilot, and I, our feet braced against the instrument panel, were both struggling to pull the wheel back. It was absolutely immovable, as though it were welded. Second by second the mountains were coming nearer. Finally the Dakota yielded to the wheel. We could do nothing but climb straight ahead into the cloud and pray there were no mountains in the way.

The whole adventure was probably over in minutes — I have no idea. All the while we were fighting the fury of that cloud, my dander was up. This was a battle, and I was going to win. When it was over, my feet were trembling on the rudder bars. Chas reset the gyros and we climbed homeward.

Perhaps the Burton crew had a similar adventure, but without the happy ending. At 7 o'clock on the morning of February 12, they set out to deliver a load of ammunition to a place called Budalin and never arrived. The exigencies of war kept the Squadron at its duty, but crews scanned the jungle on each sortie for some sign of Burton's aircraft. Nothing was ever found. Some months later another aircraft disappeared in the same way. On June 21 Bill Rogers flew off in KN563. With him were William Joseph Kyle, co-pilot, David McLean Cameron, navigator, Charles Peter McLaren, wireless operator, Stanley James Cox, second wireless operator, and Cornelius John Kopp, crewman and kicker. They took off in the morning for what, but for the monsoon clouds, was a routine trip to Myitkyina, and then they disappeared. The squadron spared a few hours for a search, but the weather, the vast expanse of mountain and jungle, and operational demands defeated their efforts.

Forty-five years later a native hunter chanced upon the wreckage of an aircraft and picked up a curious bit of metal, a wrist watch. The face was rusted away, but on the back an inscription was still decipherable, the name of William Kyle and a service number that began with an 'R'. The missionary to whom the hunter gave the watch eventually brought it to the Taukyan Cemetery of the Commonwealth War Graves Commission where a chance visitor remembered that a service number with an 'R' prefix signified a Canadian. Even with that clue, it was July 1995, fifty years after the Rogers aircraft was lost, before word of the find came to Veterans Affairs, and a year after that again before an investigative team from Ottawa could thrash through an agony of red tape and diplomatic negotiating and miles of jungle to establish that KN563 had been found. The aircraft had burned and there was very little left of the men who had been its crew. One wing was found three kilometres from the crash site, suggesting that it had been torn from the fuselage before the crash occurred.

In February 1997 twenty-six kin of the dead airmen and twenty-four wartime members of 435-436 Squadrons travelled to Burma to bury their loved ones and their comrades with the honour they deserved. One casket, draped with the Maple Leaf flag, represented the remains of the six airmen. The veterans and an Honour Guard from the current 435 Squadron marched behind. Across the thousands of carefully tended graves of the Taukkyan War Cemetery echoed the haunting notes of the *Last Post*, and then the piper's lament. The Honourable Lawrence MacAulay, Secretary of State for Veterans, said the final farewell:

> *Rest gently William Bennet Rogers*
> *and you, Cornelius John Kopp.*
> *You join 51 of your brothers who have been*
> *at peace here all these years.*
> *Farewell David McLean Cameron.*
> *God speed, Stanley James Cox.*
> *Your sacrifice will not be forgotten.*
> *And peace be with you Charles Peter McLaren,*
> *and you William Joseph Kyle.*
> *Your country mourns and honours you.*
> *And as surely as the sun sets, and the morning breaks,*
> *you will remain with us in our hearts.*

For the family members the Taukkyan ceremony had deep meaning. For 52 years they had lived with that twisted word "Missing," a word that promised hope and whispered "Death." Immediately after the war, Bill Kyle's mother had bought a cemetery plot in Perth, Ontario for her son and dreamed that he would one day lie beside her there. Walter Kopp, Cornelius's brother, remembers that their mother went to her grave still harbouring the hope that Cornelius would some day be found. When the ceremony was over each family was handed a carefully folded Canadian flag with the dead man's campaign medals resting on it. Margaret Janzen,

Cornelius Kopp's sister, summed up the significance of the day: "It's a huge relief that words just can't express. After 52 years of uncertainty we finally have closure."

Dicing with monsoon clouds was soon accepted as a daily challenge and the two Canadian squadrons began to feel like old hands in Combat Cargo Task Force, the American formation that administered their operations. Daily they loaded up with ammunition and petrol, food for men and for beasts, mail and newspapers, clothing and tents, indeed, everything and anything that was needed at the front and could be loaded into a Dakota. That included jeeps and mules, tank tracks and tank engines, machine guns and heavy artillery. There were annoying loads too. It greatly irked the Canadians to fly Canadian beer and Canadian whiskey to the front (under guard) and have to be satisfied in their canteen with Indian beer and Indian Three Feathers gin. On the other hand, there was a peculiar satisfaction in special deliveries such as a set of false teeth or a pair of spectacles. Crews handled ammunition with aplomb, blithely dumping bombs out the door onto the ground five feet below. Forty-five gallon drums of gas sometimes began to leak if the aircraft ventured into upper regions of the atmosphere. Matches were a dangerous cargo. Once someone stepped on a pack containing matches and the whole load started to smoulder. Thereafter matches were required to have a red warning tag. There is no record of matches and gas being carried in the same load. Ghee, the clarified butter so dear to the stomachs of the Indian troops, was sure to leak. Not only did it smell, it made the aluminum floor of the aircraft as slick as a skating rink. Bob O'Brien, a 436 pilot, claimed that his wireless operator, Johnnie McCullough, was so expert at dropping that he could ring the stupa of a pagoda with a coil of barbed wire.

Jack Barker, a 435 pilot, remembers a particularly annoying load:

> At Imphal the Indian Army had completely packed the aircraft with unwrapped, skinned goats, filling the cargo area to the ceiling. All we could see were goat carcasses piled on top of each other with the four legs sticking up. It was impossible to enter the cockpit except by the ladder through the small door by the navigator's table.
>
> We flew this prized load into a very dusty dirt strip in the forward area. Unable to get out of the aircraft we waited for someone to relieve us of our goodies. Eventually three army trucks driven by Indian troops arrived. After checking our cargo, they broke into huge fits of laughter. Then climbed back into their trucks and drove away. Obviously these fellows were of the wrong religion.
>
> The temperature was well over 100 degrees and an aircraft didn't sit too long until the insides becomes unbearable. We were trapped, and while the goat perhaps wouldn't hurt to be cooked, we didn't feel that

the cooking of four air- crew would add anything to this delicacy. Some-thing had to be figured out quickly. There was a hatch in the cockpit ceiling that we had never had an occasion to use. Now we could use it, climb out and along the length of the air-craft and, with any luck, slide down into the open cargo door.

It worked. I remained in the cockpit and as soon as the pile of carcasses got too large I would taxi ahead, cutting sharply to the left to miss the carcasses with the tailplane. When we finished, there were three huge piles of goat meat in the dust. That evening in the mess there wasn't a word of complaint from any of our crew as we sat down to another meal of bully beef.

The 435 Squadron Operations Record Book for August 11, 1945 lists an even stranger cargo: 800 white mice and 25 guinea pigs flown to Comilla for typhus research.

Dr. W. B. Stiver, a Canadian and a graduate of the University of Toronto, was Director of Malariology at General Headquarters, New Delhi. He had been away from home for nearly five years. His eight-year-old daughter knew him only from pictures and his wife was not well. Repeatedly he had tried for home leave, but there was no chance. Then a chance came, a recommendation that specimens of the scrub typhus virus that so plagued the army in Burma should be sent to Dr. James Craigie in Toronto in the hope that he could discover a vaccine. Immediately Dr. Stiver volunteered to courier the mice bearing the virus to his friend in Toronto. His offer was accepted, but there was one stringency: the mice had to be in Toronto within 72 hours, or even better, 48 hours. Dr. Stiver went to work at once. Through an American friend he got a travel order signed by Joe Stilwell: "Expedite passage to Canada of Colonel Stiver and 30 laboratory mice. Top priority is essential; must arrive at destination within 48 hours."

That note opened all doors. Dr. Stiver was given VIP treatment all the way and within 30 hours he and his mice were in Miami. He phoned his wife. They met in Montreal and spent the night in the Mount Royal Hotel, the very hotel in which they had spent their honeymoon. Next day, the Stivers travelled by train to Toronto, the mice in the baggage car despite every argument Colonel Stiver could muster. They were delivered to Dr. Craigie in good order and in good time. Unfortunately, Dr. Craigie, though he had already discovered a vaccine for classic typhus, was not successful with the mice from Comilla. Still, 435 played its small part in this medical drama by at least getting the mice to Comilla.

The mice were legitimate cargo. The snake Norm Collins and Manley Spencer carried was a stowaway. It was a routine trip from Calcutta back to Imphal when Spence called back to Norm, his navigator, "We've got a snake up here." Norm came forward and saw the little snake crawling along the top of the automatic pilot. Slightly intrigued, he tickled its tummy with his pencil then went back to his desk. Then Spencer let out a yell, and jumped away from the controls. The snake was hanging over the right rudder pedal and aimed at Spencer's foot. Norm reached back for his kukri, knocked the snake to the floor, broke its back so it could not strike, then cut off its head. With commendable modesty he notes, "The little guy was sluggish because of the lack of oxygen (we were at eight or nine thousand feet) and it was cold, for a snake." The squadron intelligence officer identified it as a Russel's viper, adding "You probably have eight minutes to live after a good bite."

If the flying was a challenge, ground operations were equally challenging. The American squadron that had flown off to China and bequeathed us their quarters also left their sign behind: CAMP PIZPUR. The name was well chosen. The squadron was deposited in the midst of a scramble of bedraggled "bashas" and told to bed down where we could. Inside the bashas there was nothing but a bare dirt floor. We stretched out our bedrolls and went to sleep. It is not in the Canadian nature to merely moan about adversity. On the second day, a pile of bamboo poles and big gunny sacks was deposited outside each hut. Slip the poles into the sack, fit a stretcher in at the top and bottom to hold the poles apart, rest this frame on a kit bag and a discarded ration tin, string the mosquito netting from the roof of the basha and, *voila*, one had a bed fit for a king. Within days each basha had invented for itself some ingenious bathing arrangement, a shower made from a five-gallon can pierced with holes and strung up on a bamboo pole, or a bath tub made from a half a petrol drum or from a Spitfire drop tank with its top side cut off. The cooks contrived a stove out of a sheet of metal and a pile of bricks. The fitters and riggers did daily inspections with a flashlight and a coin as a screwdriver. In the end, with 'A' frames and improvised hoisting equipment, they were doing engine changes as efficiently and expeditiously as rear echelon workshops, all in the open, regardless of the weather.

When 436 Squadron came forward a few weeks later, their living conditions were even more primitive. More than once, the American squadron that was still at Imphal came to their rescue. The medical officer in particular suffered from a lack of equipment and supplies. His American counterpart was embarrassingly generous, even giving him medications and ointments that the British sources did not yet know of. When Doc Barnard tried to protest, the American doctor waved him aside. "I was down at our Headquarters last week and they told me specifically, 'Look after those orphaned Canadians up in Imphal.' So that's what I'm doing." For both squadrons, one of the biggest worries for the medical officer was safe drinking water. The American squadron not only gave them clean water, but loaned them a 500 gallon water truck as well.

Gradually Canadian ingenuity supplied at least some of the amenities that made life in Burma more bearable. Thanks to the generosity of a nearby Remount Depot, 435 squadron organized a Riding Club. A swimming pool and rest area flourished in a local village pond until the medical officer discovered it was used as a laundry and for other purposes by the native population, and he condemned it for sanitary reasons. With equipment supplied by the Canadian Legion Auxiliary Services, a recreation tent was established, a badminton court, and a softball diamond, a gym, and a camera club. 436 Squadron built a luxurious outdoor cinema with seating for eighty, that is, if you didn't mind sitting on an up-ended petrol drum sunk into the sand. In both squadrons, the ground crew, of their own initiative, organized a canteen that offered "real luxury items," cereals, shoe polish, writing paper, chocolate bars, biscuits, and cheese. All squadron members made a "voluntary" contribution to the messing fund which enabled the leave kite to bring fresh fruit and vegetables from Calcutta to supplement the regular rations of bully beef and dried potatoes.

As soon as the squadrons began their work, it became clear that extra hands were needed to handle the cargo. Whether on a landing or a drop, the whole process could be speeded up if there were extra bodies to help with the loading and unloading. Ground crew were offered the chance to volunteer, and at the same time to earn a bonus of fifty cents a day. So eager was the response that the engineering officer had to set a limit of 15 volunteers per day. Not only did this arrangement speed the work, it helped integrate aircrew and ground crew in a spirit of mutual achievement that enhanced squadron pride and purpose. Kickers came to regard themselves as members of the crew and tried to fly whenever "their" skipper was flying. John Harvey, an aero engine mechanic with 436 Squadron, did it differently. He flew 250 sorties in 35 different Daks with 46 different crews. His logbook bears the endorsement "700 hour tour completed on August 14/ 45. (signed) R.L Denison, S/L, CO, 436 Sqdn." Beneath this endorsement S/L Denison has written a unique commendation: "Flying as a crewman, this airman has completed 700 operational hours without interfering with his normal duties. This is a most commendable effort and shows keenness far beyond the normal call of duty." No small part of the credit for the exceptional achievement of the two Canadian squadrons in Burma must go to John Harvey and other ground crew like him. These men shared all the perils that their aircrew comrades faced, doing work which they were not trained to do, expected to do, or adequately paid to do. Three ground crew were wounded doing this extra duty, and three were killed. To recognize the important part the ground crew played in the Squadron's activities, both as kickers in the air and as servicing and maintenance workers on the ground, the aircrew of 436 brought special food and refreshments up from Calcutta and honoured them at a splendid banquet. In addition, the officers signed their beer ration over to the airmen's canteen "for the duration."

With both 435 and 436 the strong spirit of squadron solidarity, the youthful keenness of all personnel, and the awareness, at least among the aircrew, of repatriation after 700 hours, gave them the enthusiasm and energy to top the Combat Cargo Task Force performance charts month after month. 436 Squadron, having set itself the goal of 4000 flying hours per month, actually averaged 4140 for its first six months of operation. 435 Squadron, despite the fact that all its aircraft were hand-me-downs from other squadrons, twice ranked first in Combat Cargo Task Force for all-round efficiency. In their determined effort to supply the beachhead across the Chindwin, the Canadians had provided General Slim with the kind of air support he needed. Now, as March began, they were ready to support his next move, the crossing of the Irrawaddy.

THE ROAD TO MANDALAY, VIA MEIKTILA

As the Canadian Officer Party was leaving the forward area and 435 RCAF Squadron was entering it, General Slim's Fourteenth Army began crossing the Chindwin. The war's longest Bailey bridge, completed on December 10, 1944, allowed him to visit Shwegyin and the banks of the Chindwin, still littered with the rusted tanks and trucks that his retreating forces had abandoned two and a half years earlier. In *Defeat into Victory*, he recollected that moment: "As I walked among them, resavouring in imagination the bitter taste of defeat, I could raise my head. Much had happened since then. Some of what we owed we had paid back. Now we were going to pay back the rest— with interest."

His thinking was that a good part of the enemy's force had been lost at Imphal. Now what was needed was another such confrontation, a big battle in an open setting where he could deliver the *coup de grâce*, the final blow that would finish the Japanese Army in Burma altogether. Studying his map, he found just such a spot, the Shwebo plain. Since it stretched across the northern approach to Mandalay, it also seemed likely that the enemy would choose it for the defence of that city. As his advance pushed forward, however, he sensed that the Japanese were going to set their defence line on the east side of the Irrawaddy and then force him to fight hill by hill and street by street for Mandalay itself.

Slim changed his plan. While still making every show of using Shwebo as a base for the attack on Mandalay, he made very secret plans for a river crossing in the Pakkoku-Pagan area, well to the south, and then a *Blitzkrieg* dash across country to take the large supply depot at Meiktila, thereby cutting the Japanese line of communication and isolating the Mandalay defences. To mislead the enemy, Slim devised an elaborate scheme of deception. Under the surprisingly unsubtle code name of *Cloak*, a furious

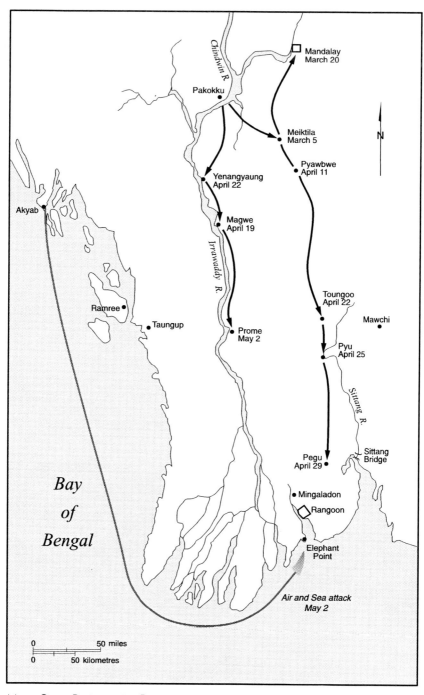

Map 8 — Return to Rangoon

exchange of phony signals between a dummy corps headquarters and actual field units persuaded the Japanese that Slim's main Irrawaddy crossing was to be in the Shwebo area. Small skirmishes and patrol encounters were enhanced with "canned battle," loud, recorded sounds of extensive fighting, to suggest significant forces were involved. To further confuse the enemy, canned battle noises and devices that simulated the fireworks of an attack were floated down the river. Spurious plans and maps disclosing a plan to cross the river and then head south to the oil fields of Yenangyaung were "lost" in a night raid.

All this time, huge tonnages of supplies were accumulated at Shwebo for the attack on Mandalay. Day after day during the last week of January crews of 435 and 436 Squadron flew two and three sorties per day into the dry and dusty strip. One crew counted 50 aircraft in dispersal and 10 more in the circuit waiting to land. To confound the confusion, there was only one runway so that aircraft landed north to south and took off south to north. This activity above Mandalay further drew the enemy's attention away from the preparations to cross in the Pakkoku-Pagan area and speed to Meiktila.

While the airwaves on the Irrawaddy above Mandalay were filled with misleading signals, 4 Corps maintained radio silence and, avoiding roads and main tracks, pushed 300 miles through mountains and jungle to get into position at Pakokku and Pagan. Slowly and quietly the bridgehead force collected, their presence still undetected by the Japanese.

One problem above all plagued the planners. Although in February the Irrawaddy was low and slow, it was still a formidable barrier, especially since it was filled with sandbars that were constantly shifting their shape and their location. If they were not accurately plotted, if the river depths were not plumbed to determine where boats could operate, if the opposite shore was not reconnoitred to ascertain if it could take tanks, the whole crossing might well fail. Fortunately, an underwater reconnaissance party was available to provide this information.

It was known officially as the Sea Reconnaissance Unit, and its presence in Burma was the consequence of an unusual set of events. In January 1941 the regular commander of the small vessel that patrolled the harbour entrance at St John's, Newfoundland was ill, and Bruce Wright, a young sub-lieutenant of the Royal Canadian Naval Volunteer Reserve, was asked to take his place. Huddled over the wheel in the dark cold, his collar turned high against the drift of wet snow, Wright fell to pondering how anyone or anything could subvert the harbour's defences. The one submarine attack that had been attempted failed, perhaps because the net that drooped down from the boom had deflected its torpedoes. Any boat or submarine attempting to enter the harbour would be detected by the large asdic loops on the ocean floor. But a swimmer? Bruce was a champion swimmer and the thought turned round and round in his head as he waited out the night. A swimmer could come in undetected and do a good bit of damage. Next morning he talked about the idea with his superior. "Put it on paper and we'll send it on," said his Captain, and he did.

Surprisingly, the paper made its way upward and eastward until it landed on the desk of Admiral Mountbatten, Chief of Combined Operations. It was just the sort of off-the-wall but promising notion that Mountbatten loved and under his auspices Bruce was empowered to recruit and train a Sea Reconnaissance Unit. The recruiting was easy when it was learned the unit would train in California and the Bahamas. By the time it was ready for action, Lord Mountbatten was in SEAC as Supreme Commander and the Navy, not knowing what else to do with such an odd outfit, shipped it to SEAC as well. Thus, when the Fourteenth Army needed to discover the secrets of the Irrawaddy, it was on hand and available, a motley collection of Army, Navy, and Air Force officers, Canadians and British, but all trained to fight like commandos and to swim like fish. Half the group was sent off to help with the taking of Ramree Island and the other half was sent to survey the Irrawaddy.

Bruce Wright, in his book *The Frogmen of Burma*, tells how he spent two nights crossing the Irrawaddy near Pagan, charting its sandbanks, sounding its depths, and drawing sketches for the British troops. The project had its tense moments. Swimming silently in the darkness, Bruce sensed something was wrong. He stopped and listened, and discovered he was sharing the channel with an enemy frogman. When he reached the far shore, a Japanese war dog loudly announced his arrival. Fortunately the sentry did not investigate. On the way back he revisited a sandbank where he had rested on the way over and found definite signs that a Japanese sentry had been there between his first visit and his second. It was a scary operation, but it was worthwhile. The platoon commander was ecstatic with Bruce's report. Never had he had such detailed and accurate information about the obstacles in his path. Unfortunately, this was not the area that had been chosen for the final crossing.

Harry Avery, in charge of a second frogman section farther up the river, found himself in the thick of the Irrawaddy crossing. Harry was born in Ottawa in 1917. He had spent his summers at the family cottage on the Ottawa River and winters getting a BSc in agriculture. Then he joined the RCAF and was posted overseas as a radar officer. He was on a lonely station on the Welsh coast when word came that volunteers with good aquatic skills were required for an interesting assignment. Harry volunteered and trained with Bruce Wright's crew in California. February 1945 found him on the banks of the Irrawaddy. The Army gave him four days to reconnoitre the river and report. As Bruce Wright had done, he crossed the wide expanse of the Irrawaddy repeatedly, sometimes with swim fins and pad-dleboard, sometimes just swimming, always of course in the dark of night. He sketched the sandbars, charted the safe channels, tested the firmness of the far shore and recorded what access it gave to the territory beyond. The crossings were strenuous, the water was cold, and the British commando who accompanied him almost gave them away with his chattering teeth and exhausted breathing. They were shot at, but their low silhouette in the darkness offered a difficult target.

The Allies had accomplished a more northerly crossing ten days earlier. Opposition was fierce and the beachhead was only eight miles long and two miles deep, but it was still hanging on. The determination of the British convinced the Japanese that this was the main attack and they moved their defensive forces northward to meet it. That was what Slim was hoping for. The more the enemy became interested in the northern beachhead, the fewer men they had available for the real one.

On the night of February 24-25, Harry sat in the lead boat and directed the flotilla through the channels and the currents. Lacking the resources to provide air cover for all the crossings, the Air Force simulated a fighter attack by having the Americans dive their Canadian-built Norsemen out of the low cloud with their propellers in fine pitch. That covered the sound of the approaching tanks and forced the Japanese to keep their heads down for a moment, but it was not altogether effective. The Allies were in the middle of the river when they encountered a vicious volley from the other side. Part of the fleet got caught on a sandbar and dug in there. Another section met such heavy fire they were forced to turn back. Many of the outboard motors failed, some of the boats leaked badly. The battalion Harry Avery was with gained a tentative foothold on the eastern shore, but reinforcements were desperately needed. The next amphibious truck to come ashore brought only 30 men; twenty were dead and the other ten were wounded. The radio did not work. The medical officer had been killed and Harry was busy bandaging the wounded.

As daylight came the beach commander asked Harry to swim back with a message for the General. The first half of the swim was tense. Japanese rifle and light machine gun fire sought him every time he raised his arm. Then the smoke the engineers were laying covered him and saved him. Moreover, under its cover, more men were ferried over, order was established on the beachhead, and the fighting began to run in favour of the British. At noon, the General called Harry and two other frogmen to him and announced; "On recommendation from the field, as well as from my own observations, I am pleased to announce that I am recommending you for the Military Cross." This was one of the rare instances of a Military Cross, an Army decoration, being awarded to an Air Force officer.

Although this crossing was opposed and almost failed, the whole plan of deception had done its work. The Japanese generals were convinced that the more northerly crossings were the real threat and that the crossings and hints of crossings well below Mandalay were simply feints. Between February 18 and 21, two brigades of the 17th Indian Division, the very one that had fought the bitter retreat from Rangoon in 1942, crossed in the Pagan-Nyaungu area and dashed off toward Meiktila. Five days later, leaving the infantry to control the road, the tanks sprinted ahead and captured the airstrip at Thabutkon, just 13 miles from Meiktila. The next day, 17th Division's air transportable brigade, the 99th Indian Brigade, flew in from Palel, where it had been parked, and consolidated control of the strip. Dunstan Pasterfield was one of the officers of that Brigade.

Dunstan was born at Bethune, Saskatchewan in 1917, the son of an Anglican clergyman. When war broke out, he was a theological student in England, but, wanting to do his part, he immediately went to London and tried to join the Canadian Army. At that early date, the Canadians had no facilities for recruiting and training in England, so Dunstan joined the British Artillery and was then transferred to India and to the Indian Army. At one stop on the long, hot, dusty train journey from Calcutta to Dimapur, he walked up to the front of the train. The locomotive looked familiar. "Where does your engine come from?" he asked. "From Canada," the driver replied. "So do I," said Dunstan, "Can you spare me some hot water?" The driver gave it willingly, and Dunstan had a nice hot bath right there in his compartment.[1] His Canadian boyhood came to the fore again when he was appointed regimental messing officer. "In future, every one will have to eat what I want," he wrote in his letter home. "I'm looking for corn-on-the-cob."

From February 27, Dunstan and the 6/15 Punjabs occupied the airstrip at Thabutkon and skirmished along the road to Meiktila. He was on the strip on March 1 when a Mitchell bomber arrived. In his days with an anti-aircraft battery in Britain, Dunstan had been the company aircraft recognition officer and his curiosity about different planes remained. He walked over to examine the Mitchell close up, and was surprised to see General Slim emerge. Only later did he hear the story behind that event. Because it was vital to his overall plan that the Meiktila attack go forward in coordination with the attack on Mandalay, Slim wanted to see for himself that there was no hold–up on the road to Meiktila. But the RAF absolutely refused to fly him there. As Slim tells the story: "I was very angry when the RAF told me

---

[1] Slim tells how the capacity of the railway from Calcutta to Dimapur had been increased nine-fold with the arrival of 4700 American railway men and "more powerful locomotives from America and Canada." Locomotives were scarce since they were a prize target for strafing pilots, and local production could not supply replacements; in 1942, India produced only three locomotives and, in 1943, only 40.

with utmost politeness, but with equal firmness, that they would not fly me to Meiktila — it was too dangerous! I was told the RAF would be delighted to fly any of my staff anywhere at any time, but not me, not Meiktila, not now." Just then an American general flew in. Slim, wily as ever, asked, "Would you like to see the Meiktila battle?" "Sure," said the American heartily, "Let's take my plane." And they did. That is how Slim foiled the RAF and assured himself that the Meiktila battle was going ahead as planned. And that is how Dunstan Pasterfield got to inspect a Mitchell close up.

After three days in the Thabutkon area, Dunstan's regiment, with the tanks again leading, set out for Meiktila, 13 miles down the road. All the way from the beachhead at Pakokku there had been resistance, but nothing that the tanks had not been able to set aside fairly quickly. Now, just ten miles short of their objective, a strong and stubborn roadblock reinforced with wire, mines, a blown bridge, and even artillery, blocked their advance. The tanks came straight on in a determined frontal attack while the infantry skirted around the blockade and came at it from behind. The roadblock faded, and the advance toward Meiktilla resumed. Meiktila was a huge depot complete with stockpiles of food and ammunition, workshops, and a hospital. Patrols that night revealed that all around the perimeter and even in among the piles of rice and ammunition, the enemy had constructed his usual heavy defences — deep trenches and thickly roofed bunkers. The garrison was strong.

For Slim, speed was essential if he were to exploit the surprise that had thus far been his ally. But at just this point, word came through that Chiang Kai-shek was demanding the immediate return to China of the three remaining American transport squadrons and of Chinese troops in the Northern Combat Area. The implications of this demand were enormous; Slim would lose a good portion of his air supply force, his right flank would be exposed, and the Japanese forces now engaged against the Chinese could be transferred to the Central Burma front. On top of all that, he would have to take over defence of the newly opened Burma Road and the RAF, with its much reduced resources, would have to supply the defenders. All this at the very moment when the Meiktila bow was drawn taut and ready to launch its arrow. Fortunately Mountbatten once again pulled strings that reached all the way to the seats of power in London and Washington and got from the Americans the assurance that their transport squadrons would stay till Rangoon fell or till the first of June, whichever came first.

Even before he was assured that his transport squadrons would stay, Slim ordered the attack on Meiktila to begin. From all sides, infantry and tanks tore into the defences. The Japanese replied with artillery, anti-tank weapons, heavy and light machine guns, and snipers on every vantage point. The tank commander drew back, called for air support and watched while a veritable armada from the air attacked the bunkers and fortified houses in the town. Then they moved forward again and established a shaky line along the town's edge. That night, the Japanese infiltrated and retook their old positions. Next morning the tanks came in again and this time they stayed. By now the airstrip was in their hands and Dunstan Pasterfield was with his company in the Box alongside it. They were there for the whole of the month of March, holding the perimeter to keep the strip open for supply planes or sending out patrols to push the enemy away. In a letter home, written in May, after censorship was relaxed, Dunstan describes life in the Box at Meiktila:

> *Once the Japanese got over the shock of us going behind their front and disrupting their lines of communication, they began to take offensive action. Though the attacks on our perimeter were never successful, they caused a good deal of trouble with their shelling. For upwards of a fortnight we had shells dropping in on our Box on the airstrip nearly every day. Some of it was mighty close and we had some casualties from it. Towards the end of the month, however, we carried out a big attack on the positions they had dug in the north and cleared them out, and after that there was no more trouble.*

The important thing is that, in spite of the mortaring and shelling every day and the jitter raids every night, the Box held. And Dunstan Pasterfield still has a red silk dressing gown made from one of the parachutes that was dropped to him in Meiktila.

As with the Admin Box in the Arakan and the strongholds of Kohima and Imphal, the Box at Meiktila held because the ground forces were determined and because they knew they could count on air supply. Both 435 and 436 Squadron were fully operational, indeed, were now old hands at the air supply game. Throughout February they had been dropping or landing at Shwebo, Onbauk, and Kyaukmyaung above Mandalay, and at Alon, Monywa, Allagappa, and Ondaw, west of Mandalay. As the month progressed and the Army moved southward toward the Pakokku crossing, so too did the air supply activities. On March 2, 435 Squadron aircraft landed at Thabutkon, the strip on the eastern side of the Irrawaddy just 13 miles from Meiktila. Two days later, they flew into Meiktila itself. On every sortie the crews were aware that they were getting closer to the enemy. To reach Meiktila, aircraft were required to fly to Pakkokku and from there fly a three-mile wide corridor straight to Meiktila. The corridor was relatively safe; to stray from it was definitely not. As they approached the strip they could watch the bulky Thunderbolt dive bombers streak straight down on the enemy lines, drop their bombs, and then soar upward for a new attack. On the strip itself, crews were advised not to linger and overnight visits were out of the question. In fact, the ground forces abandoned the strip each night rather than to try to defend it. That meant the Royal Air Force

Regiment had to spend as much as four hours next morning first retaking the strip and then repairing cratered runways and painstakingly searching for mines, booby traps, and cunningly concealed snipers. When, on March 18, Bob Quigley of 435 Squadron blew a tire at Meiktila, the aircraft was stripped of its radios and then left to its fate. Fortunately, that was one time when the enemy did not take over the night shift and Bob's kite was repaired and retrieved next day. When the enemy did take the strip at night, incoming aircraft had to circle next morning till a green Verey flare indicated that the RAF Regiment had done its job and the runway was clear.

In February Shwebo had been Burma's busiest airstrip; now it was Meiktila's turn. With a total strength of 250 Dakotas, Combat Cargo Task Force was flying in 2000 tons of supplies each day, at least half of it to Meiktila. With very little air support available to him and with his tanks decoyed to the Mandalay area, the enemy fought back by concentrating on the Allies' air delivery system. The Japanese forces pressing around Meiktila aimed their guns and mortars at the transport planes when they were most vulnerable, that is, when they were landing, taking off, or at dispersal. On March 20, seven Dakotas were destroyed in this manner. 435 and 436 Squadron planes were late arrivals that day and were recalled before they reached Meiktila. For a time thereafter landings were eschewed and all delivery was by dropping. Then the sweep that Dunstan Pasterfield described pushed the Japanese back and by the end of March landings were again possible.

The fighting for the Meiktila area was as vicious as a desperate and suicidal defending force could make it. Even a month after it was taken, the scars of battle were everywhere. Norm Collins, the navigator from Windsor Ontario who killed the snake in the cockpit, had the day off on April 3. With his friend, Tom Lee, a radar mechanic from Aylmer, Ontario who had a deep interest in anthropology and a great facility with a pencil, he hitched a ride to Meiktila. Norm's diary records what they saw:

> We looked at the remains of some Jap fighters, but there wasn't very much left of them. A bit further on we came on our first dead Jap, one that was almost completely burned up. Some distance again and we reached what seems to have been the main Jap position and we learned later that from here they had launched their final attack. How they were stopped by three walls of firing — two of rifles and one of machine guns — was a cunning piece of strategy on our part. Rotting, decaying bodies covered with flies were lying all around but a great number had already been buried in bomb craters and covered over with the help of bulldozers. We picked up a few souvenirs and walked on, coming later to a gun crew where we were offered a cup of tea and a bit of friendly conversation.

All the time the Meiktila advance was going on, the troops that had crossed the Irrawaddy farther north were closing in on Mandalay. There were two features of Mandalay that would attract the attention of any force trying to conquer it, the Mandalay Hill and Fort Dufferin. The Hill, towering almost 800 feet above the city and covered with pagodas and temples, was tackled first. For three days, a Gurkha regiment and two British regiments combined to storm its slopes, pressing forward and upward by sheer strength of grenades, tommy guns, and determination. The Japanese defended till they were all killed, and they were all killed only when petrol drums were rolled into their caves and set alight with tracer. Then the attackers turned their attention to Fort Dufferin.

Fort Dufferin was a large park area containing barracks, administration buildings, official residences and the impressive teak palace of King Thibaw, Burma's last king. It was enclosed by an exceedingly stout brick and earth embankment, twenty feet high and sixty feet thick at its base. In front of the wall was a wide moat filled with water and lotus plants. All attempts to cross the moat were turned back by a fierce fusillade of defending fire. Artillery shells were ineffectual against the thick walls of the enclosure. Even dambuster attempts to breach the embankment with aerial bombing were only partially successful. Allied casualties were mounting and still the Japanese held out. Unexpectedly, on the fourth day of the siege, Burmese natives appeared on the stockade waving white flags. The Japanese defenders had decamped during the night, crawling away through the drains from the moat. In a short-lived echo of the days of the Raj, General Pete Rees, who had commanded the siege, raised the Union Jack above Fort Dufferin. There was still some mopping up to be done, but basically, Mandalay had been taken. It was March 20, 1945.

On March 22 aircraft from 435 and 436 Squadrons flew into the newly taken city. The sun was shining brightly and somehow there was a sense of jubilation in the air. Aircrews flying into forward strips were used to getting down, getting their loads off, and getting out as soon as possible. The only ground troops they saw were Indian Army Service Corps men. Now the feeling of tension and of hurry was relaxed and, quite unusually, front line troops, the kind the transport crews had not met before, were at hand and delighted to talk to them. They were as pleased to meet the fliers that had fed them as the aircrews were to see them. Stories were told, and souvenirs exchanged — shoulder flashes of XXXIII Corps and the 14th Army, captured Japanese flags, Japanese currency (called banana leaf currency to underline its worthlessness).[2] Proudly, with a sense of personal relationship, they told

---

[2] The Japanese occupation forces had printed over 5 billion "Burmese" rupees in cheap paper currency and the military administrators were now faced with the question of what to do with it. To accept it would be to seriously affect the value of the Indian rupee; to reject it would work a hardship on the Burmese tribespeople who held it. Finally it was decided to replace it with silver coinage as soon as possible. Military personnel and civil administrators then burned the currency in front of the Burmese to emphasize its worthlessness.

the Air Force men "General Slim is on the strip," and the Air Force men felt he was their general too.

That unexpected feeling of relaxation and triumph came, not from a notion that it was all over, but from the realization that the black days were behind us and that what was yet to be done, we could and would do. Military historians have named various pivotal points in the Burma Campaign — the Admin Box which proved that the enemy's road block and hook no longer worked, the Chindit expeditions that showed Indians and British could fight in the jungle too, Kohima and Imphal where the grit and stubborn determination of the Allies more than matched that of their adversaries. The truth is, all these are turning points, cumulative ones, each adding a few more degrees to the turn. So it was too with Mandalay and Meiktila. Repossession of Mandalay was pivotal for the sentiment and prestige attached to the place. Meiktila was pivotal because it was a central depot and a main communications node. Together they meant the road to Rangoon was open, final victory was at hand. The only question left was — could it be grasped before the monsoons broke?

For 435 and 436 Squadrons the taking of Mandalay and Meiktila had an additional meaning. The return flight from their Imphal base to the front took four hours and stretched the economical range of the Dakota. Clearly there would have to be some moves. The generals had of course foreseen this development and had plotted the advance in the Arakan with the idea of establishing an air supply centre at Akyab, a place that offered a shorter flight to the Burma front and a sea connection to Calcutta. Both squadrons had outstanding operational records and extremely high morale, but because of the small problem with the dismissal of Herb Coons, 435 had a lesser reputation at Headquarters and that is probably why 436 got the nod to move to Akyab. In the week of March 10 to 17, 436 Squadron moved itself to its new home while at the same time continuing to operate at better than half capacity. Despite the time taken for the move, 436 flew 3913 operational hours in March. 435 Squadron did slightly better at 4001 hours.[3] That has to be understood in the context of Combat Cargo Task Force's original target of 2500 operational hours per month.

For the remainder of the campaign, 435 stayed at Imphal and took on the task of re-supplying the forward depots. Increasingly however, its job came to be flying rice to places in the northern area — Bhamo, Lashio, Mytkyina and even Mu-se in China — to feed the local populace. In the aftermath of

---

[3] Melnyk (p.132) makes the point that, because of differences in number of aircraft and crews and availability of loads, statistical comparisons of the performance of 435 and 436 Squadrons are not meaningful. Both squadrons set serviceability and operational records and were very highly regarded in the Group.

war the civil administration of pre-war Burma had collapsed and, though the British were working to restore some vestige of organization and order, food procurement and distribution was a military responsibility. After the excitement of front-line involvement, rice runs were dull. Occasionally however the Squadron was given a chance to observe the restoration of civil administration at the village level.

For me this came when the Army Liaison Officer (ALO) told me "Your load today is 50,000 silver rupees. An Army paymaster will go with you." We had carried all manner of supplies in the last six months, but this was something new. "Why?" I asked. The ALO explained, "The Japanese paid the natives in banana leaf currency and now they won't accept anything but hard money." We found our destination, just a clearing in the jungle with a small wooden hut beside the strip. A young Burmese, looking upright and alert in a quasi-military uniform, greeted us in his language and of course we did not understand. One phrase he kept repeating as though it contained all the information we needed: "Dee-es-pee, dee-es-pee." We gathered we should wait, and we did. Very soon a jeep drove up, a smart young Brit in uniform introduced himself as the DSP, the District Superintendent of Police, and signed for our cargo. "Would you like to see my station?" he asked. We would indeed and he drove us a short distance through the verdant green jungle to a large barn-like structure of unpainted wood. We stepped over the threshold onto the dirt floor of a cavernous room that occupied the entire lower area of the police station. Two or three fires burned in the gloom, and around each squatted a motley collection of dispirited little men. "These are my prisoners," explained the DSP. "They're dacoits, natives who got hold of weapons left as the war moved on and terrorized the neighbourhood." Terrorized! They looked as though they hadn't the strength or spirit to herd goats. "Don't be fooled," said the DSP. "They are vicious and heartless. Come upstairs."

We followed him up the wooden stairs to the loft, another huge room the size of the one below. There was nothing in it but armaments, all manner of gun and weapon — Bren guns and Sten guns, Thompson machine guns and big anti-tank guns, pistols and side-arms, grenades and grenade launchers and, off in one corner, a big pile of Japanese swords. "This is what we have taken from the dacoits. Would you like a souvenir?" He meant it. Each of us chose a weapon as a memento of the day we delivered 50,000 silver rupees to the new Civil Administration of Burma. I was tempted by the Samurai swords but put off by the thought of carrying it home. Instead I chose a Mauser pistol because it had German printing on one side and Japanese on the other, a reminder of the long reach of the Axis. Three inches had been raggedly sawn from the barrel, but it still worked. We flew back to base with our souvenirs, a heaping basket of mangos and papayas and new appreciation for a very young Brit who was willing to live alone on the edge of the jungle for the sake of law, order, and Empire.

436 Squadron, having settled in at Akyab during the last week of March, began at once to supply the Fourteenth Army as it raced the monsoon to Rangoon. Three weeks later it moved again, this time to Ramree Island, a location that put all parts of southern Burma within easy range. The strip at Ramree was almost at sea level and the camp area was little higher. The monsoons, with as much as 10 inches of rain in a day, were imminent and the whole squadron, officers included, immediately set about making tent-stands, rectangles cribbed about with bamboo to a height of 14 inches and then filled with sand dug taken from the drainage ditches that surrounded each tent. The air was always saturated and shoes left under one's bed turned green with mould overnight. The airstrip, surfaced with pierced metal plates laid on the sand, handled the heavy rains fairly well, but any pilot landing before the last deluge had had a chance to soak in was liable to be blinded by the spray. In spite of all the hardships and handicaps 436 Squadron set delivery records in June and again in July that far exceeded the performance of all other transport squadrons in Burma.

Now began a period of intense operation. To supply the 1800 tons of matériel that the Army needed each day Dakotas that were rated to fly 125 hours per month were flying twice that. 436 continued to be the high performing squadron of the Group, achieving in one month an all-time record of 4800 operational hours, and that was flying from "the wettest and most difficult base in all Burma" and over the most hostile route. The Arakan Yomas, the mountain range that lay between Ramree and the central plain, represented a particular threat throughout the monsoons. 436 met the danger by permanently positioning an aircraft, named *Watchbird*, over the hills to guide the squadrons' planes to the most favourable crossing. Soon all the aircraft in the area were availing themselves of *Watchbird's* advice.

For a short time in April, 436 Squadron's performance faltered. It had been ordered to change from T-type engine oil to X-type. Serviceability dropped, oil consumption soared, and aircraft began to stagger home with engine failure. The rumour was that X-type oil was actually oil that had been drained from fighter aircraft and then reclaimed for the transports. When the Squadron's engineering personnel complained, oil experts from HQ were flown in to convince them there was no problem. Then the Air Chief Marshal himself came down to placate the crews. On the day of his visit, the engineering officer upped the ante by declaring all his aircraft unserviceable and he flourished his statistics to prove that T-type oil gave better performance and safer flying. Despite strong pressure to use the cheaper oil, the Squadron remained obdurate. It took two months for the experts to acknowledge that they had been wrong.

The aggressive enthusiasm of the aircrew of both Canadian squadrons was one of the ingredients of their operational success; the other was the equal eagerness of the ground crew. In their new quarters at Akyab, and later at Ramree, 436 Squadron kept an all-ranks mess. In April 1945 an RCAF Staff Officer inspecting the Squadron found it to be a very happy place but complained that "no Officers or Sergeants Mess had been set up, and that all officers and NCO's ate with the airmen or lined up with the airmen for their food." A remonstration to the Commanding Officer only brought the response that he and the Squadron liked it that way; it was good for morale. The staff officer took his unhappiness up to RAF Wing headquarters and got a similar response: "We are not going to interfere if the Canadians wish it that way." Eventually, because of congestion, separate messes did evolve, but the spirit of egalitarian cooperation had been established and remained.

It was a spirit that paid off in unexpected ways. The servicing crews of both squadrons put their all into their work. Toiling outside with no protection from the broiling sun or the pounding rain, they worked overtime to do engine changes and other maintenance chores that under normal circumstances would have been done in rear echelon workshops and, when their ground duties were done, they proudly flew as kickers with "their" aircraft. In the air, rank differences were almost irrelevant; function and responsibility defined inter-personal relationships. It truly was the case that "we are all in this together." In a light-hearted way the story of the "Brick Bomber" illustrates the point.

Art Adams was a corporal rigger with 436 Squadron. On the morning of April 23 he was standing by aircraft KN210 and pondering the news that, having barely settled into the camp at Akyab, the Squadron was now to move to Ramree. S/L Dick Denison, the deputy CO of the Squadron approached and asked, "Adams, how much does a brick weigh?" "I haven't a clue, sir. Maybe two or three pounds," Art replied. Then Denison laid out what was on his mind: "You know, Ramree Island has been bombed to bits. There is nothing there, no tents, no bashas. Not even bricks for the cooks' stove. I've arranged for an Indian Army lorry to bring over a load of bricks. If a brick weighs three pounds, we can take 2000 of 'em, so load 2000. Put a tarp down on the floor first." Art did as he was told. Dick Denison came back, looked at the load of bricks, said, "That's enough. Hop in and go to Ramree with us." Dick started the engines, did his pre-takeoff check, swung onto the runway and opened the throttles. Halfway down the strip, the tail was still on the ground. "We'll have to take another run at it," grunted Dick as he throttled back and turned around. This time, he went to the very end of the strip, stood on the brakes, and opened the throttles till the aircraft shuddered. They were still bouncing as the end of the strip came upon them. "We've got to get off," said Dick and hauled back on the control column. The aircraft staggered off the ground, climbed to 5000 feet and wouldn't go any higher. Halfway to Ramree, Art, standing at the back door, saw a Japanese seaplane on the beach of a tiny island. "Let's get rid of some bricks," he shouted. Dick banked the plane and turned on the green light while Art and the wireless operator threw out bricks as fast as they could. At Ramree, Dick landed the aircraft as light as a feather.

After the war, Art weighed a brick — four pounds even. A Dak could take off with 7000 pounds, but its maximum load for a landing was around 6000 pounds. At 8000 pounds, they were dangerously overweight. Bombing the seaplane probably saved their lives. Art won't say whether or not they hit the target, but he does boast of being the only corporal rigger in World War II who bombed a seaplane with a brick.

Ross Huston fought for his squadron in a different way. When Ross, a Prairie farm boy, joined the RCAF in Regina in 1941, he wanted to be an Air Gunner. Because he didn't have Grade Twelve, he did not qualify for aircrew. He had taken a course in diesel engines. Could he be a mechanic? The RCAF was not recruiting mechanics at the moment. So he joined as General Duties and swept hangar floors in Brandon, Manitoba until he found his calling, Fire and Crash Truck attendant. After a few courses and a few exams, he became a Sergeant Fire Fighter and was posted to 436 Squadron in Burma. His skill at scrounging, deal-making, and "acquiring" enabled the Squadron to get the tents, tarpaulins, lumber, and bithess needed to make the swampy wastes of Ramree into a habitable camp. His tentmate was a cook and Ross became interested in the cook tent's sanitation problems. With no heating and cooking facilities except the smoky fire of used engine oil dripping on a steel plate, hot water was always in short supply. Neither the cooking utensils nor the men's mess tins were ever really clean. As a Saskatchewan farm boy, Ross was well aware that the hissing white light of a pressure gas lamp depended upon the fuel being pre-heated and vaporized in a generator. He took a length of conduit, the bendable aluminum tubing used to lead wiring through the aircraft frame, sealed one end, then drilled small holes four inches apart along the first four feet of the tube. With a "U" bend he led the next four feet back along the first bit so that it was about six inches above the holes. The final length of the tubing he fitted into a small barrel of kerosene hung up in a tree. When the kerosene flowing through the holes was lit, it pre-heated the fuel in the supply tube above it, and shortly the apparatus was burning like a blowtorch. Three barrels cut in half lengthwise, filled with water, and mounted above Ross's blowtorch gave 436 the cleanest cutlery on the island.

The next challenge was rat control. The lack of disposal facilities for the dirty waste water from the kitchen meant rats were everywhere. Ross buried four barrels with their lids removed in the ground and connected them with a drain that led from the bottom of one barrel to the top of the next. In each barrel the water portion of the effluent drained to the next barrel and eventually out to a septic pit, while the grease rose successively to the top. Every morning the cooks removed the grease and buried it and the rat problem disappeared. This system attracted the attention of the Chief Medical Officer of a nearby hospital. He came to ask if Ross would install a similar system for him. "I don't come cheap," Ross bargained. "Well," said the MO, "I'll take your appendix out for free." "The hell you will," responded Ross, and they settled on a weekly invitation to the nurses' dances at the hospital.

That, however, was just the beginning. Ross was busily at work one day when he heard a voice, "Sergeant Huston!" Turning around, he saw he was surrounded by three strange officers with lots of gold braid on their shoulders. He thought he had done something wrong, but all they wanted were the specification for his heating system. This time, Ross didn't bargain and his invention was used eventually in camps and hospitals throughout the area.

When repatriation came at the end of the war, Ross got pneumonia and was delirious in the ship's hospital for the six day transit from Britain to Canada. He was taken off the ship as a stretcher case and put in hospital in Montreal. When, finally, he was allowed out of bed, his brother phoned to congratulate him. "I only stood up for a minute," Ross responded, "but it sure felt good to be on my feet." "Well, that's good, but that's not what I'm congratulating you for. The King's New Year's Honour List says you have been awarded the British Empire Medal for outstanding dedication to duty with the RCAF in the Far East." Today Ross Huston, farm boy, scrounger, and inventor, wears the BEM with pride, one of only 230 Canadians entitled to that honour.

Ross contributed to the domestic economy of the squadrons. George Sims contributed to what might, in some sense, be called the national scene. When an unexploded bomb was found in a Naga village, George, as head of the 435 Armament Section, was sent to defuse it. With two companions and a British Army interpreter he set out by jeep up a rough mountain track For the last three miles they had to walk along a narrow game trail through thick jungle till they came to a small collection of bashas on a hilltop. At the entrance stood two totem poles, each bearing a weathered buffalo skull. At the base of the totems was a collection of smaller skulls. "Monkeys, and probably humans too," George speculated, aware that the Nagas had only abandoned the sport of headhunting thirty years before. The entire village, men, women, children, dogs, and pigs, led the armament party down a series of game trails till they came to a 500 pound bomb. It was easily defused and then the colourful parade returned to the village for a celebration. Five bone stools were set in front of the headman's house and George was led to the middle one. The headman's wives brought *zhu,* rice wine in bamboo mugs and everyone toasted everyone. As the jollity of the celebration took hold, the Nagas, all black-haired, felt free to examine George's blond locks. "The natives all laughed and talked and soon some of them were examining my chest growth very closely," George remembers. "Through the interpreter I learned that the chief considered me a very powerful and famous sahib and hoped that I would stay in his village for a long time. The way it looked, some of the girls seemed to have the same idea." On being told that this was impossible, the chief declared that Sergeant Sim was an honorary member of the village, free to come back at any time and enjoy all the privileges of village life. Everyone shouted approval and drank another toast with *zhu*.

With their easy-going adaptability and mechanical inventiveness Canadian airmen were always at work improving their lot. They found, for example, that by wrapping their beer in burlap, soaking the burlap in high octane fuel, and turning on a fan, they could have cold beer despite the heat of Burma. At Ramree the airmen had a regular yacht club with fighter drop-tanks as their sailing craft. That venture faded, however, when the Navy let it be known that they were tired of rescuing these airmen turned sailor. The fitters and riggers of 435 Squadron vied with one another in crafting miniature motorcycles out of fighter tailwheels and small gas engines. With no dhobi wallah to do their laundry, 436 suffered until Jim Green hooked a makeshift agitator to a small electric motor with a Pitman rod, fixed it in half barrel and began to take in the Squadron's washing. Jim was also one of the stars of 436's variety show, *Monsoon Follies*. His song of the life of a rigger, done in the style of Stanley Holloway, brought the house down.

These were small attempts to lighten the hardships and shorten the hours of a group of young Canadians far from home and enduring the privation of inadequate food, insufferable weather, abysmal accommodation, and demanding work schedules, and they were all part of what kept morale high. Aubrey "Dutchie" Dutch, a rigger with 435 Squadron, expressed it well: "I feel that I had a small job, but I put in all my best efforts, and that could be multiplied over and over again until it became a big job with lots of effort, and that is what eventually won the war." In the intense flying that was necessary to ensure the success of the drive for Mandalay and Meiktila it was the aircrew and ground crew together, each doing his small job with his best effort that carried the day.

XVI

RADAR, CLANDESTINES, AND IRREGULARS

ENERAL SLIM's plan was to take Mandalay and Meiktila and then consider the advisability and possibility of aiming for Rangoon. But though the airfield at Meiktila was taken on March 2, 1944 and Mandalay on March 20, the area was not consolidated until the end of the month. Since the monsoon could be expected any time after May 15, Slim had only six weeks to reach Rangoon, six weeks to fight along more than 350 miles of roadway and paddy to take what would undoubtedly be a well-guarded city. If Rangoon was to be his goal, he would have to hurry. In our narrative however, we can break for a moment to explore the activities of Canadians who were involved in ways that stood apart from the normal front-line action, some on radar, some working clandestinely behind enemy lines, and some doing irregular jobs that were difficult to classify.

Chief among these, certainly in numbers and arguably in importance, were Canadians on radar. Radar was new and very secret in the early days of the war. It began in 1935 when a Scot, Robert Watson-Watt, demonstrated that radio waves could be sent out to bounce off an object such as a ship or airplane and then be detected on their return. The military quickly recognized the value of this discovery; it could, for example, help night-fighters find their target, or help pilots find their way home. Britain, unable to recruit enough radar technicians at home, asked for help from Canada. A thousand ham operators and radio service-men were sent. The call came for four thousand more. To find this many, Canada recruited young men who had some university or normal school education, even some straight from high school, and sent them to university for an intense short course on physics, mathematics, and the fundamentals of radio. Recruits rejected for aircrew because of colour blindness or other such causes were prime candidates for radar training. The trainees still did not know what they were being trained for, so great was the secrecy adhering to the magic of radar. In Britain the Canadians were given further specialized training and then sent out to various stations for experience. In the end, six thousand RCAF radar personnel served overseas with various army, navy and air force units, and over seven hundred of them ended up with the RAF in South East Asia Command. Until Angus Hamilton's book *Canadians on Radar in South East Asia 1941-1945* appeared in 1998 very little was known about these seven hundred, for, as Hamilton remarks, "During the war none of us was allowed to say where we were or what we were doing, and, after the war, no one cared."

There were at least sixteen Canadian radar mechanics in Malaya before the Japanese attacked on December 7, 1941. During the fighting on Singapore, Java, and Sumatra one was killed and twelve were taken prisoner (and four of these died in prison). Only three escaped to Ceylon. Before they fled or were captured, however, they did good service. A portable radar unit on the Malayan coast commanded by F/O Branston "Stan" Martin of Kitchener, Ontario was the first to warn of the Japanese bombers approaching Singapore, and he kept his set operating even as Singapore fell. To do so, he had to erect and dismantle his station five different times in five different locations, each time dodging the bayonets of the Japanese Army to make good his withdrawal. For this he received the OBE "in recognition of gallant and distinguished services rendered during the period of operations against the Japanese in Malaya and the Netherlands East Indies." When Singapore fell, he escaped, first to Java, and then to Ceylon. At Ceylon his Early Warning station was not yet operating when the Easter Sunday attack came in. Fortunately, Len Birchall and his Catalina crew had already given the alert that saved the island, and perhaps India.

Canadians on radar continued to arrive in SEAC throughout the war. Hal Snell, born in England, came to Canada as a seventeen year old to study engineering at McGill. A dismal first year and a summer job in a gold mine, convinced him that engineering was not for him. He switched to Arts, graduated, worked for a while with Eaton's, then decided to enlist. Having been with the COTC at McGill, he had an Army commission, but he resigned that to apply for aircrew. He was rejected for pilot training because of poor eyesight. How about navigator? No. Well then, air gunner? No, but they would take him as a cook. As Hal remembers it, "Things were looking grim till someone suggested: 'You've got a good education and there is this new thing. We can't tell you much about it, but it's called RDF [radio direction finding]. Want to try it?' Well, why not? I could never cook anyway." After basic training, he was sent to back to McGill, back to the very physics prof with whom he had failed physics so dismally four years earlier. This time he applied himself, passed the course, and went on to further training in Canada and then in Britain.

In 1943 he was the Technical Officer in charge of building a radar station at Silchar, the small town at the end of the track that leads westward from Imphal. When the Imphal siege was over and the Fourteenth Army began to move toward the Irrawaddy, Hal's job was to establish mobile stations as far forward as possible. One such venture was a bit too far forward: "We were on a remote track leading down to the Irrawaddy. Suddenly soldiers jumped out at us — ours fortunately — telling us that we were now passing though their front lines toward the enemy, that we were well forward of the artillery, and that an attack was to begin at dawn. Well, we turned around, and when it was light enough to see, set up our station in an abandoned Jap revetment on a small airfield a mile back. In the morning the army moved ahead as planned, and this time we followed."

As the war progressed, Hal became the Technical Officer at Wing HQ responsible for all mobile radar units in Burma, travelling constantly to set up new sites or visit established ones. At the end of the war, Hal was repatriated from Rangoon.

Gwyn Owen ended up in radar because a diagnosis of colour blindness (incorrect, as it turned out) kept him out of aircrew. His career followed the usual path of compressed study at a university, then a posting to a station in Britain. Gwyn left Scotland at the end of May, 1942, as part of the largest convoy ever to leave Britain during the war. In Capetown he was taken off the ship delirious with malaria and it was six weeks before he resumed his journey. In India he chased back and forth across the continent trying to find where he belonged. In Calcutta he had a second bout of malaria and a second bout of hospitalization and convalescence. Finally he reached his active station, and four days later malaria struck again. After his third hospitalization, he was given command of an AMES[1] at Comilla. His assignment was a gentle one, scanning the skies for possible air attacks aimed at Calcutta. Gwyn was here for a year, the only Canadian with thirty Englishmen. In fact when he made a duty run to Chittagong and met two friends from Canada, they were the first Canadians he had seen in three years. In March 1945 his repatriation orders came through, and by July he was back in Canada. His last posting was as Commanding Officer of a small station at Cape St. James on the southern tip of the Queen Charlotte Islands. At the end of the war, he closed the station and retired to civvie street, taking with him as tangible evidence of his service years a kukri from Darjeeling and the last RCAF flag to fly over Cape St. James.

While Gwyn Owen's career in India was fairly static, Bill Corcoran swears he never spent longer than five weeks in any one place. He arrived in

---

[1] AMES = Air Ministry Experimental Station. All radar stations were given this name since radar was still a word that could not be spoken.

Bombay in August, 1943 and was posted to Dimapur. After a month there, Bill asked for a transfer to a more active front and he was posted to Imphal, there to take charge of a mobile Light Early Warning station that was to travel with the Army. His diary records the adventures that ensued:

> Dec 17/43 – Crossed into Burma [at Tamu] at 09:13 this morning. Jungle so thick you can't see through it. Road merely 2 tracks. Very forward position. Must carry arms at all times. No lights or talking except whispers at night.

For their Christmas celebration, an admin officer brought his little group two ducks and two bottles of rum. Two weeks later there were indications of a new Japanese offensive aimed at Tamu and Bill Corcoran and his van were recalled to Imphal. A month at Imphal, and then they were ordered back to the Tamu area. Again Bill's diary records what happened:

> Mar. 22 — Started for Moreh. Part way down road, had to turn back. Japs on road.
>
> Mar. 23 — Tried road again – OK. Finally arrived at site. Situation pretty grim.
>
> Mar. 24 — Shell fire all day. Most of time spent in slit trenches.
>
> Mar. 25 — Quiet all day but Japs resumed shelling in evening.
>
> Mar. 26 — Quiet day – shelling all going toward Japs.
>
> Mar. 27 — Quiet day. Japs opened up about 18:15 hrs. Over to tech gharry [truck]. Shelling intense and very close. During lull ran for dugout. Just in when shelling resumed. Japs using whiz-bang mortars, medium and heavy artillery. 18:50 hrs. direct hit on Bofors gun ammo dump about five yards from tech gharry. Fire started – Phillips and I went to try to save equipment. Driven back by exploding ammo. Gharry burned for hours. Luckily no one hurt but everyone's nerves shaken.

Corcoran and his unit moved back to Imphal around April 1 without ever having set up their station. Imphal was in a panic. The Dimapur road had been cut and the siege was on. In his diary Bill noted: "Half rations — 24 hour stand-to, guards posted at all times. Everyone concerned but confident the army can handle the situation." Very quickly they were moved out of Imphal with other non-combatants.

They were then instructed to get ready to join the Chindits but this move was cancelled and instead they found themselves once more on the road to Tamu, this time with Slim's forces on the way across the Chindwin. As the Fourteenth Army moved down through Kalemyo. Kalewa and Meiktila, Bill kept pace and eventually, early in July, ended up in Rangoon. On 11 July, his repat orders came through. Looking back now, Bill claims his peripatetic life in Burma taught him two useful lessons: (1) How to pack a kit bag,

(2) Never complain about where you are because there is always somewhere worse — and you'll likely be there soon.

During the second Arakan campaign, the RAF found that radar stations on the coast of the Mayu peninsula were fairly useless. The mountains, rising abruptly from the sea, made the radar blind in its eastward-looking eye and of course the Japanese air raids came from the east. Bases located a few miles out to sea would give them the scope to view the mountain tops, but the Navy could not spare any craft that would serve as offshore bases. The radar boys in Calcutta solved the problem by making their own. Four old coal barges, mere steel hulls 98 feet long, were fitted with sleeping quarters and operating facilities in the hold, mess room and galley above that, and all topped off with a massive antenna installation. They were ungainly, awkward, top-heavy, hot as Hades below decks (despite air conditioning), and they had no motive power, but they would have to do.

Bill Kerr, an RCAF corporal, joined his barge as it sat in the Hooghly River in Calcutta, and promptly christened it The Hooghly Belle. On the appointed day, a tug took them alongside and moved them through the serpentine channels of the Sundarbans and across the northern tip of the Bay of Bengal to Chittagong, 150 miles in all. It was quite an experience, especially going through the Sundarbans where they shot a deer and enjoyed venison instead of the usual bully beef. Later they moved from Chittagong to Akyab and here they scored their first victory. A high-flying Japanese reconnaissance plane came onto their screen and the operator alerted a nearby strip. The radar crew could watch as two Spitfires scrambled; they could watch as the Spitfires followed the intercept orders they gave, and they could hear on their radio when the pilots locked onto the invader and shot him down. They had trained to do exactly this, and it was satisfying to see their training finally put into operation.

On New Year's Day 1945 Bill's barge was slated to join a convoy and move farther down the coast. The corvette was manoeuvring to get them alongside when two fast-moving cruisers cut across their bow. Within minutes the heavy wake hit them. Yoked side-by-side, the corvette and the barge began grinding together and rocking apart, lifting as much as six feet and then dropping again. The barge, top-heavy and unstable even in calm conditions, tilted to an alarming angle and threatened to overturn. "This was the only time I saw rats deserting what they thought was a sinking ship," remembers Bill. "They jumped off the barge and clung to the ropes of the corvette." The steep pitch of the barge's deck flung one of the radar men, a non-swimmer, into the sea between the two vessels just as they were threatening to grind together again. Without thinking, Bill Kerr jumped in, grabbed his mate, and swam with him the length of the barge till he got to open water. There a sailor from the corvette threw them a life preserver and pulled them to safety. Bernard Holt, from Moose Jaw, the CO of the barge, put Bill in for a medal. In the King's New Year's Honour List for 1946 the story of Bill's bravery is told and the award of the British Empire Medal is announced.

More than was the usual case for RCAF personnel attached to the RAF, Canadian radar mechanics were not merely attached, they were subsumed, to the extent that Canadians with radar in Britain were not even deemed to be overseas. In India and Burma their isolation from things Canadian was even more complete. They were scattered in very small units in a hundred different locations. Many of them had come to SEAC before there was a Canadian administrative headquarters in the East. Even after a Canadian headquarters was established, contact with Canadian radar personnel, scattered singly or in twos and threes over the whole sub-continent, was infrequent and unsatisfying. Imagine, therefore, the excitement of two Canadians isolated in the Arakan when they were told that Air Marshal Breadner, the RCAF's top officer, was touring India and would be in their area. The two rearranged work schedules, got up early in the morning, endured a long, hot, dusty, and bone-crushing ride in the back of a truck, hunted for two hours on back trails for the right squadron, and were then handed a note: "Upon reconsideration, Air Marshal Breadner has decided to omit Comilla from his itinerary." They were not merely forgotten, they were scorned.

Over time the constant association with the RAF had its effect. Doug Gooderham, the senior Canadian on radar in SEAC (and the recipient of the OBE and the American Bronze Star Medal), recalls his visit to an American station. He appreciated the coffee and the ice cream, but he would gladly have traded the incessant canned music in the Officers' Club for a dart board or a shove ha'penny board. Bruce Aikenhead and Jake Wright set out in delight and anticipation to visit the two Canadian squadrons who had just arrived in their neighbourhood. They returned puzzled and perplexed: "After our long immersion with the RAF, they all seemed quite foreign and really seemed to speak a different language. I don't remember going back to visit them a second time."

For all that, they kept their Canadian identity, or at least some part of it. Rather than learning to play cricket, if there were at least three Canadians on the station, they recruited the RAF boys for a game of softball. The cricketers learned the art of fielding with surprising ease, though they had more trouble with the batting. For one unit, the highlight of their baseball season was beating an American Navy team 13 to 4. Gordon MacPhail of Carleton Place, Ottawa, got a chuckle out of hearing one of the Yanks say: "Imagine being beaten by a bunch of Limeys at our own game." Gordon didn't tell them there were three Canadians on the RAF team.

Mail from Canada was always a problem and one they could do little about. Promotion was even more irksome for promotion came slowly in the RAF. Even when the RCAF did promote its members, the newly-promoted man could not be accommodated in the RAF establishment. Hence came the habit of shadow rank that we have already met with Neil Turnbull at Broadway. The good thing about shadow rank was that, though it did not show on the uniform, it was entered in one's paybook and did show on pay parade. But the real sticking point for Canadians on radar in SEAC was repatriation. For a long time there was no set or announced duration for an overseas tour; the airman or officer simply lived in the hope that someone, somewhere would eventually remember him and send him home. When the tour limit of three years from the day of leaving Canada was eventually set, most of the radar men were beyond that limit and orders went out for Canadians to be repatriated. By February, 1945 repatriation was in full swing, but it was a slow business, first a posting to a transit camp at Bombay, a wait for sea transport, and then the long tiresome voyage to Liverpool or Southampton. In Britain there was leave and another wait for a ship to Halifax, Montreal or New York. By October, all Canadian radar personnel had left India. On the boat going home, one of the airmen summed it all up: "I wouldn't have missed it for a million dollars, but I wouldn't do it again for ten million."

At the beginning of 1942 when the RAF's few Brewster Buffaloes and worn out Hurricanes together with the AVG's handful of Tomahawks were trying to defend the skies over Rangoon, there was only one radar station and the Air Officer Commanding categorically stated "The lack of adequate RDF equipment exerted a critical influence on the air battle in Burma." By the end of that year there were 53 installations and at the end of the war there were more than 120 AMES's as well as other installations with squadrons and wings. There is no question but that they exerted a critical influence on the final victory in Burma, and one could argue that without the Canadians it could not have been done, for more than twenty-five per cent of the men on radar in Burma came from Canada. A disproportionate number of the radar officers, the men who gave leadership and example, were Canadians, including Doug Gooderham, the Senior Signals Officer in SEAC. On the AMES's many of the RAF men were radar operators whereas the Canadians were all radar technicians, men trained to maintain and repair equipment, to improvise and invent, to mend and make-do. The best estimate of what they contributed to the work of the radar units in Burma comes from their RAF colleagues. Ken Yabsley of Plymouth, UK wrote to the present author: "I found all the Canadians chaps good company and of course, when one reflects that they were to a man all volunteers, we must give them full credit for their patriotism." Alan Cooper of Devon elaborated on that opinion:

"The Canadians were a good influence on these small units. They were on average better educated than many in the RAF, and were used to the wild, open-air life we had to live. It was thought that the RCAF were paid like film stars, and good luck to them. They appeared to have a maturity and self-confidence we lacked — but more important, they were very pleasant colleagues and good company." This sums up the experience of Canadians on radar in India. They fitted in with a minimum of the "colonial" friction that was so often generated when Canucks and Limeys met; they did their job well and were quietly appreciated. They brought home an attitude and a legend that sets them apart so that even today, decades after the war is over, they regularly meet to reminisce and remember.

In all theatres of war there were will-o'-the-wisp troops operating in secret behind the lines. In the Burma campaign they were known as V Force and as Force 136. V Force was organized very shortly after the retreat in 1942 with intelligence gathering as its main purpose. When the Allied forces straggled into Imphal, shaken, disorganized, and confused, there was every reason to think that the Japanese would continue to press forward, either in strong open attack or in furtive infiltration. To monitor Japanese intentions, a volunteer officer from the Army or the police, or a former trader or administrator with local knowledge was inserted immediately behind the lines. He took with him a small force of the Assam Police.[2] Few Canadians were involved in this work, but we do know that Ian MacPherson missed the first Chindit expedition because he was with a V Force detachment.

There were two other officers with V Force who seem to have been a Canadian and who were vividly in the memory of the men they worked with. The first is Evan Darlington, and we have met him already in Keith Muir's chronicle.

It will be remembered that, on the retreat, Keith Muir took the long, northern route that led through the swamp of the Hukawng Valley. For this part of the trek the Assam Tea Planters Association had provided a string of overnight camps and at one of these Keith chanced to meet a Mr. Stewart. In his memoirs, Keith wrote: "On learning that I was a Canadian, Stewart led me to a basha to meet Mr. and Mrs. Darlington and their infant daughter. They were missionaries from Toronto who had been working among the Kachins. They intended to continue their journey in the morning, riding on an elephant." And indeed, next morning, Muir watches as the Darlington family mount their elephant and continue to India. When they finally crossed the border to safety, all they had left was the clothes they stood in, for his wife a shirt and a pair of shorts, for him, just a pair of shorts. Their baby daughter was only three weeks old.

[2] The Assam Police were a pre-war border patrol force of Gurkhas recruited and paid by the Assam civil administration.

The other Canadian is David Darlington, Evan's younger brother. Very little is known of them, but, because they were working as V Force operatives, guiding and translating for a group of American clandestines, they are mentioned in three books written American veterans, and each tells a few details of the lives of this mysterious pair. First in time is *KC8 Burma: CBI Air Warning Team 1941-1942* by Bob Phillips. It tells how, in late 1942, a small American unit struggled across the hills and swamp from Ledo to set up an early warning radio station in northern Burma. The group was feeling particularly forlorn and forsaken when a stranger came to them:

> *The stranger turned out to be a British civilian with a very tropical appearance. He was wearing a sun helmet that almost completely obscured his face, a pair of sunglasses, a white sleeveless shirt, and a skinny pair of khaki shorts. He was skinny, too, but when we heard him speak in an American style of language, instead of some kind of Cockney, we completely forgave his appearance.*
>
> *"Mr Darlington is my name," he said. "I have been assigned to make the trip into the hills with your party as interpreter and political officer.*
>
> *In the ensuing conversation, the Americans offered him a cigarette.*
>
> *"I love American smokes," he admitted. "I had a lot of them when I was in Canada and I have missed them ever since."*

David is, in Bob Phillips' phrase, a "gabby person," and they soon have his story. He was born in Burma of English parents who were missionaries in this area. He and Evan were sent to Canada for their education when they were in their mid-teens, attended theological college in England and then came back to Burma. In the weeks that follow, David is an invaluable mentor and protector to the small group of Americans. He speaks Kachin fluently (his wife is a Kachin), he knows the country, and when he does not know the trails, he knows how to find someone who does. Moreover, he knows the people. In village after village, the natives come out joyously and noisily to greet him. In each case, David can explain who the Americans are and vouch for their *bona fides.* Conversely, he can assure the Americans that the Nagas are no longer interested in collecting their skulls, and that the Kachins expect a bountiful distribution of cigarettes. Without David Darlington's help, the radio unit might never have reached its destination and begun reporting on Japanese air traffic.

Evan Darlington we last saw taking his little family to India by elephant in 1942. In the fall of 1943 he was back in Burma as the British liaison officer assigned to help Merrill's Marauders make their way into the Myitkyina area. In *Burma: The Untold Story,* Won-Loy Chan, a San Francisco Chinese and a major with the American Army, describes him as being of medium height and build, with a thin, well-trimmed moustache. Oddly, whereas the Americans who travelled with David remarked on his North American accent, Chan notes particularly that Evan's British accent was most pronounced, "though that didn't seem to affect his ability to converse with the Kachins in their own dialect." In March 1944 Evan conducted a second group of Americans through the Hukawng Valley, as Charlton Ogburn relates in *The Marauders*. Ogburn and Chan both agree that they could not have survived without Evan's expert guidance. "Evan was indispensable not only as a supplier of guides but as a guide himself," wrote Charlton Ogburn, and Won-Loy Chan added: "His knowledge of the Hukawng Valley and its inhabitants was invaluable to the Northern Combat Area Command staff." For his unique contribution to the efforts of the Marauders, Evan was awarded the Legion of Merit by the American government.

After the war, Evan returned for a while to the Burmese mission field, while David was from 1949 to 1954 the incumbent of the Anglican Church in Engelhart, Ontario. He then returned to England to join his brother in parish work there. The brothers were probably not Canadians in any legal sense, and therefore they belong only marginally in our story. But their lives do demonstrate how strangely a Canadian connection winds its way into odd corners of the Burmese conflict.

They also demonstrate one aspect of the work V Force people were doing in the Burma campaign, that is, helping to introduce clandestine forces into their behind-the-lines locations. Other V Force operatives were more focused on gathering information about Japanese troop dispositions and movements or harvesting battle plans from enemy couriers waylaid on a jungle path.

While V Force was mainly an intelligence gathering network and thus ancillary to the operational side of military affairs, Force 136 was a clandestine, behind-the-lines operational organization, the Burma arm of what was known in Europe as Special Operations Executive (SOE). Force 136 did collect and pass on intelligence, but its mandate also included raising and training indigenous cadres and using them in all manner of sabotage and guerrilla activities. V Force, especially at the beginning, worked right behind the lines, whereas Force 136 operatives were parachuted into locations anywhere in occupied Burma. In the intelligence gathering sphere, for example, its informers and operatives in occupied Rangoon could monitor and even accelerate the growing rift between Aung San, the leader of the Burmese National Army, and his Nipponese masters. By the end of March 1945, Force 136 was able to bring General Slim and Aung San together to hammer out an understanding that saw the Burmese National Army defect from the Japanese side and ally itself with the British.

As the Fourteenth Army pushed southward from Mandalay and Meiktila toward Rangoon, Slim became increasingly troubled with the thought of his open left flank. In an operation called *Character,* Force 136 undertook to provide the protection he was looking for by organizing and arming the Karens along the Sittang River. Organizing them was not difficult, for the Karens were extremely loyal, but it was also necessary to hold them in check until the hour had come, for if in their enthusiasm they moved too soon, the Japanese could send in a punitive force and end their usefulness. In its double role of training and restraining, *Character* was taxing the resources of Force 136 and more operatives were needed. Nine French-Canadian agents recently retrieved from France volunteered to go behind the lines in Burma. In most respects they were ideal candidates for the job; they were experienced saboteurs, accustomed to hard living, trained in code work and wireless operation, adept at laying ambushes, skilled in woodcraft and survival, and experts in unarmed combat. A short course at an Eastern Warfare School in India added some knowledge of junglecraft to their catalogue of skills, but there was no time to supply their deficiency in the local languages. They would have to depend on interpreters.

Leonard Jacques Taschereau was one of the first Canadian volunteers to drop into Burma. Born in Saskatchewan, brought up in Montreal, Leonard had worked pre-war as a surveyor, a bush pilot, and a bookkeeper to keep himself afloat during the depression years. For a time his job in an aircraft factory prevented him from joining the Army so that, when he finally began his life behind-the-lines, first in France and now with Force 136, he was older than most of his colleagues. In March 1945 he was dropped into the Karen Hills area somewhere east of the Sittang. In his book, *Canadians behind Enemy Lines, 1939-1945*, Roy MacLaren tells of Taschereau's reception:

> *Taschereau had the singular good fortune to be observed landing by an elderly Karen who emerged from the jungle to inform him that he had served as a batman in the British Army during the First World War. After proudly showing to the astonished — and relieved — Canadian his carefully preserved 1914-1918 medals, he led Taschereau along the jungle paths to a remote Italian mission.*
>
> *Its Roman Catholic fathers warmly welcomed him, providing food and shelter, and helping him to reconnoitre a nearby rail line and the mountain paths used by the Japanese.*

These were the paths and the jungle trails the enemy troops were now resorting to as they fled from Slim's determined push toward Rangoon and tried to escape into Siam. While Karen volunteers lined the edges of the trail with sharply pointed bamboo stakes angled into the ground, Taschereau buried his explosives and connected lengths of cordite fuse line. Then they hid till the Japanese and their mules toiled up the path. When the mines exploded, the Japanese jumped to the side. Those that escaped impalement were quickly despatched by Bren gun fire, and Taschereau and his friends ran off to mine another path.

In April Joseph Ernest "Rocky" Fournier and Paul-Emile Thibeault joined Leonard Taschereau in the Karen Hills. Rocky was a short, stocky hard-rock miner from New Brunswick, used to hard living, but gentle withal. When he joined the Royal Canadian Corps of Signals in 1942 the recruiting officer noted that he was a "very willing, agreeable chap. Anxious to do whatever will be most useful in the Army." In August 1944 he had parachuted into France to begin his clandestine career. Now he was to continue it half a world away. It was well that he was accustomed to hard living, since on his first Burma adventure he found himself living in a Karen village, sleeping on the floor of a native hut, eating a constant diet of rice with an occasional addition of chicken or pork, and enduring unending rain. Fournier's specialty was radio communications. When Japanese encampments or supply caches were located, he could call up an airstrike and then inform the pilots of the effectiveness of their strafing. If supplies were required, his radio was ready to arrange an airdrop. At the end of his tour, his superior assessed him as "one of the best and most useful officers under my command." Suffering from malaria and dysentery, Rocky walked out to Toungoo and was flown to hospital in Calcutta.

Fournier had been operating in the Karen Hills between the Sittang and the Salween Rivers. With a British officer, a radio operator and two Burmese guerrillas, Pierre Meunier was dropped into the Pegu Yomas, well to the west of the Sittang. Hardly had the small group settled in, when they were ordered to operate in the Toungoo area, 150 miles to the south and on the other side of the mountains. It was a demanding trek, especially since the group had to exist on the rations they had arrived with until they could set up in their new area and arrange a drop. Then they began their task, recruiting and training Karen guerrillas, leading their recruits on ambushes, and gathering whatever information they could about the whereabouts of enemy troops. Within ten days they had a levy of 150 Karens under training and an intelligence network that kept them informed of all enemy troop movements within a radius of 100 miles. On at least twelve occasions they found ammunition and supply dumps, called in airstrikes, and watched as the RAF blew their target to pieces.

The British officer accompanying Meunier, emboldened by news of Slim's success on the road to Rangoon and by their local success along the Sittang, decided to attack a small Japanese garrison in a nearby village, even though offensive action was not usually a sanctioned tactic for a clandestine force. The approach to the village was over open country and for two hours Meunier painstakingly crawled forward to observe. As he watched, it became clear the Japanese were already preparing to withdraw. On the spur of the moment, Meunier devised an audacious plan. Perhaps he could accelerate their withdrawal. He drew up his small army into a column and boldly marched them onto the village as if they were the van of an advancing force. The ruse worked beautifully. The Japanese fled from the village and right into the arms of the guerrillas he had stationed on the escape route to receive them. Soon thereafter the advance guard of the Fourteenth Army overtook them, and Meunier moved with the troops to Rangoon from whence he was flown back to Calcutta and eventually to Canada.

With such exploits as these the French-Canadian agents, though they came late to the Burmese Campaign, contributed to a greater extent than is commonly known to the eventual success of Slim's march to Rangoon. But there is another Canadian connection to the clandestine activities in Burma. When Meunier climbed aboard an aircraft in Calcutta for his trip into Burma, he was surprised to discover that the entire crew was Canadian. "Needless to say," he remarks in his memoirs, "we had a good chat about Canada — which eased the tension considerably."

An all-Canadian crew was actually not that surprising. The rapid growth of the clandestines, both Force 136 and a more secretive group known only as the Inter-Services Liaison Department (ISLD), had required that a squadron be devoted entirely to their care and feeding. Thus in January, 1944, 357 RAF Squadron was formed and designated as a Special Duties squadron. Based near Calcutta and flying ten Liberators and ten Hudsons (soon exchanged for Dakotas), the squadron concentrated first on dropping agents and operatives behind the lines, and then on keeping them supplied. In January, 1945 a second Special Duties Squadron, 358 Squadron, was formed to share the work. Both squadrons were heavily dependent upon the RCAF for aircrew personnel. At the height of its operating activities in April, 1944, 357 Squadron carried 83 Canadians on its roster. If we estimate the total aircrew on the Squadron to number about 240, one third of them were Canadians. Tommy Lee, an ex-instructor from Toronto, was Flight Commander of the Liberator flight, his deputy flight commander was Doug Lamb from Vancouver, and the favourite relaxation of off-duty crews was a game of horseshoes.

It was in the nature of Special Duties operations that casualties would be heavy. Almost all drops were done at night and into remote and inaccessible areas where there was less likelihood of discovery. On the night of March 14, 1944 a Hudson set out from Calcutta to drop to a Force 136 group near Bhamo, a round trip that pushed the limits of the aircraft. The crew battled through ferocious weather to locate the DZ, a small clearing halfway down a mountainside and in a steep, narrow valley. The first circuit went well. Pulling up for the second circuit in the dark, the Hudson lost an engine, hit a tree, and cartwheeled into the jungle. The pilot and three crewmen were killed. The co-pilot, F/L Ponsford, though himself injured, pulled the Canadian navigator, F/O W. Prosser, from the burning wreckage.

Ironically, both were tour-expired and had gone on the trip only because they had been there before and knew the area. When the Force 136 men who were to receive the drop came to the crash, they found both Prosser and Ponsford barely clinging to life.

It is a tribute to the efficiency of the clandestines' radio network that the call for medical aid evoked two responses. An American behind-the-lines group despatched a doctor at once — and estimated it would take him five days of mule travel to get there. Back at Calcutta, Dr. Graham, 357 Squadron's medical officer, volunteered to go immediately even though he had never jumped from a plane before. "They were men from our squadron," he later explained, "so of course I had to go." The squadron's flight-sergeant parachute instructor volunteered to jump with him for encouragement.

The parachute instructor went out first and, as Dr. Graham says, "He was sort of waiting in air for me as I came down." Following the flight-sergeant's mid-air instructions, Graham controlled his swaying chute and landed safely and the two then set about tending Prosser's badly smashed leg and doing what they could for his fractured skull. For Ponsford they could do nothing. He died that afternoon. A warning came that the Japanese were approaching. Doctor Graham and the flight-sergeant fashioned a litter for Prosser and carried him quickly from the crash scene. They hid in the jungle for two weeks, afraid to move their patient because of his injuries. Then, for four days, twelve coolies carried their patient, painwracked and almost drained of life, through enemy-held territory as they headed for an American airstrip where they could all be lifted to safety. Once over the border into China, the coolies balked, fearful of being conscripted into the Chinese army, and only an offer of money, rum, and aspirin persuaded them to continue. On April 5, three weeks after the crash, the group reached an American outpost. The Americans hired a new set of coolies and put them on the path to the airstrip. The coolies, having been paid in advance, immediately decamped.

While they rested and awaited a new set of coolies, Prosser had moments of lucidity, his first since the crash. He spoke in a dispirited tone of his weariness and despair. "What makes the grass grow in Texas?" Graham jokingly rejoined. The answer of course was "Bullshit," and it was the Squadron's little formula for puncturing pomposity or lightening solemnity. "Perhaps there won't be a crop this year," Prosser whispered, but his tired little grin gave the lie to his pessimism. On April 11, after a lengthy march over mountain passes in atrocious weather, the group reached the airstrip. Five days later a rescue plane came in; on take-off its landing gear malfunctioned and they had to abort the mission. Next day all went well. Graham, Flight-Sergeant White and Prosser returned to their base and Prosser eventually made a full recovery. For their part in this epic of jungle survival, Graham received an immediate DSO and White a DCM.

The rugged, remote terrain, the need to operate in darkness, the unfriendly weather, these were dangers in themselves, but they were all enhanced by an additional consideration more felt in the Special Duties squadrons that in regular supply flights – the awareness that the troops they were supporting were in enemy-occupied territory and that the Special Duties squadrons were their only lifeline. If a crew were told at briefing that "This plasma has to be there today," they took chances beyond the ordinary to ensure that the plasma got there. Not always, however, was the extra pressure justified. F/L Tommy Lee, the Canadian flight commander, was an experienced and conscientious flier and at the time he held the record for the longest Liberator sortie, 22 hours and 45 minutes. Thus he felt keenly the "special duties" pressure when he was handed a wrapped package and told that it was vital that it be delivered that night. Carefully he stowed the package and took off. He had been to the DZ before; it was in a valley cradled by five thousand foot peaks and on previous visits he had done well to get his Liberator down to two thousand feet for the drop. Tonight he would take special care with his special package. Gently easing off on the throttles, curving his flight path and playing with the flaps, he floated down to fifteen hundred feet to let the parcel fly. Then flaps up, full power at once, hard back on the wheel, over onto one wing to get up out of the valley and clear of the mountains. Tom felt particularly good as he settled onto his homeward course. Some time later he discovered by chance that the vital package was fresh meat and that the urgency was to preserve its freshness.

In 1939, Art Coy, born and brought up in North Vancouver, was a gold refiner with the Canadian Mint in Ottawa. When war was declared, the Head Refiner and Smelter, who was a Reserve Army officer, was called up and Art stepped into his job. In 1941 he joined the RCAF and did the usual stint of "guard duty" in the cold of an Alberta winter while waiting to get on course. After graduating from #3 SFTS, Calgary with a commission, he instructed at Vulcan until his agitation for a more active posting brought him to the Liberator Operational Training Unit at Abbotsford. At the end of the course he had his nine-man crew and a posting to 357 Special Duties Squadron in India. Eight other crews from Abbotsford O.T.U had the same posting, and thus 45 Canadian airmen arrived together at 357 Squadron in March, 1945.

The Coy crews' first operational sortie, March 17, 1945, was a humble six and a half hour trip to drop a million nickels over Mandalay. Art's diary notes gun flashes over Mandalay, but no flak or opposition. "Dropping nickels" was Special Duties' jargon for scattering propaganda leaflets and it was done on each supply trip to obscure the sortie's real purpose. There was a tendency to spurn this activity as a waste of time, and indeed the leaflets aimed at winning over the Japanese soldiers were probably totally ineffectual. On the other hand, pamphlets warning the Burmese rail workers of an upcoming bombing raid had their effect. The workers stayed home and the Japanese supply trains did not travel that day.

Their next trip was "the real stuff." They dropped four men, eleven canisters and five packs to the *Character* unit and then returned via Meiktila to fling out 10 packs of leaflets and watch a fighter strike directed at the Japanese who were still besieging the strip. Art liked to assess each trip and learn from it. For this one his judgment was: "Good trip but dropped too high. Radio altimeter not accurate so didn't take chances. Navigation perfect; everything on the nose. Two poor devils fell in the lake. 12 hours 10 minutes; 2230 air miles." Just as he assessed each trip, so he assessed his crew. Like many Liberator captains, Art took a very particular, even paternal, interest in the eight Canadians who flew with him and in the way they worked together. After a month on operations, his diary recorded his judgment:

> So far I feel satisfied that we are doing quite well. Nav. team is really tops. Chuck and George very keen and darned accurate. Ray more confident all the time, still a bit jumpy in a pinch, has to be hollered at occasionally. Yank really quick and keen. Ted easier going but darn good. Fred's dispatching good. Curly and Jim in there pitching. Reports OK so far.

Art's pride in "Coy's Boys," as the Squadron designated them, still shines when he talks of them today: Curly Despres, his completely bald French-Canadian gunner, Italo "Yank" Palumbo, an American in the RCAF and the man who undertook to scrounge all the food for every trip, and bomb-aimer George McGregor who became unusually proficient in taking star- and sun-shots for the navigator. Art particularly remembers his navigator: "Charlie Campbell was recognized as exceptional and received the DFC for his efforts. He was never still and was very accurate in his work. He literally worked himself to exhaustion and when we finished our last trip he went to bed and slept for 72 hours, so soundly that we couldn't wake him even though he had received numerous letters from his beloved wife Jean." Art's pride in his crew seems well justified. In his diary he recorded that Major Tyce, the Army Liaison Officer, "says we are the best crew on the squadron."

In mid-April they had another short trip, eight hours to Toungoo to drop a French-Canadian captain — this was probably Peter Meunier, who, it will be remembered, eased the tension of his fly-in by having a good chat about Canada with his all-Canadian crew. Normally the crew does not know who it is dropping, and it is even considered bad form in the shadow world of clandestines to seek any information about the passengers. In this case it would have been unnatural if they had not talked about Canada. On a second occasion, the Coy crew dropped Major Bunny Warren, an operative so exalted within the ranks of infiltrated agents that, as Art's navigator, Charlie Campbell from Red Deer, Alberta, reports, "eight jeeps and trucks filled with big shots came to give their regards and farewells." They also dropped Colonel D. Smiley, another famous operative, into Siam to organize the Siamese resistance force for a possible uprising against the Japanese. It seems that the crew was selected for the big name drops.

In his book, *The Moonlight War*, Terence O'Brien underlines the dangers of special duty flying by pointing out that casualties were far higher among the air crew who serviced the clandestines than among the clandestines themselves. In fact, one airman was lost for every three agents dropped and aircrew of the Special Duties squadrons suffered 40 times greater loss of life than the operatives on the ground. As a measure of the perils of this sort of flying, consider that the two Special Duties squadrons, 357 and 358, lost 27 aircraft in an 18 month period (and 358 was operational for only six months of that time), only one of these to enemy air action. In those 27 aircraft, 28 Canadians were killed. The loss of the Stockwell crew brings these facts home to Art Coy.

Len Stockwell and his crew were among those who were posted from Abbotsford to 357 in March, 1945 so the two crews knew each other well. On April 1, scarcely two weeks into their tour, both Coy and Stockwell were briefed for a trip to south Burma. Stockwell was assigned KH323, U for Uncle. Coy remembered it as the aircraft he had taken on his first operational solo and tried to avoid ever since. Everyone called it "the gutless wonder." As soon as Coy and his crew return from their trip, they are told the news: Len's aircraft had crashed on take-off killing all 9 crew and 6 Burmese paratroopers. Art's diary entry for April 2 tells the rest of the story:

> Had grim job of loading Len's crew and Burmese onto truck for transfer to cemetery. Heat already at work on bodies so very disagreeable. Storkey's shoelace hanging out of casket didn't help much either. Buried in cemetery back of our quarters, will take snaps tomorrow. Very brief service, only mumbled committal ceremony, three volley salute and Last Post, all lowered hastily into graves about a foot apart in a row. Can't believe they are gone — Len Stockwell, crazy humour but very likeable; Brian Millar, stubborn, keen and intent on being first pilot soon, continuing after war; Jack Friesen, Nav, real wit, smart, always said "Might as well die, nothing to live for." Karl Merriam, Bomb Aimer, big feet, good sport, athletic; Sgts. Storkey and Steventon, Wireless Air Gun-

ners, Brett, Green, and Rickert, Air Gunners, all good. They shouldn't have had to die.

All nine of the crew members Art named were Canadians. Next day, Art, as a member of the Committee of Adjustment, had to go through the dead men's personal effects. That was even harder to take than Storkey's show lace hanging out of the coffin the night before — Karl Merriam's right-hand baseball glove, Brian Millar's books on aero engines and his letter to Trans Canada Airlines enquiring about future employment. Hardest of all were Mrs. Stockwell's letters to her husband and her worries about his safety. Art undertook to write to Mrs. Stockwell, telling himself "It's a difficult job, but I believe it's appreciated."

Still shaken by this all-too-sudden confrontation with the lethal reality of operational flying, the Coy crew returned to their routine of dropping agents into the jungle and then dropping supplies to keep them there. Their goal now is to get in the 300 hours required to complete their operational tour. Art's diary keeps a running record of their progress toward that goal:

> *10 May, 1945 — 209 ops hours, over 3/5 through.*

> *24 May, 1945 — still 38 hours to get in and the monsoons only 13 days away.*

> *27 May, 1945 — only 17 hours to go.*

Then came the triumphant entry:

> *2 June, 1945 — My time now 314:50, tour-ex soon I hope.*

The next entry shattered that hope:

> *3 June, 1945 — Word has come for tour extension to 400 hours as of June 1, same day we went over 300.*

They tried to argue that they had technically completed a 300 hour tour before the 400 hour tour was in effect, but they were overruled. There was nothing for it but to put in another 100 hours.

Rules seemed to be all important now. Art thought of what had happened to his roommate, the jovial Jack Blinkhorn. Jack made his drop and then, in response to a request from the ground, he landed at Dien Bien Phu to evacuate some severely wounded French soldiers to Calcutta. When he returned to base, he was placed under open arrest for "making an unauthorized landing and thereby endangering one of His Majesty's aircraft." "We all think he did a good show," snorted Art in his diary, "Probably get a reprimand and a DFC."[3]

---

[3] What actually happened to Blinkhorn the records do not say, but instances of rules trumping battlefield common sense are legion. Tom Watson was reprimanded for escaping Singapore in a battered old Brewster Buffalo since he was not checked out on the Buffalo. Joe Curtiss was reprimanded for bringing home his Dakota on one engine rather than landing at some inadequate interim drome. And in the First World War, Air Chief Marshal Sir Robert Brooke-Popham was censured for endangering his Bleriot flying machine by attempting to mount a machine gun!

The days of eight hour flights to Burma were rare now for 357 Squadron. Eighteen and twenty hour flights to Malaya or Siam were more common.[4] For Art and his crew this was good news for the hours mounted up quickly. On the other hand, long trips were very demanding. They had to get up at 3 in the morning for a 5:30 takeoff, land at Cox's Bazar to top up all tanks, including those in three of the bomb bays, and then set off to fly to Malaya and back, non-stop, 3400 air miles in 22 hours. To avoid weather, radar and enemy aircraft, they flew between 300 and 500 feet, most of it on automatic pilot if they had dependable equipment, otherwise the pilots had to fly the whole time. In theory one pilot could sleep, but one close call put an end to that possibility for Art.

What with the long flights and the difficulty of sleeping in the Calcutta heat, the crews were often on the edge of exhaustion. Art noted that even when the automatic pilot was on and all he had to do was scan the horizon, he sometimes slept for an instant and then woke with a start, once to find himself in a 40 degree bank and 60 degrees off course. The next time, he gave in to his fatigue and, handing over to Ray Jorgenson, the second pilot, and went back to the flight deck for a snooze. Rain drops falling on him from where the upper turret had been removed (to save weight) woke him abruptly. He looked out the front windscreen and could see only water. Shouting "Pull up!" he flew to the cockpit and, in one swift, unthinking motion, knocked the automatic pilot off, and heaved back on the wheel. They had been within seconds of crashing into the waves. Art called the rain drops providence, but it is equally likely that, as a conscientious and experienced pilot, even in his sleep he was aware of the attitude of his plane and alert to the danger.

Coy's Boys finished their tour as the war ended. They were offered an opportunity to fly a few extra sorties, but they were tired and tired crews make mistakes. The long flights, the restless nights, and the memory of the near calamity had taken their toll. Art's diary entry for 7 June 1945 makes the point: "Woke again to find myself sitting up in bed, reaching for the throttles, couldn't seem to get off the deck." It is time to go home.

En route by rail to Bombay, they capped their Burma adventure with an unusual encounter. Chuck Campbell noticed that a VIP car had been hitched on next to them and he recognized the VIP, Jawaharlal Nehru. Audaciously they sent a message back "Please come and visit the Canadians in the next car." Graciously, Nehru invited them to come visit him instead, and they did. In his diary Art recorded how Nehru explained why the

---

[4] According to John R. W. Gwynne-Timothy's book, *Burma Liberators,* the longest operational flight of the war occurred when Canadian F/L J. A. L. Muir flew from Ceylon to Malaya, 3735 miles in 24 hours, 10 minutes, to drop two operatives.

orange-white-green Congress flags were waving so wildly, then he summed up his impressions of their illustrious host: "His English was excellent, a Cambridge student, his personality very friendly. Is a fine-looking man and very sincere. Said the Congress Party is open to all, that we could join by paying subscription. Dislikes present franchise as it covers only 10% and all controlled. Had amazing grasp of Canada's problems. Thought we had less tolerance there with French than shown in India."

In the last months of 1944, 357 Squadron found that it was overworked. Force 136, V Force, the highly secretive Inter-Services Liaison Department (ISLD), the American Office of Strategic Services (OSS), and even secret agents of de Gaulle's Free French — all this uncoordinated web of underground activity was demanding to be serviced in Burma, Malaya, Siam, French Indo-China, or the Dutch East Indies. To ease the burden, a second Special Duties squadron, Number 358, came into being. In the six months it operated there were 51 Canadian aircrew on its rolls and nine of these were killed. One Canadian name is followed by the rare and puzzling entry: "Missing, returned." This is Harry V. Smith from Winnipeg, and his unusual story bears retelling.

In May 1945 Harry had just turned 21, the war in Europe had ended, and he was one long trip away from finishing his tour in Burma and going home. At briefing that day he got the one long trip he wanted — drop four American OSS agents at Korat in central Siam. They were to take off at midnight so that the drop could be made at dawn. That was fine, but it did mean that they would be returning 600 miles over enemy territory in full daylight. They would just have to pray for cloud cover. Like all Special Duties Liberators, their aircraft had been stripped of its front turret, ball turret, beam guns, and armour plate for the sake of longer range.

All night they flew through rain and turbulence. The sky was filled with cloud, and static made the radio almost useless. At 6:30 they crossed the coastal range and began to descend to the DZ. The sun came out and the sky cleared. Not a cloud in sight. At that moment, nine Japanese fighters attacked. They came from all directions, but the frontal attacks were the worst. Straight into the cockpit their canon fired. The second pilot was killed at once, and the navigator. The mid-upper gunner tried to fight them off, but they got him too. With his engines controls knocked out, radio shot up, starboard elevator useless, half the crew dead, and the airspeed falling off rapidly, Harry gave the order to prepare for a crash landing. He tells us what happened next:

> The only hope was to try the tree top landing technique used by Canadian bush pilots. I lowered the flaps to reduce airspeed and dropped the under-carriage to absorb some of the energy of the impact. When the trees began scraping along the belly of the aircraft I braced both feet

*against the instrument panel and hauled back on the control column
with all my might. There was a colossal rending of metal as the plane
crashed through the trees. The wings, with their load of fuel, sheared
right off. Good riddance, I thought. The fuselage careened on, hitting
more trees before coming to rest deep in the forest.*

"Rest" is hardly the right word; the wreckage was burning, the ammunition was exploding, and the Japanese fighters were still strafing them. Slowly they gathered and took stock. Four were dead and, of the nine survivors, one was near death, two were seriously injured, and the rest were "walking wounded." They heard voices and Harry sent those who could walk off to hide while he stayed with the dying American corporal. His own scalp wound must have overcome him, for when he next sensed what was happening, he was surrounded by natives intent upon rescuing the whole party.

It turned out that, although the Siamese government had made an "arrangement" to allow the Japanese to occupy their territory, the whole Siamese army, navy, air force, and police force had secretly formed itself in a Free Siamese underground with the Regent of Siam as its commander. Harry Smith and his crew had, in fact, been rescued by a police patrol sent out with specific orders not to let them fall into the hands of the Japanese. They slept that night on straw mats in a cell of the Siam Police Headquarters. The next morning the Siamese police and the local OSS Headquarters revealed a plan to spirit the OSS men and Harry out of the country. The rest of the crew, the injured members, would be safe in a Siamese internment camp. The story was to be that the five graves at the crash site and the four airmen interned represented the whole crew of a relatively innocent meteorological flight.

From this point on, Harry's adventures border on the fantastic. With the four Americans, he is taken by car to the OSS headquarters located in the palace of the Regent of Siam. On the Regent's elegant dining room table, two Siamese doctors, one educated in England, one in America, swab out his scalp wound with a battery tester, then use a curved shoemaker's needle and a pair of pliers to sew him up. To put plaster casts on the broken bones of the two Americans they have to risk a quick trip to the local hospital. The Regent even suggests they recuperate for a spell in the guest house he has bought especially for the purpose. It is stocked with fine wines, gourmet food, and even female companionship. Unfortunately the OSS high command considers the proposition too dangerous and the group has to make do with the first-class room and restaurant service of the Regent's palace.

When the time comes to move out, the five are inadequately disguised in large conical straw hats and put in a bus with curtained windows. The driver gets them past the first Japanese patrol with the story that he is transporting prisoners to jail, but then the bus gives out and they have to return to the palace and start again. Next night, in a convoy that includes their bus, a tow truck, and a follow-up bus, they reach the small airport where they are flown to a larger strip, picked up by a Dakota from 357 Squadron, and flown back to Calcutta. Three weeks after he took off, Harry is back in India and, after a short leave, back on the squadron. On the squadron's nominal roll the scribe adds the word "Returned" after the previous entry "Missing." Such is the strange world of clandestine operations.

Almost as strange is the story of Roland Bacon's assignment and fate in Force 136. In 1931 Roland and his wife Pearl, both from Nova Scotia, were sent to Korea as missionaries by the United Church Board of Foreign Missions. They were a true husband-and-wife team. Roland taught in the Boys' Academy, but took greater pleasure in the evangelical work, supervising rural churches, nurturing new congregations, and helping Korean Christian leaders. His sincere interest in the Korean people, not just as potential converts, but as human beings, won him the affection and admiration of all who met him. Pearl was kept more than busy at the mission station as director of the church's choir, as principal of the kindergarten, as secretary of the mission station and as mother to an ever growing family. She was even closer to the Korean people than Roland, for her parents had been missionaries in Korea for almost 40 years. Both, of course, became fluent in Korean. They would have been very happy if it were not for the increasing political tension in daily life.

The Japanese had taken over Korea in 1910 and thereafter had had to contend with an underground independence movement led by Korean and Chinese communists. Year by year the situation grew more difficult and more dangerous. Food was severely rationed, freedom of speech was curtailed, and no one was immune from immediate arrest as a spy. Foreigners, especially the British, and more especially still, British (and Canadian) missionaries, were particularly threatened. Roland's job required that he travel a good deal, and Pearl, in a letter written in 1941, after they had left Korea, painted a vivid picture of the circumstances she had to cope with when he was away:

> We couldn't write about conditions as they actually were and we had a hard time keeping our chins up when the military police made themselves at home in our home any time they felt like doing so. The officer used to come to our house nearly every day and if Roland was not at home he ordered the servants to tell me to make an appearance. He often came quite drunk and would order me to play the piano and entertain him, sometimes he would suggest that I teach him to dance and then he would wander all over the house as though he was searching for something (and he probably was).

When the rumour came that 24 missionary women had been arrested for spreading anti-war propaganda, the Bacons realized they would have to leave Korea. They did so in January, 1941.

Even though they had the support structure of the mission field in finding a job and accommodation, it was difficult re-establishing in India. The climate was trying, there was a new language to be learned, and a new child, their fourth, had just arrived. Moreover, the awareness of the war was now closer to them, and Roland soon felt the call to volunteer his services to the Indian Army. Commissioned as a Second Lieutenant, he was sent on a cipher course, and then allowed a scant three days leave before being posted as British Cipher Officer to an American Air Force unit in the Imphal area.

In photos taken during the war, Roland Bacon is seen as a smallish, almost frail man. His round glasses, small moustache, and straightforward gaze suggest a scholarly mien and a quiet and sincere conscientiousness. What we know of Roland beyond that derives from his letters to his parents back in Nova Scotia and in them we see, above all, a man dedicated to family. He writes to them, especially to his mother, as often as the unpredictabilities of service life allow and never fails to inquire about and comment on the activities of all his siblings and to give a full account of his own family, how each of the four children is progressing, how Pearl is bearing up with the stressful task of raising four "Kiddies" in a foreign land without a "Daddy," and above all, how much he is looking forward to his next leave.

Leaves are rare during war time so all leaves are cherished. Of his leave at Christmas 1943 he wrote: "What a welcome of ten days. Impossible to express it in words, the tree, the trimmings, good eats and the merry laughter of the Kiddies." Pearl, who is a livelier letter writer than Roland, evokes the special meaning of Christmas in her letter to his mother. After having offered particular thanks for each individual gift, she puts all her gratitude into the last sentences: "The big box of Moirs [chocolates] caused an uproar of "Hurrahs" as soon as it made its appearance and what a lot of "smacking" of lips went on over every taste! Can you believe it, we went home-sick over every thing and felt that we were back in dear old Nappan again."

As the war goes on and the end comes more clearly into view, Roland's letters reflect increasingly an interest in returning to Canada "to see you all and to get our bearings once again and to get adjusted for the work we love and have dedicated ourselves to doing." At times he lets himself dream: "I'm going to buy myself a small place all my own, have a garden, cows, pigs, and chickens." But he makes realistic plans as well. In October, 1944 he petitions to be released from the Army in March 1945, and at the same time he asks the Board of Foreign Missions for home furlough. To complete the rehabilitation plan, he applies to Union Theological Seminary in New York for a fellowship to further his professional studies. A future without war is beckoning brightly, and he is enthusiastically preparing for it.

On March 4, 1945, his mother's birthday, Roland wrote his parents again, a shorter letter than usual. It contained the ominous line: "Very likely I shall soon find myself back in the front line again," but most of the letter spoke of returning to his work in Korea and of returning to Canada in the spring: "At home it will soon be springtime and the Mayflowers in full bloom. Well I remember the days we found the first blooms. Those are vivid memories." He closed the letter: "Once again, greetings and many, many more years of happiness. Love Roland." That is the last letter in the collection. The next page contains only a six-word telegram to Clinton Bacon, Amherst, Nova Scotia: "Roland died of wounds Mandalay Thirteenth." It is signed, Pearl Bacon.

Exactly what Captain Roland Bacon was doing during his time with the Indian Army in Burma is not clear. As is proper, and as the censor demands, he gives no precise information about his activities. In the letter of April 17, 1943 he tantalizingly drops the news that he is on Active Service "up closer to the Front." Three months later he writes: "Things are moving these days and we find ourselves very busy. 24 hrs. duty seven days a week. I've kept going straight time since Feb. with no breaks." It is September before he is withdrawn — eight months of continuous action and yet we have no idea what he is doing. He is apparently in the Imphal valley area, but since the first half of 1943 was a relatively quiet time, it is not clear why he is so very active.

For the next three months he enjoys a respite from actual fighting in the quiet of a Delhi headquarters. From his army record, we learn he is now a Liaison Officer with the Korean National Army Liaison Unit and is attached to the Training School of the Indian Field Broadcasting Unit, a fact that only makes the puzzle more puzzling. What are Koreans doing in the Indian Army? What does a Field Broadcasting Unit do?

During this period his letters reflect the relaxed tension that comes from being out of the fighting, but they also reflect his constant awareness that he will have to return to it. This realization haunts his thoughts and unwittingly echoes in his letters — in December 1943: "I expect that it will be necessary to return to the Front soon;" January 1944: "I may find myself at the Front again;" February, 1944: "Long ere you receive this I shall be at the Front again." Each time he adds, either for his parents' benefit, or for his own, the assurance that there is no need to worry. His letter of 26 August 1944 sums up his thought: "I am hoping that this will prove to be the last lap for me and that my Irish luck will hold true. So far so good, but we have a lot to do yet."

Young men go into battle, so we are told, confident that they will return, that death cannot happen to them. Roland Bacon is a mature man with a lot to live for, and he knows it can happen to him. He is not by nature a fighting man eager to get back into battle; he is a married man with four children and a sincere dedication to the missionary cause. It is natural that he does not relish the idea of returning to the bloody business of war, but it is to his credit that he returns without demur, and that, having returned, he acquits himself well. There is a quiet confidence and an unassuming courage in this man that is not readily perceived in reading his letters. A Confidential Report on Captain Bacon, completed July 1, 1944, lets us see him more wholly:

> REPORT ON OFFICER'S EFFICIENCY AT PRESENT WORK: *Quite good at coping with the Koreans, who are a handful and then some. No military training but will do any job given to him.*
>
> FOR WHAT OTHER TYPES OF WORK IS THIS OFFICER SUITED: *Propaganda to the Japanese.*
>
> NOTE ON OFFICER'S CHARACTER AND PERSONALITY: *Showed a lot of guts and persistence both in the retreat from TIDDIM and in later work against Japanese 15 Div. Very much a Canadian and a missionary, tends to be hearty at all times and does not take kindly to the more British forms of discipline.*

This report deserves slow perusal and pondering, for there are insights and information in it that we have not seen before. We know now that he has been closely involved in the Tiddim Road battles that began in 1944 and continued in bloody ferocity for four months. But in what way are the Koreans a handful? And who are "the Koreans," any way? What does the reviewer mean when he says Roland is "very much a Canadian and a missionary"? Is that a compliment or a complaint? In what way has Roland balked at British discipline? In the aftermath of his death, some of these questions are answered.

During the latter part of the Far East campaign, the Japanese developed an active psychological warfare initiative. American and British service men who could tune in to Tokyo Rose listened and laughed, but the Japanese broadcasts intended to soften up the Indian citizenry for the proposed invasion were having their effect. The British determined to fight back and the Indian Field Broadcast Units (IFBU) were part of that fight. The IFBU which Roland Bacon was asked to lead comprised six Korean officers along with a few Gurkhas for protection. Because they had grown up under Japanese occupation, the Koreans were fluent in Japanese and therefore ideally suited to their task of "combat propaganda." The unit used its mortars to distribute propaganda leaflets in Japanese to the Japanese forces and in Burmese to the indigenous population and it used its loudspeakers to broadcast the news in English and Urdu to the Allied troops. But its main task was to whisper defeatist propaganda into the ears of the enemy. Sneaking up as close as possible to the enemy lines, the Broadcast Unit set up its huge loudspeakers, known by the quaint name of "ampradiograms," and through them the Japanese-speaking Korean officers delivered their message. Taking their cue from Tokyo Rose, they usually began with evocative Japanese music or nostalgic reminiscences and a news report that emphasized the successes of the British. Then came the offer of safe conduct and good treatment for any sons of Nippon who were ready to surrender.

In his drive to Mandalay, Slim had taken Monywa on January 22, 1945, and had even moved his Headquarters there in early February. Mandalay lay a scant 75 miles down the road but it took the Fourteenth Army exactly two months to cover those 75 miles, such was the obstinacy and the ferocity of the Japanese defence. It was into this bloody, pummelling battle that Roland Bacon's IFBU was launched. On March 13 the Korean officers pushed their equipment as far forward as they could and set to work. Every movement, however, brought a burst of machine gun fire. They were pinned down with no cover. Roland crawled over to a small tree and eased himself up so he could use his field glasses to spy out the sniper. A machine gun rattled and he fell with multiple wounds across his stomach. By the time they had got him to the Civilian Hospital in Monywa, a five hour ambulance ride away, it was too late. He was buried two days later in the Military Cemetery in the small village of Alon, just up river from Monywa.

Ironically, in a letter written February 2, the Director of the Union Theological Seminary had granted Captain Bacon admission and a fellowship. Had he received it in time, it is likely that he would not have returned to the Front. Since his release was pending, he had that option. Pearl was against his returning in any event, but he felt it his duty to go.

Now she was left alone in India with four small children. Her grief is great. To his family she wrote: "Roland is always in my heart. My great regret is that I cannot see his resting place in Burma." In the same letter, however, we see the strength of her character and her courage; "Life can be difficult if one looks at it in many ways but it has a great deal to offer if we look for the good things." Troubled by grief and loneliness, she is also distressed to know how she can survive until some pension money comes, either from the Army or the Church. Help for both her troubles comes from an unexpected quarter. Comforting letters arrive from four of the Korean officers with whom Roland had served. Not only do the letters contain sympathy and sincere expressions of their admiration for Roland, they contain money that the Korean officers have contributed because they can imagine her need. They continue to write and they persuade their Headquarters to take her on as a liaison officer, a job for which her ability with the Korean language fully qualifies her.

With the work with the Korean Army and later as manager of a British Army leave hostel at Darjeeling, Pearl managed to support her family until pension arrangements could be made and passage found for her return to Canada. Years later, the Korean government still remembers the dedication and affection Roland Bacon showed for the Korean people as a missionary and for the Korean Army as a soldier. In October 2002, Elsa Dickson, Roland's youngest daughter, was invited by the Minister of Patriots and Veterans of South Korea to participate in a formal ceremony commemorating her father at the Tomb of the Unknown Soldier in the National Cemetery in Seoul. With a few other honoured guests, also relatives of men who had fought for Korea's independence from Japan, Elsa participated in the dedication of a room in the magnificent Independence Hall in Cheonan. Prominent in the Hall is a photo of her father and the six Korean officers, recognition of the fact that he had died fighting with the Korean National Army.

Roland Bacon died on March 13, 1945. Exactly one week later the Fourteenth Army took Mandalay. General Slim now realized that it might be possible to push straight through to Rangoon before the monsoon came and he determined to make that push.

XVII

THE BURMA BOMBERS

To this point a good deal has been said of the role of fighters and transport planes in Burmese skies, but nothing of the part played by bombers. The reason for this silence is that bombers were a scarce item in Burma, and heavy bombers were almost entirely absent for the first part of the campaign. The twelve Blenheims that gathered in December 1942 to attack Mandalay (and then had to abort because of weather) were a typical display of the bomber strength of the RAF in Burma at that time. Pilots had a saying: "the Blenheims were so old and the squadron's spirits so high, that the planes flew on happiness alone." Later fighter-bombers — Vengeances, Beaufighters and Thunderbolts — appeared and did good service in supporting the land forces and disrupting the enemy's lines of communication, but even in 1945 the old Hurribomber with a bomb tucked under each wing was still doing yeoman service.

Mosquitos appeared in late 1944 and when the war ended seven squadrons in Burma were equipped with them. In 1941 Stan Johns from Swift Current, Saskatchewan quit his $600 a year job with the Royal Bank to become a pilot in the RCAF. After getting his wings he was sent to Summerside, PEI for an astro-navigation course, to England for night flying and instrument training, to an OTU to convert to Wellingtons, to Italian Somaliland to patrol for submarines, and finally to India to illuminate Japanese naval targets with flares so that Beaufighters could come in for the kill. None of these postings led to any action so when the word came out that pilots were wanted for a Mosquito squadron, Stan and five of his Canadian chums jumped at the chance. On June 14, 1945 he began his operational tour of low level strafing and bombing in support of the ground forces. "The Japs had run out of fuel," Stan remembers, "so their planes were sitting ducks on their airstrips. We had a ball shooting at trucks, trains, anything that moved." His logbook for the next ten days records successful attacks on bridges in the Sittang area and on Japanese encampments. Then "unscrambling" struck. After just four sorties, all five Canadians were abruptly taken off ops and posted away. A terse one-line entry in Stan's logbook, signed by the Squadron commander, tells the story: "Operational tour terminated due to unscrambling of Dominion personnel." "I think," laments Stan, "I was the most overtrained and underutilized pilot in the RCAF."

As for the Mosquito, every pilot enjoyed its speed and manoeuvrability , but in Burma the humidity played havoc with its structure. The main spar, made of Canadian spruce, was put together with a non-waterproof glue and tended to delaminate. A plastic inspection panel was installed over the joint so that its integrity could be assured before each flight. But the Mossie had another problem: the powerful Merlin engines heated up very rapidly in the tropical temperatures. Pilots had to do an abbreviated engine run-up as they taxied and then take off as soon as they turned into wind. Despite its shortcomings, the Mosquito was popular in Burma. Indeed, the first man to land at Mingaladon and discover that Japanese had fled from Rangoon was flying a Mosquito.

Mosquitos were fine as light bombers and there were a few Wellingtons in the theatre as medium bombers, but the question of heavy bombers was still open. Because the British bombers, Lancasters, Halifaxes and Stirlings, were all needed in Europe, the American Liberator was chosen for SEAC. One squadron of Liberators appeared in December 1942 and another within the year. By the end of 1944, five Liberator squadrons were operating in Burma. The USAAF claimed the Liberator with a load of 3000 pounds had a range of 1200 miles. That was a good start, but those statistics did not please the RAF — the Mosquito could do better than that. With experimentation and modification, they upped the range to 3000 miles and the load to 8000 pounds. With that capability Liberators changed the nature and tempo of aerial warfare in Burma.

Thousand bomber raids such as Europe knew did not happen in SEAC; there was neither the concentration of industry nor dense centres of population to warrant them. But with the advent of Liberators, targets that had previously been beyond the range of Allied aircraft were now vulnerable. The Japanese fighters that had fled Magwe and Mingaladon for Chiengmai and other Siamese fields found that they were no longer immune to attack. Major cities like Rangoon and Bangkok were now within range. Mines could be laid in the Rangoon River, the Mekong Delta, and even in the harbour at Singapore, a 3350 mile round trip from the Calcutta area bases. Even the shipping lanes that conveyed supplies from the Japanese homeland could be attacked. A favourite target was the Bangkok-to-Burma railway. All of these missions represented long and tedious hours in the air, as much as 24 hours, but now, thanks to the Liberators, they were possible.

Given the huge aircrew losses in Europe and the need for new crews in SEAC, training Liberator crews became a priority issue and to meet the need a new Operational Training Unit was set up at Boundary Bay just below Vancouver. With 17 Liberators on strength plus 27 Mitchells for transitional training, 5 OTU began operating in April 1944. The students were a mixed lot, veterans from England training for a second tour, instructors released from the Commonwealth Air Training Plan, or inexperienced aircrew straight from the training schools. Since the courses were assigned alternately to the RAF and the RCAF, at least half of the graduates were Canadians. With the argument that squadrons on the east coast of Canada needed crews for their anti-submarine operations, RCAF Headquarters wanted all Canadian graduates from 5 OTU for itself. The British were adamant: "Until the full output of RAF crews becomes effective it is essential to operations in ACSEA [Air Command South East Asia] that all RCAF crews trained in 5 OTU should proceed to ACSEA squadrons. Therefore request assurance urgently that these crews will proceed to ACSEA as previously arranged. Failing agreement with the RCAF we would wish to take the matter up at government level." That was a heavy threat and the result was that many Canadian Liberator crews arrived in India in the 1944-45 period. In his book *The Forgotten Air Force*, Henry Probert, acknowledges the Canadian contribution when, in commenting on the growth of the Burma bomber force, he concludes by remarking "it should be remembered that the RAF squadrons included a substantial number of men from the Royal Canadian Air Force."[1] When Roy Borthwick, a Vancouver boy, joined 159 Squadron in January 1945 he estimated half the aircrew was from Canada and, in fact, over the three years 159 Squadron operated in Burma a total of 237 Canadian names appeared on its rolls. Had they all been there at the same time, it would have been an all-Canadian squadron. In March 1945 there were 49 Canadian aircrew on 354 Squadron, enough to carry out a basketball schedule with a game almost every evening. The Squadron Sports Report for March 18 told of Eastern Canada losing 23 to 18 to Western Canada.

But there were Canadians with the Liberator crews in Burma even before Boundary Bay began operating. John Dey from Swift Current, Saskatchewan joined 159 Squadron as a rear gunner in December 1943. On the night of April 1, 1944 his aircraft, "T" for Tommy, took off to bomb Rangoon. As they approached Mingaladon red tracer from light anti-aircraft fire streaked up

---

[1] Probert is one of the few military historians to acknowledge the prominent role RCAF personnel played in Burma. In describing the success of air supply he goes out of his way to characterize the two Canadian squadrons as "very welcome" and "invaluable."

toward them and the probing fingers of eight searchlights stabbed the sky. Over Rangoon the intensity of the defences increased. The blue beam of the master searchlight found them and the smaller searchlights flocked around it. The anti-aircraft fire became heavier and more accurate, following the searchlight beams to seek out the marauding aircraft. Now they were on their run-in. The rail-yard was dead ahead. "Looking good," cried the bomb-aimer, "Hold her steady for just 15 seconds!" as the pilot fought the buffeting of the heavy flak. At that moment John Dey, isolated in the rear turret, saw the black form of an enemy fighter dead astern and 100 yards away. A long burst from the fighter wounded Dey, put his turret out of order, and severed his inter-comm connection with the crew. Twice more the enemy fighters came at them, but the pilot held the Liberator straight and level for a further five seconds till the bombs were gone. Then he put the nose down and began to corkscrew.

"T" for Tommy had started its run at 13,500 feet. It was at 8,000 feet when it escaped the searchlights' cone and turned for home. Taking stock, the skipper found that Dey and two other crew members had been wounded and that one of his engines had been knocked out. That was all right; they could get home on three engines. In the middle of the Bay of Bengal, a second engine stopped. On two engines they crept homeward, losing height all the way and finally crashing at Alipore, an airdrome near Calcutta, but a hundred miles short of their base at Digri. "T" for Tommy was the first Liberator on 159 Squadron to have self-sealing gas tanks and looking back now, John Dey remarks; "If we hadn't had those tanks, we never would have made it."

John Dey's April Fool's Day attack on Rangoon was not the first and it certainly was not the last, for the city was a central node in the Japanese supply line to Burma. Its harbour and docks were thronged, the Irrawaddy, navigable to Bhamo on the border with China, was a major water route to the north, and all the trains chugging up the central plain left from the Rangoon rail yards. Accordingly the area was provided with the best defences Japan could muster — searchlights, anti-aircraft guns, and fighters. After almost three years of waiting and training and waiting, on November 4, 1944 Wallie Frazer did his first operational sortie, destination: Rangoon.

In November 1941 Wallie was 20 years old and working as a "sort of bookkeeper." He earned $12 a week, paid half of it for his board, three dollars on his car loan, and still had enough left to enjoy life. He joined the RCAF and in January 1942 found himself bunking in with a hundred other recruits in the stables at the CNE grounds in Toronto. In due course, and that means after many months of tarmac duty, guard duty, and flying training, Wallie shouldered his kit and marched up the gangplank on to the *Louis Pasteur.* In England there was more waiting and then a posting to an OTU — for operation training on twin-engined aircraft, even though he had graduated on Harvards! At the end of the course he and his crew expected to be posted to a Wellington squadron in England. Instead, the crew was broken up and Wallie found himself on the troopship *Stratheden* bound for Bombay. A month later, on the last day of March, he was in India. After six weeks of waiting he was posted to a Heavy Conversion Unit to acquire a new crew and to learn how to fly a huge four-engined Liberator bomber. Finally, at the beginning of June 1944, he was posted to an operational squadron, No. 215.

Eager and apprehensive at the same time, Wallie looked forward to his first operational sortie. After three years of waiting and training, here was the chance to do what he joined up to do, and he wasn't at all sure he was ready for it. The CO tried to reassure them: "For those going on your first operational flight, just remember you are well-trained crews flying an excellent aircraft that is exceptionally well armed. If you remain alert, keep your wits about you, you should have no problems whatsoever." If the CO gave them confidence, the Intelligence Officer shook it again: "Expect heavy anti-aircraft fire over the target. And you're virtually certain of meeting enemy fighters ... If you are shot down, it would be difficult to make it back on your own. Five hundred miles of mountain, jungle and swamp ... Stay away from the hill tribes ... They may be cannibalistic ... And we're not sure about the natives here either." Obviously it's better not to get shot down. Then the curtain covering the map is pulled aside and there's the red tape leading to their target: Rangoon. They are to go for the marshalling yards at Innsein, the northern suburb of the city. Just where the defences are concentrated.

The sky is blue and the sun is bright as they churn across the Bay of Bengal. When they pick up the coast of Burma they also pick up a comforting umbrella of friendly fighters, RAF Thunderbolts and American Lightnings. Wallie and his crew in "P" for Peter are way out on the left edge of the formation and they tuck in a bit closer for safety. It feels better there. Now they are on the run-in. Fifteen seconds to go. Flak, white puffs of it that look so innocent, come closer and closer. The bomb-aimer screams for Wallie to hold her steady but the mid-day turbulence and the explosive whumps of flak toss them all over the sky. One explosion is closer than all others and P for Peter shudders. Wallie does his best to "hold her steady," till he feels the aircraft leap up like an unleashed puppy as two tons of bombs drop free. Then all hell breaks loose. Enemy aircraft come at them from every side. Five of the Liberator's ten machine guns are hammering at once, each spewing out a stream of big half inches slugs of lead. The whole aircraft is full of their noise and the stink of cordite. Suddenly all is quiet. The flak and the fighters have been left behind and they can concentrate on eating their bully beef sandwiches and getting home. On the way they chatter about the bombs that dropped just about where they were supposed to, the flak that almost hit them, and the fighters that they may have shot down. There is a high-pitched elation in their voices. They've done it, survived their first ops, their baptism of fire.

Wallie makes the softest, sweetest landing he has ever made. He could hardly believe they were down. Then a devil took over. The aircraft veered fiercely to the left and he could not correct it. "Get off the brakes," he screamed to the second pilot. "I'm not on them," came the terrified reply and P for Peter tore across the infield, headed straight for a strong clump of palms. It kept swinging viciously to the left, missed the palms, crashed and thudded across a series of drainage ditches, and came to rest on its knees. Shaken and quiet the crew got out. The fire truck, the Engineering Officer, the CO speeded up to the crash scene. Wallie Frazer repeatedly asked himself "What happened? What did I do wrong?" The Engineering Officer had the answer: "A cannon shell right through the engine nacelle and the tire. You've landed with a flat tire." Next day at debriefing the CO made the whole crew feel good: "If Flying Officer Frazer had not made a damned good landing, he would have been in a lot worse trouble."

On November 4, as Frazer and crew were bombing Rangoon, Andy Duncanson, the Canadian infantry officer with the Royal West Kents, was leading his company against an equal Japanese force about 20 miles south of Tiddim on the road to Kalewa. His diary records the result: "6 Japs killed — own casualties NIL." In *Defeat into Victory*, General Slim notes that on 4 November resistance at Vital Corner crumbled and Kennedy Peak was taken. The Fourteenth Army was pushing persistently toward the Chindwin, and what Frazer and his crew were doing was speeding their advance. Indeed, throughout the push to Rangoon the Liberator squadrons arranged their sorties to coincide with the Army's needs. While the Army was making its swift dash to Meiktila, the RAF distracted the enemy with a series of raids on Rangoon.

With the advent of the Liberator squadrons, the Air Force was able to add a new tactic to its offensive strategy, the laying of mines, and harbours that had previously been too remote could now be infected with this invisible underwater virus. 160 Squadron, stationed on Ceylon, became a specialist mine-laying unit and its CO could wax eloquent about the efficacy of mines, stressing how they not only played havoc with shipping, but also occupied a good number of Japanese sailors and mine-sweepers.

With an all-Canadian crew, Percy Waddy flew a Liberator from Montreal to India to join 160 Squadron and to drop mines in the harbours of the Kra Isthmus and Sumatra. Then came the order to mine the harbour at Singapore. The RAF had not been back to Singapore since it fell in 1942; this would be a first attempt. Stripped of gun turrets and oxygen equipment, and with extra fuel tanks installed in the forward bomb bay, Waddy's Liberator and seven others set out on March 26. They were over Singapore at midnight, found the place lit up like a peace-time port and laid their mines with no opposition. The RAF brass were elated. The Squadron was congratulated and allowed to bestow a decoration on one member of each crew.

When submarine surveillance and air reconnaissance indicated that a mined harbour was back in operation, the Squadron would visit it again. On 24 April they went back to Singapore. "This time," says Waddy "the natives were not too friendly." The mines were laid down with parachutes and for accuracy they had to be dropped close to the water. As Waddy and his crew skimmed along at 350 feet, flak ships in the harbour and anti-aircraft guns on shore opened up with all they had. Over his intercom he heard the plaintive voice of Mercer, his Canadian wireless operator: "Skip, those boys are shooting at us!" Somehow the guns missed, but just at that instant Waddy saw the black shape of a twin-engine fighter coming straight at them. "He was above us," says Waddy, "and I think the nose of his aircraft must have cut off his view because he did not open fire." But he turned to come in again. Waddy was on his run-in and couldn't take evasive action. The moment the navigator cried "Mines away!" he put his aircraft down to 30 feet and they streaked for the harbour entrance and for Ceylon, strafing an incoming tanker as they went. The whole trip took 22 hours and 15 minutes.

Unique to the Burma campaign was the use of lumbering Liberator bombers in a close attack role that in other theatres would be assigned to Hurribombers, Beaufighters or Mosquitos. Thus Liberator squadrons in Burma were charged with the interdiction of water traffic, particularly coastal shipping. The targets were almost all small, 300 tons being considered a large vessel, and the attacks were made, not from ten thousand feet, but from down among the waves. V. R. Ensom of Toronto got a bit closer than he planned, however, when he led five Liberators on a mission against a small coastal convoy in April 1945. Ensom sighted the convoy, a 350-ton motor vessel and its sub-chaser escort, off the Nicobar Islands. He dived down at it out of the sun and straddled the rear of the ship at a mere 25 feet. Something hit his inboard engine. The navigator's cabin was also damaged and splinters flew into the navigator's eyes. Oil was streaming from the damaged engine and, fearing a fire, Ensom feathered the propeller. The second pilot took over as navigator and gave him a course for base, 900 miles away. "We came home on three engines and used a lot of petrol," says Ensom, "and when we landed we had only sufficient for another half hour's flying." They also discovered they had brought home a souvenir of their trip, a piece of mast stuck in their damaged engine.

W. A. McKay of Elmira, Ontario was the third man to attack the convoy. Since the motor vessel was already sinking he came down onto the sub-chaser. Unfortunately his bomb bay doors did not open. Disregarding the intense anti-aircraft fire, he turned and came in again, this time with good success. Despite a badly perforated aircraft, he got home safely. That was exciting, but the next mission was even more interesting. He was so keen on pressing home the attack on shipping in the Andaman Sea that he scarcely noticed that they had flown through a heavy anti-aircraft barrage. When they pulled out, McKay discovered one engine had been damaged, the brakes were out of order, and a canon shell had ripped a large-size hole in the tail. "Fortunately," McKay summed it up, "the engine was all right, but it was obvious that the landing was going to be a nasty business." As they approached base, he got the gunners to tie a couple of parachutes to the beam guns and instructed them to throw them out as soon as they touched down. The scheme worked and they made a good landing with no brakes and a shattered wheel.

Although locomotive hunting was usually reserved for Beaufighters and Mosquitos, in Burma Liberators assumed the role of agile fighters and swooped down to ground level to strafe engines, troop trains and goods wagons that dared to move during daylight hours or to blast bridges, rail yards and trackage. As a vital link in the Japanese line of communication the 244 miles of the Bangkok-to-Burma railway received special attention. Between January and April 1945 twenty-seven hundred tons of bombs were dropped on it, and the crews estimated that at least 8 of its 688 bridges and viaducts were out of action at any one time. The tonnage delivered to the Japanese front dropped from 750 tons per day to 150. This sort of strategic action did much to hasten the end of the war in Burma, and it was only possible because the Liberators had arrived.

Tom Watson, the man who flew the last plane out of Singapore in 1942, who did a tour with the RAAF in Australia, and who then graduated from the Boundary Bay OTU, did his third and last tour with 159 Squadron on Libera-tors. There were 97 Canadian aircrew on the squadron when he joined in February 1945. "It was a first-class squadron in every way," Tom remembered. "We destroyed important targets at Bangkok and other areas in Siam and mined harbours in the Tenasserim Peninsula from Burma to Malaya." He also helped sink the King of Siam's private yacht that had been converted by the Japanese to a submarine tender, and to destroy what he named the "Kanchanaburi Bridge," also known as the bridge on the River Kwae.

Kanchanaburi, one of the first way stations on the railway, was the central supply depot and manning centre for the area. Just north of it a sizable bridge had to be built to cross, not the Kwae, but its conjunct river the Maekhlaung. This is a quibble, however; since David Lean's ever-popular film the bridge is the Bridge on the River Kwae and we will name it so. In fact, however, there was a total of 14 kilometres of bridging on the completed railway and any one of the lesser bridges could be casually and generically identified as the Bridge on the River Kwae by the Allied airmen intent upon disrupting the railway. All of them were constant targets for the Liberator bombers and which one Tom destroyed is open to debate. Each RAF Wing had a model of the whole railway and photos of the bridges were constantly being updated. The Japanese for their part tried occasionally tried to discourage aerial attacks by lining the bridges with prisoners of war.

Roy Borthwick and his all-Canadian crew, also of 159 Squadron, made a low-level attack on the bridge at the Three Pagoda Pass, the point where the railway crosses from Siam into Burma. The defensive fire was intense and he was not altogether surprised when one of the gunners announced, "Skipper, we've been hit in number three (engine) and we've got black smoke pouring from it." Roy's attempts to feather the engine failed and he realized the oil needed for feathering was streaming out behind him. The engine, stuck in coarse pitch and turning at high revolutions, was giving him nothing but drag and he could do nothing about it. The heat of the engine, just before it seized, started a fire that could not be controlled. Roy's only option was to tell the crew to prepare for ditching.

Because the impact would immediately cave the fragile bomb-bay doors and let the ocean flood into the enormous cavity of the fuselage, a Liberator is not a good candidate for ditching. Roy ordered the crew to the back of the aircraft where they had some small chance of getting out alive while he and the co-pilot strapped themselves tightly into their seats. The flames were fierce now and spreading quickly along the wing. Roy let down to 50 feet and cut back to stalling speed. They were at 20 feet and on the very point of splashing down when Roy noticed out of the corner of his eye that the flames had disappeared. He thrust the throttles of the three good engines forward and gently coaxed the huge aircraft upwards.

The rate of climb was agonizingly slow. Between them and their base lay miles of ocean and after that the tangled mangrove swamp of the Sunderbans with its infestation of crocodiles. Akyab had recently been retaken and was much closer. He raised the station on the radio and got the news — Akyab was a short strip with no lighting but they could put two flares out at the beginning of the strip. He lined up on the two flares and, with as much control as three engines gave him, made his landing as short as he could. With brakes full on, the plane shuddered to a stop with its nose against the jungle wall. An army officer came aboard with a bottle of whisky. "Here, chaps, I expect you could use this," he said. Next morning the crew surveyed the strip and marvelled that they had somehow missed all the bomb craters that pockmarked it.

Given the number of Canadians on Liberators in Burma it is not surprising that a Canadian should rise to lead a squadron. Hugo Beall from Lindsay, Ontario was named Commanding Officer of the newly-formed 356 Squadron in April 1944. It was to be the first Liberator squadron in Burma to bomb by day and Hugo was the right man to bring a new squadron into shape for the precise formation flying that day bombing required. He had gone to England in 1936 to join the RAF and had flown in the Battle of Britain before coming to Burma. A trim, serious man he insisted upon thorough training and upon striving for perfection. When a new bombsight was introduced, he and his crew were the first to train on it and he instructed the rest of the squadron on its intricacies. In the main the aircrew saw him as a hard master, but his own crew knew him as a warm man and eventually everyone recognized that, while he demanded absolute loyalty, he gave absolute loyalty as well, and the morale of the squadron grew with their operational experience. The squadron flew its first mission in July 1944 and Hugo led it, as he did all subsequent missions if he possibly could. When Wing Commander Beall left the squadron at the end of January, Group Captain Reg Jordan summed up his term as Commanding Officer: "When he was awarded the Distinguished Service Order on the completion of his tour, no one doubted it was thoroughly deserved."

Hugo Beall's successor was another Canadian, Wing Commander G. N. B. Sparks, known to the whole squadron as Sparky. Sparky was a friendly man with a broad smile and, like Beall, he led from the front. On one mission the squadron is detailed to bomb an enemy naval force, a cruiser, four destroyers and a supply ship. Wallie Frazer grows increasingly apprehensive as they fly along. He remembers a reconnaissance course he once took where they were told that a cruiser "is basically nothing but a floating gunplatform." Then he takes comfort from the thought that the CO is there too: "Good old Sparky. He's been doing his share of ops lately, could have skipped this one, sent one of the Flight Commanders instead. But he's right here with us. Everyone going has noted that, appreciates it." In this case, Wallie is spared any further worries; the flight is recalled because the enemy fleet has disappeared.

The great part of the Liberator action in Burma took place within the twelve month period mid-1944 to mid-1945. During that time the big bombers contributed significantly to Slim's advance to Rangoon. For example, when, in February 1945, the Army was fighting down the coast toward Ramree, Strategic Air Force dropped 750 tons of bombs on Kangaw to silence the Japanese artillery and blast open the defensive bunkers. Two weeks later Hugo Beall led a force of 85 Liberators on a massive low-level bombing raid on Ramree, so low in fact that one of the air gunners, Bernard Ronnellenfitch of Creston, B.C. declared "We didn't fly over the target. We bounced over it." When they arrived they could see the naval guns pounding the shore and the fighters strafing the beaches. As they were leaving they saw the infantry streaming ashore from the landing barges. Thus did the Army, the Navy and the Air Force combine to take Ramree. This action took place January 21, 1945 but the Japanese resistance on the island was so stubborn that it was not until three weeks later that the last remnant of the defenders was driven into the swamp and into the jaws of the crocodiles so that 436 Squadron could move in.

There are fairly accurate figures available for the Canadian personnel of twelve of the Liberator squadrons. Taking casualties, tour expiries and repatriation into account one can estimate that there was a total of about 3000 aircrew on these twelve squadrons over that year of intense activity. Of these, 1672 were Canadians, just over 50%, and of these, 176 were killed. After the war a group of Burma Liberator veterans formed the Burma Bomber Association; at the inaugural meeting one of the members remarked, with a trace of bitterness but with full justification, "You can search Burma Command records and the fact is never mentioned that Canadians played such a healthy part in the Burma Campaign."

XVIII

DRACULA AND THE RETAKING OF RANGOON

IT WAS now the last week of March 1945. In his Headquarters newly relocated to Mandalay, Slim sat down to do some very careful calculating. The monsoon could break in as little as 45 days. Rangoon was 350 miles from Meiktila. He would have to average between eight and nine miles each day. That was possible, but it meant leaving his line of communication exposed on the left and it meant that he would be more than ever dependent upon air supply. What would he do if he reached the gates of Rangoon just as the monsoon broke? He could well find himself at the very point of victory and lacking the certainty of supply that would enable him to seize it. He conferred with Mountbatten and they decided to take out contingency insurance — *Dracula*, the scheme for an amphibious and airborne operation against Rangoon, would be reinstated. There would then be a welcoming committee on hand to greet him when he reached his goal. With these arrangements in hand, Slim issued the order for the drive to Rangoon.

It was to be a two-pronged advance with the westerly thrust brutally butting its way southward along the Irrawaddy to recover the oil fields at Yenangyaung and the airfield at Magwe from which the RAF had fled in March 1942. That thrust would end at the beginning of May at Prome, still well short of Rangoon. The easterly advance, the main one, would follow the road and the railway straight south from Meiktila to Rangoon. Retaking Rangoon should be possible. The futile counter-attack on Meiktila had cost the Japanese dearly; their strength was a third of what it should be, they had few guns and little ammunition, and the RAF was harassing their line of communication.

Despite their desperate circumstances, however, the Japanese soon let Slim know that his march to Rangoon was not going to be a springtime stroll. They withdrew down the road and railway for twenty miles and, with an obstinacy that denied reality, set up new defences at Pyawbwe. In the normal course of living, Pyawbwe was an inconsequential little town, but as armies live and move it was important, for the road and the railway intersected there and on the north edge lay a decent fair-weather airstrip backed up by a fairly strong garrison. From Meiktila, Dunstan Pasterfield set out with his battalion to occupy the airstrip. It was only twenty miles away but it took them five days of skirmishing to cover the first ten miles and another five days to reach Pyawbwe and work their way around it. In those ten days they killed 1750 Japanese. The British casualties had been light — just over 100 men killed. On April 10 the town was completely surrounded and the attack could go in. Dunstan's battalion, with help from the Brigade's tanks, took the airstrip and then joined with the other attackers to move into the town itself. There they met further resistance. Their first attack on the bunkers that protected the water works was repulsed and a second was successful only after the tanks again came to their rescue. So it was for the besiegers all around the outskirts of the town. A maze of trenches and bunkers stood against them and the gaunt defenders within were not about to give up. At the end of the day, the British held the railway station and half the town; it took another day of heavy fighting to secure the other half. There were five thousand defenders in Pyawbwe. When the fighting was over 1100 were dead and those who survived were scattering southward, pitifully disorganized, lacking their guns, low on ammunition, and in uncertain communication with their commander. "It was certainly a very strenuous fortnight," Dunstan wrote to his family, "and we were mighty glad when the victory at Pyawbwe gave us a welcome rest." Slim saw the encounter from a different perspective: "For its size," he wrote, "Pyawbwe was one of the most decisive battles of the Burma war. It shattered Honda's army, but it did more than that — it settled the fate of Rangoon."

But it had also put Slim well behind schedule and the menace of the monsoon loomed larger. He still had 312 miles to go and, if he were lucky, four weeks to do it. With his planners he surveyed the situation. The troops were feisty and ready for anything. Morale and momentum were with him. If he jumped down the road in giant strides, quickly establishing airfields for his supplies but not stopping to mop up and consolidate, it could still be done. Now he blessed the good work Fournier, Taschereau and the other agents had done in training the Karen levies of operation *Character*. They could be counted on to protect his left flank.

The Japanese, of course, did the same calculation and plotted their strategy. From this point on they would not seek the big victory that could change the whole course of the campaign, but rather hinder and delay till the weather became their ally. Their handicap was that their "army" had in fact scarcely the strength of a brigade and coordinated, coherent command was feebly uncertain. Despite this handicap, the war-weary remnants of the Japanese army continued to exploit every opportunity for resistance that presented itself. The morning after the victory at Pyawbwe the Allied column wheeled down the road and by nightfall had taken the next town. In the darkness, a Japanese suicide patrol, 400 strong, infiltrated and dug in, so that, when morning came they were back in the town and in charge of the road. It took the British two days to dislodge them, and once more the timetable was tightened. Further south, the road led through a narrow defile, a perfect spot for an ambush. The Japanese brought in fresh troops to arrange a trap. Fortunately Slim had anticipated such a move. He sent a hook wide around the cliff and surprised the enemy even as they were digging in, but he lost another day. So it went, all the way to Rangoon. How do you beat an enemy that doesn't know when he is beaten?

Outguessing and outfighting the enemy in this way, Slim still figured he had a better than even chance of beating the monsoon to Rangoon and he pushed forward with all possible speed. I had an opportunity to measure that speed when, on April 19, I was detached to a small airdrome control unit as "Forward Strip Commander." "What does a Forward Strip Commander do," I asked, for the title sounded daunting. "There's no flying personnel there," was the reply. "All you have to do is wash out flying if the strip gets too wet." In the week I was with the 28th AACS, USAAF (I never did find out what all the initials stood for), it never rained.

The unit was small — Lieut. Andy Anderson, Corporal White, and ten men — with a large square tent for sleeping, a marquee with a field cooker beside it for eating, a jeep and two trucks. One of the trucks, equipped with an Aldis lamp and a wireless set, was parked at the end of the bare, dusty strip as the control tower. We each took turns cooking. Traffic was constant but not overwhelming. At the end of my first day I felt I was going to enjoy my Burma holiday and a respite from the daily grind of flying. That night we got an order to move to Tatkon, about 100 miles down the road. Next day Andy Anderson and his crew, with an efficiency that indicated they had done this many times before, folded their tents, threw their kit bags in the trucks and set off. We operated for two full days at Tatkon. The second night as we lay in our cots in the tent with the sides rolled up, we heard the heavy thunder of artillery just off the edge of our camp. The flashes of the guns illuminated our bivouac. "There's an attack going in," said Andy. "We'll move again tomorrow."

He was right. We packed up and drove another 90 miles to Toungoo and were soon welcoming Dakota after Dakota, each with its three and a half tons of food, petrol, mail, and ammunition. The cargo was loaded straight out of the planes onto trucks and driven way to the Army Service Corps

distribution point. It made us feel good to see this efficient system in operation and to know that we were a part of it. We were aware, too, of the other
end of the operation, for on the southern edge of our strip we could watch
the Thunderbolts fly across at about 800 feet, dive almost vertically to bomb
and strafe the enemy lines, then pull up steeply and come around again.
The sky was clear blue and the sun glinted off their silver cowlings. It was
beautiful to see, an unusual and impressive combination of brute strength
and bright gracefulness.

My detachment to the forward strip had been for one week only, but in
that week the front had moved about two hundred miles and air supply
had moved along with it. It was April 23 when we moved to Toungoo and
Rangoon was still 177 miles to the south. If the monsoon held off till May
15, Slim had just 22 days to cover that distance. If the monsoon came early?
Well, he had *Dracula* to fall back on. But he would much rather that the
Army retook Rangoon. The 17th Indian Division, his Division, had been
the last out of Rangoon in 1942, and it would be sweet justice to see them
leading the return. A few things were working in his favour: Aung San's
Burmese National Army had revolted against their Japanese masters and
had joined the British forces, a good part of Subhas Chandra Bose's Indian
National Army had defected and were now hard at work building new air
strips for the RAF, and the Karen levies were actively obstructing the Japanese columns trying to force their way toward Rangoon on jungle tracks to
the east of Slim's line of advance.

From Toungoo Slim moved quickly southward, covering thirty miles in
one day and twenty miles the next. Twenty-three days left to cover 125
miles. If the monsoons held off till mid-May it could be done. On 28 April,
ten miles north of Pegu, the 17th Indian Division met heavily mined roads
and strong Japanese defences and a precious day was lost battling through
the roadblock. In Pegu itself the resistance was even stronger and more
desperate. Finally, on May 1, the British troops broke into Pegu — and on
the same day, the monsoon broke over their heads.

For two days the rain came down in torrents, overflowing every river, filling every chaung, washing out every road and bridge, and flooding every
paddy field. Slipping, sliding, wading, rafting, the 17th Division continued
to slog toward Rangoon, but the monsoon, coming two weeks before its
time, spelled the end to their hopes of being first back into the city. Fortunately, there was still *Dracula,* the plan to attack Rangoon from the south,
from the sea and from the air.

The decision to launch *Dracula* was a difficult one, for it meant withdrawing troops and transport squadrons to India for training and both were
sorely needed where they were. Moreover, the Americans were lukewarm
because they were not convinced it would "make a timely contribution to

the opening of the China Road." Sir Oliver Leese, the Commander-in-Chief of the Allied Land Forces in SEAC, was hesitant because he felt the army could and should take Rangoon. Mountbatten on the other hand was ecstatic because it played into his specialty, Combined Operations. Slim, sober, thoughtful and realistic, accepted the operation because he saw that, from a strategic point of view, he had to. As he put it, it felt right to "have someone hammering at the back door while I burst in at the front."

The attack was to come from the land, the sea, and the air, what Churchill delighted to describe as a "triphibious" attack. The Navy would throw a huge arc of defence around the area to keep enemy ships away (even though Japan's naval strength was meagre), sweep the mines from the Rangoon River, and then deliver the Army to the paddy fields below Rangoon in assault landing craft. Since the off-shore approaches were too shallow to allow for a naval bombardment, RAF bombers were to soften up the Japanese land defences. Gurkha and Indian paratroops would land first to take and hold the Rangoon shores till the seaborne troops arrived. The USAAF was to supply the planes that dropped the paratroopers and the bombers that gave immediate cover to the drop.

The dithering and delay in coming to a decision meant that everything now had to be done "on the double." The date, May 2, chosen to ensure that the landing craft were not hampered by monsoon-induced waves and surges in the Rangoon River, was only weeks away. The Navy was in a good position to manage its side of the operation and the RAF was ready. The USAAF was not. It was probably a political decision to have Americans do the paradrop. There is evidence that the British had doubts about the ability of their allies to deliver a successful, accurate drop and there is evidence that this suspicion put the Americans on their mettle to show they could. Whatever the reason, the decision was made and on April 18 the Gurkha paratroops gathered at Hailakandi airfield near Silchar to meet for the first time the aircrew who were to deliver them to the target.

Immediately problems became evident. The Americans in SEAC had never made a live drop before, they had never worked with the Gurkhas they were to drop, and their aircraft were not equipped to carry externally the ammunition, medical supplies, wireless equipment, picks and shovels the paratroopers needed. To overcome these problems the authorities turned to the Canadian squadrons, 435 and 436. All the armourers from the two squadrons were detached to Hailakandi to modify the American Dakotas for the drop and twenty-five wireless operators from each squadron were sent along to act as jumpmasters.

The armourers were told they were being sent to Gujrat for a special course. They wondered about that; it didn't make much sense. They wondered even more when they were put aboard an American plane and not until they arrived at Hailakandi were they told the whole story — they had fourteen days to modify forty-five American Dakotas for a paradrop on Rangoon. The group went to work at once, labouring night and day to do the job. First all the equipment had to be sorted out — special containers for the each of the various supplies, cradles and pararacks to hold the containers, straps to affix the containers to the aircraft. The containers were weighted with sandbags and dummy drops were made to test them. Then the supplies had to be checked, sorted and packed — ammunition in special containers with red parachutes, medical supplies with orange chutes, wireless equipment with black chutes. The armourers had to check the jumpmasters' switches and then check that the container release switches let go instantaneously and infallibly. Just before the fortnight was up they were ready for the final test, a full-scale practice drop.

The paratroopers too were getting ready. It is puzzling at first that Canadians were chosen as jumpmasters for *Dracula* rather than Americans, but as Howie Cuming, the Senior Jumpmaster, explains, the Americans did not have anyone trained in an equivalent role. American paratroopers could be depended upon to put on their own equipment, shout "Geronimo!" and get out of the plane in good time and in proper order. Jumpmasters weren't needed. In the RAF system of paradropping, jumpmasters were all-important. A good jumpmaster could get a "stick" of twenty paratroopers off in 18 to 20 seconds, and that meant they all landed together in a small area and near their arms. It helped if the jumpers and the jumpmasters knew each other and could work well together, and that is why Canadians were chosen to drop the Gurkhas on Rangoon. In late 1944 the Canadian squadrons and the 50th Gurkha Parachute Brigade had trained together at Chaklala. The Gurkhas, with good memories of that time, specifically asked for the jumpmasters they knew and trusted for this, their one and only opportunity to show the results of their training. In consequence, the Canadians turned up at Hailakandi and trained with the Gurkhas again. For the next two weeks they helped the Gurkhas put on their equipment, adjust their packs, arrange themselves in "sticks" and emplane in proper order. Over and over the routine was practised until it became second nature. Once in the air, it was the jumpmaster's job to check the exit sequence, to make a final inspection of each man's equipment and to ensure that each static line was properly hooked to the small overhead cable. This last was most important. The static line was simply a length of light rope with one end attached to the small cable that ran along the top of the fuselage and the other attached to the parachute pin. When the paratrooper left the aircraft, the static line pulled the pin that released the chute and the man dropped away beneath his billowing canopy while the line was gathered in by the jumpmaster and slid aside to make room for the next static line and the next jumper. In training they had already had one near tragedy when a paratrooper jumped and found himself dangling at the end of his static line because it had been caught under his webbing. Fortunately the jumpmaster and the crew were able to reel him back in but that mistake ought not to have happened.

By the time the preparations and training were over there was time for only one full-scale practice drop. It went very well, all on time and on target. The camp stood down for one day of rest and then took off for final assembly and briefing at Akyab.

For the Canadians, the two weeks at Hailakandi had been hectic and pressured, but there were compensations. Howie Cuming, the Signals Officer for 436 Squadron, had been put in charge of the group. On joining the Air Force, Howie had opted for pilot training. After the usual stint of tarmac duty he was posted to Winnipeg, billeted in what had been the School for the Deaf, and enrolled in a wireless operator/air gunner course. When he protested that he wanted to be a pilot, the Adjutant soothed him, "Well, look, you're here now. Just do the course and we'll apply for a remuster later." The remuster of course never came and Howie went overseas as a WOP/AG, wireless operator/air gunner. He began his operational career doing submarine patrols on Hudsons from Sierra Leone. It was miserable. After a half slice of fried bread for breakfast the crew set out for an eight-hour patrol with no nutrition but a package of Chiclets gum. They came home to a supper of bully beef. In the middle of his tour he was detached for a short time to an American base and discovered a mess tent that specialized in steaks, apple pie, ice cream and even lemonade-flavoured iced tea.

Howie remembered that experience when he and his group were posted to Hailakandi and billeted with the British Army. He persuaded the American messing officer that, in the interests of getting to know each other and thus being able to work together more effectively, the Canadians should eat in the American mess. The Americans agreed, and the Canadians enjoyed not only the excellent American cuisine, but also jam sessions and sing-songs in the mess that carried over to easy cooperation in the air. The Canadians eased the way for the Indian Army as well. As one British writer explained: "Liaison was not easy between the Americans and the Gurkhas, both being unfamiliar with each other's language and equipment, but liaison was greatly helped by the presence of Canadian jumpmasters from 435 and 436 Squadrons." When the training period was over, the entire group, Americans, Gurkhas, and Canadians moved to the "perching area" at Akyab.

The seventy hours spent at the perching area were filled with briefing and last-minute preparations. The armourers were busy checking and rechecking equipment and securing the containers to the pararacks. The operations people, jumpmasters, and jumpers were getting final details about arrangements for a second wave and what to expect on arrival. At midnight it began to rain and as the downpour increased, the armourers, huddled in the war-wrecked skeleton of a hangar, speculated that the operation would be scrubbed, but at 3:10 am eighty Pratt & Whitney engines thrashed into action and forty aircraft took off for Rangoon. The information at the last briefing had been that the crews on the big coastal guns had been evacuated and that opposition would be light. As they flew through the darkness and the deteriorating weather one of the Gurkhas approached Howie: "If there are no Japs, can we kill Burmese?"

Apart from a few minor injuries — a few sprained ankles and torn shoulders — the drop was perfect. One British commander claimed it was the only perfect paratroop drop of the whole war and for his part in it Howie Cuming was awarded the DFC. Ironically, the drop was unnecessary. Contrary to all expectations, and indeed contrary to the explicit instructions of his commander to hold Rangoon to the last man and the last round, General Kimura had withdrawn from Rangoon two days before. The night before the paradrop the defences on both banks of the Rangoon River had been heavily bombed. Wallie Frazer and his Liberator were there that night and he had seen his second stick of bombs take out one of the big guns on Elephant Point. Perhaps that had helped to speed the enemy on their way.

The POW's in Rangoon Jail knew on April 23, a full week before *Dracula* took place, that the Japanese had evacuated Rangoon but they had difficulty getting the word out to the rest of the world. From the earliest days of the Burma Campaign the Japanese had housed prisoners in the old Rangoon Jail and at the end there were about 1300 there. Of these, at least 13 were Canadians and Major Norman Irwin McLeod was one of them.

Norrie McLeod was the son a prominent Kingston pharmacist and a member of the socially elite of old Kingston. After graduating from Queen's Medical School in 1934 he joined a surprising number of recent medical graduates in volunteering for the Royal Army Medical Corps, later transferring to the Indian Medical Service. When the Japanese invaded Burma he was serving as Deputy Assistant Director of Medical Services (DADMS) to the 17th Indian Division near Moulmein. In the chaos and confusion of Japan's blitzkrieg advance, he and his boss, Colonel K. P. Mackenzie, a rugged, no-nonsense Scot, were taken prisoner in February 1942, almost before they had time to understand what was happening. A third doctor was captured at the same time, Major Charles Gamble, also a Canadian.

Charlie Gamble's captivity was brief. While Mackenzie and McLeod were sent off to the local HQ in Sittang village, Gamble and the other five officers in his group were trussed up and given to understand that they were going to be executed on the spot. Charlie's particular offence was that, contrary to the Geneva Convention that forbade medical officers from carrying weapons, he had a revolver. This, it seems, was the only article of the Geneva Convention that the Japanese recognized for in their treatment of prisoners they contravened all its other strictures. A British counterattack caused momentary distraction in the Japanese camp and Gamble and the other officers wriggled free and fled. The others were recaptured and indeed executed. Charlie slipped through the jungle, made good his escape, and lived to fight another day.

McLeod was kept with his hands tightly tied, at first behind his back and then in front of him, for two days. During that time he had neither food nor water. He was taken to Moulmein jail and later, after Rangoon was captured, to Rangoon Jail. There conditions were deplorable. The prisoners were locked in small cells, five feet by eight, with no furniture but a board to sleep and an old ammunition box as a latrine bucket. They called the latrine bucket a banjo and once a day they were allowed out of their cells to empty it, but even then they were forbidden to speak to anyone. After a time this regime was relaxed; they were put in an open barracks with other prisoners and allowed to cook their own food, what little there was. Slappings and beatings, with fists or with clubs, were the regular means of communication. Orders were given in Japanese and roll call was in Japanese. If a prisoner did not understand and respond at once, he was beaten, often to the point of insensibility. If a prisoner did not bow to the correct angle whenever a Japanese guard appeared, he was again beaten. Dysentery left men so weak they could not move. They simply opened their bowels where they lay and lived in indescribable filth. It was inevitable in these circumstances that the men's well-being should suffer and even the doctors could not keep themselves healthy. Norman McLeod was wracked with dysentery despite everything he did to prevent it.

Despite his own troubles, McLeod worked tirelessly for the welfare of the prisoners and he is still remembered by them for his selfless dedication. Jim Leonard of Liverpool, England was taken prisoner in March 1944. He was interrogated daily and whenever his answers were deemed unsatisfactory he was required to spread his hand, palm down, on the table while the interrogator beat his knuckles with an iron bar. Each day another finger was broken and each night Norrie McLeod set it as best he could. To this day Jim tells how, when he got home, he refused to have the fingers reset, saying "What Major McLeod did is good enough for me." In his book, *Operation Rangoon Jail*, Colonel Mackenzie records that Norman McLeod performed some remarkably difficult operations under extremely primitive conditions and with excellent results. In one case, with no anaesthetic and with make-shift instruments, he amputated the leg of Corporal Usher, a sturdy little Welshman, just below the thigh. Corporal Usher made an excellent recovery.

Most of the Canadian prisoners were Air Force people who had been shot down over enemy territory. Richard Corbettt, Alfred Cuddy, Mel Haakenson, Herb Ivens, Ken Wheatley, and John Joseph Yanota have been identified as Canadians in Rangoon jail; there were others. Ken Wheatley, it will be remembered, was the Hurricane pilot who went on the first Chindit expedition and was captured while out cutting firewood. He escaped, was recaptured, and sent by train to Rangoon jail, his home for the next two years. He was interrogated of course, but he played dumb, told them he was an absolute newcomer to the theatre and knew nothing. "It worked too," said Ken after his release, "despite the Johnny with the club." He also remembers that rice was the prisoners' entire diet: "We had rice for breakfast, again at lunch with a clear soup, and again in the evening." He estimated that at least 40% of the Rangoon prisoners died of malnutrition. One of his friends in the prison had an infected sore that smelled so bad that he asked to be taken from the "hospital" to spare the other patients the discomfort. Ken Wheatley would sit with him for hours, on occasion so long that he was physically ill when he left. When his friend died, he was there to hold his hand. Ken was the first Canadian to be released from Rangoon and returned to his home in Banff, Alberta.

At the end of 1944 there were three Thunderbolt squadrons on one Burmese airfield. That meant there were six flight commanders, and five of them were Canadians, including Herb Ivens. Herb grew up in Wilkie, Saskatchewan, joined the RCAF after one year at university, got his wings and did a tour of duty on Kittyhawks at Annette Island, Alaska before being sent to Burma. 146 Squadron had just got its Thunderbolts when Herb arrived and he revelled in them. "It's like driving a Rolls," he enthused. "There's nothing in Asia that compares with it." That was how he felt when he took off on the morning of December 11, 1944 to bomb and strafe Meiktila. An hour later he was shot down by groundfire. In the ensuing crash his beautiful Thunderbolt burned but Herb was thrown clear of the wreckage. He tried to flee but, with a broken leg, there was no hope. The Japanese captured him, sent him to Rangoon, and put him in a small solitary cell and forbade any communication with his fellow prisoners.

A period in solitary was standard Rangoon jail treatment for all new prisoners, but for aircrew it was extended and more punishing because, ever since Japan itself had been bombed, they were classified as "common criminals" who murdered women and children. "The weeks that followed are not pretty to tell about," Herb wrote in an article that appeared in the Wilkie paper on December 21, 1945. "I was beaten, threatened, cursed and kicked 'til I began to wonder if it was worth the effort to try to live. The thoughts of a quick and painless death became a hope, sometimes a prayer." The prisoners had developed a system of "air writing," spelling out messages through mirror writing in the air to the prisoners they could see, the two on the opposite side of the corridor, and thus transmitting rumours, gossip, and news throughout their cell block. As Christmas approached the word went round that something was going to happen.

The anticipation grew palpable, inflamed by speculation: would they get an extra ration of rice, a sliver of meat, or even, even a cigarette? All day long Herb waited for Christmas, more eager and anxious than ever he had been as a child. It was evening before the clack of the wooden sandals of the Chinese prisoner who delivered their food echoed down the corridor. Herb held out his pan and got his rice, still steaming, and a bit more than usual. Then came another Chinese, a bent old man with a plate of cookies, and one of these went on top of the pile of rice. It had been months since the prisoners had tasted anything sweet. Herb stared at the little brown cookie. Another Chinese came and put something else on his plate — the fore-leg of a cow. There was no meat on that 2½ foot bone of course, but to Herb it was more than a whole Christmas turkey. "A panfull of steaming rice, a cookie and a bone!" exulted Herb, "Before I lifted my pan into my cell I breathed a very sincere thank-you," and he carefully set the bone aside so he could add its marrow to tomorrow's rice.

But there was more. A Japanese officer walked slowly down the corridor, opening cell doors as he went. He swaggered to the centre of the block and loudly announced: "Today is Christian Christmas. My commanding officer has said today you will smoke. Tonight, when roll call has been taken, you will sing your Christian songs. This will be for one day only. You will not talk. The Nippon Masters are good." Then the guards doled out big Burmese che-roots, five to each prisoner. They smoked their cheroots, laughed giddily, and coughed as the smoke of the harsh green tobacco entered their lungs. Slowly and tentatively at first, then with ever increasing confidence and fervour, the whole cell block joined in every carol and Christmas song they knew.

Next day a new prisoner came into the cell across from Herb. He was hungry and there would be no rice till next morning. Herb offered the newcomer his bone. But — a bare, meatless bone? The stranger scorned it, not recognizing the magnanimity of the gesture. The stranger was Wing Commander Lionel Hudson, an Australian pilot who had come to grief and been taken captive simply because he flew too low over the Irrawaddy. In the book he wrote after the war, *Rats of Rangoon*, he tells how Herb Ivens schooled him in the protocol of prison life: Never look a Nip in the eye when he is beating you; jump up and bow whenever a Nipponese of whatever rank approaches; never be caught sitting or lying down; wear your boots day and night because when they come to take you out for question-ing, they will not give you time to put your boots on. Later, when the rules for solitary confinement were lifted, Herb and Hudson were cell-mates. At first they found they had a good deal in common, but as time wore on the constant togetherness grated and in the end they were barely speaking.

As the spring of 1945 passed and the monsoons approached, the prisoners became aware of changes in the atmosphere of the jail. Most noticeable was the frequency of raids by the RAF. It was an ambiguous experience, to be bombed and strafed by your own troops. Still, they recognized that the docks, the rail yards and the enemy HQ were nearby and they were in the line of fire. Over all, about a dozen bombs fell on the jail and thirty prisoners were killed. There were other signs of something untoward happening. The Japanese were storing quantities of firewood in the jail-yard. They were burning documents and issuing new uniforms. Then came the day when the prisoners were asked to hand in a list of all those fit to march. On April 25 this group, led by the Japanese commandant, marched out of the prison gate with no notion of their fate or destination. It was a ragged column. The cooks pushed hand carts piled high with rice, the marchers wore parts of Japanese uniforms and carried their few belongings in old rice sacks. Some wore Japanese boots, some wore make shift wooden sandals, most were barefoot.

Major McLeod stayed behind as medical officer for the camp. Over the years of confinement beri beri had affected his eyesight and hampered his usefulness as a doctor, though throughout he had continued to operate and to repair his weary shirt with vari-coloured patches sewn on with neat surgical stitches. Ignoring his own uncertain health, he fretted about the condition of the prisoners in his care and yearned for medicines to treat their many illnesses. The new guards were all too obviously raw recruits who had no thought of enforcing discipline in the manner of their predecessors. Gradually the prisoners became aware that the guards had all left Rangoon; they were on their own. They also became aware that the British Army did not know this. Lionel Hudson, as the senior officer left in the jail, took charge and undertook to inform the British forces of the new situation. A large sign was printed on the roof: JAPS GONE. BRITISH HERE. Next day it was apparent that their message was not believed for Rangoon was bombed again. A new message was added: EXTRACT DIGIT, a bit of RAF slang that would confirm the authenticity of the roof-top messages.

The stratagem worked. A Mosquito pilot landed on the bomb-pitted runway at Mingaladon, made his way to the jail and heard the news. Knowing that *Dracula* was now launched, he commandeered a sampan and went down the Rangoon River to exhort the seaborne troops to hold their fire. Thus was Rangoon retaken, not by the 17th Indian Division marching into the city in triumph or the 26th Division charging up the Rangoon River, but by a Squadron Leader in a wrecked Mosquito and a Wing Commander who was technically still a prisoner of war.

The column that marched out of Rangoon Jail proceeded north in a series of forced marches that left many of the so-called "fit" unable to keep up. Colonel Mackenzie, Norman McLeod's superior, was one of these. He had gone with the column, not because he was fit, but because he felt the column needed a medical officer. It was not long before he had to be put on one of the overloaded rice wagons. Later in the march the carts had to be abandoned, and two of the men, themselves exhausted from months of malnutrition and days of relentless marching, volunteered to carry the Doc. There was often glass on the road and those with no footwear suffered badly. The column straggled on for four more nights — they moved only at night because of the threat of air attacks. The Japanese Commandant pressed them relentlessly, refusing to allow them to stop at wayside puddles to assuage their raging thirst. Finally the British brigadier balked and announced they would go no further. Surprisingly, the Commandant agreed and the whole troop moved off to the cover of a clump of trees. During the night the Japanese slipped away and next morning the Brigadier called the group together and made an announcement: "At last I can tell you something you have been waiting to hear for years: we are all free men."

To this point the prisoners had feared that when the chips were down, they would probably all be shot. To hear that they were merely abandoned was cause for ecstatic celebration. They spread out a Union Jack they had pieced together out of rags and remnants and waited to be rescued. There was immense excitement when the planes came over. The prisoners cheered and waved their rags. The planes came lower and circled and returned. Then, misled by the Japanese uniforms, they bombed and strafed. Miraculously there was only one casualty, the Brigadier. That night Major Lutz, an American aircrew officer, sneaked through the lines, made contact with the British forces and arranged a rendezvous. A Gurkha patrol then led them to a bivouac where they were fed, reclothed, and lined up for evacuation by Dakotas.

Bob O'Brien, a native of Vancouver and a pilot with 436 Squadron, was the last to leave the forward strip near Prome on the evening of May 1, 1945. He was taxying out for take-off when an American officer stepped in front of his aircraft and waved his arms vigorously. Bob stopped and the officer climbed up into the cockpit. His request was that the O'Brien crew fly back down the railway about 60 miles to a small strip bulldozed out of the paddy and pick up a load of POW's. "I have no authority to do that," demurred Bob. "This aircraft has to be serviced and on the line for tomorrow's work." "You have my authority, and I'm a colonel." "Yes sir," answered Flying Officer O'Brien, and set off down the railway.

At the strip he found about 140 men. Colonel Mackenzie was the senior officer, but he seemed to be beyond logical thought so Bob dealt with Major

Lutz. "I'll take 20," said Bob. "There are only 20 seats." "We don't need seats," replied the Major, "and you can take 35. We're all skin and bones and we don't have any luggage." Bob looked at the wan troop. It was true, none weighed over 120 pounds, they had no luggage; they didn't even have shoes, just rags wrapped around their bloody feet. He agreed to take 30 and to solve the problem of who should go and who should stay, he decided upon half Americans and half British. It never occurred to him to ask about Canadians and so he missed the three that were there. "Take the Colonel," said Lutz. "He has had a hard time of it and he saved a good many lives in the camp." Bob took both Colonel Mackenzie and Major Lutz.

It was a rough trip back to Ramree, what with the darkness and extraordinarily heavy rain. When they reached the base, Colonel Mackenzie was so completely worn out that he hardly knew what was happening, but Major Lutz immediately went to the information table in the operations tent to catch up on all the war news he had missed. There was a light directly over the table, but the major could not decipher a thing and asked Bob to read to him. He desperately wanted to return to flying and Bob later asked the Medical Officer what his chances were. "No chance at all," responded the MO. "A pure white rice diet has left him with a Vitamin A deficiency from which he will never fully recover." Bad news for the major, but at least he and the other 29 members of his group were now on their way to hospital and home.

As for Rangoon itself, despite the news that the occupying forces had left, Mountbatten and Slim decided to stick to the original plan of taking the city with the assault troops who had landed on the river. The banks of the Rangoon River are swampy at the best of times; with the monsoon full upon them, they were almost impassable. It was not until May 3, twenty–four hours after they had been dropped, that the troops were able to march in triumph through the streets of the city.

XIX

MOPPING UP

THE FALL of Rangoon and the almost coincident end of the war in Europe brought a short flush of deflation into the energy and tempo of the Burma Campaign. But it was a false flush; the war in Burma still had three murderous months to go, murderous, that is, from the point of view of the Japanese. The race to beat the monsoon to Rangoon meant that the Fourteenth Army had spurted down two narrow pathways. The westerly one followed the Irrawaddy River for two hundred miles into enemy territory. The easterly one thrust southward from Mandalay to Pegu. It was three hundred miles long and on average only two miles wide. General Slim called it "the longest and narrowest salient in history."

Scattered to the east and to the west of these two triumphal slashes and in the low mountains between them there were still more than 50,000 Japanese troops with another 25,000 across the Sittang in the Moulmein area. Their intention was to consolidate in the area east of the Sittang River and around Moulmein. Slim's intention was to annihilate as many of them as possible before they ever got there.

With the monsoon now in full flourish, neither side had easy going, but it was of course harder for the Japanese. What followed was a fox hunt on a massive scale. The enemy west of the Irrawaddy tried to cross the river and enter the Pegu Yomas, a range of low but heavily wooded hills, from whence they hoped to escape south and east toward Moulmein. Those east of the Sittang tried to filter southward into the same area. Occasionally there were set battles, some lasting as long as four days, but in the main, the Japanese tried to sneak across the river or out of the hills and across the Rangoon-Mandalay Road and the British waylaid them and slaughtered them. Around Pegu the enemy fled through the flooded paddy fields harassed by continuous air strikes and pursued by eager British troops. The Gurkhas had a hard time of it for the water was often up to their armpits, but their blood was up and they pressed on. By chance the whole Japanese plan for a concerted escape fell into the hands of the British. In it the points for preliminary gathering were identified, as well as the escape avenues across the Mandalay-Rangoon Road, and even the date for the breakout, July 20. The British made sure they were ready.

Dunstan Pasterfield describes his part in the show in a letter written at the end of July:

> The last ten days have been ones of continuous dawn-to-dusk activity, slogging across country through mud and water and rain in a grand endeavour to finish off this campaign as quickly as possible. Water everywhere. Ankle deep, knee deep, hip deep and armpit deep. And the rain every day. I've been commanding the Punjabi Mussalman company in this show and have had plenty of fun. We're all very glad to be back in camp. Got a great welcome on our return, battalion pipe band playing, five-gun salute, congrats from the Brigadier all round. The Battalion recorded over 1000 Japs killed in 10 days ... grisly business though, and I can't glorify it.

After a very short break in camp he is back in the field, and his next letter, written August 12, continues the story:

> After one of the most tiring days I've had for a long time – slogging across the same old paddy fields, soaked to the skin and chilled to the marrow by the rain, directing artillery fire in the enemy positions, withdrawing the company out of a ticklish spot – I got back to our base at about ten at night to be told that Japan had started surrender negotiations. Which cheered me up more than somewhat, and as a result, having to sleep on a hard floor with just one blanket didn't affect me as it would normally have done.

Before the mopping up was finished, Dunstan was stricken with malaria and taken to hospital in Rangoon and then repatriated.

The tag ends of the enemy forces that escaped the Gurkha pursuit and the road ambushes fell victim to the Sittang River and a fierce epidemic of cholera that followed. The Japanese losses during the whole breakout are horrible to contemplate. Twelve hundred sailors of a Naval Guard Force attempted to cross the Mandalay road and the Sittang River in late July. By the time they reached the Sittang their number had been reduced to 400, and of these, only three managed to cross the river. Ten thousand Japanese tried to break out from the Pegu Yomas; 8300 of them were killed.

While this pursuit and slaughter was going on in the flooded and swampy area of the Pegu-Sittang Bridge sector, a smaller but parallel pursuit took place in the Shan Hills further north. The remnants of the Japanese army that had been pushed eastward as the British fought down the road to

Mandalay were now struggling along the ridge of the Shan Hills to join their fellows far to the south. The Karen levies that had been recruited by Taschereau and Meunier were the only British troops in the area and it fell to them to stop this southward flow. The Karens were eager to do that, but how were they to be supplied? That problem was solved by asking 436 and 435 Squadrons in turn to supply a small detachment to the Toungoo strip. 436's contribution, two aircraft, two crews and the necessary complement of ground crew, arrived at the beginning of August and began operating at once. What they did and how they did it cannot be better told than by quoting the diary of a member of the crew:

> *Aug. 2. Once again early call and away we go to 721[1], a satellite for 677; this one is also parked bang in the middle of some four- and five-thousand foot peaks. D.R.[2] wouldn't work, so we tried valley crawling from Sittang Valley. Almost made it, but a blank wall nearly had us — Whew!*
>
> *Over the top we go to the Salween, down it to the Papun where the slant- eyes are pretty thick, over a ridge into the Yunzalin Valley and up it rather shakily into the DZ. This we practically dive-bombed as our circuit was partly in cloud and almost solid rain. Windshield wipers packed up and it was no fun groping around in there.*
>
> *Aug. 3. Away to satellite 2005; no joy with D.R. again, so up the Yunzalin we grope and damn near missed the run into the DZ, situated on a creek. Made it, though, and back the boys went to toss out the rice. Had to drop short sticks because the DZ was about the size of a postage stamp. Almost lost the crew out the door on one split-hair turn over the ridge. Back to base, reload with rice, BOR's, rum, ammunition and a radio, set out for 67, away north of the Mawchi Road and again smack in the middle of nowhere. More valley crawling, but about three miles from the DZ the ceiling closed in and we got out of it, but fast! Tried the same tactic from the Sittang side, but had the same result, so we packed it up for the day. We weren't exactly sorry when we climbed out.*

The diary entries show vividly how treacherous this sort of flying was and how stubbornly the crews fought to deliver their loads. One can also sense how personally the airmen feel it when they hear that the troops at a DZ they have tried repeatedly and unsuccessfully to reach are almost starving.

The crews are taking enormous risks, but what makes the risks worthwhile are the appreciative "chitties" they get from the troops on the ground. One of them reads: "Otter Red reports splendid drop, also good drop Mongoose

---

[1] The numbers identify Dropping Zones.

[2] D.R.: deduced reckoning, that is, navigation based on deducing one's position by applying wind speed and direction to a course plotted on a map.

White. 'Canucks Unlimited': splendid show!" A second chitty reveals the unique empathy that developed between the crews in the air and the troops on the ground: "Personal to today's pilot. V for Victory! Bloody good show. We were dead scared you would hit some cloud-covered hills. How did you feel upstairs?" The ultimate recognition for the work the 436 crews did and the chances they took came in the form of immediate DFC's for F/L H. W. Pearson and Warrant Officer D. G. Parker. The recommendation for these awards is long and laudatory, but the final paragraph says it all: "The manifest courage shown by Pearson and Parker, their determination in supplying these guerrilla troops regardless of the danger in the hidden peaks and the enemy fire, and their superb skill in dropping their ammunition and supplies on the most difficult of DZ's has been a truly exceptional record in Transport Supply operations."

In the last half of August a detachment from 435 was sent to Toungoo to relieve the 436 crews. The Squadron's Operations Record Book entry for August 30, 1945 hints at the difficulties the detachment encountered: "Returning pilots say that the drops were the most difficult they had had to do since arriving in the theatre, sometimes on mountain peaks, sometimes in narrow valleys, and almost invariably covered in 9/10 or 10/10 cloud." Despite these difficulties the crews were determined to deliver and, as the Operations Record Book has it, "added a few more laurels to our record." In recognition of their effort, Major Tice, the Senior Army Liaison Officer with Force 136 sent the following communication: " To all members of 435 Squadron Detachment. You have in four days broken all previous records. TACHQ are grateful beyond words for your efforts. Field reports are slow to arrive, those received so far report excellent drops. Canucks, we wish you a good trip home and happy landings!"

In all of these appreciations one feels a deep sincerity. The men of Force 136 were completely isolated in the mountains and the jungle. They were fighting a wily and stubborn enemy inflamed by desperation. Without supplies from the air, Force 136 had no food and no ammunition; they would either starve or be killed. Knowing this, the men in the air took desperate chances to get through. The men on the ground could see the chances they took and they were grateful.

The Toungoo Detachment was the last operational activity for 435 Squadron. The majority of its crews were tour-expired and the Japanese had surrendered on August 14. Squadron personnel were invited to enjoy VJ Day celebrations on the Maharaja of Manipur's palace grounds — fireworks and dancing girls, a parade of gaudily-adorned elephants led by a Manipuri pipe-band — and then, at the end of August, firm word came that an RAF squadron was coming to replace them and the jubilation spread through the bashas on Sentinel Hill. But there was a wee hint of sadness in the celebrations, as the last entry in the Squadron's Operations Record Book makes clear:

We shall leave our valley with mingled feelings. We are a bit deliri-
ous at the thought of going home, but many of us have developed a
strong attachment to this beautiful green valley enclosed on all sides by
mighty mountains, and its always happy people with their gleaming
white clothes and shining faces ... After getting to know the Manipuri
people one is inclined to wonder whether they haven't got something we
haven't got. And with that thought we bring to a close our diary for the
month of August.

436 Squadron too was winding down its operations and preparing for the flight back to England but one more mission came their way. On August 25 they were asked to fly to Hong Kong with emergency medical supplies for recently released POW's. There was no actual need for the flight — it was more a case of showing the flag since there were so many Canadians in the Hong Kong POW camps. Al Aikman was chosen for the job. Al was a Toronto native who had already earned a DFC and Bar for his exploits as a Spitfire pilot in North Africa. The DFC citation described him as "a keen and tenacious pilot who has shown a rare zest for battle." After complet-ing the Transport OTU course at Comox he began a new career with 436 in Burma, enlivening Squadron life with occasional single-engine passes across the strip at less than tree-top height. As a recently-appointed Flight Commander he was given the privilege of the flight to Honk Kong. S/L Bill Irving, the Protestant padre, went along too; after all, he was a qualified navigator. Because of the Dakota's relatively short range they had to take a round-about route — Ramree to Calcutta, to Bombay, back to Calcutta, then Rangoon, Bangkok, Saigon and finally Hong Kong. In the event an engine failure at Bangkok forced the crew to abort the mission, but after eight months of lower Burma they had at least had a minor adventure to a new part of the exotic East. When it was over 436 began preparations to fly itself back to Britain. The last sentence in the 436 Operations Record Book was less sentimental than 435's but no less full of affect: "Rainfall at base during August totalled 57.34 inches."

The Canadian Government thought it had an understanding with the British that "unscrambling," that is the extraction of Canadians from RAF squadrons, and repatriation of all Canadians in SEAC would begin as soon as the war in Europe was over. The British however dragged their feet and repeatedly resisted all requests and demands for the wholesale release of Canadians with the argument that the exigencies of the campaign would not allow it. In particular they insisted that the transport squadrons simply could not be spared for they were needed for the continued supply of the forces in the field. The dropping of the atomic bomb on August 6 changed everything. Whereas there had been over 1000 Canadians still with the RAF in June, plus another 1000 with the two RCAF squadrons, by the end of August there were only 325 RCAF aircrew left in SEAC. At that time the RCAFHQ in Delhi stopped keeping statistics on Canadians in Burma.

The Canadians on radar had gone to India with the understanding that they would be repatriated after three years overseas, measured from the moment they left Canada. Soon after their arrival in SEAC they were told that their tour would be four years, but in fact a repatriation draft of 84 radar mechanics left for the UK in December 1944 carrying homeward men who had embarked from Canada three years earlier. In February of 1945 an even larger draft left and, as with aircrew, in August large-scale repatriation began. Britain was then inundated with Canadian servicemen boisterously eager for a boat to Halifax or New York. Each man was given a repat number based on his months of overseas service and though to the men the wait seemed interminable, the wholesale transfer of thousands of impatient and anxious soldiers, airmen, and war brides was handled with remarkable dispatch.

For all the British troops in Burma, but especially for the Air Force, the official Japanese surrender on August 14 did not signify the end. Isolated pockets of enemy troops had to be persuaded, often by force, that their God-Emperor had indeed been defeated, civil order had to be restored in remote areas where banditry reigned, and, above all, prisoner of war camps all over South East Asia had to be found and succoured. In the main this task fell to RAF personnel but a few Canadians got temporarily lost in the labyrinthine channels of bureaucracy and missed the main wave of repatriation. One of these was Ian Traquair. When Ian left the family farm at Dafoe, Saskatchewan the Air Force trained him as an aero engine mechanic, but he insisted he wanted to fly and so he was remustered to Wireless Operator/ Air Gunner and in that trade he completed a tour of operations with a ferry unit based in Cairo. He came late to the Burma theatre and was posted to a newly-formed RAF transport squadron in May 1945. In August the squadron moved from Akyab to Rangoon. Shortly thereafter Ian and his chums watched the local Japanese commander hand over his sword to the British. From that point on, Ian's flying was all connected with rescuing POW's. These flights Ian calls "the most unforgettable of our Burma experience." Having located an isolated POW camp in Siam, they flew low over it to reconnoitre. Hundreds of men waved and cheered, so loud they could hear them from the air, and it was with a tremendous sense of satisfaction that they dropped their load of clothing and medical supplies. For the next trip their aircraft was fitted with stretchers for this time they were to land. Ian's diary describes what happened:

The strip was very near their quarters and by the time we came
to a stop all who could walk were out to greet us. There were 600
of them and they were like scarecrows. As I stood in the doorway
of the aircraft one of them yelled "Hi Canada!" He had spotted
the cigarettes in my shirt pocket. He was from Toronto and the
only Canadian there. We had a good visit and I left him my cigs
along with some chocolate bars that had arrived in a parcel. I
had never seen human beings as thin before. Their eyes were
sunken and one could count every bone .... The POW's had
organized themselves into groups and they did a variety of things
to stimulate positive thinking and one group had the responsibil-
ity of clearing and preparing a landing strip because as they
said: "We knew you would come for us sometime."

One of the prisoners gave Ian a scrap of paper with a name and address
on it. "Just write them and say I'm alive. They haven't heard from me in
two and half years." That started an avalanche. Every piece of paper the
prisoners could find was torn into little scraps and before he left Ian had
about 600 addresses. Then his crew loaded as many of the very sick as they
could and took off. All the way back to Rangoon, Ian pondered how he was
going to deal with 600 addresses. Of one thing he was sure — it would be
done. The Red Cross felt they could not help so he turned to the Knights
of Columbus and they agreed to look after the whole thing. After one more
such trip, this one to Singapore, Ian's Repatriation Directive came through
and on September 16, 1945 he flew out of Burma.

Like Ian Traquair, Mel Little, a Canadian from Viking, Alberta, was
stranded in a RAF squadron after the war had ended. He ended up with an
all-Canadian crew on a RAF transport squadron stationed at Rangoon and
involved in bringing Allied POW's, mostly Australians, back from Malaya.
On one occasion they were asked to fly a delegation of high-ranking
Siamese officers from Bangkok to Mountbatten's headquarters in Ceylon.
Mel has little recollection of the Lieutenant Generals, Rear Admirals and
Wing Commanders, but the ladies in the group impressed him for "they
were much more attractive than Indian or Burmese women and their
voices were like tinkling bells." In a letter written to the author in February
2001, Mel told of a bit of shopping he did in Ceylon before he returned
to Rangoon: "I bought a magnificent set of satinwood elephant bookends.
The shopkeeper kindly offered to mail them home to Canada so I would
not have to carry them. They haven't arrived yet." The fantastic collection
of Burmese rubies and emeralds that he bought on the streets of Rangoon
he kept with him for safekeeping. Once again he experienced the Oriental
shopper's luck: "Appraisal back home was sobering," Mel wrote. "My only
consolation was that my friends got swindled too."

After Mandalay had been retaken and final victory in Burma seemed assured, Mountbatten began to plan for the next phase in the SEAC war, the invasion of Malaya. Aware that there was a strong Chinese component in Malaya, his planners decided to set up a behind-the-lines network using Chinese from the Commonwealth countries. To man the network, they turned to Canada, the only Commonwealth country with a significant Chinese population, and they selected Major Mike Kendall as their recruiter. Mike Kendall was a mining engineer from Vancouver who had worked long enough in South China to acquire fluency in the language and a Chinese wife. Now a major in the British Army, he toured across Canada seeking likely young Chinese to be trained as agents for clandestine work in Malaya or China.

Although some Chinese were embittered by the shoddy treatment they had received when they tried to enlist in the Canadian Army, others persisted, hoping that in the end their service would earn them and all their fellows enfranchisement and full citizenship. Kendall found his first recruits from among the Chinese-Canadians already in the Canadian Army and sent them off to train at the camp he had founded on the east shore of Lake Okanagan just north of Penticton. There they were taught the secrets of the guerrilla's trade — radio and wireless, unarmed combat, weapons and explosives. When they were ready, they were shipped to Australia for further training and deployment. But deployment was delayed time and time again, thanks to the objections of the Americans and the Chinese, who both smelled in the Kendall project a Trojan horse for the return of British imperialism. In the meantime, the bomb fell on Hiroshima and most of Kendall's Chinese Canadian recruits returned home without getting into action.

A second wave of Chinese Canadians trained in India for clandestine work in Malaya. Henry Fung, only nineteen years old, was dropped behind the lines in June 1945 and was soon hard at work blowing up bridges and rail lines, disrupting telephone communications and harassing Japanese convoys. After the war ended the team he was with had their hands full trying to persuade the Japanese troops to surrender and the Malayan communists to cooperate with the British. A number of Chinese Canadians followed Henry Fung into Malaya — Bing Lee, Ted Wong, Victor Louie and Harry Ho.

Harry Ho's story does not rightly belong in this narrative for he was inserted into Malaya, not Burma, but it deserves to be told. Harry, born in Vancouver in 1922, was sent to school in China at the age of eleven. On his return to Canada he worked in a shingle mill till 1944 when he was called up for military service. He volunteered for "special duties," and ended up in India learning how to use plastic explosives and various weapons and how to jump from a plane. In July 1945 a Liberator dropped Harry and a guerrilla team led by the French Canadian Pierre Chassé into Malaya. Harry was the interpreter and the demolitions instructor for the group. Most of them landed in a dry riverbed, but the British captain got caught in a tree and the rest worked anxiously all night to get him down.

Then they began the work they had come to do, carrying out sabotage and harassment throughout the Kra Isthmus. For more than a month the small group slipped down the chaungs and through the jungle to pester the enemy as much as they could. The enemy pestered them too, and on one occasion, after a narrow escape from a Japanese patrol, Harry threw off the radio pack and stretched out to catch his breath. His back began to itch ferociously and he asked his companions to check. The battery acid had etched through his backpack, through his web belt, through his clothing and through his skin. It took over a month for the wounds to heal and Harry still has the scars. In August they got the news that the war was over but it was June of 1946 before Harry was home in Vancouver and a civilian once more. Today he is very proud of his service in Malaya and proud too that his service in Malaya was in some small measure a factor in the decision to grant him and his fellows all the rights of Canadian citizenship.

The Japanese held more than 220,000 POW's in large and small camps in numerous unknown locations throughout south east Asia and the great fear was that, as the ring tightened around them, they would kill their prisoners. It was important to know in advance as much as possible about the whereabouts of the camps and have some indication of the numbers involved so that mass annihilation could be forestalled. To that end, Arthur Stewart was sent into the area. Arthur Stewart, born in China, came to Vancouver at the age of 20 and joined the police force where his fluency in both Cantonese and Mandarin was useful. When he joined the Army and went to England, the Special Operations Executive, the English spy people, chose him for clandestine work in Yunnan province on the China-Burma border. From his base in Paoshan he launched *Operation Vancouver* and somehow helped a total of 550 Indian troops to get back to India and the Indian Army. By December of 1944 he had moved south and west into the Shan states to find escapers and evaders and arrange their return.

On August 24, 1945, ten days after the Japanese surrender, he and Bill Lee, a young Chinese-Canadian also from Vancouver, were dropped into the Johore area with instructions to get to Singapore and feel out the readiness of the Japanese authorities there to accept the reality of surrender and capitulation. They commandeered a rickety truck from a pineapple farm and beat their way down the road. At the Singapore causeway they waited while the Japanese guard held his machine gun on them and sent for his superior. The superior allowed them to proceed, but only after he had reminisced with Bill for a moment about his earlier life in Vancouver's

Chinatown. Arthur Stewart and Bill Lee went first to Changi prison to catalogue the main medical needs of the inmates and, more importantly, to tell
the prisoners about the end of the war and the possibilities for repatriation.
For a few days at the beginning of September Lieutenant Colonel Arthur
Stewart of the Canadian Army was the ranking Allied officer in Singapore
and he established his command by raising the Union Jack over the city
despite the protests of the Japanese. At the same time, Bill Lee was the only
radio operator in Singapore and his broadcasts to Ceylon were the only
window Mountbatten had on developments in the area. Bill worked twenty-
hour days coding, sending, receiving and decoding the wireless traffic that
informed the world about happenings in Singapore.

For all the various schemes dreamed up to involve Chinese-Canadians
in the Far East war a total of 150 men were enlisted. Most of them did not
get into action, partly because the war ended before they were fully ready
but also because the Americans and Chinese strongly resisted their involvement. As Herb Lim, one of the men trained at Commando Bay, Penticton
says: "It wasn't my fault I didn't get into action. I was ready to fight for my
country." That was true of a good many Canadian-Chinese.

Japanese Canadians had a far harder row to hoe before they were
recognized and recruited. During the First World War Japan was an ally,
indeed, was entrusted with the defence of Canada's west coast, and almost
two hundred *Nisei*, Canadians of Japanese parentage, fought overseas. Fifty
-four never came back. During the Second World War however, even before
Pearl Harbour, a Special Committee on Orientals in Ottawa "reluctantly
and not unanimously" recommended that Japanese Canadians should not
be given military training. After Pearl Harbour, although they found absolutely no evidence of disloyalty or betrayal, Canadian authorities expelled
Japanese Canadians from the coastal region of British Columbia and seized
their property. Repeatedly Japanese Canadians who applied to enlist were
scorned and rebuffed. All the while Australia was pleading for people
with Japanese language competence and battles in Burma were being lost
because captured Japanese documents could not be quickly translated.

Don Mollison, a captain in the Indian Field Broadcasting Unit, the
same organization that had employed Roland Bacon, had an idea: Why
not recruit Japanese speakers in Canada? He was sent to Canada to try his
hand at recruiting only to discover that the Canadian Army did not enlist
Japanese Canadians. Shocked and dismayed, he argued with the military
and persuaded them of the need. Still the Canadian War Cabinet refused
to change its mind. Mollison played his trump card; he asked his North
American superior, William Stephenson, the man known as Intrepid, to
get Mountbatten to ask Churchill to intervene. Whether this high-level
intervention occurred or not we do not know, but the Cabinet did eventu-

ally give permission to recruit 100 *Nisei*, half to go to SEAC and half to Australia.

The peculiar lever that moved the Canadian government to enlist the *Nisei* was of course the need for Japanese speakers. Since many of the potential candidates were not fluent, some remedial language instruction was required. In 1943 a Canadian Army Japanese Language School had been organized in Vancouver; typically the staff were almost all Caucasian. So too were the students at first, Canadian Army personnel like the politician Judy Lamarsh and the architect Arthur Erickson who were willing to tackle the almost impossible task of learning Japanese in one year. Later *Nisei* whose Japanese was inadequate were sent to the school, which meant, for some of them, being sent back to the very city from which they had been expelled. Some of the school's graduates were of course sent to SEAC. Peter McKenzie, the son of the school's commandant, toured Burma after the war ended, counselling Japanese Canadians on what to expect when they returned home. Dick Adachi slogged through the 1945 monsoon screening Japanese prisoners and doing field security. Fred Kagawa, one of the twelve Mollison recruits to be sent to Burma, actually got into action before the campaign ended.

Fred was working in a pulp mill on Vancouver Island when the war with Japan began. When the Canadian government ordered all Japanese Canadians to move at least 100 miles from the BC coast, he opted to go to a road camp in northern Ontario and then, four months later, to London, Ontario. In London his first job was shovelling coal into sacks for home delivery, but after a month, thanks to his Vancouver Technical School Training, he found work in a machine shop making steam winches for American Liberty ships. That is what he was doing when the foreman came to him and said, "Fred, take of your coveralls and come with me. There's a guy in the office wants to see you." The "guy" was Captain Mollison and the proposition was that he join the British Army as a corporal and go to Burma as an interpreter. Having already offered himself to the RCAF and been rejected, Fred jumped at this second chance. When he told his mother what he had done, she cried and scolded: "Why do you want to go after the way they treated us?" All Fred could answer was that this was what he had to do.

There was a switch in plans; because the Canadian Government had now decided to (or been pressured into) accepting *Nisei* recruits, Fred became a private in the Canadian Army rather than a corporal with the British. Even so, when the time came for Fred and the other eleven who had volunteered for Burma to leave Toronto, they were paraded in stealth through Union Station and told to identify themselves as Chinese. A troopship took them to England and another took them to India. Fred was then posted to the

Psychological Warfare Broadcasting Unit in Rangoon. His supervisor was an American in the Canadian Army and his CO was Major Johns, a Montrealer in the British Army. The unit was housed in a large dwelling in Rangoon and daily they were taken to their "studio," a trailer on the outskirts of the city. Fred's job was first to translate the day's news into Japanese then open his microphone and intone "This is Headquarters Radio South East Asia Command. Here is the news," and read the communiqué. Once he was also asked to prepare a Japanese-language leaflet to be dropped over the front lines. Because Japanese was his second language Fred had frequent recourse to the dictionary, but never was it more needed than when the bomb fell on Hiroshima. How do you say 'atom bomb" in Japanese? They found *genshi*, atom, and *bakudan*, bomb and *genshu bakudan* became the accepted terminology thereafter.

After the surrender Fred put in time for a while supplying English commentaries for a local Rangoon station's "swing" music hour. He was then sent to New Delhi to work at the U.S. Army South East Asia Translation and Interrogation Centre. Here he was billeted in a British Army camp where Italian POW's did all the menial chores, even bringing him hot water for his morning shave. He was still there when Christmas 1946 came round, and Fred remembers it as "the loneliest Christmas I ever knew, no music, no feast, no celebration. I wandered into the local YMCA and played table tennis." Shortly after that he joined a draft of other Japanese Canadians who had been in Burma and started the long voyage back to England and to Canada.

Whether there was any reaction to his propaganda efforts, Fred never knew but the likelihood is strong that at least the Japanese equivalent of Special Operations Executive was monitoring his broadcasts. Then again, perhaps they weren't. All the news that Fred sent out told them what they already knew — that the Japanese Army in Burma was broken and battered and in truth no longer existed. Fred was one of the last Canadians active in SEAC and his job was simply to tell the world that the Burma Campaign, the longest campaign of the Second World War, was over.

XX

CONCLUSION

W HEN THE fighting was over and the mopping up finished, a question remained: What had the Burma Campaign accomplished? Raymond Callahan entitles the final chapter of his *Burma 1942-45* "Barren Victory," and he concludes that Slim "forged an army that won a victory immense but almost meaningless." A dismal thought! Were those thousands of British and Indian soldiers sacrificed to no purpose? Did this war bring nothing about? If nothing else, one could claim that it hastened the end of an outmoded and tainted system of colonial imperialism, and if the independence that came at the war's end was not as Utopian as the dream had promised, that was surely not the fault of Slim's victory.

But one other consequence of the Burma War has been generally overlooked.

When, in July 1937, General Mutaguchi inflated the incident at the Marco Polo Bridge into a full-scale attack on China, he launched the flood of Japanese force that rolled like a tidal wave over Siam, Malaya, Borneo, Java, Sumatra and Burma. In March 1944 he stood on the border of India with the dream of riding in triumph into Delhi gleaming in his eyes. Behind him stood an invincible army, every one of its soldier dedicated to fight to the death for his God-Emperor and for the Greater East Asian Co-Prosperity Sphere.

General Slim and the Fourteenth Army shattered that dream. Slogging through heat and dust, through rain and mud, the British Army and the Indian Army, with the Royal Air Force, the United States Army Air Force and the Royal Canadian Air Force above them, ground the proud soldiers of Japan into abject submission. Of the 305,501 troops Japan sent to Burma, only 118,352 ever returned to their homeland. It was the dropping of the atomic bomb that ended the war, but it was the complete and absolute defeat in Burma that killed the *samurai* and *bushido* spirit of the Nippon Army. Had it not occurred, it is possible that Japan's military cadres would have reasoned that their army was nullified by an act of the gods of technology and never defeated on the battlefield, just as the German Army in 1918 declared it was betrayed by its generals and marched forth in 1939 to redeem its sullied honour.

Does the Burma Campaign mean anything to Canada or to Canadians who were not there? Perhaps not much. Canadian-built trucks are still hauling teak out of Burmese forests today, a small reminder that the demands of war were responsible for Canada's post-war trade and development. The tug and tussle by Britain to get Canadian troops into Burma and by Canada to get them out again played some small part in extricating Canada from the colonial relationship, and the need for Chinese- and Japanese-speakers in Burma and Malaya was instrumental in eventually bringing Chinese and Japanese Canadians into full citizenship.

But it is difficult to assess the significance of the Canadian involvement in the Burma Campaign because no one knows how many Canadians were involved. The strength of the three Canadian squadrons, 413, 435 and 436, was, of course, known, and the RCAF regional HQ in Delhi, established in late 1943, tried to track RCAF personnel in RAF squadrons and in radar units. On the basis of this accounting, military historians and government officials have estimated that somewhere between seven and eight thousand Canadians served in SEAC.[1] But there is no record of the Canadians who joined the RAF or of the missionaries and doctors and soldiers of fortune who served in the Indian or British Army. Men like Ian MacPherson, Charles Hoey, Dunstan Pasterfield, Roy McKenzie, Norman McLeod, Charlie Gamble, Keith Muir, Andrew Taylor, Seton Broughall, Walter Anderson, Jacob Markowitz and George Faulkner — and there were many others — are not counted into the Canadian total.

We can assume then, that despite Mackenzie King's veto on Canadians fighting to restore Britain's empire, approximately eight thousand Canadians served in Burma. All of them were involved operationally; no Canadian troops served in ancillary roles. Generally speaking, one third of the RAF's aircrew were Canadians, and in the Liberator and transport squadrons the proportion in the end was higher. After the war in Europe ended, the Canadian government asked repeatedly that their nationals be repatriated and repeatedly the British refused, pleading that the Canadian bomber and transport crews were essential to the successful conclusion of the war in Burma. How essential the transport squadrons were is evident

---

[1] Since Hong Kong was not part of SEAC, Canadians in the Hong Kong action are not included in this tally.

in the statistics: during the 1944 race to Rangoon — from January to May — the Army received 210,000 tons of supplies by air and only 5500 by road. In his post-war analysis of the campaign, Major General F. J. Loftus, a West African divisional commander, laid bare the skeleton of victory when he proclaimed: "We had two match winners which the Japanese did not have, the mule and the Dakota." As we have seen, Canadians played a strong part in providing the Dakota contribution.[2]

When 435 and 436 Squadrons were eventually repatriated, the Air Officer Commanding generously acknowledged their contribution: "On the eve of your departure I wish to thank all ranks for their fine record of operations in Burma. You have added a shining page to the history of 232 Group and transport operations. No commander ever had the privilege of commanding a more loyal or gallant unit." That of course is nice to hear, but it is only the usual farewell from a commander to a departing unit. More hearty and heartfelt is the acknowledgment Group Captain Reg (Lucky) Jordan, a skipper with 356 Liberator Squadron expressed in *To Burma Skies and Beyond*:

> *By the time I left the squadron at the end of May 1945, the majority of the aircrew were RCAF. In due course, contact with the new crews confirmed my view that Canadians make excellent airmen, with their robust outlook and generally unflappable temperament. They were also to bring with them new social habits with which they enlivened Mess life. It was not long before the less staid of us 'oldies' joined them on our knees in a corner of the ante-room to play craps, the dice game I had first encountered during my training in Canada.*

Tributes such as these show how much the Canadian contribution, in its various guises, was valued. So too do the DFC's awarded to Canadian airmen in Burma, some 120 in number. A full list of all awards won by Canadians in Burma, both Army and Air Force, is difficult to come by, but even a conservative tally is impressive: one Victoria Cross, 3 Distinguished Service Orders, 3 Military Crosses, 4 Orders of the British Empire, 2 British Empire Medals, 3 Air Force Crosses, 2 George Crosses, and 6 Mentioned in Dispatches.

These honours came at a cost. In May 1944 there were 12 Canadians flying Beaufighters with 211 RAF Squadron. By the end of August, nine of them were dead. In the Liberator squadrons losses were particularly high

---

[2] Canadians played a significant part in assuring the mule contribution as well. Most of the mules came from the United States and in their journey by sea from New York to Karachi they were tended by "mule-skinners" from the ranks of the Veterans Guard of Canada. Between March 1944 and May 1945 one hundred and seventy-nine members of the Veterans Guard "conducted" 1300 mules to India.

since some crews were all-Canadian crews so that the loss of one aircraft could mean the loss of ten or eleven Canadians. Between May and December 1944 thirty-five RCAF aircrew were lost from 354 RAF Squadron. Even with the transport squadrons, losses were greater than expected; 435 RCAF Squadron lost 18 personnel in eight months of operations, half to enemy action and half to the hellish weather. In all at least 500 Canadians who fought in Burma are still lying in remote jungle graves or in the well-tended Commonwealth War Cemeteries of East Asia, two hundred more than were killed in the Korean War. Surely that fact alone is reason to protest that the involvement of Canadians in the Burma Campaign ought not to be forgotten.

Among the Burma veterans, their involvement is not forgotten. Their war experiences had little in common with the experiences of those who fought in Europe; they were in a strange and distant land that very few of their fellow Canadians knew, and while they were there, their focus was intense — the war was always with them, there were limited opportunities to escape it. Just as John Knowles felt that all Chindits were marked forever, so too, though in a lesser way, Canadian veterans of the Burma Campaign still feel a uniqueness and a special bond. The Burma Star Association, the British organization of Burma vets, has branches throughout Canada, the Burma Bombers Association was founded in Canada and has spread across the Commonwealth, and the 435-436 and Burma Squadrons Association still publishes a quarterly newsletter and has held reunions every year since the war ended. In Vancouver the Chinese-Canadian War Museum features the exploits of Chinese Canadians in the Far East. There are cairns erected in memory of the Burma vets in Edmonton, Trenton, Scarborough and in Arakan Park near Charles Hoey's birthplace on Vancouver Island. Each year veterans gather at these stones to remember their comrades and recite the Kohima Epitaph:

When you go home
Tell them of us and say
For your tomorrow
We gave our today.

Bibliography

UNPUBLISHED MATERIAL

Barnard, James. *435 Squadron at Imphal.* Unpublished diary. Handwritten.

Brouse, Barbara. *Dr. Andrew Copeland Taylor.* Unpublished ms.

Corston, Albert R. Unpublished memoirs.

Day, Anthony. *The Air War over the Arakan.* Unpublished typescript.

Dickson, Elsa. *Letters of Captain Roland Clinton Bacon, 1941-1945, India and Burma.* Unpublished typescript.

Hearn, Owen. *Bing.* Privately published memorial to A. J. M "Bing" De Cruyenaere, nd.

Huston, W. L. Ross. *World War II Experiences of W. L. Ross Huston, BEM.* Unpublished typescript.

MacGregor, Neill M. *Wings Over Burma.* Unpublished typescript.

Muir, R. Keith. *Memoirs of a Medical Officer.* Unpublished typescript.

Waddy, P. B. *Memories of World War II.* Unpublished typescript.

OFFICIAL HISTORIES

Ehrman, J. *Grand Strategy.* Vols. IV and V. HMSO, 1956.

Greenhous, Brereton. *The Crucible of War 1939-1945,* vol. III of *The Official History of The Royal Canadian Air Force.* Toronto: U of T Press, 1994.

Kirby, S. Woodburn. *The War Against Japan,* vols. II – IV. HMSO, 1957-1965.

No. 413 Squadron Operations Record Book. National Archives of Canada.

No. 435 Squadron Operations Record Book. NAC.

No. 436 Squadron Operations Record Book. NAC.

Saunders, Hilary St. G. *The Royal Air Force,* 3 vols. HMSO, 1954.

Stacey, C. P. *Arms, Men and Government: the War Policies of Canada, 1939-1945.* Ottawa: Queen's Printer, 1970.

SELECTED BIBLIOGRAPHY

Anders, Leslie. *The Ledo Road.* Norman, Oklahoma: The University of Oklahoma Press, 1965.

Allen, Louis. *Burma, The Longest War.* London: Dent, 1984.

Allison, L. and Harry Hayward. *They Shall Grow Not Old.* Brandon, Man.: Commonwealth Air Training Plan Museum, 1996.

Allison, L. *Canadians in the Royal Air Force.* Published by the author. Roland, Man.: Friesen Printers, 1978.

Baker, D. J. *A History of 413 Squadron.* Burnstown, Ont.: General Store Publishing, 1997.

Beauchamp, Gerry. *Mohawks Over Burma.* Stittsville, Ont.: Canada's Wings.

Bierman, John and Colin Smith. *Fire in the Night: Wingate of Burma, Ethiopia and Zion.* New York: Random House, 1999.

Bidwell, Shelford. *The Chindit War.* London: Hodder & Stoughton, 1979.

Bowen, John. *Undercover in the Jungle.* London: Kimber, 1978.

Bradley, Dr. Neville. *The Old Burma Road.* London: Heinemann, 1945.

Brooke-Wavell, Derek. *Lines from a Shining Land.* London: The Britain-Burma Society, 1998.

Brookes, Stephen. *Through the Jungle of Death: A Boy's Escape from Wartime Burma.* New York: John Wiley & Sons, 2000.

Bryan, Arthur. *The Turn of the Tide,* London: Collins, 1956 (based on the War Diaries of Viscount Alanbrooke).

Brown, Atholl Sutherland. *Silently into the Midst of Things.* Lewes: The Book Guild, 1997.

Callahan, Raymond. *Burma, 1942-1945.* London: Davis-Poynter, 1978.

Calvert, Michael. *Prisoners of Hope.* London: Leo Cooper, 1971.

Campbell, Arthur. *The Siege: A Story from Kohima.* London: George Allen & Unwin, 1956.

The Canadians at War. Vol II, Reader's Digest, 1969.

Castle, Colin. *Lucky Alex: The Career of Group Captain A. M. Jardine.* Victoria: Trafford, 2001.

Chalker, Jack. *Burma Railway Artist.* London: Leo Cooper, 1994.

Chan, Won-Loy. *Burma: The Untold Story.* Novato, Calif.: Presidio Press, 1986.

Chinnery, Philip D. *March or Die: The Story of Wingate's Chindits.* Shrewsbury: Airlife Publishing, 1997.

Colvin, John. *No Ordinary Men: The Battle of Kohima Re-assessed.* London: Leo Cooper, 1976.

Cooke, O . A.. *The Canadian Military Experience, 1865-1995: A Bibliography.* Ottawa: DND, 1997.

Cotton, M. C. *Hurricanes over Burma.* London: Grub Street, 1995.

Cruikshank, Charles. *S.O.E. in the Far East.* Oxford UP, 1983.

Day, David. *The Great Betrayal: Britain, Australia and the Onset of the Pacific War, 1939-42.* New York: Norton, 1988.

Everard, Hedley. *A Mouse in my Pocket.* Picton, Ont.: Valley Seaplane Publishing, 1988.

Fergusson, Bernard. *Beyond the Chindwin.* London: Collins, 1945.

Franks, Norman. *Hurricanes over the Arakan.* London: Patrick Stephens, 1989.

_____. *Spitfires over the Arakan.* London: Kimber, 1988.

Frazer, W. W. *A Trepid Aviator: Bombay to Bangkok.* Burnstown, Ont.: General Store Publishing, 1995.

Grant, Ian Lyall & Kazuo Tamagama. *Burma 1942: The Japanese Invasion.* Chichester: Zampi Press, 1999.

Grant, Peter. *A Highlander Goes to War.* Edinburgh: Pentland Press, 1995.

Gwynne-Timothy, John R. W. *Burma Liberators: RAF in SEAC,* 2 vols. Toronto: Next Level Press, 1991.

Hamilton, Angus. *Canadians on Radar in South East Asia.* Fredericton: ACH Publishing, 1998.

Hemmingway, Ken. *Wings over Burma.* London: Quality Press, 1944.

Hempsall, Leslie. *"And don't Forget to Put Paper on the Toilet Seat"*. Surrey, B.C.: Coomber Publishing, 1999.

Herbert, Patricia. *Burma: An Annotated Bibliography*. Oxford: Clio Press, 1991.

Hudson, Lionel. *The Rats of Rangoon*. London: Leo Cooper, 1987.

Innes, David. *Beaufighters over Burma*. Poole: Blandford Press, 1985.

Ito, Roy. *We Went to War: The Story of Japanese Canadians who Served during the First and Second World Wars*. Stittsville, Ont.: Canada's Wings, 1984.

Izumiya, Tatsura. *The Minami Organ*. Rangoon: University Press, 1981.

Kelly, Terence. *Hurricanes over the Jungle*. London: Kimber, 1977.

Lavender, Emerson & Norman Sheffe. *The Evaders: True Stories of Downed Canadian Airmen and their Helpers in World War II*. Toronto: McGraw-Hill, 1992.

Lomax, Eric. *The Railway Man*. London, Jonathan Cape, 1995.

Lu, David. *From the Marco Polo Bridge to Pearl Harbor*. Washington: Foreign Affairs Press, 1961.

Lunt, David. *A Hell of a Licking*. London: Collins, 1986.

McLure, Robert B. *China's New Highways*. Cambridge: British Fund for the Relief of Distress in China, 1939.

_____. *Tales from the Burma Road*. Toronto: United Church of Canada, 1945.

Melnyk, T. W. *Canadian Flying Operations in South East Asia. 1941-1945*, Ottawa: DND, 1976.

Moyles, John T. *Short Bursts*. Brandon, Man.: Ex-Air Gunners Assn. of Canada, 1994.

O'Brien, Terence. *The Moonlight War: The Story of Clandestine Operations in South East Asia, 1944-1945*. London: Collins, 1987.

Ogburn, Charles. *The Marauders*. New York: Harpers, 1956 .

Phillips, Bob. *KC8 Burma: CBI Air Warning Team*. Manhattan, Kansas: Sunflower University Press, 1992.

Pittet, Richard G. *Determined on Delivery, the History of 435 Squadron*. No publisher given: 1994.

Pringsheim, Klaus. *Neighbors Across the Pacific*. Westport, Conn.: Greenwood Press, 1983.

Probert, Henry. *The Forgotten Air Force: The Royal Air Force in the War against Japan, 1941-1945*. London: Brassey's, 1995.

Rooney, David. *Burma Victory: Imphal, Kohima and the Chindit Issue*. London: Arms and Armour, 1992.

_____. *Wingate and the Chindits: Redressing the Balance*. London: Arms and Armour, 1994.

Scott, Munro. *McClure, The China Years*. Toronto: Canec Publishing, 1977.

Shores, Christopher, Brian Cull & Yasuho Isawa. *Bloody Shambles*. vol. 2, London: Grub Street, 1992.

Slim, William. *Defeat into Victory*. London: Cassell, 1956.

Street, Robert. *Another Brummie in Burma*. Grantham, UK: Barny Books, nd.

Terraine, John. *The Life and Times of Lord Mountbatten*. London: Hutchinson, 1968.

Thomas, Lowell. *Back to Mandalay*. New York: Greystone Press, 1961.

Thompson, Julian. *The Lifeblood of War: Logistics in Armed Conflict*. London: Brassey's, 1991.

Turnbull, Patrick. *Battle of the Box*. Shepperton, Surrey: Ian Allen, 1979.

Van Wagner, R. D. *Any Time, Any Place, Any Where: The 1ˢᵗ Air Commando in World War II*. Atglen, Pennsylvania: Schiffer Military History, 1998.

White, Theodore H., ed. *The Stilwell Papers*. New York: Wm. Stone Associates, 1948.

Williams, Douglas. *194 Squadron, Royal Air Force: the Friendly Firm*. Braunton, Devon: Merlin Books, 1987.

Williams, J. H. *Elephant Bill*. London: Hart-Davis, 1950.

Wong, Marjorie. *The Dragon and the Maple Leaf: Chinese Canadians in World War II*. Toronto: Pirie Publishing, 1994.

Wright, Bruce S., *Frogmen of Burma*, Toronto: Clarke Irwin, 1968.

Ziegler, Philip. *Mountbatten*. Glasgow: Fontana/Collins, 1985.

Index

An asterisk before a name indicates a Canadian who served in Burma.

ISBN 1412015367

9 781412 015363